KU-442-401

Accounting Theory and Policy Making

BRIAN UNDERDOWN
BA, MA, ACMA

PETER TAYLOR
BA (Econ)

HEINEMANN PROFESSIONAL PUBLISHING

Heinemann Professional Publishing Ltd
Halley Court, Jordan Hill, Oxford OX2 8EJ

OXFORD   LONDON   MELBOURNE   AUCKLAND   SINGAPORE
IBADAN   NAIROBI   GABORONE   KINGSTON

First published 1985
Reprinted 1987, 1989

© B. Underdown and P. J. Taylor 1985

British Library Cataloguing in Publication Data
Underdown, B.
Accounting theory and policy making.
1. Accounting
I. Title   II. Taylor, P. J.
657   HF5635

ISBN 0 434 91914 4

253704

UNIVERSITY OF BRADFORD LIBRARY	
3 0 MAY 1991	
...CESSION No.	CLASS No.
0340049953	E 657·01 UND
LOCATION	Man. Centre Library

Printed and bound in Great Britain by
Redwood Burn Limited, Trowbridge, Wiltshire

CONTENTS

1 Accounting Theory and its Environment   1
Accounting Theory   1
The Notion of 'Good Theory'   2
The Conventional Approach to Accounting Theory   2
Accounting Research Methods   4
The Nature of Accounting Controversies   5
The Environment of Financial Reporting   6
Should Accounting be Regulated?   8
Developing the Objectives of Accounting   10
The Accounting Policy-making Process   12
Questions   20
References   20

2 The Conventional Approach   24
A True and Fair View   25
Developments in Company Law   25
The 1948 and 1967 Companies Acts   27
The Legislation Lag   27
Additional Disclosures   28
Implementing a 'True and Fair' View   29
The Structure of Accounting   30
Questions   36
References   37

3 Accounting Standards   39
The Need for Accounting Standards   39
Types of Accounting Standards   40

The Emergence of Accounting Standards in the UK   41
The Aims of the Accounting Standards Committee (ASC)   42
The Accounting Standards Programme   43
Evaluation of the ASC Approach   46
Changes in the Standard-setting Process   49
Statements of Recommended Practice (SORPs)   53
International Accounting Standards Committee (IASC)   53
Questions   56
References   56
Appendix: ASC's Work Programme as at 1 November 1984   57

4 Company Legislation   61
Background to the 1980 and 1981 Acts   61
Companies Act 1980   62
Companies Act 1981   63
Companies Act 1985   70
Questions   70
References   72
Appendix 1: Balance Sheet Formats   73
Appendix 2: Profit and Loss Account Formats   78
Appendix 3: Distributable Profit   82
Appendix 4: Stock Exchange Listing Agreement   84
Appendix 5: The City Code on Take-overs and Mergers   88

5 The Decision Usefulness Approach   90
                I A Priori Research   91
Conceptual Framework—The FASB's Approach   93
The ASC's Approach   102
                II Empirical Research   104
Economic Consequences Research   105
Capital Market Research   105
Efficient Markets Research   107
Implications for Accounting Policy Makers   110
Increasing Disclosure   111
Research on Other Economic Consequences   111
Predictive Properties of Accounting Numbers   113
Behavioural Research   116
Questions   118
References   120

6 Income Concepts   125
Income, Capital and Wealth   126
Economic Income   127

	Net Assets	135
	Capital Maintenance	144
	Questions	147
	References	149
7	**Recognition, Realisation and Matching**	151
	The Matching Concept	152
	Revenue Recognition	156
	Expense Recognition	160
	Evaluation of Recognition Criteria	162
	Questions	163
	References	163
8	**Accounting for Price Level Changes**	165
	The Development of Inflation Accounting in the UK	165
	Current Cost Accounting	167
	Current Cost Profit in SSAP16	168
	Evaluation of SSAP16	185
	FASB Statement No. 33	189
	Questions	191
	References	195
9	**Funds- and Cash-flow Statements**	196
	Funds-flow Statements	196
	Reporting Cash Flows and their Components	201
	Questions	208
	References	210
10	**Specific Issues in Financial Reporting**	211
	Extraordinary Items and Prior-period Adjustments	211
	Earnings Per Share (EPS)	216
	Deferred Taxation	230
	Contingencies	241
	Post Balance Sheet Events	242
	Stocks and Work-in-progress	243
	Depreciation	250
	Intangible Assets	255
	Leases	265
	Pensions	276
	Foreign Currency Translation	283
	Value-Added Statements	296
	Questions	299
	References	307

11   Accounting for Inter-company Relationships   311
    Trade Investments   311
    Associated Companies   312
    Subsidiary Companies   315
    Acquisition Versus Merger Accounting   318
    Consolidated Financial Statements   323
    Questions   327
References   327

12   Increasing Disclosure   328
    Reporting Income Components   329
    Reporting by Segments   330
    Interim Reporting   333
    Reporting Forecasts   335
    Conclusion   338
    Questions   339
    References   339

Index   341

PREFACE

Interest in accounting theory and policy making has grown considerably over recent years reflecting criticisms voiced both inside and outside the accounting profession of the procedures followed in drawing up the published financial statements of companies. Traditionally, accounting theory developed as a structure of accounting principles which described financial reporting practices. This conventional structure developed in a piecemeal, pragmatic fashion and tended to follow practice rather than lead it. Although user needs played an important role in this process they were not explicitly recognised in the literature until comparatively recently. In contrast, contemporary developments in accounting theory place the emphasis on the needs of users for making economic decisions.

Over time financial reports have come to be more closely regulated by accounting policy makers. Government and government agencies have for many years exercised some control over financial reporting and have latterly been joined by accounting standard-setting bodies. Whereas government bodies have mandated certain aspects of financial reporting, standard setting bodies have sought to standardise the practice underlying financial reports. Ideally, accounting theory should provide accounting policy makers with guidance in choosing the best solutions to procedural problems and in establishing accounting policies. The ability of accounting theory to do this has not been helped by the absence of a single universally accepted accounting theory. Instead, a collection of theories exists which frequently conflict. Difficulties in formulating generally acceptable theories arise from disagreements over the objectives of financial reporting. Furthermore, even when objectives are agreed there remains the substantial problem of obtaining agreement on the means of achieving objectives.

The aims of this book are two-fold. The first is to provide an understanding of the main contributions which have been made in the development of theory in accounting. We shall see that there has been a wide variety of approaches taken by theoreticians and that the term 'theory' is subject to a number of interpretations. A chief concern is the specification of the criteria for judging the quality of alternative theories. The second aim of the book is to identify how accounting policies to guide practitioners are formulated, and how accounting theory may help policy makers in their deliberations and choices.

The book consists of twelve chapters. Chapter 1 considers accounting theory and its environment and attempts to present an overview of the topics covered by the book. Chapter 2 examines the conventional approach to accounting theory and policy. Chapter 3 discusses some of the background to the setting of accounting standards and the institutional detail of the process. Chapter 4 provides a brief review of recent law affecting accounting and financial reporting. Thus, the first four chapters review theoretical and institutional issues relating to accounting theory and policy. Chapter 5 concentrates on a very important approach to accounting theory, namely decision usefulness. The next three chapters are devoted to various aspects of income measurement—Chapter 6 considers approaches to income measurement from a conceptual viewpoint, while Chapter 7 examines the problems of recognition and realisation under the conventional approach and Chapter 8 is devoted to accounting for price changes. Chapter 9 extends the discussion of issues raised in earlier chapters by concentrating upon funds and cash-flow reporting. Chapter 10 is devoted to specific issues in financial reporting. This very long chapter is split into a number of sections each relating to a particular issue. The sections need not necessarily be read in sequence and most are aimed to be self-contained. The purpose of Chapter 10 is to apply some of the ideas developed in the previous chapters to practical issues. Chapter 11 looks at certain of the issues raised by the need to account for inter-company investments. Finally, Chapter 12 discusses extensions to disclosure and serves as a concluding chapter.

Accounting Theory and Policy Making is intended for use by the following:

(*a*) Students attending university and polytechnic undergraduate courses in financial accounting and accounting standards.
(*b*) Students attending MBA courses in business schools.
(*c*) Students studying for the examinations of the professional accountancy bodies.
(*d*) Practising accountants who wish to acquire a broader viewpoint of the accounting process.

We express appreciation to Ann Butchers, Frank Hall and Michael Nardone for their constructive comments on this work and to Kathryn Johnston for typing the manuscript.

Brian Underdown
Peter Taylor

May 1985

CHAPTER 1

Accounting Theory and its environment

Accounting Theory

Accounting theory has been defined as 'a cohesive set of hypothetical, conceptual and pragmatic principles forming a general frame of reference for a field of study' (American Accounting Association, 1966). Within this definition accounting theory may serve one or both of the two ends which all theories serve, namely to explain or to predict. Theories which explain may set out principles of what ought to be, in which case they are normative. Alternatively, theories may explain observed phenomena, and are termed descriptive. Theories of both types may be found under the heading of accounting theory.

The purpose of accounting theory is to provide a framework for (1) evaluating current financial accounting practice and (2) developing new practice. Whenever the need for a new application of practice arises, the general frame of reference of accounting theory should provide accountants with guidance on the most appropriate procedures to adopt in the circumstances. If accounting practice emerges from the application of rigorously constructed accounting theory, then practice has been tested for logic, consistency and usefulness. At present no single general theory of accounting exists which all agree can fulfil these objectives. Instead, numerous alternative theories have been proposed, and continue to attract support (AAA, 1977). However, in recent years much effort has been directed towards developing a general theory for the guidance of practice. Such a general theory has come to be known as a conceptual framework.

So far we have stressed the nature of accounting theory in only two of the three senses contained in the AAA definition quoted above, namely hypothetical and conceptual. It is in these senses that scientists, both natural and social, understand theory best. However, accounting theory has traditionally been viewed as the set of pragmatic principles which describe the structure of accounting practice which has evolved over many decades. As such it is composed of principles and rules which guide accountants in drawing up financial reports. The development of this pragmatic accounting theory has been a piecemeal process of trial and error in response to changing social and economic forces. Typically, principles have been evolved from observations of existing practice, and practice (and hence theory) has assumed a strictly utilitarian function. In this book we shall term this approach to accounting theory the conventional approach.

The Notion of 'Good Theory'

The many alternative developments in accounting theory may be evaluated against a standard of 'good theory'. Good theories have the following characteristics:

1. They explain or predict phenomena, that is, they are empirical.
2. They generate implications which are capable of refutation by empirical testing. Theories are tested in order to determine their ability to explain or predict observable phenomena. Theories which fail tests (are refuted) are clearly not of universal applicability and must be replaced by non-refuted theories. Theories which are not capable of refutation by testing are not scientific but speculative.
3. They are consistent both internally and externally. Internal consistency is present if the propositions or statements making up the theory are logically consistent with each other. Internal consistency is concerned with the analytic properties of theory and ensures that a theory predicts the same outcome for every identical situation. Externally, a theory should be consistent with theories in other disciplines.
4. They are helpful in providing a focus for guiding and directing research into empirical problems.

The Conventional Approach to Accounting Theory

The conventional approach to accounting theory dominated accounting thought in the period before accounting standard-setting bodies began to be established in various countries. Theory developed using the conventional approach is essentially concerned with what accountants do. In developing such theories, reliance is placed upon a process of inductive reasoning which consists of making observations and drawing generalised conclusions from those observations. In making observations of phenomena the theorist is seeking similarities of sufficient frequency as will induce the required degree of assurance needed to develop a theory concerning the phenomena.

The conventional approach has emphasised accounting practice as the basis from which to develop theory, and theory is, therefore 'primarily a concentrate distilled from experience . . . it is experience intelligently analysed that produces logical explanation . . . and . . . illuminates the practices from which it springs' (Littleton and Zimmerman 1962). Thus, conventional theory is descriptive in character.

When compared with the characteristics of good theory the conventional approach exhibits severe limitations. The subject matter of conventional accounting theory is composed of man-made constructs rather than natural phenomena. Accounting theory is none the less empirical since by 'empirical' it is generally meant 'that the subject matter . . . must, at least in the minds of the scientists concerned, represent some real phenomena capable of being observed' (Ryan, 1980). However, the conventional approach concentrates upon the behaviour of practising accountants rather than the behaviour of real-world phenomena (Sterling, 1967). The conventional approach duplicates the role of auditing in the accounting process. The accounting process takes observable occurrences (transactions), translates them into symbolic form (money values) and makes them inputs (e.g. sales, costs) into the formal accounting system where they are manipulated into outputs (financial statements) which are examined by an auditor. Auditing 'is not a verification of the outputs; instead it is a recalculation of the outputs . . . and a check on the accuracy or verity of the inputs. Thus, the auditing process focuses on the inputs to the system and the way in which these inputs are manipulated. It does not verify the output of the system' (Sterling, 1970). Similarly, conventional theory is not concerned with judging the usefulness of the output of accounting practice, but concentrates upon judging the means of manipulation of input into output.

Good theory should generate testable implications. The conventional approach fails to distinguish between the construction of accounting theory and the testing of the implications of theory. Indeed construction and testing are essentially the same process. Principles are selected as part of accounting theory because of their general acceptability (construction) and their general acceptability serves to validate their selection (verification).

The consistency of the conventional approach may be questioned. Inconsistencies in conventional theory have given rise to alternative accepted principles and procedures which give significantly divergent reported results. Accrual accounting results in allocations which provide a variety of alternative accounting methods for each major event—e.g. LIFO (Last In First Out) and FIFO (First In First Out) valuations of stock—and different accountants may prefer different methods depending upon how they are affected. Moreover, the conventional approach is inconsistent with theories developed in related disciplines. For example, the historical cost concept of valuation is externally inconsistent with valuation concepts from economic theory.

Finally, good theory should provide for research to assist advances in knowledge. The conventional approach tends to inhibit change, and by concentrating upon generally accepted principles, makes the relationship between theory and practice a circular one.

The mounting dissatisfaction with existing accounting practice which has resulted partly from an acceleration in the rate of environmental change in recent years, and partly from a growing recognition of the inherent weaknesses of the conventional approach, has lead to much research aimed at developing new accounting theories. It is to this research that we now turn.

Accounting Research Methods

Research is necessary in order to improve and develop theories. Accounting research embraces two activities: **a priori research** and **empirical research**. Many accounting writers have viewed these activities as separate, but in the light of our criteria of good theory, they are closely connected and complementary.

A priori research involves logical deduction directed towards the building of models and the generation of hypotheses. A priori research in accounting begins with the establishing of the objectives of accounting. Next, certain key definitions and assumptions are set out. The researcher must then develop a logical structure which leads to the specification of the means by which the objectives of accounting are achieved. These means will be the procedures and practices of accounting and form the conclusions of a priori theorising. The conclusions depend upon the assumptions made and the soundness of the reasoning following from those assumptions. Given the empirical character of accounting, a priori theorists must pay careful attention to the empirical testing of the implications derived from their theories, for without such testing theories are to be viewed as speculative.

Bedford (1978) has categorised a priori theories as follows:

1. Attempts to develop basic postulates and principles of accounting (as in Moonitz, 1961 and Sprouse and Moonitz, 1962).
2. Attempts to broaden the base of accounting by relating it to those fundamental disciplines such as economics, behavioural science and measurement theory (as in Chambers, 1966; Edwards and Bell, 1961; Ijiri, 1978; and Sterling, 1970).
3. Attempts to formalise accounting theory into a more abstract form (as in Mattesich, 1977; Williams and Griffen, 1969; and Demski, 1973).

4. Attempts to politicise accounting theory for practical use in bargaining by preparers and users of accounts (as in Horngren, 1972).
5. Attempts to develop a conceptual framework for accounting (Financial Accounting, Standards Board, 1976).

These categories identify the evolution of a priori theory.

Empirical research begins with observations of phonomena from which a problem is defined. Data relevant to the problem are collected and hypotheses are formulated. Finally, the hypotheses are tested by an independent process. Empirical research in accounting may be categorised as follows.

1. Predictive ability research. This examines the usefulness of financial reports for past periods in enabling investors in particular to make estimates of the future.
2. Research into the behaviour of individual users of accounting information. Such research attempts to apply concepts from the behavioural sciences such as psychology and sociology.
3. Aggregate user (or efficient markets) research. This examines how information, particularly accounting information, affects the formulation of share prices in stock markets. This approach is based in economics and the theory of finance.

One reason for the rapid growth of empirical research in accounting in the 1960s and 1970s was disillusionment with speculative a priori research. In contrast empirical research was seen as being concerned with facts rather than abstractions. Unfortunately much empirical research can be criticised as measurement without theory. As Beaver (1981(b)) has pointed out, 'The empirical research on market efficiency . . . preceded a formal conceptual development of market efficiency'. A priori theorising is a necessary complement to empirical research since it provides a framework of definitions, concepts and hypotheses to guide empirical researchers. Without such a framework it is difficult to interpret the results of empirical research. Also, as we have already pointed out, it is necessary to test a priori theory against the experience of reality by empirical research.

The Nature of Accounting Controversies

Many controversies in accounting arise because there is no single, generally accepted theory of accounting. Until this metatheory (Bedford, 1978) is developed, a multiplicity of alternative theories will continue to exist. Conflict between alternative theories is partly due to methodological disputes between theorists and partly due to misunderstandings of the proper (complementary) relationship between a priori and empirical research.

However, other, perhaps more important, controversies arise from the political nature of accounting policy-making (Horngren, 1973). By necessity, the concepts and assumptions of accounting are rooted in the value system of the society in which it operates. They are socially determined and socially expressed. Controversy in accounting originates as much from these considerations as from theoretical differences or disputes about technical applications since the choice of a particular accounting policy from amongst alternatives almost inevitably requires judgements to be made about whose interests are to be served, and what trade-offs are to be made between the interests of different groups. Problems of this kind cannot be settled by logic or reference to a metatheory of accounting. Rather, their resolution depends upon the exercise of political power by those who possess it or by the achievement of consensus among all interested parties. For example, the double entry system of data recording and classification can be learned and applied. But when it is necessary to interpret and evaluate economic events for financial reports the concepts change from debit and credit to more complex forms such as matching, allocation, and revenue recognition. It is here that controversy arises because judgement is needed.

The fundamental debates in accounting revolve around socially significant and value-laden concepts such as fairness, objectivity and disclosure. When such concepts are involved, there are no universal truths or general laws. The universality or generality of value-laden concepts depends upon their acceptability to the majority of people affected by them.

The Environment of Financial Reporting

As we have stressed, accounting is greatly influenced by the social, political, and economic forces which make up the environment in which it functions. This is especially true of the preparation of external financial reports. Figure 1.1 illustrates the relationships between the main elements which comprise the financial reporting environment.

Figure 1.1 shows the various groups which are interested in the contents of financial reports (Accounting Standards Committee, 1975). There are different views between groups and within groups on the information which should be disclosed in financial reports. For example, the information demanded by financial analysts may not be the type that management is willing to disclose.

Demands for information are directed to the suppliers. Figure 1.1 shows that two groups are responsible for the amount and method of disclosure.

1. Financial report preparers. The primary responsibility for financial reporting rests with management. In an unregulated environment

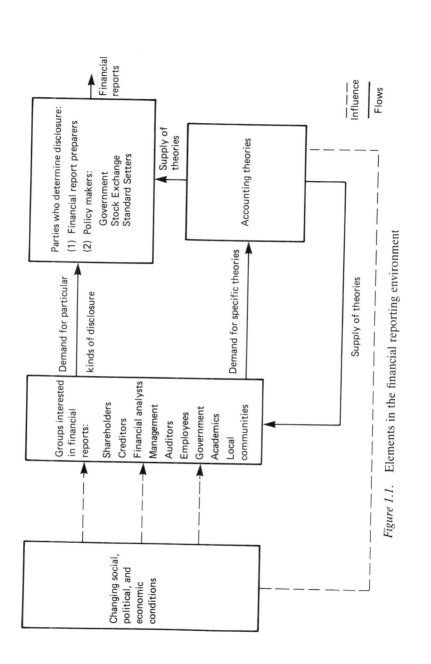

Figure 1.1. Elements in the financial reporting environment

management prepares reports in response to the dictates of market forces (Watts, 1977 and Watts and Zimmerman, 1978) and in accordance with the principles and rules which have evolved through time.
2. Policy makers. They regulate financial reports by imposing disclosure requirements upon preparers. Governments impose legal requirements (Companies Acts) and the Stock Exchange requires minimum disclosure as a condition of allowing a company's shares to be traded (Listing Agreement). More recently, professional accounting bodies have been established to regulate financial reports through the promulgation and enforcement of accounting standards (ASC, FASB).

Users of information, preparers, and regulators, all make use of accounting theory. Users may require theories to support their case for disclosure whilst preparers and regulators use theories to support their choices of what to disclose or what to require to be disclosed.

There is some dispute over how the supply of accounting theories arises. One might argue that theories emerge from a process of more or less scientific endeavour stimulated by influences arising from the environment. Alternatively it has been argued (Watts and Zimmerman, 1979) that theories are developed by compliant or self-interest theorists in response to demands by individuals and groups who subsequently employ the theories in pursuit of their own interests.

However they have arisen, it is clear that accounting theories have developed to cope with existing problems rather than to anticipate new or emerging ones. For example, the rapid growth of leasing as a source of finance has stimulated interest in accounting for leases. Perhaps more strikingly, inflation accounting is a product of the distortions introduced into the financial system by changing prices.

Should Accounting be Regulated?

Accounting disclosure is regulated by a combination of public sector (governmental) and private sector (e.g. ASC, FASB) institutions. Regulatory institutions and the relationships between them will be discussed in Chapter 3. Here we shall examine regulation in more general terms.

Regulation of the provision of any commodity, including financial information, implies that a freely-functioning market is not thought able to ensure an appropriate allocation of that commodity. In a free-market setting, the demand for financial statements would come from users of such statements (chiefly investors and creditors) and companies would supply such statements at a price. Thus, market forces would ensure that information would be produced and communicated at a level consistent with the equation of marginal costs and benefits. According to this view, the processes which exist for generating financial information would create an adequate supply without compulsion (Benston, 1973). On the demand side, investors would bid for information relevant to their investment decisions. On the supply side management would have strong incentives to provide adequate and reliable financial information which would attract investment; companies which did not furnish information adequate to the disclosure standards applicable to companies generally would have a limited existence due to their inability to attract and retain investment.

Supporters of a free-market approach to financial reporting present evidence that voluntary disclosure and auditing of financial information took place before legal regulation existed (Watts, 1977), and continue to occur (Leftwich, 1983). The tendency of accounting practice to evolve to meet current needs is well established and lends support at a macro level to the micro analysis of agency theory contained in the works just cited.

However, there are important reasons for doubting the ability of a free market to provide an optimal solution to financial reporting problems. The efficacy of a private-market solution has been questioned empirically:

> There have been many instances known to members of the Committee which demonstrate that falsified financial statements and other abuses of the disclosure process have endured for a long time without market forces in any way bringing about sufficient, reliable, or timely disclosure.
>
> (Securities and Exchange Commission, 1977)

The question of market failure may be approached from a conceptual point of view if the characteristics of disclosed financial information as a commodity are considered. Disclosed financial information has the attributes of a public good. A public good is one which, if supplied to one person, is available for all others. Thus, unlike pure private goods, the exclusion principle cannot be applied in consumption, and the public good is subject to joint consumption. Non-exclusion creates a reluctance on the part of the consumers to reveal preferences for a public good in the hope that others will demand the good and thereby ensure supply for all. This is the free-rider problem. If financial information is published its total supply is not diminished by use since the same information may be used by all. Moreover, the production of financial information (like other public goods) is subject to declining cost since additional users may be supplied at no incremental cost once the first user has been supplied. The declining cost of financial information strengthens the free-rider impulse. Thus, the problems which have long been identified with public goods such as defence seem applicable to financial information. A solution to these problems is offered by public provision in the case of commodities like defence, and regulation in the case of accounting information. However, the question of the level and type of provision (regulation) is transferred from the market to the policy maker and this creates its own problems.

Developing the Objectives of Accounting

Having established a case for the regulation of accounting disclosure we now examine the problems of reaching agreement on the objectives of regulation. Several advantages may be identified for having an agreed set of objectives for accounting regulation (Sorter and Gans, 1974):

1. The proper evaluation of current practice requires a set of objectives. In the absence of objectives policy makers may be forced to apply inadequate criteria to the evaluation of practice. For example, practice may be judged against existing regulations or standards. Such an evaluation merely establishes how far existing regulations or standards are being applied, not whether existing regulations or standards are achieving their objectives. More generally, this has been stated as follows:

   > Articulation of social goals is important for ascertaining whether they are being reached and even for reaching them. It is improbable, to say the least, that any goals can be reached by chance.   (Terleckyj, 1970)

2. The evaluation of proposed changes in accounting regulations or standards requires the establishment of stated objectives if a rational choice is to be made between alternatives. This merely extends a tenet of the classic economic-decision model to accounting regulation.
3. The need to respond appropriately to changing circumstances implies objectives against which responses may be evaluated. In the absence of articulated objectives accounting regulations or standards may become dogmatic and ends in themselves, rather than means to ends.

Despite the importance of developing accounting objectives there are serious problems in formulating objectives:

1. Lack of knowledge about user needs. The objectives selected will inevitably reflect knowledge or perceptions of the needs of those who are thought to use financial reports. Unfortunately, as Stamp (1980) sees it:

   > One of the great difficulties in producing standards and financial statements that are truly free of bias is our general ignorance of the nature and variety of user decision models, so that it may be difficult to be sure whether information is biased or not.

   Objectives are normative in character and will tend to reflect the value judgements of those who formulate them. This tendency will be greater, other things being equal, the more ignorance there is of user needs. Research which has sought to investigate user needs (Lee and Tweedie, 1975; Cooper and Essex, 1977) has done little to blunt this criticism.
2. Different users have different needs. Each user group will make its own

decisions and different decisions will require different information. Moreover, within given user groups the value of information will vary between individuals depending, amongst other things, upon their level of understanding and access to other information sources. Therefore, if user needs were known their variety would impose its own problems.

3. Conflicts of interest. The interests of various groups are likely to be in conflict. Formulating objectives for accounting depends upon resolving such conflicts. Cyert a. ' Ijiri (1974) consider the interaction between three groups: users, corporations and the accounting profession. Their analysis is contained in Figure 1.2.

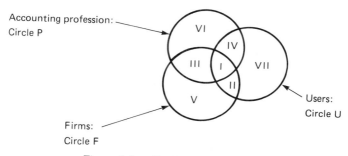

Figure 1.2.   Conflicts of interest

Figure 1.2 represents information sets for the three groups. Circle U represents information useful to users of accounts, circle F information which the management of firms agrees to disclose, and circle P information which the accounting profession is capable of producing and verifying. Area I is the feasible set acceptable to all groups. That is, such information is perceived as relevant by users, is disclosed by firms, and can be produced and verified by accountants. Areas II to VII inclusive represent areas of conflict.

Given these conflicts Cyert and Ijiri suggest three approaches to the formulation of accounting objectives. The first considers the set of information which firms are willing to disclose and attempts to find the best means of measuring and verifying it. Thus, circle F is kept fixed and circles P and U are moved towards it. The second approach takes circle P as fixed and attempts to accommodate users and firms through various accounting options. This involves moving circles F and U towards P. Finally, the information considered relevant by users, circle U, is considered central and accountants and firms are encouraged to produce and verify that information.

Simply stated, the first approach is firm-orientated, the second profession-orientated, and the third user-orientated. At the present time the user-orientated approach is in the ascendancy. The *Corporate Report* (ASC, 1975), the *Trueblood Report* (American Institute of Certified Public Accountants, 1973), *The Stamp Report* (Stamp, 1980), and the FASB's conceptual framework programme have each adopted such an approach to determining the objectives of accounting.

Securing agreement on the objectives of accounting is not the only problem facing policy makers. Accounting regulation requires the implementation of objectives through the application of a set of rules and principles. Much a priori research has been devoted to the derivation of such sets of rules and principles and they have come to be known as conceptual frameworks (Peasnell, 1982). A conceptual framework is an a priori theory whose validity depends upon its consistency with stated objectives of accounting and its logical structure. None of the attempts at constructing a conceptual framework have proved entirely successful. This is not to say that their logic has necessarily been in question. Rather, it is their normative character that has proved controversial. Indeed, although objectives create conflict, they may be less controversial than the principles or assumptions of a conceptual framework since the former are more general (and hence more likely to gain general acceptance) than the latter. This is illustrated if we consider the reception given to two documents issued by the Accounting Principles Board (APB) in the USA, namely (Moonitz 1961) and (Sprouse and Moonitz, 1962). These two studies were intended to provide the foundation for subsequent work and for the issue of statements by the APB. Postulate B–2 in Moonitz (1961) stated that 'accounting data are based upon prices generated by past, present or future exchanges which have actually taken place or are expected to'. Clearly, no-one would dispute this assertion. On the other hand, the principle set out in Sprouse and Moonitz (1962) that assets be shown at their current values (derived in part from postulates B–2) received a very critical reception.

The Accounting Policy-making Process

Our discussion so far has considered some of the justification for accounting policy making and some of the influences on it. Now we shall extend this discussion by examining the accounting policy-making process.

The complexity of the accounting policy-making process is illustrated in Figure 1.3 derived from May and Sundem (1976). Figure 1.3 is divided into four sections as follows:

I Policy makers.
II Firms and auditors.
III Individuals.
IV Markets.

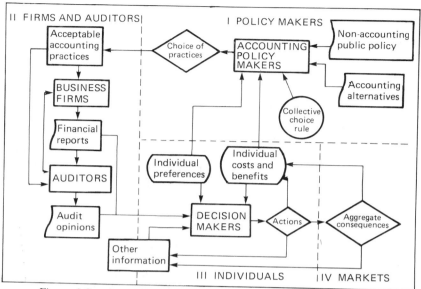

Figure 1.3. A model of the accounting policy making process

A priori, one would expect the accounting policy making process to proceed in an anti-clockwise direction. Thus, accounting policy makers choose accounting practices which are applied in business firms in the preparation of their financial reports and by auditors in auditing those reports and forming opinions on them. Audited reports, together with other information, are used by individual decision makers to make their decisions, which through the media of markets, generate economic consequences which create costs and benefits, which in their turn influence decision makers. Policy makers may be influenced in their policy decisions by their perceptions of the costs and benefits of economic consequences flowing from accounting practices; by the preferences of individuals; by public policy; and by knowledge of accounting alternatives. Accounting policies are chosen by the application of a choice rule, thereby turning the process full circle. How policy makers choose between alternatives is not clear, neither is it obvious how they should choose. Moreover, we cannot be sure that our a priori explanation is the only one, or indeed the most valid. Many interpretations have been placed on the elements of this policy-making process and we may distinguish five approaches to policy making. Although these perspectives are not inconsistent the emphasis is different. They are:

1. Reporting economic reality.
2. Decision usefulness.

3. Agency theory.
4. Political approach.
5. Social welfare.

Reporting Economic Reality

This approach attempts to measure the results of economic events in an objective, neutral manner. Accounting controversies are viewed in terms of technical issues. Such an approach was very popular in the 1960s when accounting theorists were mainly concerned with a priori theorising about the best means of reporting the results of economic transactions. Proponents of this approach do not accept that accountants should become involved in a political process and question the wisdom of implementing policies which are designed to affect human behaviour. They take the view that accounting measurements should be as neutral as they can be made (Solomons, 1978), for, if they are not neutral, accountants will lose their credibility.

The approach is based upon the assumption that users' needs are known and that reporting accounting income and asset values will meet those needs. As we shall see in Chapter 6, the various income measures which have been suggested all have advantages and limitations and it is not possible to judge them on technical grounds alone. Rather, the value of an income measure depends upon its utility to those who use it rather than its relationship to some notion of ultimate truth.

Decision Usefulness

Supporters of this approach adopt an information-systems approach aimed at satisfying the requirements of decisions. The information may or may not be economic in nature. Two perspectives may be distinguished: (1) decision models and (2) decision makers. The decision-models perspective focuses on the information needs of decision models whilst the decision-makers perspective emphasises the information used by decision makers. The former is normative and the latter positive. The decision-models perspective specifies normative characteristics such as understandibility, relevance, reliability, timeliness and comparability for information which will enhance its usefulness in normative decision models. The policy makers' choice amongst accounting alternatives is based upon a priori reasoning often expressed in a conceptual framework. As with the reporting of economic reality, only a portion of Figure 1.3 is considered relevant under this approach to accounting policy making.

The decision-makers perspective is positive in character and considers how decision makers actually behave. It involves empirical research into decision making at both the individual and aggregate level to which we have already referred. Thus, individual-user research seeks to identify individual decision makers' actions and preferences in section III in Figure 1.3), whilst aggregate-user research investigates section IV. The decision-usefulness approach is discussed further in Chapter 5.

Agency Theory

Agency theory stresses the incentives within the private-sector market system for management to disclose financial information to owners. Agency theory is a formal version of the arguments against accounting regulation which we discussed above (Jensen and Meckling, 1976; Watts and Zimmerman, 1978). Agency theory assumes that individuals seek to maximise their own utility. An agency is defined as a relationship by consent between two parties whereby one party (the agent) agrees to act on behalf of the other (the principal). Within the context of a firm the accepted view is of management as the agent and suppliers of capital as the principals. The principal's task is to elicit optimal behaviour from the agent given his (the principal's) expectations about an uncertain future and he attempts to do this by monitoring the agent's activities. If the agent can produce financial information for monitoring purposes at lower cost than the principal, the utility-maximising agent will voluntarily agree to supply such information and thereby reduce the costs of maintaining the agency relationship to the advantage of both parties. Because of the diversity of contractual arrangements accounting procedures based upon agency relationships will vary. Moreover, if alternatives are available agents will tend to choose the procedure which is most favourable in the light of contractual arrangements.

The agency-theory approach argues that decentralised market arrangements can adequately control the supply of financial disclosure. Indeed, some empirical studies have concluded that intervention by accounting policy makers in this free-market arrangement has not proved to be in the interests of the shareholders and bondholders (Benston, 1973; Chow, 1983). Proponents of agency theory see the best behaviour for accounting policy makers to be benign neglect; their most useful function is to make and protect the general rules by which markets for financial information function, and to provide a legal framework offering opportunities for redress. Thus, the only influence which section I of Figure 1.3 has is through an overseer's role on section IV. The process by which acceptable accounting practices emerge begins in section IV and proceeds in a clockwise direction.

We have already summarised arguments in support of accounting regulation based upon ideas of market failure. These arguments are clearly directed against the agency-theory approach. It must be emphasised that agency theory is essentially descriptive in character and does not provide a basis for promoting change. Furthermore, its emphasis upon the utility-maximising behaviour of managers and suppliers of credit has caused it to be politically and socially unacceptable to some writers (Tinker, 1982).

Political Approach

This approach found an early and vigorous advocate in Horngren (1972, 1973) who wrote that:

> the setting of accounting standards is as much a product of political action as of flawless logic or empirical findings. Why? Because the setting of standards is a social decision. Standards place restrictions on behaviour; therefore they must be accepted by the affected parties. Acceptance may be forced or voluntary or some of both.   (1973)

This observation is undoubtedly true and applies whether accounting policy making is conducted in the public or private sectors (Dopuch and Sunder, 1980). Clearly if governments or governmental agencies such as the SEC establish accounting regulations, political considerations are important, but the same considerations are present if private-sector bodies like the ASC or FASB set accounting standards. Although supporters of neutral accounting recoil from such an explicit view, others see an explicit concern with the politics of accounting regulation as desirable:

> a politicization of accounting rule making [is] not only inevitable, but just. In a society committed to democratic legitimization of authority, only politically responsive institutions have the right to commend others to obey their rules . . . when a decision making process depends for its success on public confidence, the critical issues are not technical; they are political. In the face of conflict between competing interests rationality as well as prudence lies not in seeking final answers, but rather in compromise.   (Geborth, 1972)

The virtues of the politicisation of accounting are, according to this view, to be found in the democratic process and compromise. This in its turn implies a particular approach to policy making, namely incrementality. This is typical of policy making generally in democracies and policy makers will, as Lindblom (1977) points out, 'turn their limited analytical energies in some small part and sometimes exclusively to the analysis of citizen volitions rather than the substance if the policy decision at hand'. A danger, therefore, is that of emphasis is placed largely on acceptability, accounting policies may be very general and may lack intellectual rigour.

Thus, the political approach emphasises the institutions and choice processes of section I of Figure 1.3. A democratic political process for accounting policy making involves the establishing of institutional arrangements for the consultation and involvement of interested or affected groups. In the Netherlands, as Muis (1977) comments: 'the two principal social partners, employers and trades union organisations are put in one standard setting boat with the profession. The over-riding criterion is whether or not these practices are acceptable to the business community'. In the USA and the UK quite elaborate consultation processes have been developed to try to ensure democratic influence on policy makers. However, even with ostensibly democratic institutions, certain groups may wield disproportionate amounts of power and influence, and policy makers may unduly favour some groups. There is an increasing body of evidence on the extent to which groups have engaged in the lobbying of policy makers (Hagerman and Zmijewski, 1979; Hope and Gray, 1982).

Social Welfare

This is an extension of the political approach and involves an assessment by policy makers of the effects of accounting policies on the behaviour of user groups and others and thereby upon the economy. The social welfare approach is closely related to the issue of the economic consequences of accounting policy which began to emerge in the 1970s. Zeff (1978) defined economic consequences as follows:

> By 'economic consequences' is meant the impact of accounting reports on the decision making behaviour of business, government, unions, investors and creditors.

A number of writers have presented a priori studies of the likely economic consequences of accounting policies (Rappaport, 1977; Beaver 1981(a); Selto and Newman, 1981). Much more attention has been devoted to empirical analysis seeking evidence of the existence of economic consequences (FASB, 1978; Abdel Khalik, 1981). Such research has encompassed both individual and aggregate approaches.

A major issue which arises from both a priori and empirical research is the role which evidence on economic consequences should play in the decisions of accounting policy makers. Recognition of economic consequences raises a number of questions. What constitutes desirable or undesirable economic consequence? What is an appropriate balance between economic consequences and other, for example, technical considerations? How are the economic consequences on different groups to be compared? Does a private sector regulatory body have the right to make such judgements?

Some writers (May and Sundem, 1976) take the view that accounting policies should be set so as to maximise social welfare rather than the welfare of any particular interest group or groups. This suggests rather broad objectives for financial reporting such as those set out by Mautz and May (1978):

1. Improve capital formation.
2. Assist in the allocation of resources.
3. Encourage innovation and risk-taking.
4. Facilitate domestic enterprises to meet foreign competition.
5. Provide benefits which are greater than costs.

There may be conflicts between these objectives. For example, information which is necessary to attain the most efficient allocation of resources within the economy may be detrimental to companies in international competition. The implementation of these objectives places a heavy burden on policy makers who would have to:

(*a*) Specify the effects of accounting policies on total investment within the economy. For example, an alleged economic consequence of reporting the effects of inflation could be to alter the rate of capital formation within the economy. Similarly, an accounting policy that required research and development expenditure to be capitalised might reduce such expenditure and constitute a threat to economic progress. The profits of small firms might be particularly affected and this policy might have the additional effect of adversely affecting their access to the capital market.

(*b*) Specify the costs of providing information from accounting and other sources.

(*c*) Identify the effect on the allocation of resources from various accounting alternatives. For example, reporting the effects of inflation may alter the allocation of resources among various sectors of the economy.

(*d*) Identify the impact on the welfare of all members of society from accounting policy decisions. For example, increasing the disclosure of financial information may improve the welfare of the sophisticated investor; but the additional costs of disclosure may be borne by shareholders generally through reduced dividends, by the consumers of the products of the reporting enterprise in the form of higher prices, and by the tax payer through the tax deductability of such costs.

Thus for each accounting policy alternative it is necessary for accounting policy makers to identify all the costs and benefits involved, a process which imposes severe information requirements on policy makers.

Once costs and benefits have been identified, there remains the problem of how to combine them in order to compare and select alternative accounting policies. If an accounting alternative which is Pareto optimal (i.e. one which improves the welfare of some whilst leaving no-one else worse off) could be identified, then this would be selected. Unfortunately, it will be much more likely that there will be gainers and losers under each alternative and, as we have already noted, a desirable characteristic of a policy-making process is that it takes into account the preferences of affected groups. Thus, the problem of accounting policy making is one of social choice. For this reason, there has been a growing interest in the application of welfare economics to accounting policy making. Demski (1973) provides a demonstration that it is not possible to choose unambiguously between accounting alternatives about which individuals have individual share preferences (deriving from potential gains and losses). This *Impossibility Theorem* has been taken to preclude any acceptable choice between accounting policy alternatives and hence seriously to call into question the possibility of accounting regulation. However, it has been argued that there are strong grounds to believe that socially acceptable accounting policies are possible (Cushing, 1977). Optimal accounting policies may be identifiable if individuals exhibit considerable homogeneity in their preferences for accounting alternatives, or if areas of general agreement may be identified. Furthermore, the tendency to agreement may be strengthened if the mechanisms and institutions for policy making are acceptable, particularly to those who may be adversely affected by policy choices.

Despite the considerable difficulties both theoretical and practical which are emerging from studies of accounting policy making, it remains one of the most important areas of accounting. On the subject of future research in the area May and Sundem (1976) argue:

> The most promising use of any given research strategy in the area of financial reporting policy is not in selecting optional alternatives; rather it is in contributing, along with all other available strategies, to developing theories that they may be used by policy makers to settle specific issues.

Taking Figure 1.3 as a framework they go on to detail the implications for future research as follows:

Section   I — Researchers should produce theories to show policy makers the effects of their policies on social welfare.

— How accounting policy fits into the public policy framework.

— Developing and clarifying accounting alternatives.

— Feedbacks on the impacts of policy decisions on individuals.

Section II — Prediction of effect of alternative rules on accounting
statements.
— Empirical work on the effects of alternative rules of
accounting statements.

Section III — Tracing the effect of financial reports on individual actions.

Section IV — Determining how individual actions combine to yield
equilibrium prices with accounting numbers as variables.
— Determining effects of different equilibrium price sets on
resource and wealth allocation.

QUESTIONS

1. Distinguish between descriptive and normative theories.
2. Explain the four characteristics of 'good theory'.
3. Define 'conventional approach'. Compare the characteristics of the
   conventional approach to accounting theory construction with those of
   good theory approaches.
4. Differentiate a priori research and empirical research. Why should
   they be viewed as complementary?
5. Name the three categories of empirical accounting research.
6. Why is accounting policy making political in nature? To what problems
   does this give rise?
7. Which two groups are responsible for the amount and method of
   financial disclosure?
8. Consider the arguments for regulating financial reporting.
9. (a) What advantages may accrue from an agreed set of objectives for
      financial reporting?
   (b) Consider the problems inherent in the process of formulating and
      implementing such objectives.
10. What is meant by a 'reporting economic reality' approach to
    accounting policy making? What problems are involved in
    implementing this approach?
11. Distinguish between a decision model's and a decision maker's
    perspective
12. What is 'agency theory' and what are its characteristics?
13. Define economic consequences. In which areas of accounting are
    economic consequences likely to arise?
14. What problems are involved in attempting to identify all the costs and
    benefits of accounting policy making?

REFERENCES

Abel-Khalik, A. R., *The Economic Effects on Lessees of FASB Statement No. 13, 'Accounting for Leases'*, FASB, 1981.

Accounting Standards Committee, *The Corporate Report*, Institute of Chartered Accountants in England and Wales, 1975.

American Accounting Association, *A Statement of Basic Accounting Theory*, 1966.

American Accounting Association, Statement on Accounting Theory and Theory Acceptance, 1977.

American Institute of Certified Public Accountants, *Report of the Study Group on the Objectives of Financial Statements*, (*Trueblood Report*) 1973.

Beaver, W. H., *Financial Reporting—An Accounting Revolution*, Prentice Hall, 1981(a).

Beaver, W. H., 'Market Efficiency', *Accounting Review*, Vol. 56, 1981(b).

Bedford, N. M., 'The Impact of a Priori Theory and Research on Accounting Practice, in Abdel-Khalik. A. R., and Keller, T. F., *The Impact of Accounting Research on Practice and Disclosure*; Duke University Press, 1978.

Benston, G. J., 'Required Disclosure and the Stock Market: An Evaluation of the Securities and Exchange Act of 1934', *American Economic Review*, 1973.

Chambers, R. J., *Accounting, Evaluation and Human Behaviour*, Scholars Book Company, 1966.

Chow, C. W., 'The Impacts of Accounting Regulation on Bondholder and Shareholder Wealth: The Case of the Securities Acts', *The Accounting Review*, 1983.

Cooper, D. J. and Essex, S., Accounting Information and Employee Decision Making', *Accounting Organisation and Society*, 1977.

Cushing, B., 'On the Possibility of Optimal Accounting Principles', *The Accounting Review*, 1977.

Cyert, R. M. and Ijiri, Y., 'Problems of Implementing the Trueblood Objectives Report', *Journal of Accounting Research*, Supplement, 1974.

Demski, J., 'The General Impossibility of Normative Accounting Standards', *The Accounting Review*, 1973.

Dopuch, N, and Sunder, S., 'FASB's Statement on Objectives and Elements of Financial Accounting: A Review', *The Accounting Review*, 1980.

Edwards, E. O., and Bell, P. W., *The Theory of Measurement of Business Income*, University of California Press, 1961.

FASB, *Scope and Implications of the Conceptual Framework Project*, 1976.

FASB, 'Economic Consequences of Financial Accountancy Standards', *Selected Papers*, 1978.

Geborth, D. L., 'Muddling Thro' with the APB', *Journal of Accountancy*, 1972.

Hagerman, R. L. and Zmijewski, M. E., 'Some Economic Determinants of Accounting Policy Choice', *Journal of Accounting and Economics*, 1979.

Hope, A. J. B. and Gray, R., 'Power and Policy Making: The Development of an R and D Standard, *Journal of Business Finance and Accounting*, Winter, 1982.

Horngren, C. T., 'Accounting Principles: Private or Public Sectors?', *Journal of Accountancy*, May, 1972.

Horngren, C. T., 'The Marketing of Accounting Standards', *Journal of Accountancy*, October, 1973.

Ijiri, Y., *The Foundations of Accounting Measurement*, Scholars Book Company, 1978.

Jensen, M. C. and Meckling, W. H., 'Theory of the Firm: Managerial Behaviour,

Agency Costs and Ownership Structure', *Journal of Financial Economics*, October 1976.

Lee, T. A. and Tweedle, D. P., 'Accounting Information: An Investigation of Private Shareholders Usage', *Accounting and Business Research*, Autumn, 1975.

Leftwich, R., 'Accounting Information in Private Markets: Evidence from Private Lending Agreements', *The Accounting Review*, Vol. 58, January, 1983.

Littleton, A. C., and Zimmerman, V. K., *Accounting Theory: Continuity and Change*, Prentice Hall, 1962.

Lindblom, C., *Politics and Markets*, Basic Books, 1977.

Mattesich, R., *Accounting and Analytical Methods*, Scholars Book Company, 1977.

Mautz, R. K. and May, W. G., *Financial Disclosure in a Competitive Economy*, Financial Executive Research Foundation, 1978.

May, R. G. and Sundem, G. L., 'Research for Accounting Policy: An Overview', *The Accounting Review*, 1976.

Moonitz, M., *Accounting Research Study Number?: The Basic Postulates of Accounting*, AICPA, 1961.

Muis, J., 'Accounting Standard Setting: the Pit and the Pendulum', *Accounting and Business Research*, 1977.

Peasnell, K. V., 'The Function of a Conceptual Framework for Corporate Financial Reporting', *Accounting and Business Research*, Autumn, 1982.

Rappaport, A., 'Economic Impact of Accounting Standards—Implications for the FASB', *Journal of Accountancy*, 1977.

Ryan, R. J., 'Scientific Method', Chapter 2, in *Topics in Management Accounting*, J. Arnold, B. Carsberg and R. Scapens (eds.), Philip Allan, 1980.

Securities and Exchange Commission, *Report of the SEC Advisory Committee on Corporate Disclosure*, 1977.

Selto, F. H. and Newman, B. R., 'A Further Guide to Research on the Economic Consequences of Accounting Information', *Accounting and Business Research*, 1981.

Solomons, D., 'The Politicization of Accounting', *Journal of Accountancy*, 1978.

Sorter, G. H., 'An Events Approach to Basic Accounting Theory', *The Accounting Review*, 1969.

Sorter, G. H. and Gans, M. S., 'Opportunities and Implications of the Report on Objectives of Financial Statements', *Journal of Accounting Research Supplement*, 1974.

Sprouse, R. T. and Moonitz, M., *Accounting Research Study Number 3*, 'A Tentative Set of Broad Accountancy Principles for Business Enterprises', AICPA, 1962.

Stamp, E., *Corporate Reporting: its Future Evolution*, Canadian Institute of Chartered Accountants, 1980.

Staubus, G. J., *Making Accounting Decisions*, Scholars Book Company, 1977.

Sterling, R. R., 'A Statement of Basic Accounting Theory, a Review Article', *Journal of Accounting Research*, Spring 1967.

Sterling, R. R., 'On Theory Construction and Verification', *Accounting Review*, 1970.

Terleckyj, N. E., 'Measuring Progress towards Social Goals', *Management Science*, 1970.

Tinker, A. M., *The Nationalization of Accounting, Social Ideology and the Genesis of Agency Theory*, Graduate School of Business Administration, New York University, 1982.

Watts, R. L., 'Corporate Financial Statements: A Product of the Market and Political Processes', *Australian Journal of Management*, April 1977.

Watts, R. L. and Zimmerman, J. L., 'Towards a Positive Theory of the Determination of Accounting Standards', *The Accounting Review*, 1978.

Watts, R. L. and Zimmerman, J. L., 'The Demand for and Supply of Accounting Theories: the Market for Excuses', *The Accounting Review*, 1979.

Williams, T. H., and Griffen, C. H., 'On the Nature of Empirical Verification in Accounting', *Abacus*, December, 1969.

Zeff, S., 'The Rise of Economic Consequences', *Journal of Accountancy*, 1978.

CHAPTER 2

The Conventional Approach

In Chapter 1 we considered the operation of the financial reporting function in both a regulated and unregulated manner. Also, we discussed some of the ways in which accounting policy makers could approach their decisions on accounting regulation. Once a decision has been made to adopt a particular approach there remains the question of its implementation. Two approaches to establishing and enforcing accounting rules and procedures are:

1. A pragmatic approach, similar to the way common law has developed. This 'piecemeal or case-by-case approach' (Storey, 1981) has been adopted by the conventional approach, the subject of this chapter.
2. A comprehensive or conceptual framework approach, beginning with the establishment of the objectives of financial reports and ending with the derivation of a set of rules for implementing these objectives. This approach has been adopted by the FASB and will be discussed in Chapter 5.

In Chapter 1 we defined the conventional approach as that which dominated accounting thought in the period before mandatory standard-setting boards were established. In the present chapter we examine the development and structure of conventional theory and illustrate the nature of the controversies which it has raised. During the twentieth century the focus has moved away from the importance of the suppliers of financial information towards the interests of users. Controversies surrounding the conventional approach relate to its ability to adopt adequately to this new perspective.

A 'True and Fair' View

In the UK financial reporting has followed an approach which leaves it to the independent judgement of those qualified by training and experience to confirm that within the legal and social framework financial reports follow a general principle prescribed by the law (Flint, 1982). The responsibility for published financial reports rests upon the judgement of directors and auditors. By 1970 the framework for guiding that judgement had been established by developments in (1) company law which prescribes a required minimum level of disclosure and (2) accounting principles of measurement and communication. The 'general principle' prescribed by the law is that the central and overriding objective of financial reporting is to give a *true and fair view*. This requirement was introduced by the Companies Act of 1948 and superseded the previous reference to a *true and correct view* which first appeared in 1844. The 1948 Companies Act provided that the requirement to give a *true and fair view* shall override all other requirements of the Companies Act as to the matters to be included in a company's financial reports.

Developments in Company Law

The flexible nature of *true and fair* or *true and correct* may be appreciated by considering how company law has changed over time. In 1844 accounting was underdeveloped and there was no theory on which legislators could draw for devising standards of reporting. During the twentieth century the movement in financial reporting has been towards increasing the disclosure of information. The period 1900 to 1970 saw successive Companies Acts which added to the level of disclosure required from companies. The impetus for this movement came from the changing economic and social conditions which brought demands for better protection for investors and creditors and a wider social role for the financial reporting function. These demands arose for three main reasons.

1. Changes in General Philosophy The shift from the *laissez faire* ideas of the nineteenth century to a wider notion of social responsibility in the twentieth century had important implications for financial reporting. A *laissez faire* philosophy meant that a businessman's financial affairs were considered to be his private concern and the disclosure of information was thought to assist his competitors (Benston, 1976). In sympathy with this view the 1856 Joint Stock Companies Act abandoned the compulsory accounting requirements and audit introduced in 1844. With few exceptions there was a complete absence of statutory regulation in matters relating to accounting and audit in the period 1856 to 1900. Those exceptions included insurance and railway companies, and building societies, where failure would cause loss to the general public.

The development of a broader social awareness during the twentieth century focused attention on the role of financial reports for encouraging the efficient allocation of capital. It has long been widely assumed that the needs of society regarding financial disclosure can be broadly identified with those of investors looking for the maximum return. Thus, legal disclosure requirements sought to satisfy society's needs for information to allocate capital by seeking to satisfy those of investors and creditors. Subsequently, as attention shifted to encompass economic and social needs in addition to capital accumulation, the specific disclosure requirements of company law were changed accordingly. For example, the 1967 Companies Act included disclosure requirements relating to charitable and political contributions, and the value of goods exported.

2. The Growth of Companies As the Industrial Revolution progressed, and as internal sources proved insufficient to meet the demands of financing large-scale production and rapid technological change, external borrowing became important. The early emphasis on the creditors as the main source of supply of funds is reflected in the importance that was given to the balance sheet. The importance of the shareholder was not formally recognised by law until the 1929 Companies Act. Before 1929 the laws focused on creditor protection. The 1900 Act made an annual audit compulsory by requiring auditors to report on whether, in their opinion, the balance sheet represented a *true and correct* view of the company's affairs. The 1907 Act required the annual filing of the balance sheet with the Registrar of Companies, although private companies were exempt. But the form the balance sheet was required to take was not clearly defined. The objective of this legislation appeared to be to inform users of the existence, in book asset form, of the original capital.

The 1929 Companies Act made it compulsory to submit a profit and loss account to shareholders. But the auditor's duty was not extended to expressing an opinion on the profit and loss account until the 1948 Act. No guidance was provided regarding its contents and the legislation was silent with respect to the use of secret reserves. Furthermore, there was no legal provision for the publication of consolidated financial statements. The 1929 Act extended the requirements regarding the form and content of the balance sheet. Thus, fixed and current assets, preliminary expenses not yet written off, goodwill, patents, and trade marks were to be shown separately.

3. Scandals and Business Failures As Rose (1965) points out much of the legislation to 1948 was simply a response to scandals that lead to public demands for regulation. For example, the failure of the Royal British Bank in 1856 was followed by the Prevention of Fraud Act 1857 and the Joint Stock Banking Act 1858; the Life Assurance Companies Act of 1870 followed a rash of insurance failures; and the collapse of the City of Glasgow Bank in 1878 was followed by the Companies Act 1879. More recently, the Royal Mail case in 1921 revealed the use of secret reserves to manipulate income and caused many companies to greatly improve their reporting procedures (Edwards, 1976).

The 1948 and 1967 Companies Acts

The 1948 Companies Act marked a departure from previous legislation which had emphasised creditor protection and secrecy or had sought to respond to specific scandals or crises. It focused on the needs and rights of shareholders, by emphasising the importance of the provision in financial reports of information for investment decisions. The Act was based upon the recommendations of the Cohen Committee on company law reform, whose report published in 1945 stated:

> We consider that the profit and loss account is as important as, if not more important than, the balance sheet, since the trend of profits is the best indication of the prosperity of the company and the value of the assets depends largely on the maintenance of the business as a going concern.

The 1948 Companies Act required every company to present annually to its shareholders a copy of its audited profit and loss account and balance sheet together with copies of auditors' and directors' reports. The 1948 Act specified a long list of items which were to be disclosed. Therefore, the Act introduced minimum levels of disclosure and the 1967 Companies Act increased the detail to be shown. The 1948 Act stated that where a company has subsidiaries it was required, in addition to its own accounts, to prepare consolidated accounts which were to show the combined financial statements of the group. Also, the Act specified that auditors must be professionally qualified.

The Legislation Lag

Excluding the response of legislators to scandals, legislation in the UK has tended to lag behind the apparent need for change. There are several reasons why the law has evolved more slowly than some commentators requested:

1. The desirability of a change in the law is the result of a consensus that change is necessary. Because of the conflicts of interests discussed in Chapter 1, such a consensus cannot be achieved quickly. A similar

problem arises in the promulgation of contentious accounting standards.

2. As we discussed in Chapter 1, management, competing with one another for investors' funds, have incentives to provide financial information to the investment community. This explains why the practice of reporting tends to move ahead of the law despite the fact that the disclosures required by the law have become more comprehensive. Empirical evidence supports the view that directors voluntarily publish a great deal more financial information than the law requires. For example, Edwards (1981) found that companies were publishing directors' reports and profit and loss accounts decades before this became a legal requirement in 1928.

3. Disclosure required by the law has tended to follow in the wake of what was considered to be best practice by the more progressive companies. It was considered inappropriate to legislate in the absence of such a body of acceptable accounting knowledge. Edwards (1976) concludes that 'legislation without proper thought and experiment would probably have done more harm than good' in explaining the lack of legislation in the two decades before 1948.

Additional Disclosures

Another reason for the legislation lag has been the role of other bodies in requiring the regular supply of adequate information both to shareholders and the investing public. The provisions of the Stock Exchange Listing Agreement, which is signed by every listed company, go far beyond the requirements of the Companies Acts. Many disclosure requirements have been imposed before the Acts made them applicable to all limited companies. For example, in 1939 directors of holding companies were first required to enter into an undertaking to issue consolidated accounts as a condition of granting permission to deal. It was not until the Act of 1948 that legal provision was made for the publication of consolidated accounts. At the present time the Listing Agreement imposes upon listed companies disclosure requirements in addition to those required by statute and accounting standards. These include a statement by the directors as to the reasons for any significant departure from an accounting standard; the financial relationship of directors with their companies; an explanation in the event of trading results differing materially from any published forecast; information about the tax status of a company; and half-yearly interim reports.

In 1959 the Bank of England set up the City Code on Takeovers and Mergers to require companies to provide shareholders with sufficient information for them to assess a proposed takeover or merger connected with companies with which they are involved. Further details of these additional disclosures are given in appendices to Chapter 4.

Implementing a 'True and Fair' View

Although the Companies Acts 1948 and 1967 and the Stock Exchange Listing Agreement prescribe the disclosure of specific items, what constitutes a true and fair view is not specified. In 1958 the Institute of Chartered Accountants in England and Wales stated in one of its recommendations that 'a true and fair view . . . implies the consistent application of generally accepted principles'. These principles provide a framework, or structure, for guiding the judgement of accountants. The development of these principles began in the second half of the nineteenth century, a process which, it has been argued, resulted from the growth in the number and importance of companies (Yamey, 1960). The computation of income became important from an early date, because it quickly became the practice that dividends to shareholders should not exceed profits. The income figure, therefore, set an upper limit to payments to shareholders. The contemporary importance of this notion is examined in Chapter 4 where we consider the attempt of the 1980 Companies Act to clarify the definition of *distributable profit*.

In 1942 the Institute of Chartered Accountants in England and Wales began a procedure of issuing recommendations to members on particular practices to adopt in particular circumstances. In effect, the aim was to identify and codify *best* practice so that accountants might apply the principles therein to the construction of financial reports. The approach to theory construction adopted during this period was normative, but this was constrained by accounting practice. It was an attempt to get 'what should be' from 'what is?'. Figure 2.1 illustrates the process. The objective of theory construction during this period was to increase the degree of uniformity in accounting practice. Between 1942 and 1953 the Institute approved fifteen recommendations. These dealt with subjects such as income tax charges, disclosure of reserves, consolidated accounts, the content of balance sheets and income statements, depreciation, valuation of stock, accounting for chancing price levels and accounting reports for prospectuses. From 1953 to 1969 fourteen additional recommendations were issued, of which four replaced earlier ones.

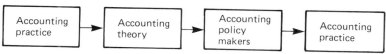

Figure 2.1. The conventional approach to accounting policy making

The Structure of Accounting

The conventional approach resulted in the establishment of a structure which could be used to identify better accounting practices. The term 'accounting principles' refers to this structure, but there exists a great deal of disagreement about terminology. Terms such as 'assumptions', 'concepts', 'conventions', 'doctrines', 'postulates', 'principles', 'propositions', are often used interchangeably in the accounting literature. We shall describe the structure in terms of its assumptions (propositions or concepts), methods (procedures or bases), and policies (recommendations), as illustrated in Figure 2.2.

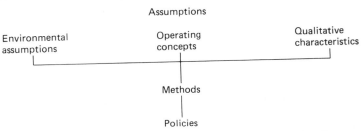

Figure 2.2.   The structure of accounting under the conventional approach

Accounting Assumptions

Given the nature of the conventional approach to theory discussed in Chapter 1, it is not surprising that accountants have found themselves differing over what exactly constitutes the structure established. Several writers have described conceptual frameworks of accounting but their presentations do not coincide. Paton (1922), Sanders *et al.* (1938), Gilman (1939), Paton and Littleton (1940), Littleton (1953), and Grady (1965), have all published their views of conventional accounting theory.

Our classification of assumptions presented in Table 2.1 is adapted from Bierman and Drebin (1978). The items classified as qualitative characteristics provide a useful comparison with a similar classification for the decision-usefulness approach which is discussed in Chapter 5.

Table 2.1   A classification of accounting assumptions

Environmental assumptions	*Operating concepts*	*Qualitative characteristics*
Entity	Cost	Objectivity
Going concern	Realisation	Consistency
Money measurement	Accruals	Conservatism
Periodicity		Materiality
		Full disclosure

Environmental Assumptions
Constraints are imposed on accounting by certain aspects of the environment in which accounting operates. Environmental assumptions are the basic assumptions made by accountants about these constraints.

The entity concept. The idea that accounting communication be confined to a specific accounting entity is fundamental to financial reporting. Clearly, a prerequisite for describing economic events is some notion of the enterprise being reported upon. However, agreement on this concept exists only at a very general level. Furthermore, disagreement exists over whether accountants should adopt a proprietary or entity approach to reporting the affairs of a business entity. A proprietary approach adopts the owners' point of view while the entity approach is concerned with the performance of the business entity. Different interpretations of the entity concept result in different views on inflation accounting (Lee, 1980). These controversies will be discussed in Chapter 8.

The going-concern concept. The function of this concept is to provide an assumption upon which to base accounting methods. As such it is not regarded as a future concept but as a present one. Unless evidence exists to the contrary, it is assumed that the entity will use its resources as planned. The implications of adopting this assumption are central to accounting practice. They justify deferring costs such as closing inventories, prepaid expenses, and undepreciated asset balances which are to be charged against the revenues of future periods. They also justify the use of cost-based, rather than realisable, values. Under a liquidation approach for example, asset values should be stated at net realisable value. In recent years the going-concern concept has been used to support the introduction of current-cost accounting on the grounds that it necessitates the maintenance of corporate capital.

Much controversy surrounds the auditor's role in alerting the public to illiquid situations which may produce self-fulfilling prophecies (Backer and Gosman, 1980). That auditors are reluctant to take this action is shown in one investigation into company failures that found that only 22 per cent of a sample of the 46 quoted (and none of a sample of 31 unquoted), manufacturing companies which failed had been qualified on going-concern grounds prior to failure (Taffler and Tisshaw, 1977).

The money measurement concept. The use of money as a medium of exchange and as a store of value has long been established in human history. Specialisation and the division of labour are made possible by the use of money as a common denominator.

However, commitment to this concept imposes a limitation on the scope of accounting for dealing with real-world events. Not all significant variables in an entity are readily expressed in money amounts. For example, the quality of management, competitive position, morale of employees and potential for growth, are not readily quantifiable. Therefore, the comprehensiveness of financial statements is limited in that, not-quantifiable in money terms may be omitted.

The periodicity concept. The economic events in which an entity is engaged occur continuously. Most of these events are the results of others which have taken place earlier and may have implications for future events. The periodicity concept assumes that the economic activities of an enterprise can be divided into artificial time periods. This enables accountants to prepare short term financial reports to interested parties. The periodicity assumption underlies the whole issue of accruals and deferrals which distinguishes accrual base accounting from cash base accounting. If there were no need for periodic reports during the life span of an entity, accruals and deferrals would be unnecessary.

Operating Concepts
Operating concepts provide guidelines which the accountant follows in recording and manipulating data in accordance with the environmental assumptions.

The cost concept. The traditional approach to accounting focuses on historical exchange prices. This ensures that the value of economic resources is reflected in financial statements at their original costs. Accountants have been reluctant to depart from the historical cost basis of valuation because it has an important advantage over other valuations in that it is definite and determinable. As a result, users of financial statements know that a substantial portion of the information is based on objectively determined amounts. The main criticism of the practice of using historical costs is that they remain static when prices change. Thus, historical cost valuation may be inconsistent with the notion of capital maintenance. The inconsistency does not create serious difficulties so long as the environment is relatively stable, but when instability increases, difficulties become serious. As this became apparent, the rules of conventional theory were adjusted to maintain the going concern concept at the expense of historical cost valuation. Accountants in the UK and other countries were revaluing assets long before the arrival of mandatory current cost accounting so as to maintain the notion of going concern. As the report of the Sandilands Committee of Inquiry put it:

> The increasing extent of revaluations in recent years shows that the accounting

convention that the balance sheet should be a statement of costs rather than values is becoming more honoured in the breach than the observance.'

(Sandilands Report, 1975)

The realisation concept. In the conventional accounting model the realisation concept has played an important role in revenue recognition, i.e. 'the process of formally recording or incorporating an item in the accounts and financial statements of an enterprise' (FASB, 1980). The realisation concept states that revenue is recognised in financial statements in which (1) the earning process is complete or virtually complete and (2) an exchange has taken place (APB Statement No 4, 1970). Critics of the realisation concept view it as a 'barrier to reporting' because it precludes any reporting of increases in wealth which have not been confirmed directly by an external market transaction (Weetman, 1980).

The accruals concept. The realisation concept focuses upon external transactions as the key set of economic events to the exclusion of the acts of production and holding. This focus is maintained in the treatment of costs by the accruals concept. Thus, the accruals concept derives from the realisation concept and the two provide the central pillars of the conventional income measurement process. The accruals concept states that revenues recognised in a particular accounting period should have deducted from them the expenses associated with the generation of that revenue and implies a correlation between costs and revenues. According to many observers, the conventional approach placed too much emphasis on achieving good matching rather than on the usefulness of the resulting information to financial statement users (Storey, 1981).

Qualitative Characteristics
These are the characteristics which accountants seek to apply to the operating concepts to ensure their measurements exhibit particular qualities.

Objectivity. Different definitions of objectivity have been used for some time in the accounting literature (Wojdak, 1970). Accounting is not objective in keeping with the everyday notion of the term because many measurements shown in financial statements contain elements of judgement. For example, measurements of depreciation, write-downs of inventories for possible obsolescence, provision for bad debts, and the accrual of pension costs all involve estimates. In recent times the definition of objectivity by Ijiri and Jaedicke (1966) as 'the consensus among a given group of observers or measurers' has received attention. Although this definition agrees with that normally held by accountants (verifiability by a third party), further analysis is required if this broad view of objectivity is to be made more useful at the operating level (Ashton, 1977).

Consistency. Consistency requires the consistent application of methods from one accounting period to the next. Consistent application in accounting is important so that the financial statements of an entity for successive periods are reasonably comparable. This application of consistency differs from that defined by 'good theory', discussed in Chapter 1. A good theory consistently predicts the same outcome for every similar situation. Accepted accounting principles which allow the use of LIFO, FIFO, variable and full-cost methods of inventory valuation, are inconsistent in themselves.

Conservatism. At the beginning of this chapter, we saw that conservative accounting was considered good accounting during the period when the prime objective of financial reports was to communicate information to creditors. From the lender's viewpoint, there was more to lose by making an unsatisfactory loan (the costs of default and opportunity costs), than by not granting what would turn out to be a good loan (lost interest and goodwill). However, the standard of conservatism may no longer be so relevant to users' needs, because of the shift from creditors to investors as the main users of financial statements (Sorter, 1973). Investors have as much to lose by not making a good investment as from making a bad investment.

Conservatism has been called 'the most influential principle of valuation in traditional accounting' (Sterling, 1967), and the conservatism concept does appear to dominate other concepts when conflicts arise between them. For example, conservatism requires the abandonment of the historical cost concept when it would produce a higher value for inventories than would market value. Further, the realisation concept is violated when obsolete inventory is written down, and the matching concept in the writing-off of advertising and research and development expenditures, rather than capitalising them.

Materiality. Materiality is an elusive concept which lacks a strict operational definition (Brault and Houle, 1982). Most definitions stress the accountant's role in interpreting what is, and what is not, material but exclude a formal consideration of the objectives of financial reports. In later chapters we argue that agreement on the objectives of financial reports is required before the accountant can make judgements and decisions on what is material to users, and what is not. Furthermore, research studies that have attempted to compare evaluations of materiality (for given situations) by various groups have led to the conclusion that there are not only differences between groups, but also within any given group (Pattillo, 1976).

Full Disclosure. Full disclosure may be viewed as an extension of the materiality concept. According to Flint (1982):

> The fundamental principle of reporting in company accounts is that the primary responsibility rests on the directors to make a full disclosure to enable the company and the directors to be judged as to whether what they have done is acceptable to shareholders, to other relevant interest groups and to society, and to enable these groups to take such decisions about the future as are competent to them.

This is a general concept which raises many questions and, similar to materiality, may be interpreted in different ways. A systematic determination of user needs, their level of sophistication and their ability to process information is required before the full disclosure concept can be made operational in a meaningful way.

Accounting Methods and Policies

Accounting methods are the procedures or bases which have been developed by applying the assumptions to particular events, e.g. methods of depreciation and inventory valuation.

Accounting policies refer to the recommendations issued during the period under review. A characteristic of the recommendations was the variety of alternative methods which were generally acceptable. It is interesting to note that Grady's (1965) framework included 'diversity in accounting among independent entities' among his basic concepts. Diversity arises from the accruals concept, whereby revenues and expenses are allocated among the periods during which an enterprise is in operation. For virtually every major event that could affect the financial statements of a particular firm there exists a variety of allocation methods.

Another characteristic of conventional accounting was its focus on **stewardship**. Under traditional stewardship, the need was to communicate information on such matters as tax assessment, the legality of dividend distributions, remuneration by share of profit, and the restriction of borrowing by reference to income or asset valuation. These matters relate directly or indirectly to the sharing of the rewards derived from events. As the Institute of Chartered Accountants in England and Wales (ICAEW) expressed it in 1952:

> the primary purpose of annual accounts of a business is to present information to the proprietors showing how their funds have been utilised, and the profits derived from such use.
> (ICAEW)

Stewardship necessitates the employment of highly verifiable data in financial statements. If a legal dispute arises, both parties require reasonable certainty of the facts of the case. This explains why the qualitative characteristics of the descriptive approach: objectivity, consistency, conservatism and materiality, take a legalistic view of the events which are included in financial statements. Many writers distinguish between the different information needs for stewardship and investment decision purposes (Gjesdal, 1981). Critics of the conventional approach argue that accountants should pay less attention to whether financial statements have complied with the concepts discussed above and more to whether they provide relevant information to decision makers (Chau, 1978). A 'true and fair' presentation from management's point of view, it is argued, may be of little significance to the user.

Many of the issues raised in this chapter are discussed in the remainder of the book where the results of more recent research are considered. In recent years both researchers and policy makers have given much attention to improving conventional accounting to meet changes in circumstances and in particular to making the true and fair requirement more useful to users.

QUESTIONS

1. Distinguish between pragmatic and comprehensive approaches to enforcing accounting rules.
2. Describe the framework which has developed under the conventional approach for guiding the judgement of the preparers of financial reports.
3. Consider how
   (a) changes in general philosophy
   (b) the growth of companies
   (c) scandals and business failures
   have provided the impetus for increasing the disclosure of financial information.
4. How did the Companies Act 1948 mark a departure from previous legislation on accounting disclosure?
5. What additional disclosure requirements are imposed upon listed companies by the Stock Exchange Listing Agreement?
6. Distinguish between a proprietary approach and an entity approach to the entity concept.
7. Why is the going concern concept central to accounting practice?

8. What limitations does the money measurement concept impose on accounting.
9. Consider the advantages and limitations of the historical cost concept.
10. How does the realisation concept affect revenue recognition?
11. What does objectivity mean to accountants?
12. Illustrate the role of conservatism in financial reporting.
13. Why is materiality an elusive concept?
14. What is meant by 'full disclosure', and what problems arise in making this concept operational in a meaningful way?
15. How do accounting methods relate to accounting policies?
16. Show how conventional accounting has focused on stewardship. What are the characteristics of traditional stewardship reporting?

REFERENCES

Accounting Principles Board, *Basic Concepts and Accounting Principles Underlying Financial Statements of Business Enterprise* Statement No. 4, AICPA, 1970.

Ashton, R. H., 'Objectivity of Accounting Measures: A Multirule—Multimeasurer Approach', *The Accounting Review*, July, 1977.

Backer, M. and Gosman, M. L., 'Audit Reporting and the Illiquided Firm', *Journal of Accountancy*, February, 1980.

Benston, G. J., *Corporate Financial Disclosure in the UK and the USA*, Saxon House, 1976.

Bierman, H. and Drebin, A. R., *Financial Accounting: An Introduction*, W. B. Saunders Company, 1978.

Brault, R. and Houley, 'Why Materiality Matters', *C. A. Magazine*, May, 1982.

Chau, T. T. M. C., 'Accounting with Integrity', *C. A. Magazine*, February 1978.

Edwards, J. R., 'The Accounting Profession and Disclosure in Published Reports, 1925–1935', *Accounting and Business Research*, 1976.

Edwards, J. R., 'Changing Legislation and Changing Patterns of Disclosure in British Company Accounts 1900–1940', ICAEW, 1981.

Financial Accounting Standards Board, *Elements of Financial Statements of Business Enterprises*, Concepts Statement No. 3, 1980.

Flint, D., *A True and Fair View in Company Accounts*, Gee and Co. Ltd., 1982.

Gilman, S., *Accounting Concepts of Profit*, The Ronald Press Company, 1939.

Gjesdal, F., 'Accounting for Stewardship', *Journal of Accounting Research*, Spring, 1981.

Grady, P., *Inventory of Generally Accepted Accounting Principles for Business Enterprise*, AICPA, 1965.

I.C.A.E.W., *Accounting in Relation to Changes in the Purchasing Power of Money*, Recommendations No. 15, 1952.

Ijiri, Y. and Jaedicke, R. K., 'Reliability and Objectivity of Accounting Measurements', *The Accounting Review*, July 1966.

Lee, T. A., 'The Accounting Entity Concept, Accounting Standards, and Inflation Accounting', *Accounting and Business Research*, Spring, 1980.

Littleton, A. C., *Structure of Accounting Theory*, AAA, 1953.

Paton, W. A., *Accounting Theory*, The Ronald Press Company, 1922.

Paton, W. A. and Littleton, A. C., *An Introduction to Corporate Accounting Standards*, AAA, 1940.

Pattillo, J. W., *The Concept of Materiality in Financial Reporting*, The Financial Executives Research Foundation, 1976.

Rose, H., *Disclosure in Company Accounts*, 2nd edition, The Institute of Economic Affairs, 1965.

Sanders, T. H. *et al. A Statement of Accounting Principles*, AICPA, 1938.

Sorter, G. H., *Purpose and Need for Objectives in Financial Statements*, AICPA, 1973.

Sterling, R., 'Conservatism, the Fundamental Principle of Valuation in Traditional Accounting', *Abacus*, December, 1967.

Storey, R. K., 'Conditions Necessary for Developing a Conceptual Framework', *Journal of Accountancy*, June 1981.

Taffler, F. J., and Tisshaw, H., 'Going, Going, Gone—Four Factors which Predict', *Accountancy*, March, 1977.

Weetman, P., 'Accounting Far Value Companies—The Barrier of Realisation', *Accountant's Magazine*, October, 1980.

Wojdak, J. F., 'Levels of Objectivity in the Accounting Process', *The Accounting Review*, January, 1970.

Yamey, B. S., 'The Development of Company Accounting Conventions', *Three Banks Review*, 1960.

CHAPTER 3

Accounting Standards

In Chapter 1 we discussed the theoretical foundations of accounting policy making by considering the case for the regulation of accounting. The purpose of this chapter is to examine the institutional aspects of accounting regulation in the form of accounting standards by concentrating upon the activities of the Accounting Standards Committee (ASC). In Chapter 4 we shall examine the legal regulation of accounting.

Our discussion of accounting regulation in Chapter 1 was conducted in general terms and in this chapter we shall consider four specific issues, namely, the factors which lead to the setting up of standard setting bodies in the UK; the types of accounting standards which might be set; the process of accounting standard setting and the means by which standards are enforced.

The Need for Accounting Standards

Accounting standards may be defined as '. . . uniform rules for external financial reporting applicable either to all or to a certain class of entity'. (Bromwich, 1981). As we have noted, accounting standards may be a response to a failure of the market for information. Also, they may be viewed as a method of resolving potential conflicts of interest between the various user groups which have access to company accounts. The various groups will have different objectives, information needs, and capacities for the generation and interpretation of information and, therefore, conflicts may arise between groups outside the entity. For example, inflation accounting may benefit existing shareholders if corporate tax payments are reduced as a result of lower reported profits. It may also benefit society by improving the allocation of certain resources. On the other hand, employees may suffer if lower wage settlements are justified by lower reported profits.

More generally, there may be conflict between the preparers of accounts and users. Accounting principles have been developed to provide a system of financial reporting to reflect management's description of the financial performance of an entity. In order to do this, they allow flexibility and choice in both accounting policies and the amount of disclosure. External users, on the other hand, may require consistency and comparability between the financial reports of different enterprises. It is a role of accounting standards to attempt to reconcile the conflict between flexibility and choice, and comparability and consistency.

Before the introduction of mandatory accounting standards some writers expressed fears that they might inhibit experiment and the development and introduction of new ideas, either by constricting thought or by forbidding innovation (Baxter, 1962). But 'far from quelling discussion, the formulation and issue of standards has brought about a great increase in the amount of open argument and controversy in British accountancy' (Edey, 1977).

Types of Accounting Standards

Accounting standards may be classified by their subject matter and by how they are enforced (Benston, 1980). According to their subject matter Benston classifies standards as follows:

1. **Disclosure Standards**. Such standards are the minimum uniform rules for external reporting. They require only an explicit disclosure of accounting methods used and assumptions made in preparing financial statements. As Edey (1977) pointed out 'the case for this type of disclosure seems overwhelmingly strong'. Such a standard is unlikely to be controversial or create conflicts of interest, particularly since it does not constrain the choice of accounting policies or items to be disclosed.
2. **Presentation Standards**. They specify the form and type of accounting information to be presented. They may specify that certain financial statements be presented (e.g. a funds-flow statement) or that items be presented in a particular order in financial statements. Such standards place only a little more constraint upon the choice of accounting policies than disclosure standards and aim to reduce the costs to users of utilising financial statements.
3. **Content Standards**. These standards specify the accounting information which is to be published. Benston recognises three aspects to such standards:
   (a) *Disclosure-content standards* which specify only the categories of information to be disclosed. The UK Companies Acts, as we shall

see in Chapter 4, are examples of such standards.

(b) *Specific-construct standards* which specify how specific items should be reported in accounts—for example, a standard which specifies that finance leases be capitalised and disclosed in balance sheets.

(c) *Conceptually-based standards* which specify the accounting treatment of items based upon a coherent and complete framework of accounting. Such standards would ideally be based upon our notion of 'good theory' as set out in Chapter 1.

Another classification of accounting standards may be based upon their method of preparation and enforcement. Benston identifies:

1. **Evolutionary and Voluntary Compliance Standards.** Such standards have evolved as best practices and represent the conventional approach to accounting. As such, their general acceptability implies voluntary compliance by individual companies.

2. **Privately Set Standards.** Private accountancy bodies such as the ASC or FASB may formulate standards and devise means for their enforcement. Other bodies, such as trade associations or stock exchanges may set accounting standards for companies as a condition of membership or listing. Enforcement powers are thus more readily available.

3. **Governmental Standards.** These standards may be laws relating to company accounting practices and disclosures, as in the case of the UK Companies Acts, or tax rules defining taxable profit. Alternatively, governmental departments or agencies may regulate accounting practices for certain industries. Finally, accounting standards may be set by governmental equivalents of the private accountancy bodies of (2) above, such as the SEC.

The two classifications are complementary and not competitive. In Chapter 2 we considered both voluntary compliance standards and the governmental standards of the UK Companies Act prior to 1980. Those standards were found to be primarily disclosure-content standards. In Chapter 4 we shall examine the UK Companies Acts 1980 and 1981, which place a greater emphasis upon specific content. In Chapter 5 we shall consider the attempts by private accountancy bodies to develop conceptually-based standards. In the remainder of this chapter we shall examine the disclosure-content and specific-construct standards which have been set by private accountancy bodies, in particular the ASC.

The Emergence of Accounting Standards in the UK

As we saw in Chapter 2, private accounting standards in the UK date from 1942 with the appearance of the first guidance statement on accounting principles issued by the Institute of Chartered Accountants in England and

Wales (ICAEW). These statements were subjected to a complicated exposure period among the membership of the Institute and required the approval of a majority of the Institute's governing Council. These pronouncements were conservative, prudent, based upon conventional practice and were well-received by the accountancy profession (Bromwich, 1981). However, as Leach (1981) has observed these recommendations were 'in no way mandatory and not much help to the auditor in persuading his client to accept best accounting practice. In fact, there were often alternative approaches, none of which was sufficiently out of line to distort a true and fair view'.

This facility for management to select alternative policies for the presentation of financial reports allowed earnings to be manipulated and made it possible to conceal economic realities. The deficiencies of such permissive standards were highlighted by the increasing frequency of take-over activity in the 1950s and 1960s. The existence of alternative accounting bases for statements of past profits and forecasts of future profits by offerer and offeree companies could lead to significant differences as the GEC-AEI merger illustrated. Reflecting a widespread mood, Professor Stamp wrote in *The Times* in 1969, 'the word 'principles' now lends a spurious air of authority and accuracy to a situation which is in fact almost chaotic.' The President of the ICAEW at the time said he was 'besieged by members demanding action from the Council to stem the mounting criticism of the profession in the press' (Leach, 1981). The Institute's response was to set up the Accounting Standards Steering Committee (ASSC) in January 1970 with the intention of advancing accounting standards.

This was the first occasion upon which the term *standards* was used in place of 'recommendations' or 'opinions'. Shortly after the founding of the ASSC, the ICAEW was joined by the Scottish and Irish Institutes and in 1971 the Association of Certified Accountants and the Institute of Cost of Management Accountants joined and were followed in 1976 by the Institute of Public Finance and Accountancy. In that year the ASSC was reconstituted as a joint committee of the six member bodies who collectively act through the Consultative Committee of Accounting Bodies (CCAB) and renamed the ASC. The ASC is responsible for preparing draft accounting standards for the consideration of the six member bodies of the CCAB. The CCAB bodies are responsible for approving, issuing and enforcing accounting standards.

The Aims of the Accounting Standards Committee (ASC)

In establishing the ASC, the ICAEW stated its intention to advance accounting standards along five lines as follows.

1. Narrowing the areas of difference and variety in accounting practice. This was to be achieved by publishing authoritative statements on best accounting practice.
2. Disclosure of accounting bases. This was to be required when accounts include significant items whose values depend upon judgement.
3. Disclosure of departures from established definitive accounting standards.
4. Wider exposure for major proposals on accounting standards.
5. Continuing programme for encouraging improved accounting standards in legal and regulatory measures.

In order to direct the ASC along these lines of development, the committee was given the following terms of reference:

1. To keep under review standards of financial accounting and reporting.
2. To publish consultative documents with the object of maintaining and advancing accounting standards.
3. To propose to the councils of the governing bodies statements of standard accounting practice.
4. To consult as appropriate with representatives of finance, commerce, industry and government and other persons concerned with financial reporting.

In seeking to meet these terms of reference, the ASC has set Statements of Standard Accounting Practice (SSAPs) by a process which has entailed effectively four elements—research; drafting; evaluation; and approval. Although these elements have been present in standard setting since the inception of the committee, significant changes have been introduced into the standard-setting process in recent years. These changes have followed the publication of three reports by the ASC in 1978, 1981 and 1983. Firstly, we shall consider the work of the ASC and the criticisms which this has attracted.

The Accounting Standards Programme

Overleaf are listed the SSAPs issued by the ASC together with and exposure drafts which have not yet been turned into accounting standards.

The first standard issued reflected an important aspect of the circumstances which had called the ASC into being, namely the use of varying bases for profit forecasts in companies which held substantial equity interests in other companies amounting to less than total control. The choice of this topic for the first accounting standard is significant in that it gives clues to the motivation behind the ASC's founding. In the face of the considerable criticism of the state of accounting which was present both

Current position of ASC Subjects
Statements of Standard Accounting Practice Issued

SSAP1	Accounting for the results of associated companies (amended 1974, revised 1982)	1971
SSAP2	Disclosure of accounting policies	1971
SSAP3	Earnings per share (revised 1974)	1972
SSAP4	The accounting treatment of government grants	1974
SSAP5	Accounting for value added tax	1974
SSAP6	Extraordinary items and prior-year adjustments (revised 1978)	1974
SSAP8	The treatment of taxation under the imputation system in the accounts of companies (revised 1977)	1974
SSAP9	Stocks and work in progress	1975
SSAP10	Statements of source and application of funds	1975
SSAP12	Accounting for depreciation	1977
SSAP13	Accounting for research and development	1977
SSAP14	Group accounts	1978
SSAP15	Accounting for deferred taxation (revised 1985)	1978
SSAP16	Current cost accounting (made non-mandatory 1985)	1980
SSAP17	Accounting for post balance sheet events	1980
SSAP18	Accounting for contingencies	1980
SSAP19	Accounting for investment properties	1981
SSAP20	Foreign currency translation	1983
SSAP21	Accounting for leases and hire purchase contracts	1984
SSAP22	Accounting for goodwill	1984
SSAP23	Accounting for Acquisitions and Mergers	1984

Exposure Drafts in Issue

ED28	Accounting for petroleum revenue tax	1981
ED32	Accounting for pension information in company accounts	1983
ED34	Pension scheme accounts	1984
ED36	Extraordinary items and prior year adjustments	1985
ED37	Accountancy for depreciation	1985

outside and inside the profession, the ASC had, in the words of its first chairman, 'to show evidence of its intentions' (Leach, 1981). This defensive reaction produced SSAP1 and has been apparent in much of the ASC's work since.

The second was an attempt to provide a framework which the ASC could use in setting subsequent standards. SSAP2 is addressed to the relationship between accounting concepts, accounting methods and accounting policies. The relationship is illustrated as follows—it is seen that accounting concepts provide the foundations to both accounting methods and policies.

Accounting Policies

↑

Accounting Methods

↑

Accounting Concepts

SSAP2 distinguishes between fundamental accounting concepts, accounting bases and accounting policies:

Fundamental accounting concepts are broad general assumptions which underlie the periodic financial accounts of business enterprises.

Accounting bases are the methods which have been developed for expressing or applying fundamental accounting concepts to financial transactions and items. By their nature, accounting bases are more diverse and numerous than fundamental concepts since they have evolved in response to the variety and complexity of types of business and business transactions and, for this reason, there may justifiably exist more than one recognised accounting basis for dealing with particular items.

Accounting policies are the specific accounting bases judged by business enterprises to be most appropriate to their circumstances and adopted by them for the purpose of preparing their financial accounts.

SSAP2 states that there are four fundamental accounting concepts which should be regarded as established standard concepts. They are as follows:

1. The **going-concern concept** implies that the enterprise will continue in operational existence for the foreseeable future. This means, in particular, that the profit and loss account and balance sheet assume no intention or necessity to liquidate or reduce significantly the scale of operation.

2. The **accruals concept**, which requires that revenue and costs are accrued or matched with one another so far as their relationship can be established or justifiably assumed, and dealt with in the profit and loss account of the period to which they relate, provided, generally, that where the accrual concept is inconsistent with the prudence concept the latter prevails. The accruals concept implies that the profit and loss account reflects changes in the amount of net assets that arise out of the transactions of the relevant period, other than distributions or subscriptions of capital. Revenue and profits dealt with in the profit and loss account are matched with associated costs by including, in the same

account, the costs incurred in earning them, so far as these are material and identifiable.
3. The **consistency concept**, which requires that there should be consistency of accounting treatment of like items within each accounting period and from one period to the next.
4. The **concept of prudence**, which requires that revenue and profits are not anticipated, but recognised by inclusion in the profit and loss account only when realised in the form either of cash or of assets (usually legally enforceable debts), the ultimate cash realisation of which can be assessed with reasonable certainty; and that provision be made for all known liabilities (expenses and losses), whether the amount of these is known with certainty or is a best estimate in the light of the information available.

SSAP2 is concerned with ensuring that accounting bases are disclosed in financial reports, whenever significant items are shown which have their significance in value judgements, estimated outcome of future events or uncompleted transactions, rather than ascertained amounts. SSAP2 states:

> in circumstances where more than one accounting basis is acceptable in principle, the accounting policy followed can significantly affect a company's reported results and financial position, and the view presented can be properly appreciated only if the principal policies followed are also described. For this reason, adequate disclosure of the accounting policies should be regarded as essential to the fair presentation of financial accounts.

Evaluation of the ASC Approach

The 1978 Report (ASC, 1978) acknowledged that the ASC has attracted both praise and criticism. The principal intention of the ASC programme has been to secure greater uniformity in the preparation of financial reports in order that there should be more comparability between different companies in this respect. This has resulted in the ASC restricting itself to making fairly minor changes in financial reporting. The ICAEW publication *Annual Survey of Published Accounts* which surveys the reporting practices of a sample of UK companies shows that, within these confines, it has enjoyed some success, encouraging the production of a more standardised type of financial statement.

The ASC's approach attracted the following criticisms in the 1970s:
1. Failure to develop an agreed conceptual framework A major criticism levelled at the ASC's programme has been that it has failed to establish objectives for financial reports and failed to develop an agreed comprehensive conceptual framework for standards. In particular, the lack of adequate research prior to the introduction of SSAP2 has attracted

criticism. As we pointed out in the case of SSAP1, the ASC began its standard setting defensively and has continued so, following a 'fire fighting' philosophy by addressing specific accounting problems which were of current concern. In their submissions to the ASC most of the major accounting firms argued for a more positive approach—especially in regard to the need for a conceptual framework. These firms argued that many of the difficulties inherent in the formulation and acceptability of accounting standards result from the absence of an agreed conceptual framework (ASC, 1979).

The absence of a more comprehensive framework than that allowed by consideration of the four concepts explicitly recognised in SSAP2 has led to contradictions and inconsistencies in the accounting standards programme. Although consistency is spelt out in SSAP2 as an accounting concept, an examination of the operation of the prudence concept through published standards reveals that it is characterised with inexplicable inconsistency (Lothian, 1982). In certain circumstances prudence is interpreted in the inflexible and harsh manner that is intended by SSAP2, in other circumstances management is allowed considerable latitude. There is an inherent conflict between the prudence concept and the accruals and going-concern concepts which has led to contradiction among and between SSAPs. For example, whereas the first draft of ED14, *Accounting for Research and Development*, was based purely on prudence, SSAP9, *Stocks and Work in Progress*, was based essentially on the matching convention. Furthermore, how can all the concepts be fundamental if accruals is to be subordinate to prudence? Prudence, as we discussed in Chapter 2, is important for reporting to creditors. It may be argued, therefore, that elevation of the prudence concept subordinates the interests of shareholders to those of creditors (Tweedie, 1981). Previous studies (Moonitz, 1961; Grady, 1965) recommended the inclusion of a much larger number of concepts in their frameworks. Although much of the accounting standards programme has been built upon SSAP2, that standard does acknowledge its deficiencies as a conceptual basis by stating that it was not the purpose of that standard to establish a theory of accounting, for 'an exhaustive theoretical approach would take an entirely different form and would include, for instance, many more propositions than the four fundamental concepts referred to here.'

2. Failure to specify user needs The reader will recognise the similarity between the conventional approach of Chapter 2 and that of SSAP2. This is concerned with reporting *true income* and wealth measurements by following correct rules and procedures. As we stated in that chapter, critics of the conventional approach argue that accountants should pay less attention to whether financial statements have complied with traditional concepts and more to whether they provide relevant information to decision makers. The problems raised by the existence of the different groups considered in Chapter 1 imply that a search for the 'best method' may be fruitless. Critics of the ASC's programme suggest the user-needs approach of the Corporate Report, which will be discussed in Chapter 5, provides a more realistic framework for setting standards. Many of the problems which the ASC experienced in setting particular standards in the 1970s might perhaps have been eliminated had the user-needs approach been adopted from the beginning.

3. The composition of the ASC Those critics who argued that more regard should be given to user needs objected to the initial composition of the ASC of 23 members, part-time and unpaid who were nominated by the six governing bodies of accountants. These members represented industry and auditors but not user groups. Therefore, it appeared odd that those at whom financial reports were aimed should have so little say in laying down the rules. Grinyer (1978) suggested that the ASC be slimmed down to a more effective size and that non-accountancy bodies should be accorded some representation. This would ensure the existence of voices on the committee to advance users' opinions direct.

4. Lack of adequate consultation and explanation The wider political and social dimensions of accounting policy making, which we considered in Chapter 1, were not given sufficient attention in the standard-setting process. In that chapter we argued that these aspects of policy making must be taken into account in a democracy. In the 1970s, many complained that preparers and users of accounting statements received EDs from 'on high' with little or no explanation of alternatives considered or the reasons for the judgements leading to the proposals (Grinyer, 1978). Those who submitted comments in the EDs had no evidence that they had been considered in the promulgated standard. In some cases, controversy continued after a definitive standard had been published, e.g. SSAP 11, the original standard on deferred taxation. It was argued that controversy over SSAP11 should have taken place at a much earlier stage and this indicated that either exposure for new proposals was not made sufficiently wide or that those who received exposure drafts did not pay sufficient attention to them (Weetman, 1977).

5. Inadequate enforcement of standards Some writers criticised the ASC approach for limiting enforcement to a qualified audit report (Lafferty, 1979). Others called for legislative backing for standards, a facility enjoyed by the Canadian standard setting body:

> Since Canada enjoys the same parliamentary and legal traditions as Britain, and has an accounting profession organised on much the same lines as the British profession, it is not clear to me why the ASC should be so sure that a solution of this kind would be unacceptable to the United Kingdom Parliament. It seems to me that it is worth pursuing the idea with some vigour, because it offers a far

better way of providing teeth, and credibility, to accounting standards than the alternative that has been selected by the ASC. (Stamp, 1981)

Changes in the Standard-Setting Process

As we noted earlier in this chapter, significant changes were introduced into the standard-setting process in the early 1980s, following the publication of three reports by the ASC. These changes overcame many of the criticisms voiced in the previous section. They comprised:

1. The reorganisation of the structure of the ASC.
2. The introduction of a revised standard setting process.

The re-organised ASC

In September 1982 the organisational structure of the ASC was revised in order that it might respond more effectively to changes in the business environment. The size was reduced to twenty members, which included five users of financial reports who need not be accountants. The remaining fifteen are principally members from the profession and preparers of financial reports. Efforts were made to achieve an appropriate balance as between the preparers, users and auditors of reports, as between members from large and small organisations and as between the various sectors of the community interested in financial reports. Additionally, government representatives can be co-opted, as non-voting members.

A revised standard setting process

In 1983 the ASC approved the proposals of a working party (ASC, 1983) set up to examine the recommendations and conclusions of the final report on setting accounting standards. The working party's proposals now form the process by which the ASC will operate to set accounting standards and make other recommendations. Many significant changes have been made to the process, and three new documents have been introduced, the Statement of Recommended Practice (SORP), with a special sub-category, the franked SORP, and the Statement of Intent (SOI).

The 1981 report had recognised that the process of setting mandatory accounting standards is an essentially political activity; that it is not sufficient that standards merely have technical merit and to be workable, they must also be accepted. As Watts (1981) explained, 'the overriding need is for the standards body to operate in the open, to consult openly, to encourage debate and listen to all views, to explain its reasoning and overtly to be seen to operate in the public interest rather than in any sectional interest.' It is this philosophy on which the revised standard-setting process is based.

The ASC identifies the following fifteen stages in the process of setting accounting standards:

1. **Identification of topics**. Individual standards have always been set within a programme of work approved by the ASC. However, as we have noted, there has been frequent criticism of the informal way in which topics find their way on to the ASC's agenda and of how agenda items are selected for consideration as proposed standards. The new arrangements recognise the critical importance of these issues, and seek to formalise matters by making the review and monitoring of the ASC's programme of future work, and of the selection of topics for attention, the responsibility of the planning sub-committee of the ASC. The planning sub-committee takes account of suggestions made by other members of the ASC, groups with whom consultative meetings have been held, and the ASC secretariat. Significantly, the sub-committee should have particular 'regard to the requirements of users of accounts', subject to considerations of the cost and practicability of producing the information required.

   In further recognition of the importance of the choice of items for its work programme and of communication and consultation, the ASC published its work programme in May 1984 and invited comments on it. Following comments a revised work programme was prepared and was published in November 1984. Details of the revised programme are contained in the appendix to this chapter.

2. **Planning sub-committee**. As well as preparing the agenda, the planning sub-comittee advises on the need for research, recommends the members of the working party which is responsible for the preparation of consultative documents, and generally oversees the progress of proposals for standards.

3. **Research**. A research study on a major topic will typically include a review of the existing literature in the subject (including any overseas pronoucements); the demand for, and potential problems relating to, a pronouncement on the topic; and perhaps tentative views on the technical content of a pronouncement.

4. **Formation of a working party**. On the basis of the research, the ASC decides whether to proceed towards a final pronouncement; whether the pronouncement should be an SSAP; and what type of consultative document should be issued. Finally, a working party is selected by the planning sub-committee and given terms of reference.

5. **Consultative documents**. The ASC has three types of discussion document available. Two of them (discussion paper and Statement of

Intent (SOI)) are optional, whilst the third (exposure draft) must always be issued prior to an SSAP. The SOI is a new document.

5.1 *Discussion paper*. A discussion paper is exploratory and seeks to discuss issues as a means of stimulating debate. Although it might contain tentative conclusions, it will not set out the text of a proposed standard. A discussion paper may be issued prior to an SSAP or an SORP.

5.2 *Statement of Intent*. A SOI provides a summary of how the ASC intends to proceed with a particular accounting topic, and is in considerably less detail than an exposure draft. Its aim is to stimulate public discussion, but more promptly than with a discussion paper. At the time of writing, several SOIs have been issued on a number of topics.

5.3 *Exposure draft*. Publication of an exposure draft for general comment follows internal exposure of a proposed standard. Exposure drafts contain the texts of proposed standards and usually more than 100,000 copies are issued, inviting comment. Six months have generally been provided for public exposure.

6. **Initial feedback to the ASC**. The working party responsible for the preparation of an accounting standard provides the ASC with an outline of the technical content of the documents, and a plan of the consultation for approval.

7. **Consultation plan**. The ASC sees consensus as essential to successful accounting standards and effective consultation as having a central role in achieving consensus. A plan of consultation identifies groups to be consulted, both preparers and users of accounts. If legal problems are anticipated consultation with the Department of Trade and legal advisers will be necessary. Public hearings may be planned if appropriate. Good press coverage is planned in order to encourage debate.

8. **Technical drafting**. The working party, in conjunction with the ASC Secretariat, prepare a detailed draft over a period of six to ten months, in conjunction with the planned consultations.

9. **Involvement of the CCAB**. It is the six CCAB bodies which finally approve, publish and enforce standards. In addition to the CCAB bodies receiving ASC agendas and other documents, formal contacts take place on each topic as part of the consultation process.

10. **Consideration of the ASC and publication of the exposure draft**. After drafting and consultation the working party presents an exposure draft to the ASC for its consideration. If acceptable, the draft is approved for publication.

11. **Exposure period**. The function of the exposure period is to allow the

working party to explain and discuss the proposals of the draft to interested parties and for commentators to formulate and submit their views to the ASC. A public meeting may be held.

12. **Towards a standard**. The ASC considers the comments received during the exposure period and a decision is taken on how to proceed to a standard. Redrafting and further consultations may take place.

13. **Finalisation and issue of a standard**. A final draft of the proposed standard is presented to the ASC for approval. If approved, the proposed standard is sent to the Councils of the six CCAB bodies for their approval.

14. **Guidance notes, appendices to standards and Technical Releases**. Guidance notes and appendices relate to, but are not part of, a standard. They expand and aid the understanding of a standard but do not specify how a standard should be applied in particular circumstances. A Technical Release is normally issued in conjunction with a standard and provides background information.

15. **Review and revision of standards**. Standards may require review and even revision in the light of changes in company law or other circumstances. If a revision is thought necessary it will be preceded by an exposure draft or SOI depending upon the extent to which revision is thought controversial.

The new process has certain significant characteristics which differ from its predecessors. In particular, the process is described in greater detail. Coupled with the considerable emphasis upon formality and planning, this strongly suggests a wish on the part of the ASC to demonstrate that SSAPs emerge from what the Americans describe as 'due process'. In this regard, the ASC is following in the footsteps of the FASB. Also, increased attention is given to consultation and the importance of user needs in the standard-setting process. The US influence has additionally been apparent in the instigation of public meetings.

Three main differences between the FASB approach and that of the ASC are considered below.

1. The ASC has not devoted resources to the development of a conceptual framework. A report prepared at the request of the ASC concluded that a conceptual framework is primarily useful

   as an aid to suggesting what are the important questions to try and answer, rather than as providing a formula or set of formulas such that solutions to particular accounting problems can be readily derived.   (Macve, 1981)

   This conclusion has been criticised as 'somewhat defeatist' (Solomons, 1983). The FASB conceptual framework is considered in Chapter 5.

2. The FASB consists of seven members who are appointed on a full-time

basis and who have severed all connections with any former employment or activity. It is a highly skilled body which, it is argued, can make its decisions even handedly and in true independence. The primary reason for the full-time independent status of FASB members owes much to the view that:

> The cohabitation of an accountant with the Board and with his firm, company or industry, is an incestuous relationship.   (Trueblood, 1971)

This opinion has rarely been voiced in the UK.

3. FASB standards are enforced by the SEC which refuses the filing of financial statements with a qualified audit report. Enforcement of standards in the UK is in the hands of the CCAB. In the absence of direct and powerful enforcement measures, the ASC seeks to substitute the self-enforcement of a consensus, based upon the confidence of preparers and users of financial reports in the mechanisms by which SSAPs have been set, and agreement reached on the content of SSAPs. A similar motivation seems apparent in the new category of pronouncement, the SORP. SORPs should be self-enforcing if they represent the views of the industry concerned.

Statements of Recommended Practice (SORPs)

SORPs may be issued on topics which do not meet the criteria for SSAPs. They will deal with pronouncements which are of widespread applicability but not fundamental importance, or which are of limited applicability (e.g. to a specific industry). The former will be prepared by the ASC and the latter (to be known as *franked SORPs*), by the industry concerned. 'Franking' refers to the approval of the ASC of recommendations made for an industry by representatives of it. Unlike SSAPs, SORPs will not be mandatory and there will be no requirement on a company or other body to disclose departures from a SORP. ED34 on pension scheme accounts is the first exposure draft issued on a topic which will become the subject of a SORP.

International Accounting Standards Committee (IASC)

As standard-setting bodies are established in more countries, diversity in accounting requirements are increasingly likely in the standards facing the multinational company. The IASC was established in 1973 in an attempt to co-ordinate the development of accounting standards internationally.

Although the international accounting standards set by the IASC have no force in the UK, the six member bodies of the CCAB seek to implement their support for the IASC by incorporating the provisions of International

Accounting Standards (IASs) into SSAPs. Thus, where IASs are incorporated into SSAPs, automatic compliance is ensured.

So far twenty-four IASs have been issued. They are listed. The equivalent SSAPs which are also listed incorporate the provisions of the IASs unless otherwise indicated.

Where an IAS is in conflict with or goes beyond a SSAP, the IAS does not override the SSAP. Rather the CCAB bodies have in principle undertaken either to amend the SSAP or issue a statement setting out the differences between the IAS and the SSAP. This procedure has yet to be put into effect.

The IASC hopes to facilitate a common international approach in several ways (IASC 1983). Firstly, at any time, national organisations in several different countries may be working on an accounting standard dealing with a common topic. To avoid the development of incompatible solutions, the IASC Board has urged member bodies to invite the IASC to participate whenever two or more countries that do not share common legislation are proposing to hold discussions on accounting standards. Secondly, in some countries, where accounting standards have not previously been laid down, international accounting standards are adopted as the country's own standards. When this occurs, local accounting practices will be enhanced, and the financial statements prepared in that country should be internationally acceptable. Thirdly, in other countries the principles set out in an international accounting standard are adopted as a basis for a national standard on a particular subject, guaranteeing a certain level of quality and compatibility for the particular standard. This approach can significantly reduce both the time and the development costs required to produce a national standard and can consequently enable a country to follow a programme of standard setting more rapidly than local resources would otherwise permit. Fourthly, where national standards already exist countries may compare them with international accounting standards and seek to eliminate any material differences. Fifthly, in those countries where the framework of accounting practice is contained in law, IASC member bodies endeavour to persuade the relevant authorities of the benefits of harmonisation with international accounting standards.

There is little doubt that if international agreement on the objectives of financial reporting could be reached, many other issues could be resolved more easily, and on a less piecemeal basis, than would otherwise be the case. But as we have seen in this chapter, it is very difficult to obtain agreement on objectives within a particular country, and it will be that much harder to obtain agreement between countries. Despite this problem, minimum disclosure requirements are being prescribed in EEC member countries and the effect on UK companies is considered in Chapter 4.

International standard		Equivalent SSAP
IAS1	Disclosure of accounting policies	SSAP2
IAS2	Valuation and presentation of inventories in the context of the historical cost system	SSAP9
IAS3	Consolidated financial statements	SSAP1
IAS4	Depreciation accounting	SSAP14
IAS5	Information to be disclosed in financial statements	*
IAS6	Accounting treatment of changing prices (superceded by IAS15)	—
IAS7	Statement of changes in financial position	SSAP10
IAS8	Unusual and prior period items and changes in accounting policy	SSAP6
IAS9	Accounting for research and development activities	SSAP13
IAS10	Contingencies and events occurring after the balance sheet date	SSAPs 17 and 18
IAS11	Accounting for construction contracts	SSAP9
IAS12	Accounting for taxes on income	*
IAS13	Presentation of current assets and current liabilities	f
IAS14	Reporting financial information by segment	f
IAS15	Information reflecting the effects of changing prices	SSAP16
IAS16	Accounting for property, plant and equipment	f
IAS17	Accounting for leases	f
IAS18	Revenue recognition	f
IAS19	Accounting for retirement benefits in the financial statements of employers	f
IAS20	Accounting for government grants and disclosures of government assistance	SSAP4
IAS21	Accounting for the effects of changes in foreign exchange rates	SSAP20
IAS22	Accounting for business combinations	f
IAS23	Capitalisation of borrowing costs	f
IAS24	Related Party Disclosures	f

Notes
* No specific SSAP, conformity is ensured by general compliance with the law and SSAPs.
f No equivalent UK standard.

1. Define the term 'accounting standard'.
2. How may standards resolve potential conflicts between the groups interested in financial reporting?
3. Distinguish between:

    (a) disclosure standards,
    (b) presentation standards, and
    (c) content standards.

4. Distinguish between:

    (a) evolutionary standards,
    (b) privately-set standards, and
    (c) governmental standards.

5. Why was the ASC established in 1970?
6. SSAP 2 *Disclosure of Accounting Policies* states that there are four fundamental accounting concepts which have general acceptability. Required:
    (a) State and briefly explain each of these four fundamental concepts.
    (b) State and briefly explain three other accounting concepts.
    (c) In what circumstances might you abandon one of the concepts stated in either part (a) or part (b) when preparing a financial statement?

    (Association of Certified Accountants)
7. Why did the ASC's approach to formulating accounting standards attract criticism in the 1970s?
8. How was the ASC re-organised in 1982?
9. Identify the stages in the standard-setting process which were proposed by an ASC working party in 1983.
10. What are the main differences between the FASB and ASC approaches to setting standards?
11. How does a SORP differ from a SSAP?
12. The report *Setting Accounting Standards* (Accounting Standards Committee, 1981) affirmed that accounting standards are necessary and will continue to be necessary in order to complement the statutory regulations. Required:
    Do you agree with the statement? State your reasons.

    (Association of Certified Accountants)

REFERENCES

Accounting Standards Committee, *Setting Accounting Standards*, 1978.

Accounting Standards Committee, *Submissions on the Accounting Standards Committees Consultative Document, 'Setting Accounting Standards'*, 1979.

Accounting Standards Committee, *Setting Accounting Standards*, Final Report, 1981.

Accounting Standards Committee, *Review of the Standard Setting Process*, ASC, 1983.

Baxter, W. T., 'Recommendations on Accounting Theory', in W. T. Baxter and S. Davidson (eds.), *Studies in Accounting Theory*, Sweet & Maxwell, 1962.

Bromwich, M., 'The Setting of Accounting Standards; the contribution of research', in Bromwich, M. and Hopwood, A. G., *Essays in British Accounting Research*, Pitman, 1981.

Benston, G. J., 'The Establishment and Enforcement of Accounting Standards: Methods, Benefits and Costs', *Accounting and Business Research*, Winter, 1980.

Edey, H. C., 'Accounting Standards in the British Isles', in W. T. Baxter and S. Davidson (eds.) *Studies in Accounting Theory*, Sweet & Maxwell, 1977.

Grady, P., ARS No. 7, *Inventory of Generally Accepted Accounting Principles for Business Enterprises*, AICPA, 1965.

Grinyer, J. R., 'A Personal Perspective on Accounting Standards', *The Accountant's Magazine*, February, 1978.

I.A.S.C. *Objectives and Procedures*, 1983.

Lafferty, M., 'Why it is Time for another Leap Forward', Accountancy, January, 1979.

Leach, R., 'The Birth of British Accounting Standards' in R. Leach and E. Stamp (eds), *British Accounting Standards*, Sweet & Maxwell, 1981.

Lothian, N., 'Should we Retain the Prudence Concept?' *The Accountant's Magazine*, November, 1982.

Macve, R., *A Conceptual Framework for Financial Accounting and Reporting*, ICAEW, 1981.

Moonitz, M., *The Basic Postulates of Accounting*, AICPA, 1961.

Stamp, E., 'The Watts Report and the Enforcement Problem', *The Accountant's Magazine*, June 1981.

Solomons, D., 'The Political Implications of Accounting Standard Setting', *Accounting and Business Research*, Spring, 1983.

Trueblood, R. M., 'Why Accountants Need to Tell a Fuller Story', *Business Week*, 6 February 1971.

Tweedie, D. P., 'Standards, Objectives and the Corporate Report', in R. Leach and E. Stamps, *British Accounting Standards*, Sweet & Maxwell, 1981.

Watts, T. R., 'Planning the Next Decade', in Leach and Stamp, op. cit., 1981.

Weetman, P., 'Accounting Standards: a Pause for Reflection', *Accounting and Business Research*, Summer, 1977.

Appendix

ASC's Work Programme as at 1 November 1984

Projects are listed in the order in which they are likely to become final documents, e.g. SSAPs or SORPs and not in order of priority.

Major Projects	Document(s) published	Stage reached
Accounting for Goodwill	ED30; SSAP22	Approved by ASC, submitted to CCAB Councils for approval*
Accounting for Acquisitions and Mergers	ED31; SSAP23	Draft SSAP based on a SOI published in April, 1984 has been approved by the ASC and will be forwarded to CCAB Councils for approval**
Review of SSAP15 Accounting for Deferred Taxation	ED33	Draft revised SSAP being developed in accordance with SOI.***
Accounting for the Effects of Changing Prices	ED35	ED35 published for comment in July 1984. Comment period ends 31 December. Guidance notes to be issued in 1985 with the Standard. SOI on simplifications published 1 November, 1984. Work is in hand on applications in shipping, extractive industries, private and value-based companies****
Review of SSAP6 Extraordinary Items and Prior Year Adjustments	ED36	Draft exposure draft being developed following 1983 discussion paper*****
Accounting for Pension Costs	ED32	ED32 on disclosure of pension information published in May, 1983. Consultative SOI published 1 November 1984 dealing with measurement and disclosure issues. Comment period ends 30 April, 1985
Materiality	None	A new project. An audit brief has been published
Review of all accounting standards in the light of Companies Acts 1980 and 1981, including realised and distributable profits	None	New project. Implications of recent companies legislation have so far been considered on a piecemeal basis as new standards have developed or existing standards revised.

Major Projects	Document(s) published	Stage reached
Other projects:		
Pension Scheme Accounts	ED34	Exposure draft of a SORP published in April, 1984. Comment period ended 31st October, 1984
Review of SSAP13 Accounting for Research and Development	None	Exposure draft of a revised standard being developed
Review of SSAP12 Accounting for Deprecia-tion	Discussion paper	Discussion paper published 1983. SOI published September 1984. Exposure draft of a revised standard being prepared******
Review of Explanatory for-ward to SSAPs		Working party has developed a draft and is now considering comments from CCAB Technical Committee.
Accounting by Charities	Discussion paper	Discussion paper issued February 1984. Comment period ended 30 Septem-ber, 1984
Related Party Transactions	None	Joint working party (with APC) to consider develop-ment of an exposure draft of SSAP for ASC and of auditing guidance for APC.
Fair Value in the Context of Acquisition Account-ing	None	Exposure draft of a SORP being developed
Segmental Reporting	None	Work previously carried out by ASC but suspended. Project now to be reacti-vated
Interim Reporting	Draft guidance notes	New project. Draft guid-ance notes were published in 1982 on CCA in interim reports but did not deal fully with the topic
Review of SSAP5 Accounting for Value Added Tax	None	New project. Referred to ASC by CCAB Company Law Sub Committee. Review limited to consid-eration of group VAT liability.

Major Projects	Document(s) published	Stage reached

Research projects

High priority:

The effect of accounting standards on small business
Realised profits

Others:
Capitalisation of interest
Conceptual framework,
Accounting for investments
Review of SSAP10, State-
ments of Source and
Application of funds.

---

* Accounting Standard issued and applicable to financial statements relating to accounting periods being on or after 1 January, 1985.

** Accounting standard issued and applicable to financial statements.

*** Revised accounting standard issued and applicable to financial statements relating to accounting periods beginning on or after 1 April, 1985.

**** ED35 was withdrawn in 1985 and SSAP 16 was made non-mandatory. Revised proposals are to be issued in 'due course'. The status of SSAP16 is discussed more fully in Chapter 8.

***** ED36 issued in January 1985.

****** ED37 issued in May 1985.

CHAPTER 4

Company Legislation

The activities of UK companies are legally regulated by the Companies Acts of 1929, 1948, 1967, 1976, 1980, 1981 and 1985 and by case law. As we saw in Chapter 2, the 1929 Act required public companies to file profit and loss accounts, but made no prescriptions as to their contents, whilst the 1948 Act expanded disclosure requirements and made group accounts obligatory. Also, as we noted, the 1967 Act expanded disclosure requirements further and abolished the status of exempt private companies. As we shall see in this chapter, the 1980 Act introduced a definition of distributable profits of companies whilst the 1981 Act made a number of important changes in the presentation and disclosure of material in accounts as well as in the accounting principles underlying them. The Companies Act 1985 consolidates the Companies Acts from 1948 to 1981 without changing the law contained in them.

Background to 1980 and 1981 Acts

Since joining the EEC in 1973, company law has been significantly influenced by a series of Directives emanating from the European Commission. A Directive is a legislative document containing proposals which, once the Directive has been adopted by the Council of Ministers of the EEC, are required to be implemented by member nations in their laws. Four Directives on Company Law matters have been adopted by the Council of Ministers. The First Directive was already in force when the UK joined the EEC and its provisions were enacted into law by the European Communities Act 1972. The Second Directive was implemented by the Companies Act 1980. The Third Directive was for the most part already reflected in UK company law. The Fourth Directive was implemented in the UK by the Companies Act 1981. The rate of implementation has varied considerably amongst EEC countries (Gray and Coenenberg, 1984).

A further four Directives have been drafted and await adoption. These proposed Directives (numbers in brackets) relate to employee participation in company policy decision making (Fifth), prospectuses and quotation of shares (Sixth), consolidated accounts (Seventh), and qualifications of auditors of united companies (Eighth). Each of these Directives is related in some way to company accounts and will eventually become a part of company law.

Companies Act 1980

The Companies Act 1980 (CA80) had as its main purpose the clarification of the problem of defining the distributable profit of companies. Hitherto, the law governing distributable profit was contained in a great many cases which had been before the courts. CA80 seeks to provide a general definition of distributable profit, with modification for particular categories of company. However, it must be noted that other legal provisions may apply and companies are still governed by their memoranda and articles of association as to what may be distributed.

The basic definition of distributable profits would require a calculation of the following:

	Accumulated realised profits (both capital and revenue)
less	Accumulated realised losses (both capital and revenue)
plus	Any losses written off in capital re-organisation or reconstruction
less	Extra depreciation provided on revalued assets
plus	Items taken to reserve which may be properly included in distributable profit.

The sum total of the above is distributable profit. Because realised profit and loss is central to all the items we may conclude that it is the key to distributable profit. CA80 states that realisation is to be determined by reference to normal accounting principles. The same view is taken in the Companies Act 1981 which states that 'principles generally accepted with respect to the determination for accounting purposes of realised profit' be used to calculate realised profit. These principles are considered in Chapter 7.

Criticisms of the concept of distributable profit have arisen because profit is not accumulated in a cash balance; it is usually converted into other assets long before dividend time comes around (Eggington, 1980). Furthermore, distributable profit implies that capital should be maintained. But, as we shall discuss in Chapter 6, there are competing views of capital maintenance.

Companies Act 1981

The Companies Act 1981 (CA81) implemented the detailed provisions of the EEC Fourth Directive which was adopted by the Council of Ministers in 1978. With some exceptions it applies to the accounts of all companies for financial years beginning on or after the 15th of June, 1982.

The Act made a number of important changes to company law:

1. The detailed requirements for the disclosure of information in company accounts, most of which was set out in the 1948 Act, has been considerably extended.
2. Although the accounts still comprise a balance sheet, profit and loss account, and notes to the accounts, CA81 specifies the format, headings, and order in which items appear in the accounts with a degree of detail not so far seen.
3. Hitherto, the basic accounting principles by which accounts are constructed have been governed by the conventional approach and by Statements of Standard Accounting Practice. CA81 regulates some of these principles by the force of law. However, the legal regulation of CA81 is generally in quite broad terms and this is supplemented by accounting standards.
4. Several aspects of company accounting upon which CA81 legislates are already covered by accounting standards. In some cases the requirements of CA81 are consistent with the relevant SSAPs, whilst in others there appears to be inconsistency. However, where CA81 and SSAPs are consistent it may be said that accounting standards have been incorporated into law.
5. CA81 lays down rules for valuation in the preparation of accounts. These rules allow for the continued use of historical cost but also introduce alternative valuation rules.
6. CA81 introduces a novel distinction in accounting disclosure by specifying different disclosure requirements for accounts issued by certain categories of company to the Registrar of Companies as distinct from their shareholders. Broadly, disclosure to shareholders is the same for all companies covered by CA81 and represents the full amount of disclosure required by the act. The level of disclosure in the accounts to be filed with the Registrar varies with the size and character of companies but, except for large companies (as defined in CA81), the level of disclosure is less than to shareholders.
7. As with the earlier Companies Acts, the over-riding principle governing company accounts is the true and fair view. Thus, despite the greater degree of detail specified in CA81, companies may depart from the legal provisions in order to give a true and fair view. At the conclusion of this

chapter we review the latest legal opinion on the meaning of 'true and fair view'.

Detailed disclosure requirements

CA81 requires companies to provide balance sheet, a profit and loss account, notes to the accounts, and a directors' report. The appendices to this chapter set out the detailed disclosure requirements and below we shall consider the major changes and additions to disclosure brought about by CA81.

(a) Profit and Loss Account
CA81 requires the disclosure of major categories of costs and income. This allows not only greater details of costs and income to be seen for the first time but permits the identification of gross profit details.

(b) Balance Sheet
The following information must be given in the balance sheet:

    (*i*)   Stock is to be sub-divided between raw materials, work-in-progress, finished goods, and payments on account.

    (*ii*) Debtors are to be sub-divided between trade debtors, related companies, group companies, other items, and pre-payments. Separate items are to be disclosed for amounts due within or after one year.

    (*iii*) Creditors are to be sub-divided into the categories shown in the appendix to this chapter, distinguishing between those due within or after one year.

    (*iv*) Loans are to be disclosed separately from investments.

    (*v*)   Investments must be classified between fixed and current.

    (*vi*) Research costs, preliminary costs and share-issue costs can no longer be capitalised.

(c) Notes to the Accounts
The following information must be given in notes to the accounts:

    (*i*)   The accounting policies followed by a company in determining the amounts of balance sheet items and the profit and loss of the company must be stated.

    (*ii*) Disclosure is required of departures from the accounting requirements of CA81, together with explanations and estimates of the effects of such departures.

    (*iii*) Any change in the format adopted for profit and loss account or balance sheet.

(*iv*) Reasons for capitalising development costs and an explanation of the period chosen for the writing-off of such costs.

(*v*) Justification for the period chosen for the writing-off of purchased goodwill.

(*vi*) The capitalisation of interest on borrowed money to finance the production of assets, together with the amounts capitalised, where this has been included in the cost of an asset.

(*vii*) Any material differences between the balance sheet values of stock items and their replacement costs.

(*viii*) Differences between (or information to compare) the values of assets included at replacement cost (and associated accumulated depreciation) and corresponding historical costs.

(*ix*) Tax treatment of transfers to or from the revaluation reserve.

(*x*) Movements on fixed assets previously not disclosed, i.e. investments and intangible assets.

(*xi*) Particulars of investments amounting to 10 per cent or more, and 20 per cent or more in other companies.

(*xii*) Details of any significant items included in the balance sheet item 'provisions'.

(*xiii*) Details of any security given for liabilities, and for creditors due after five years.

(*xiv*) Details of any contingent liabilities and security provided for them.

(*xv*) Details of any unprovided-for financial commitments, such as leases.

(*xvi*) Turnover and pre-tax profits by line of business, and of turnover by geographic market.

(*xvii*) Details of employees, distinguished by categories chosen by the directors together with total staff costs.

(*xviii*) Details of extraordinary items of profit or loss, together with related taxation.

(*d*) *Directors' Report*

A number of new items of information are required for the directors' report:

(*i*) An indication of likely future developments in the business.

(*ii*) Details of important events affecting the company or its subsidiaries which have occurred since the end of the financial year.

(*iii*) Indications of the company's activities in the field of research and development.

(*iv*) Details of any acquisition or disposal by the company of its own shares.

In addition to these specific new requirements the relationship between the Directors' Report and the accounts and the Notes to the Accounts has changed. For example, directors' interests in shares or debentures can now be disclosed in the accounts, and corresponding amounts, which were allowed to be disclosed in the Directors' Report, can now appear only in the accounts. Perhaps most significantly, auditors must now examine whether the information given in the Directors' Report is consistent with that given in the accounts and, if it is not consistent, this must be reported. Under CA81 the Directors' Report has to provide what the Act terms 'a fair review of the development of the business of the company and its subsidiaries during the year and of their position at the end of it'. This extends the requirements of the 1948 and 1967 Companies Acts.

Presentation of Accounting Information

The EEC's Fourth Directive proposed two formats for the presentation of balance sheets—vertical and horizontal, and four formats for the profit and loss account. CA81 allows a choice between these six alternatives. These are set out in the appendix to this chapter. The four alternative presentations of profit and loss accounts differ in both physical presentation and detail, although the variations in the latter respect are limited. As with previous acts, CA81 requires comparative information to be given for items shown in the accounts and notes, and this is recommended for inclusion in the review of the business in the Directors' Report.

CA81 prescribes certain items which must be displayed on the face of the accounts, items which may be amalgamated or presented in notes rather than on the face of the accounts, and items which may be rearranged better to suit the nature of a business. This suggests that despite the considerable degree of prescription contained in CA81 some of the flexible characteristic of earlier Companies Acts is retained. In addition to the specific areas referred to above, flexibility is possible in that the statutory requirements still present a minimum disclosure and more detail may be given if directors so wish. Furthermore, the over-riding nature of the need to present a true and fair view allows for departures from the prescribed formats of presentation.

Accounting Principles

CA81 requires that accounts be prepared in accordance with the four basic principles of consistency, prudence, going concern and accruals. These principles are embodied as the fundamental accounting concepts of SSAP2 and this standard is now given effective statutory status. Prudence is expressed as the inclusion of only those profits which are realised, and the recognition of all losses and liabilities which are actual and potential, even if they come to light only after the end of the accounting period.

An additional accounting principle requires each asset and liability to be determined separately in arriving at aggregate amounts to be disclosed in accounts. This precludes the setting-off of gains and losses on assets against each other. Although not subject to an accounting standard this is regarded as good accounting practice in the UK. Like SSAP2, CA81 requires the disclosure of the accounting policies used to put into effect accounting principles.

Relationship with Accounting Standards

The provisions of CA81 cover a number of accounting topics upon which accounting standards have been issued. We have already referred to SSAP2 in this regard. Here, we shall briefly refer to other standards. The terms of SSAP1, dealing with associated companies, are reflected in CA81's definition of related companies for the purpose of accounting for investments in other companies. CA81 requires disclosure of any extra-ordinary income or charges, together with associated tax effects. This is the subject matter of SSAP6. Since CA81 offers no definition of 'extraordinary' SSAP6 must be a source of guidance. From the same SSAP, prior year items, whilst not included in the statutory formats of accounts, are dealt with by a requirement to adjust comparative items for the preceding year where they are not comparable.

The rules for the valuation of stocks contained in CA81 allow the purchase price or cost of stocks to be determined using any of LIFO, FIFO, weighted average approach or a similar method. Since SSAP9 does not normally consider LIFO to be appropriate there appears to be a conflict with CA81. Similarly, CA81's prohibition of the anticipation of profits seems to preclude SSAP9's treatment of profits from long-term contracts. However, in both cases, the over-riding need to provide a true and fair view necessitates the application of the standard where appropriate.

CA81 is consistent with SSAP12 on depreciation and SSAP13 on research and development is incorporated in the Act's prohibition of the capitalisation of research expenditure and the allowance that development expenditure may be capitalised only in special circumstances. As we shall consider below, SSAP16 (Current Cost Accounting) is incorporated under the Act's alternative valuation rules. SSAP17 on post-balance sheet events is included in the definition of prudence in the Act's specification of accounting principles. Finally, CA81 requires as part of the notes to the accounts information on contingencies in line with the principles set out in SSAP18.

Rules for Valuation

The Act lays down rules for the valuation of items to be included in the accounts. These may be based upon historical cost or alternative rules. The historical cost rules prescribe that fixed assets must be stated at their purchase price or production costs less any amounts written off, and current assets must be stated at the lower of their net realisable value and their purchase or production cost. Fixed assets having a limited useful life must be systematically written-off over that period.

The alternative rules allow the application of current cost principles to the valuation of fixed assets and stock. This provides for valuation at either current cost or latest valuation for fixed assets other than goodwill, valuation at either market value or an alternative chosen by the directors for fixed asset investments, and valuation at current cost for current asset investments and stock. As with SSAP16, if the alternative (current cost) valuation rules are chosen as the main medium for valuation, notes to the accounts should disclose for all categories of assets, except stock, historical values or the differences between historical cost and current cost.

Where assets are revalued to current cost valuation, differences which arise are to be taken to a separate revaluation reserve. Amounts may only be transferred to profit and loss account for distribution where they represent realised profit.

Rules for the Publication of Accounts

CA81 introduces a major innovation into company law by allowing certain companies to file different accounts with the Registrar of Companies from those which they present to their shareholders. However, the statutory rules for preparing accounts apply in full to all companies and no variation is allowed in them. Moreover, certain companies must supply the full statutory accounts to both their shareholders and the Registrar. These companies include:

(*i*)   public companies,
(*ii*) banking, insurance and shipping companies,
(*iii*) companies which are members of groups of which a company in (*i*) or (*ii*) above is also a member.

Other types of company may file less detailed accounts with the Registrar but must provide their shareholders with full accounts. These companies must meet the definition of either a small or medium-sized company, which the Act sets out in the year for which accounts are prepared, and the preceding year. These conditions are as follows:

Small Company:
1. Turnover must not exceed £1,400,000.
2. Balance sheet total (effectively total assets) must not exceed £700,000.
3. Average number of persons employed (determined on a weekly basis), must not exceed 50.

Medium-Sized Company:
1. Turnover must not exceed £5,750,000.
2. Balance sheet total (total assets) must not exceed £2,800,000.
3. Average number of persons employed (determined on a weekly basis), must not exceed 250.

A small company need not file a profit and loss account, need not prepare a directors' report, need file only a modified balance sheet, and the notes to the accounts need cover only limited items. A special auditors' report is required to state that the company satisfies the small company conditions and must reproduce the auditors' report on the full accounts submitted to shareholders.

A medium-sized company must file a full balance sheet but need file only a modified profit and loss account. A medium-sized company must prepare a Directors' Report but need not file it.

True and Fair View

As we have noted in earlier chapters, the requirement that company accounts provide a true and fair view has had an important place in company law for a considerable time. In CA81 the requirement to give a true and fair view is paramount and over-rides all other requirements to present information in company accounts. Thus, directors of companies must depart from the detailed provisions of CA81 if this is necessary to provide a true and fair view. Such departures may involve the provision of additional, non-statutory disclosures, or the use of an accounting policy other than that prescribed by law. But, where departures for the statutory provisions are necessary, they must only be undertaken to the extent necessary to provide a true and fair view, and details of the departure, the reasons for it, and its effects, must be disclosed. The obligation to provide a true and fair view does not extend to the modified accounts which small and medium-sized companies may file. This is because the omissions from such accounts are likely to prevent them from showing such a view, despite the fact that they are based upon true and fair.

In a similar vein, if a company voluntarily publishes abridged accounts, such as a preliminary announcement of results to the press or employee reports, no auditors' report may be attached to them, thereby distancing such accounts from a true and fair view. However, there is a requirement to publish with such reports a statement of whether an auditors' report has been made on the full accounts and whether that report was qualified or unqualified.

In 1983 the ASC obtained a written opinion from counsel on the meaning of 'true and fair' with particular reference to the role of accounting standards. The ASC intends to take account of the opinion in all its future work. The opinion states that financial statements will not be true and fair unless the information they contain is sufficient in quantity and quality to satisfy the reasonable expectations of the readers to whom they are addressed. But the expectations of the readers will have been moulded by the practices of accountants because, by and large, they will expect to get what they ordinarily get and that, in turn, will depend upon the normal practices of accountants. Therefore, the courts will treat compliance with accepted accounting principles as prima facie evidence that the financial statements are true and fair. The opinion states that since the function of the ASC is to formulate what it considers should be generally accepted accounting principles, the value of a SSAP to a court is:

(*i*)   A statement of professional opinion which readers may expect in financial statements which are true and fair.

(*ii*) That readers expect financial statements to comply with standards.

The opinion concludes, therefore, that financial statements which depart from standards may be held not to be true and fair, unless a strong body of professional opinion opts out of applying the standard.

Companies Act 1985

The Companies Act 1985 was one of four pieces of legislation enacted in 1985. The other three Acts concerned Business Names, Insider Dealing, and Consequential Provisions. The Companies Act 1985 consolidated the five preceding Companies Acts into one piece of legislation without amending the existing law with the intention of making its application and interpretation easier by restating the law in a more convenient form. During the preparation of the Bill which preceded the Act extensive consultation was undertaken with organisations including those representing the accountancy profession.

QUESTIONS

1. How are distributable profits defined by the Companies Act 1980?
2. What major general changes were introduced by the Companies Act 1981 (CA81)?

3. What major detailed changes and additions to disclosure were brought about by CA81 to the:

   (*a*) profit and loss account
   (*b*) balance sheet
   (*c*) notes to the accounts
   (*d*) directors' report?

4. Which accounting concepts does CA81 enshrine in law?
5. Describe the relationship between accounting standards and CA81.
6. How does CA81 define:

   (*a*) small, (*b*) medium-sized companies?

7. How do the disclosure requirements for small and medium-sized companies differ from those of large companies?
8. What is meant by a 'true and fair view'?
9. The following are details of three separate companies' summarised balance sheets at 31 March 19X2:

	Angie PLC	Betty PLC	Cathy PLC
	£000	£000	£000
Fixed assets	2,500	380	500
Current assets	900	180	300
Current liabilities	(700)	(160)	(200)
	2,700	400	600
Share capital	200	300	2,000
Reserves:			
Revaluation	1,100	(200)	—
Realised capital profit	800	—	—
Brought forward realised			
revenue profit (loss)	400	500	(1,600)
Current year realised			
revenue profit (loss)	200	(200)	200
	2,700	400	600

Angie and Betty are public companies and Cathy a private company under the Companies Act 1980. Angie's property, previously included in the financial statements at original cost of £900,000, was revalued on 1 April 19X1 at £2 million. This revalued amount is included in the figures above, subject to the full amount being written off equally over the next 50 years from 1 April 19X1. Prior to this date, no depreciation had been provided on property. At 31 March 19X2, no transfer had been made between revaluation reserve and realised revenue profit.

You are required to:

(*a*) Compare briefly the bases for calculating the maximum distribution under the provisions of the Companies Act 1980 in respect of public, private and investment companies.

(*b*) Calculate the maximum distribution that Angie, Betty and Cathy could each make under the Companies Act 1980, and

(*c*) Calculate the maximum distribution if Betty PLC is an investment company and its dividend is to be paid from bank overdraft.

(Institute of Chartered Accountants)

REFERENCES

Eggington, D. A., 'Distributable Profit and the Pursuit of Prudence', *Accounting and Business Research*, Winter, 1980.

Gray, S. J. and Coenenberge, A. G. (eds.), *EEC Accounting Harmonisation: Implementation and Impact of the Fourth Directive*, Elsevier, 1984.

Appendix 1
Balance Sheet Formats

Format 1

A. Called up share capital not paid (*1*)

B. Fixed assets
   I   Intangible assets
       1. Development costs
       2. Concessions, patents, licences, trade marks and similar rights and assets (*2*)
       3. Goodwill (*3*)
       4. Payments on account

   II Tangible assets
       1. Land and buildings
       2. Plant and machinery
       3. Fixtures, fittings, tools and equipment
       4. Payments on account and assets in course of construction

   III Investments
       1. Share in group companies
       2. Loans in group companies
       3. Shares in related companies
       4. Loans to related companies
       5. Other investments other than loans
       6. Other loans
       7. Own shares (*4*)

C. Current assets
   I   Stocks
       1. Raw materials and consumables
       2. Work in progress
       3. Finished goods and goods for resale
       4. Payments on account

   II Debtors (*5*)
       1. Trade debtors
       2. Amounts owed by group companies

3. Amounts owed by related companies
4. Other debtors
5. Called up share capital not paid (*1*)
6. Prepayments and accrued income (*6*)

III Investments
  1. Shares in group companies
  2. Own shares (*4*)
  3. Other investments

IV Cash at bank and in hand

D. Prepayments and accrued income (*6*)

E. Creditors: amounts falling due within one year
  1. Debenture loans (*7*)
  2. Bank loans and overdrafts
  3. Payments received on account (*8*)
  4. Trade creditors
  5. Bills of exchange payable
  6. Amounts owed to group companies
  7. Amounts owed to related companies
  8. Other creditors including taxation and social security (*9*)
  9. Accruals and deferred income (*10*)

F. Net current assets (liabilities) (*11*)

G. Total assets less current liabilities

H. Creditors: amounts falling due after more than one year
  1. Debenture loans (*7*)
  2. Bank loans and overdrafts
  3. Payments received on account (*8*)
  4. Trade creditors
  5. Bills of exchange payable
  6. Amounts owed to group companies
  7. Amounts owed to related companies
  8. Other creditors including taxation and social security (*9*)
  9. Accruals and deferred income (*10*)

I. Provisions for liabilities and charges
  1. Pensions and similar obligations
  2. Taxation, including deferred taxation
  3. Other provisions

J. Accruals and deferred income (*10*)

K. Capital and reserves
  I Called up share capital (*12*)

  II Share premium account

  III Revaluation reserve

  IV Other reserves
    1. Capital redemption reserve
    2. Reserve for own shares

3. Reserves provided for by the articles of association
4. Other reserves

V   Profit and loss account.

Format 2

ASSETS

A. Called up share capital not paid (*1*)

B. Fixed assets
  I   Intangible assets
    1. Development costs
    2. Concessions, patents, licences, trade marks and similar rights and assets (*2*)
    3. Goodwill (*3*)
    4. Payments on account

  II   Tangible assets
    1. Land and buildings
    2. Plant and machinery
    3. Fixtures, fittings, tools and equipment
    4. Payments on account and assets in course of construction

  III Investments
    1. Shares in group companies
    2. Loans in group companies
    3. Shares in related companies
    4. Loans to related companies
    5. Other investments other than loans
    6. Other loans
    7. Own shares (*4*)

C. Current assets
  I   Stocks
    1. Raw materials and consumables
    2. Work in progress
    3. Finished goods and goods for resale
    4. Payments on account

  II   Debtors (*5*)
    1. Trade debtors
    2. Amounts owed by group companies
    3. Amounts owed by related companies
    4. Other debtors
    5. Called up share capital not paid (*1*)
    6. Prepayments and accrued income (*6*)

  III Investments
    1. Shares in group companies
    2. Own shares (*4*)
    3. Other investments

  IV Cash at bank and in hand

D. Prepayments and accrued income (*6*)

LIABILITIES

A. Capital and reserves
   I   Called up share capital (*12*)

   II   Share premium account

   III Revaluation reserve

   IV   Other reserves
        1. Capital redemption reserve
        2. Reserve for own shares
        3. Reserves provided for by the articles of association
        4. Other reserves

   V   Profit and loss account

B. Provisions for liabilities and charges
        1. Pensions and similar obligations
        2. Taxation including deferred taxation
        3. Other provisions

C. Creditors (*13*)
        1. Debenture loans (*7*)
        2. Bank loans and overdrafts
        3. Payments received on account (*8*)
        4. Trade creditors
        5. Bills of exchange payable
        6. Amounts owed to group companies
        7. Amounts owed to related companies
        8. Other creditors including taxation and social security (*9*)
        9. Accruals and deferred income (*10*)

D. Accruals and deferred income (*10*)

Notes on the balance sheet formats

(*1*) *Called up share capital not paid*
     (Formats 1 and 2, items A and C.II.5.)
     This item may be shown in either of the two positions given in Formats 1 and
     2.
(*2*) *Concessions, patents, licenses, trade marks and similar rights and assets*
     (Formats 1 and 2, item B.I.2.)
     Amounts in respect of assets shall only be included in a company's balance
     sheet under this item if either—
     (*a*) the assets were acquired for valuable consideration and are not required
          to be shown under goodwill; or
     (*b*) the assets in question were created by the company itself.
(*3*) *Goodwill*
     (Formats 1 and 2, item B.I.3.)
     Amounts representing goodwill shall only be included to the extent that the
     goodwill was acquired for valuable consideration.
(*4*) *Own shares*
     (Formats 1 and 2, items B.III.7 and C.III.2.)
     The nominal value of the shares held shall be shown separately.

(5) *Debtors*

(Formats 1 and 2, items C.II.1 to 6.)

The amount falling due after more than one year shall be shown separately for each item included under debtors.

(6) *Prepayments and accrued income*

(Formats 1 and 2, items C.II.6 and D.)

This item may be shown in either of the two positions given in Formats 1 and 2.

(7) *Debenture loans*

(Format 1, items E.1 and H.1 and Format 2, item C.1.)

The amount of any convertible loans shall be shown separately.

(8) *Payments received on account*

(Format 1, items E.3 and H.3 and Format 2, item C.3.)

Payments received on account of orders shall be shown for each of these items in so far as they are not shown as deductions from stocks.

(9) *Other creditors including taxation and social security*

(Format 1, items E.8 and H.8 and Format 2, item C.8.)

The amount for creditors in respect of taxation and social security shall be shown separately from the amount for other creditors.

(10) *Accruals and deferred income*

(Format 1, items E.9, H.9 and J and Format 2, items C.9 and D.)

The two positions given for this item in Format 1 at E.9 and H.9 are an alternative to the position at J, but if the item is not shown in a position corresponding to that at J it may be shown in either or both of the other two positions (as the case may require).

The two positions given for this item in Format 2 are alternatives.

(11) *Net current assets (liabilities)*

(Format 1, item F.)

In determining the amount to be shown for this item any amounts shown under "prepayments and accrued income" shall be taken into account wherever shown.

(12) *Called up share capital*

(Format 1, item K.I and Format 2, item A.I.)

The amount of allotted share capital and the amount of called up share capital which has been paid up shall be shown separately.

(13) *Creditors*

(Format 2, items C.1 to 9.)

Amounts falling due within one year and after one year shall be shown separately for each of these items and their aggregate shall be shown separately for all of these items.

Appendix 2
Profit and Loss Account Formats

Format 1

(see note (*17*) below)

1. Turnover
2. Cost of sales (*14*)
3. Gross profit or loss
4. Distribution costs (*14*)
5. Administrative expenses (*14*)
6. Other operating income
7. Income from shares in group companies
8. Income from shares in related companies
9. Income from other fixed asset investments (*15*)
10. Other interest receivable and similar income (*15*)
11. Amounts written off investments
12. Interest payable and similar charges (*16*)
13. Tax on profit or loss on ordinary activities
14. Profit or loss on ordinary activities after taxation
15. Extraordinary income
16. Extraordinary charges
17. Extraordinary profit or loss
18. Tax on extraordinary profit or loss
19. Other taxes not shown under the above items
20. Profit or loss for the financial year

Format 2

1. Turnover
2. Change in stocks of finished goods and in work progress
3. Own work capitalised
4. Other operating income
5. (*a*) Raw materials and consumables
   (*b*) Other external charges

6. Staff costs:
   (*a*) wages and salaries
   (*b*) social security costs
   (*c*) other pension costs
7. (*a*) Depreciation and other amounts written off tangible and intangible fixed assets
   (*b*) Exceptional amounts written off current assets
8. Other operating charges
9. Income from shares in group companies
10. Income from shares in related companies
11. Income from other fixed asset investments (*15*)
12. Other interest receivable and similar income (*15*)
13. Amounts written off investments
14. Interest payable and similar charges (*16*)
15. Tax on profit or loss on ordinary activities
16. Profit or loss on ordinary activities after taxation
17. Extraordinary income
18. Extraorindary charges
19. Extraordinary profit or loss
20. Tax on extraordinary profit or loss
21. Other taxes not shown under the above items
22. Profit or loss for the financial year

Format 3

(see note (*17*) below)

A. Charges
1. Cost of sales (*14*)
2. Distribution costs (*14*)
3. Administrative expenses (*14*)
4. Amounts written off investments
5. Interest payable and similar charges (*16*)
6. Tax on profit or loss on ordinary activities
7. Profit or loss on ordinary activites after taxation
8. Extraordinary charges
9. Tax on extraordinary profit or loss
10. Other taxes not shown under the above items
11. Profit or loss for the financial year

B. Income
1. Turnover
2. Other operating income
3. Income from shares in group companies
4. Income from shares in related companies
5. Income from other fixed asset investments (*15*)
6. Other interest receivable and similar income (*15*)
7. Profit or loss on ordinary activities after taxation
8. Extraordinary income
9. Profit or loss for the financial year

Format 4

A. Charges
 1. Reduction in stocks of finished goods and in work in progress
 2. (*a*) Raw materials and consumables
    (*b*) Other external charges
 3. Staff costs:
    (*a*) wages and salaries
    (*b*) social security costs
    (*c*) other pension costs
 4. (*a*) Depreciation and other amounts written off tangible and intangible fixed assets
    (*b*) Exceptional amounts written off current assets
 5. Other operating charges
 6. Amounts written off investments
 7. Interest payable and similar charges (*16*)
 8. Tax on profit or loss on ordinary activities
 9. Profit or loss on ordinary activities after taxation
10. Extraordinary charges
11. Tax on extraordinary profit or loss
12. Other taxes not shown under the above items
13. Profit or loss for the financial year

B. Income
 1. Turnover
 2. Increase in stocks of finished goods and in work in progress
 3. Own work capitalised
 4. Other operating income
 5. Income from shares in group companies
 6. Income from shares in related companies
 7. Income from other fixed asset investments (*15*)
 8. Other interest receivable and similar income (*15*)
 9. Profit or loss on ordinary activities after taxation
10. Extraordinary income
11. Profit or loss for the financial year

Notes on the profit and loss account formats

(*14*) *Cost of sales : distribution costs : administrative expenses*
(Format 1, items 2, 4 and 5 and Format 3, items A.1, 2 and 3.)
These items shall be stated after taking into account any necessary provisions for depreciation or diminution in value of assets.

(*15*) *Income from other fixed asset investments : other interest receivable and similar income*
(Format 1, items 9 and 10: Format 2, items 11 and 12: Format 3, items B.5 and 6: Format 4, items B.7 and 8.)
Income and interest derived from group companies shall be shown separately from income and interest derived from other sources.

(*16*) *Interest payable and similar charges*
(Format 1, item 12: Format 2, item 14: Format 3, item A.5: Format 4, item A.7.)
The amount payable to group companies shall be shown separately.

(*17*) *Formats 1 and 3*
The amount of any provisions for depreciation and diminution in value of tangible and intangible fixed assets falling to be shown under items 7(*a*) and A.4(*a*) respectively in Formats 2 and 4 shall be disclosed in a note to the accounts in any case where the profit and loss account is prepared by reference to Format 1 or Format 3.

Appendix 3
Distributable Profit

The basis for the computation of distributable profit given on page 62 applies to all companies. As pointed out, realisation is based upon generally accepted accounting principles. SSAP2 provides guidance as follows:

> . . . revenue and profits are not anticipated, but are recognised by inclusion in the profit and loss account only when realised in the form of either cash or of other assets *the ultimate realisation of which can be assessed with reasonable certainty*: provision is made for all known liabilities (expenses and losses) *whether the amount of these is known with certainty or is a best estimate in the light of the information available.* [our italic]

The Act is retrospective in that realisation is deemed to have applied as a criterion since a company was formed.

Special restrictions apply to:

1. *Public Companies*

   Such companies must provide for any excess of unrealised losses over unrealised profits of non-current assets before arriving at the sum available for distribution. Public companies may only make a distribution if:

   (a) at the time, the value of net assets is not less than the total of called-up share capital and undistributable reserves, and

   (b) if the distribution does not reduce the amount of the company's net assets to less than the aggregate of called-up share capital and undistributable reserves.

   For this purpose:

   (a) Liabilities (included in net assets) refer to any provision not taken into account in arriving at the value of an asset.

   (b) Undistributable reserves include:

       (i) Share premium account.

       (ii) Capital redemption reserve fund.

       (iii) Any other fund which is not distributable (by statute or company constitution).

(*iv*) The amount by which accumulated, unrealised and uncapitalised profits exceed accumulated, unrealised losses, so far as not written off in a reduction or reorganisation of capital.

2. *Investment Companies*

Such a company is defined as a public company listed on the Stock Exchange whose business consists of investing its funds mainly in securities with the aim of spreading investment risk and whose constitution bars the payment of capital profits. Such a Company has an alternative basis of distribution, thus:

Accumulated, realised revenue profits
(so far as undistributed or capitalised)
less Accumulated revenue losses (both realised and unrealised, so far as not written-off)

provided that before and after the distribution, the company's assets are equal to at least one and a half times the total of its liabilities.

3. *Insurance Companies*

In general, provisions relating to distributable profits of companies other than investment companies apply also to insurance companies with long-term business. However, those amounts which have been properly transferred to its profit and loss account from a surplus or deficit on its long-term business funds are to be treated as a realised profit or loss as appropriate.

Appendix 4
Stock Exchange Listing Agreement

The securing of a Stock Exchange Listing binds a company to the Listing Agreement. This requires a company to observe certain rules and procedures regarding its status as a listed company. Some of these concern its behaviour (e.g. to register share transfers without fee), others concern the disclosure of information. The following lists the major information requirements of the Listing Agreement under three headings. 'Stock Exchange' refers to disclosures of information which must be made to the Quotations Department of the Stock Exchange; 'Financial Reports' to additional information which must be disclosed in company financial reports; and 'Press' to information to be disclosed in the press.

Stock Exchange	*Financial Reports*	*Press*

A1. Any information necessary to enable shareholders and the general public to appraise the position of the company.
A2. Details of:
  (*a*) Distributions approved.
  (*b*) Proposed changes in capital structure.
  (*c*) Drawing or redemptions of securities.
  (*d*) Preliminary announcements of profit or loss when approved.
	B1. Agreement to issue annual reports and accounts within six months of the end of the accounting period.
	B2. Additional information to be included in the directors' report:
	  (*a*) Statement of reasons for departure from accounting standards.
	  (*b*) Explanations of material differences between actual trading results and forecasts.
	  (*c*) Geographic analysis of turnover and contributions to trading
		C1. Details of allotments of securities in prospectus and other offers.

A3. Details of acquisitions or realisations of certain assets.

A4. Information required by the City Code on Take-Overs and Mergers.

A5. Information on interests in voting shares required by CA81 (section 63).

A6. Changes in the directorate.

A7. Information on purchases of redeemable securities.

A8. Information on changes in the general characteristics of the business.

A9. Copies of documents issued to holders of securities.

A10. A statement of directors' beneficial and non-beneficial interests in shares.

A11. A statement of any substantial interest (other than directors') in shares.

A12. Details of bank loans, other borrowings and interest capitalised.

results from operations outside the UK.

(*d*) Principal country of operation of each subsidiary.

(*e*) Details of each company in which an equity holding of at least 20 per cent is held:

    (*i*) Principal country of operation.

    (*ii*) Particulars of issued share and loan capital.

    (*iii*) Percentages of categories of loan capital in which an interest is held.

B3. Preparation of a half-yearly interim report to be issued to holders of securities or to be published as a paid advertisement in two leading daily newspapers. Information to be included:

(*a*) Group turnover.

(*b*) Group profit or loss before tax and extraordinary items.

(*c*) Taxation.

(*d*) Minority interests.

(*e*) Group profit or loss to shareholders before extra-ordinary items.

(*f*) Extraordinary items.

(*g*) Group profit or loss attributable to shareholders

(*h*) Dividend rates.

(*i*) Earnings per share (in pence per share) according to SSAP3.

(*j*) Comparative figures.

Stock Exchange	*Financial Reports*	*Press*
	(*k*) Any supplementary information necessary (in directors' opinion) to be necessary for a reasonable appreciation of results.	
	(*l*) Provisional figures or those subject to audit should be qualified.	
	(*m*) Current cost data (according to SSAP16) as follows:	
	(*i*) Operating profit or loss.	
	(*ii*) Interest on net borrowing.	
	(*iii*) Gearing adjustment.	
	(*iv*) Taxation.	
	(*v*) Profit attributable to members of the holding company.	
	(*vi*) Operating adjustments.	
	(*vii*) Earnings per share.	

In addition to the above (but not part of the Listing Agreement) the Stock Exchange has indicated that the following additional disclosures should be made in the annual report:

(*a*) purchase by a company of its own listed redeemable securities for the purpose of sinking fund obligations.
(*b*) statement of the total amount of such securities held.
(*c*) particulars of authority given to a company to purchase its own shares.

The General Undertaking of the Unlisted Securities Market

The General undertaking is the equivalent of the Listing Agreement for the Unlisted Securities Market. Its information requirements are broadly the same as those of the Listing Agreement. Some noteworthy differences are:

Stock Exchange	*Financial Reports*
Particulars of dealings by directors in securities of the Company traded in the USM.	Publication of interim results in one leading daily newspaper as an alternative to B3.
A statement of any interest (other than a director's) of 5% or more in share capital	

Appendix 5
The City Code on
Take-overs and Mergers

The code is issued by the Council for the Securities Industry (Composed of a number of City Institutions including the Bank of England) and is applied by a Panel. The Code has no statutory force, but is backed by the authority of the Stock Exchange and Issuing Houses Association over stock brokers and Merchant Banks respectively. Moreover, the Listing Agreement requires listed companies to adhere to the Code.

The purpose of the Code is to regulate the processes of take-overs and mergers. The Code contains principles and rules relating both to the conduct of the parties to take-overs and mergers, and to the disclosure of information. The main information requirments are summarised below:

General Principles

(a) All shareholders of the same class of an offeree company must be treated similarly and given adequate information to decide upon the bid's merits.

(b) All documents issued in connection with the bid should be drafted with the same care as the Companies Act 1948 requires of a prospectus.

Specific rules

(a) An offer must be communicated to the board of the offeree company or its advisors with secrecy in other respects.

(b) Shareholders in the offeree company must be notified of the offer by immediate press release and then individual circular.

(c) Shareholders must be told in sufficient time of all necessary facts (including any concerning the offeror) to judge the merits of the offer.

(d) Offer documents must normally communicate the offeror's intentions as to the future running of the business.

(e) Profit forecasts must be prepared with the greatest care; any assump-

General Principles	*Specific rules*
	tions must be stated; the document must contain a report by professional experts on accounting bases and calculations in the forecast. Asset valuations must be supported by independent valuers' opinions.
	(*f*) Offer documents must contain details of the offeror's holdings in the offeree, and details of the holdings of directors in either company's shares, and offeree company directors' service contracts.
	(*g*) Persons concerned with the consideration and discussion of an offer must not pass on any information to anyone else unless it is necessary to do so.

CHAPTER 5

The decision usefulness approach

The last three chapters have examined the development of financial reporting in the UK based upon the principle of a true and fair view. As we noted, particular accounting issues have been dealt with case by case on a pragmatic basis. This process has continued more or less unchanged with the establishment of the ASC, except for the additional guidance provided by SSAP2.

In recent years, policy makers have been urged to adopt a more ambitious course which focuses financial reporting on a decision usefulness objective. This approach calls into question the foundations of traditional practice and involves:

1. A priori research devoted to developing the objectives of accounting, and from them details of financial reporting. Such research has been undertaken on an *ad hoc* basis, and on a comprehensive basis by policy makers with a view to deriving a set of rules to guide their actions. Such rules have come to be known as conceptual frameworks.
2. Empirical research which develops positive models to explain actual behaviour at the individual or aggregate levels. This may be used to validate a priori research. In particular, empirical research has been recommended as a means of assisting policy makers in developing conceptual frameworks and in aiding decisions regarding desirable changes to current accounting practice. However, empirical research alone cannot lead to a set of accounting standards because empiricism is concerned with descriptive rather than normative considerations. As Hankanssan (1978) states

> Desirability in the public policy sense is a strictly logical proposition and can only be evaluated in a normative model with a full set of assumptions, including a posited criterion of 'goodness'.

This chapter considers both a priori and empirical research directed towards the decision usefulness of accounting.

I *A PRIORI* RESEARCH

A priori research places primary emphasis upon the information require-ments of normative decision models. Such models are designed to explain the procedures that decision makers follow in making particular decisions in specified circumstances. An advantage of normative decision models is that they may provide a standard of reference for the evaluation of actual decision models.

Researchers have concentrated upon equity investors and their deci-sions. Writers have typically followed the theory of finance in assuming that investors seek to maximse utility from consumption and that consumption depends upon wealth. Further, the tenets of economic rationality are assumed to be followed. The investment decision involves sacrifices and benefits each of which is normally expressed as a cash flow. Thus, investors require information which will enable them to decide whether anticipated cash flow benefits arising from investment are acceptable compensation for the sacrifice of immediate consumption possibilities due to investment. Investors are assumed to invest when the current price of the investment (and the consumption foregone) is less than or equal to the investor's valuation of the investment. Investors will disinvest when the current price of the investment and the consumption foregone is greater than the investor's valuation of the investment. Existing and potential investors are constantly evaluating the alternatives of having cash to consume presently or of investing to receive cash for consumption at various future points of time.

A model which summarises these assumptions is the single investment model which considers the decision whether or not to invest in a security. Some implications of portfolio theory are discussed later in this chapter. The single investment model is utilised by AAA (1969) and Revsine (1973) and is specified as:

$$V_o = \sum_{t=1}^{n} \frac{D_t \alpha_t}{(1+B)^t} + \frac{I_n \alpha_n}{(1+B)^n} - I_o$$

where:

V_o is the net subjective value of the gain or loss to be obtained by an investor from a specific investment at time o, that is, the investor's estimate of the current value of the investment minus the maximum price he would be willing to pay for the investment. He will increase his investment when V_o is greater than the market value of his current holdings; he will realise part of his investment when V_o falls below the market value; and he will maintain his investment at its current level when V_o equals the market value.

D_t is the dividend per share expected during the period t.

α_t is a certainty equivalent factor which adjusts the expected cash flows to a value such that a given investor is indifferent between D_t and a cash-flow which is certain to be paid. This factor is determined by each investor's attitude to risk. If he is risk averse, α_t will assume a value between 0 and 1. If the investor is a speculator and a risk-taker, α_t will be greater than 1.

B is the opportunity rate for a risk-free investment and represents the minimum return required by the investor during period t.

I_n is the expected market price of the investment at the end of the holding period n.

I_o is the price of the investment at time o, when the investment decision is made.

This simple model states that an investor's calculation of the present value of his gain from making an investment is determined by his evaluation of the utility-adjusted present value of the expected cash flows from the investment less the outlays necessary to obtain the investment. His calculation of the present value of the expected cash is determined by computing the expected value of each year's gross cash receipts, adjusted for attitude to risk. This product is then discounted by the investor's required rate of return for a riskless investment. This model does not include any personal-utility considerations other than for the investor's preference or aversion for risks evaluated on the basis of the distribution of expected cash flows. Although this investment model emphasises the assessment of future prospects and the assessment of risk and uncertainty, the investor may have other considerations in mind which may cause the model to be adapted. For example, the investor may make his investment decision in part upon an assessment of the contribution to society of the enterprise whose securities are valued using the normative investor's model.

Information needed by decision makers for the operation of this model may next be specified. Accordingly, such information relates to expectations of future dividends and the risks inherent in them. More specifically, it is necessary to prescribe financial reporting requirements for such information. A number of alternative specifications have been offered. For example, according to an AAA report (1969), dividend payments are a function of:

net cash flow from operations;

non-operating cash flows;
flows from investment and disinvestment by stockholders and creditors;
flows from investment and disinvestment in assets;
flows from random events;
management's dividend policy.

If these factors are both necessary and sufficient for investors to forecast dividends, they provide a basis for financial reports. Many different forms may be specified for financial statements to communicate such information. Figure 5.1 is one form of a cash-flow statement. In Figure 5.1, t refers to time periods, F to forecasts and A to actual cash flows, and arithmetic signs to cash in $(+)$ and out $(-)$ flows. Summaries of totals of regular and irregular cash flows may be reported for segments of a company.

In addition to a cash-flow statement, a balance sheet based on realisable values might be considered to provide relevant information to the investor for assessing the risks associated with an investment. Of prime importance for predicting the risk associated with the firm's cash flows is the degree of flexibility which the management of a firm possesses in employing its resources (Ronen, 1974). The more numerous the alternatives open to management to utilise the resources of the firm, the less it is dependent on the fortunes of current operations. One quantitative measure of flexibility is the realisable value of the firm's resources. The higher the realisable value of a firm's assets, the greater is the flexibility and the lower the risks attached to the operations of the firm.

A priori research along the lines set out above has been widely criticised. The neglect of groups other than investors is seen as a drawback, although some writers have attempted to analyse the information needs of other groups (Cooper and Essex, 1977). More fundamentally, such research is considered piecemeal. Thus, while it may be addressed to particular decisions, decision makers, or accounting issues, it is unlikely to provide comprehensive and integrated solutions to a variety of accounting problems. Consequently, policy makers have sought to create comprehensive theoretical frameworks to meet this deficiency along the broad lines of the decision usefulness approach. These conceptual frameworks are considered next.

Conceptual Frameworks—The FASB's Approach

The FASB have devised the most ambitious programme to date for developing a conceptual framework, defined as 'a constitution, a coherent system of interrelated objectives and fundamentals that can lead to consistent standards and that prescribe the nature, function and limits of financial accounting and financial statements' (FASB, 1976a). The

Figure 5.1 Specimen company cash flow statement

	$t-2$ F A	$t-1$ F A	$t=0$ F A	$t+1$ F P	$t+2$ F P	$t+3$ F
Regular Cash Flows						
Operational transactions	±	±	±	±	±	±
Non-operating	+	+	+	+	+	+
Taxation	−	−	−	−	−	−
	±	±	±	±	±	±
Irregular Cash Flows						
Sales of assets	+	+	+	+	+	+
Investment by investors	+	+	+	+	+	+
Investment in assets	−	−	−	−	−	−
Random items	±	±	±	±	±	±
	±	±	±	±	±	±
Total cash flows	±	±	±	±	±	±
Cash retained b/f	+	+	+	+	+	+
Cash available	±	±	±	±	±	±
Dividends	−	−	−	−	−	−
Cash retained c/f	±	±	±	±	±	±
Segment A						
Regular cash flows	±	±	±	±	±	±
Irregular cash flows	±	±	±	±	±	±
	±	±	±	±	±	±
Segment B						
Regular cash flows	±	±	±	±	±	±
Irregular cash flows	±	±	±	±	±	±
	±	±	±	±	±	±

objective of the conceptual framework is to help produce a body of standards that is more internally consistent than either the *ad hoc* approach just considered or the conventional approach of Chapter 2 would permit, thereby enhancing the credibility of accounting information.

The FASB's approach consists of the following components:

1. A statement of the objectives of financial reporting.
2. A specification of the characteristics that financial information must possess to qualify for inclusion in a financial report. These characteristics provide criteria for choosing among alternative accounting methods.
3. A set of definitions of the elements of financial statements.
4. A specification of the criteria for deciding when to recognise the various elements of financial statements.
5. A set of measurement rules.
6. A set of guidelines for the presentation and disclosure of the elements and other information that is useful in fulfilling the objectives of financial reporting.

These components are illustrated in Figure 5.2 and will be examined in turn.

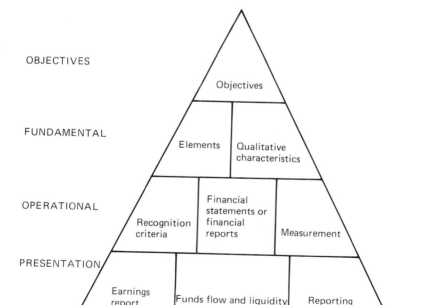

Figure 5.2. The FASB conceptual framework for financial reporting

Objectives

These are established in the Statement of Financial Accounting Concepts No. 1 (SFAC1), *Objectives of Financial Reporting by Business Enterprises* published in 1978. This states that financial reporting is not an end in itself. It is intended to provide useful information for making business and economic decisions concerning the alternative uses of scarce resources. These decisions affect the allocation of resources in the economy. SFAC1 supports the earlier Trueblood Report and, in particular, echoes and re-emphasises the objective of using financial reports for the prediction of the amount, timing and uncertainty of the future cash flows of enterprises. It should be noted that the statement applies to the whole of financial reporting, not merely to financial statements.

The three objectives which are included in SFAC1 are considered below:

Objective 1

Financial reporting should provide information that is useful to present and potential investors and creditors and other users in making rational investment, credit and similar decisions. The information should be comprehensible to those who have a reasonable understanding of business and economic activities and are willing to study the information with reasonable diligence.

This statement establishes the basic objective for financial reporting. The prominence of investors and creditors among existing user groups, their economic significance to the economy, and the fact that information which satisfies their needs is believed generally to satisfy the needs of other user groups, made them the FASB's primary choice for the purpose of defining objectives. It is interesting to note that according to the FASB, the orientation of financial reports should be towards users who have a reasonable level of sophistication.

Statement of Financial Accounting Concepts No. 4, *Objectives of Financial Reporting by Non-business Organisations*, published in 1981, concludes that it is not necessary to develop an independent conceptual framework for any particular category of entity. This statement follows the structure of SFAC1 in adopting the viewpoint that financial accounting and reporting concepts and standards should be based on their decision usefulness.

Objective 2

Financial reporting should provide information to help present and potential investors and creditors and other users in assessing the amounts, timing, and uncertainty of prospective cash receipts from dividends or interest and the proceeds from the sale, redemption, or maturity of securities or loans. Since investors' and creditors' cash flows are related to enterprise cash flows, financial reporting should provide information to help investors, creditors and others, assess the amounts, timing and uncertainty of prospective net cash inflows to the related enterprise.

Stating objectives in terms of the prediction and evaluation of cash flows provides a vehicle for assessing and evaluating all accounting information. Although none of the three objectives of SFAC1 mentions enterprise earning power, earnings are shown to retain their importance in financial reporting, for 'the primary focus of financial reporting is information about earnings and its components'. According to the reasoning of the FASB, reports of past earnings are used as a basis for the assessment of future earnings. An adjustment is assumed to be made by the user to the assessment of future earnings to derive an assessment of future cash flows. This two-stage process is considered to be perferable to the direct assessment by the user of future cash flows because the income statement is thought to provide a more comprehensive picture than a cash statement of the results of transactions of a period and of the relationship between them.

Therefore, the primary focus of financial reporting is on information about an enterprise's financial performance during a past period. Investors, creditors and others use this information in various ways and for various purposes in assessing an enterprise's prospects. These users do their own evaluating, estimating, predicting, assessing, confirming or rejecting. Financial analysis is beyond the scope of financial reporting.

Objective 3

Financial reporting should provide information about the economic resources of an enterprise, the claims to those resources (obligations of the enterprise to transfer resources to other entities and owners' equity), and the effects of transactions, events, and circumstances that change its resources and claims to those resources.

This objective is concerned with the need to evaluate enterprise performance during a period. Elsewhere, and apparently by way of emphasising this objective's cash flow implications, SFAC1 states that 'information about resources, obligations and owners' equity also provides a basis for investors, creditors and others to evaluate information about the enterprise's performance during a period. . . . Moreover, it provides direct indications of the cash flow potentials of some resources and of the cash needed to satisfy many, if not most, obligations'.

Qualitative Characteristics

The FASB approach requires that each standard setting decision be based on an assessment of the costs and benefits of various alternatives and a judgement by the standard setters on which of the alternatives is most useful in the decision-making process of the user of financial information (Kirk, 1981). The objective of Statement of Financial Accounting Concepts No. 2 (SFAC2) is to assist this process by the establishment of criteria by which financial accounting policies and procedures are to be judged. As we discussed in Chapter 2, the role of qualitative characteristics is to assist in the evaluation of information systems whenever alternative measurements or disclosure treatments are possible. The FASB presented a hierarchy of qualities, with usefulness for decision making as most important; this includes benefits and costs, relevance, reliability, neutrality, verifiability, representational faithfulness, comparability, timeliness, completeness, consistency, and materiality. This hierarchy is illustrated in Figure 5.3. The key user-specific quality is understandability. Information can only be useful if the decision maker can understand it. Understandability is partly within the control of the standard-setter but it also depends in part on the knowledge level of the user.

Certain conclusions may be drawn from Figure 5.3. The best choice, subject to considerations of cost and materiality, is the one most useful for decision making. The primary qualities are relevance and reliability which often impinge on each other, creating a need for trade-offs. Relevant information is that capable of making a difference to the decision maker by changing the assessment of the probability of occurrence of some event relating to the attainment of an objective. Relevant information must be timely and must have predictive value or feedback value or both.

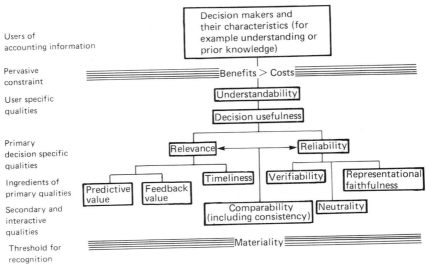

Figure 5.3. A hierarchy of accounting qualities

Information is timely when available as needed. Usually, information possesses both predictive and feedback value because knowledge about the outcomes of actions already taken will generally improve the decision maker's ability to predict the results of similar future actions.

Reliable information must have verifiability, neutrality and representational faithfulness. Verifiability implies a high degree of consensus among independent measurers using the same measurement methods. Neutrality requires freedom from bias, both in the measurer and in the measurement method. Representational faithfulness allows the user to depend on it to represent the economic conditions or events that it purports to represent. Figure 5.3 shows comparability, which includes consistency, as a secondary quality that interacts with relevance and reliability to contribute to the usefulness of information. The need for benefits to exceed costs and a materiality threshold are shown as constraints. Materiality is strongly intertwined with relevance and reliability; all the qualities of information are subject to a materiality threshold derived from the probable impact on a user's decision.

Judgement is necessary for achieving trade-offs among the characteristics. The Statement acknowledges the problem of trying to balance the needs of all users when these are in conflict, and the needs of society as a whole. The assessment of costs and benefits and who will bear and enjoy them is extremely complex and subjective (as we discussed in Chapter 1), but the Statement recognises the need to undertake the discipline of attempting the assessment.

Elements

The Statement of Financial Accounting Concepts No. 3 (SFAC3), *Elements of Financial Statements of Business Enterprises*, defines ten interrelated elements of financial statements—assets, liabilities, equity, investment by owners, distributions to owners, revenues, expenses, gains, losses, and comprehensive income—all at a high level of generality. Assets are defined as 'probable future economic benefits obtained or controlled by a particular enterprise as a result of past transactions or events affecting the enterprise', liabilities are 'probable future sacrifices of economic benefits arising from present obligations of a particular entity to transfer assets or provide services to other entities in the future as a result of past transactions or events'.

The objective of SFAC3 is to establish definitions which supplant those that have grown out of practice that do not meet the conditions of being related to real world things and events. For example, the Accounting Principles Boards Statement No. 4 (AICPA, 1970) defined assets as 'economic resources of an enterprise that are recognised and measured in conformity with generally accepted accounting principles (GAAP)'. In other words, an asset was whatever GAAP chose to report as an asset, whether or not it reflected a resource to the enterprise. However, SFAC3 emphasises that the definitions do not require upheavals in present practice, although in time they may lead to evolutionary changes in practice or in the way certain items are viewed.

Recognition and Measurement Concepts

In reviewing the status of its work towards the development of a conceptual framework the FASB identified three conclusions which were noteworthy by 1983 (FASB, 1983). Firstly, there are significant differences of opinion among board members about the concepts that should guide recognition in financial statements. These relate to concepts for recognising changes in assets and liabilities while they are held, the main disagreement concerning the extent to which current price changes should be recognised. Secondly, that recognition concepts are often inseparable from measurement considerations. For example, a decision to recognise a decline in the replacement cost or recoverable amount of inventory while it is held involves, in addition, a measurement decision. The inseparability of measurement and recognition issues caused the Board to decide that a recognition project should incorporate the question of the attribute to be measured—such as historical costs, recoverable cost, current cost and current value. Thirdly, board members' views on financial statement presentation concepts are often related to views concerning recognition criteria. For example, adopting the conventional realisation test for recognition of revenues and gains would preclude any need for a presentation concept dealing with reporting unrealised gains.

Following this interim review the FASB went on to complete its work on a conceptual framework by preparing and publishing Statement of Financial Accounting Concepts No. 5 *Recognition and Measurement in Financial Statements of Business Enterprises*. SFAC 5 sets out recognition criteria and guidance as to what information should be incorporated into financial statements and when, with particular attention being given to earnings statements and comprehensive income.

Presentation Concepts

Because the concepts for determining what is to be recognised are interrelated with the concepts for reporting the resulting amount of income, the Board has decided to defer further consideration of the issues related to reporting income until it has made basic decisions about recognition and measurement. The Board has issued discussion documents on reporting income, reporting funds flows and liquidity and financial statements and other means of financial reporting and an ED on reporting income, cash flows and financial position was published in 1981 (FASB, 1982).

Benefits of the Conceptual Framework

Several benefits are expected from the FASB conceptual framework according to its supporters (Kirk, 1981; Pacter, 1983; Solomons, 1983).

1. With a framework, the standard setter is in a better position to assess the usefulness of alternative methods.
2. It should help produce a body of standards that is more internally consistent than at present, thereby enhancing the credibility of accounting information.
3. It should help to reduce the influence of personal biases and political pressures in making accounting judgements. Given the existence of conflicting interests in the information market, one way of reducing these conflicts is to encourage a common attitude towards accounting. This may require preparers and users to subordinate their individual preferences in the knowledge that they will in the long run gain more than they lose (FASB, 1980).

In contrast to the ASC, the FASB members are not appointed by individual constituent groups and do not attempt to represent particular groups. This non-partisan behaviour is demanded by the constituents.

> From my years of experience as a practitioner and standard setter, I believe that practitioners and business managers are willing to spend money on a conceptual framework because they don't want a purely political system with the FASB acting as a power broker that comprises the positions of special interest groups. They do not want a theoretical system designed to produce rationalisations and excuses for political actions   (Kirk, 1981).

Some writers question the benefits of a conceptual framework. They argue that the policy-making process is a social choice problem. In Chapter 1 we saw that this viewpoint entails:

1. an assessment of the consequences of decisions on various constituencies and,
2. a decision on trade-offs among the groups affected.

These writers argue that the FASB takes a social choice perspective, and that the ultimate generality or specifying of the conceptual framework will be heavily affected by the relative importance the FASB attaches to its various constituencies (Horngren, 1981). Other writers question the usefulness of the statements of concepts published to date to facilitate decision making. For example, Joyce, Libby and Sunder's (1982) research finds that the qualitative characteristics fail the tests of operationality. Not only is there considerable disagreement among policy makers on what the qualitative characteristics mean in the context of particular accounting policy issues, there is also considerable disagreement on their relative importance.

The ASC's Approach

As we saw in Chapter 3, the ASC has adopted a pragmatic, political approach to policy making. However, most of the major firms of chartered accountants, in their submissions to the ASC in response to the Watts Report (ASC, 1978) suggested an accelerated effort toward reaching agreement on the broader considerations underlying accounting standards. The ASC commissioned a study to examine the possibilities of developing an agreed conceptual framework for setting accounting standards. The resulting report (Macve, 1981) concluded that 'it is unlikely that an agreed conceptual framework can be found that will give explicit guidance on what is appropriate in preparing financial statements'.

The Corporate Report

The ASC's sole initiative on establishing fundamental objectives and principles is the Corporate Report (1975) which moved in rather a different direction from the FASB and reflected the more pluralistic views of Western Europe. This report stated that:

> The fundamental objective of corporate reports is to communicate economic measurements of and information about the resources and performance of the reporting entity useful to those having reasonable rights to such information.

It identified the groups as having a reasonable right to information and whose information needs should be recognised by corporate reports as follows:

Equity Investor Group. Investors require information to assist in reaching share-trading decisions, in deciding whether or not to subscribe to new issues and in reaching voting decisions at general meetings.

Loan Creditor Group including existing and potential holders of debentures and loan stock, and providers of short-term loans and finance.

Employee Group. Employees and prospective employees require information in assessing the security and prospects of employment and information for the purpose of collective bargaining.

Analyst-Advisor Group including financial analysts and journalists, economists, statisticians, researchers, trade unions, stockbrokers and other providers of advisory services such as credit rating agencies.

Business Contact Group including customers, trade creditors and suppliers and, in a different sense competitors, business rivals and those interested in mergers, amalgamation and takeovers.

Government including tax authorities, departments and agencies concerned with the supervision of commerce and industry, and local authorities.

The public including taxpayers, ratepayers, consumers and other community and special interest groups such as political parties, consumer and environment protection societies and regional pressure groups.

The report rejected the assumption that general purpose financial statements can serve the information needs of all user groups. It proposed the following six statements in addition to those normally provided.

1. A statement of added value to show how the wealth produced by an enterprise is shared between employees, providers of capital, the state, and reinvestment.
2. An employment report showing the size and composition of the workforce relying on the enterprise for its livelihood, the work contribution of employees and the benefits earned. Employment reports should contain the following: numbers employed, changes in numbers employed and reasons, age distribution and sex, functions of employees, geographical location of major employment centres, major plant and site closures, hours scheduled and worked by employees, employment costs, costs and benefits associated with pension schemes, cost and time spent on training, names of unions recognised by the entity for the purpose of collective bargaining and membership figures, safety and health information, scheduled ratios relating to employment.
3. A statement of money exchanges with government showing the financial relationship between the enterprise and the state.
4. A statement of transactions in foreign currency showing the direct cash dealings of the reporting entity between this country and abroad. This statement will assist users to judge the economic functions and performance of the entity in relation to society and the national interest (e.g. contribution to balance of payments). It may also provide information of assistance in assessing the stability and vulnerability of the reporting entity and in estimating its capacity to make future cash payments. The degree of risk attached to foreign dealings may be significantly different from that attached to UK operations.
5. A statement of future prospects, showing likely future profit, employment and investment levels. This statement will assist users to evaluate the future prospects of the entity and to assess managerial performance.
6. A statement of corporate objectives showing management policy and medium-term strategic targets. This statement will assist users to

evaluate managerial performance, efficiency and objectives. Corporate reports should include a statement of general philosophy or policy, and information concerning strategic targets in the following policy areas: sales, added value, profitability, investment and finance, dividends, employment, consumer issues, environmental matters, other relevant social issues.

The Corporate Report caused great controversy within the business community and the accounting profession. In particular, the proposals for increased disclosure attracted much criticism. In 1977, the then Labour Government issued a Green Paper on *The Future of Company Reports* which endorsed the recommendations of the Corporate Report. This action further provoked the business community into its rejection. But, as one of the authors of the Corporate Report has stated,

> the more or less simultaneous publication of the Sandilands Report drew attention away from the Corporate Report. . . . The great inflation accounting debate has occupied the centre of the stage ever since and the more fundamental issues concerning the scope and nature of financial reporting dealt with in the Corporate Report have received scant attention. The Corporate Report has faded into history.
>
> (Peasnell, 1982)

II EMPIRICAL RESEARCH

As we noted at the beginning of this chapter, empirical research may assist policy makers in their policy choices. Griffin (1982) shows empirical research to be helpful in two ways. First, it acts as a check on the assumptions adopted in the policy-making process. For example, given the assumptions inherent in the FASB's conceptual framework, policy makers may be interested in knowing how individuals react to the information contained in financial reports and what is the relative usefulness of types of information for predicting enterprise cash flows and other relevant inputs to decision making. Second, empirical research is helpful for assessing the economic consequences of accounting alternatives for affected parties. As we saw in Chapter 1, the nature of such consequences will be important for cost-benefit assessments of accounting policies.

In this section, we consider three types of empirical research:

1. Economic consequences research which examines the potential and actual economic effects of accounting alternatives. Much of this research has been devoted to the relationship between accounting information and the behaviour of securities markets. Such research by-passes the individual decision-making process and concentrates upon the aggregate behaviour of the capital market. In recent years, analysis

of economic consequences has extended to cover other types of economic effect related to individual decisions.

2. The predictive properties of reported accounting numbers. This research considers whether accounting numbers possess properties which allow them to be used to predict the future prospects of companies.

3. Behavioural research which examines the behaviour of individual decision makers. Such research is often questionnaire or survey based and draws upon psychology and sociology to explain and predict human behaviour at the individual level.

Economic Consequences Research

As we noted in Chapter 1, economic consequences result from the effects of accounting information on decisions. Economic consequences may arise if:

(*i*)   the intended recipients of accounting information alter their behaviour;

(*ii*)   if other 'free riding' groups receive accounting information which alters their behaviour;

(*iii*)   if the behaviour of the management of the reporting company changes.

The decisions of users of accounting reports may change because their evaluation of certain factors, such as the risks associated with securities, changes. Management decisions may alter if, for example, managers' compensation plans are linked to any accounting variables, or because managers believe that users will react in particular ways to the provision of types of accounting information. This type of impact has been termed 'information inductance' (Prakash and Rappaport, 1977; Selto, 1982).

Economic consequences have been viewed as affecting resource allocation and the distribution of income and wealth (Beaver, 1981; Taylor and Turley, 1982) through the combined effects of the influences listed above.

Capital Market Research

Most empirical research on economic consequences has been devoted to the effects of accounting information on capital markets, especially on share prices. Much effort in the theory of finance has been directed to the search for a theory which explains the expected returns from individual securities. A widely accepted theory which offers such an explanation is the Capital Asset Pricing Model (CAPM). The CAPM is based upon the assumption that investors seek to hold portfolios of securities which give maximum returns for particular levels of risk, and its development is associated with Sharpe (1964) and Lintner (1965). According to the CAPM, the expected return to a security is as follows:

$$E(R_{it}) = R_{ft} + \frac{\text{Covariance } R_{it}, R_{mt}}{\text{Variance } R_{mt}} \times [E(R_{mt}) - R_{ft}]$$

where

$E(R_{it})$ = the expected return in the form of dividends and price change on security i in period t.

R_{ft} = the return available on a risk free asset.

$\dfrac{\text{Covariance } R_{it}, R_{mt}}{\text{Variance } R_{mt}}$ = the measure of the systematic relationship between movements in returns to security i and the return on the market portfolio (normally written as β_{it}).

$E(R_{mt})$ = the expected return available on the market portfolio.

β reflects the extent to which returns on security i vary with those on the market as a whole and represents the systematic risk of the security. Unsystematic risk is that which is unique to the security in question and is assumed to be diversified away by investors. Thus, only systematic risk remains and β measures the riskiness of the security. The stock market as a whole has a β equal to 1. Relatively high risk securities (e.g. β 1.5) change more rapidly than the market when it changes. If the expected excess return on the market portfolio during a period is 10 per cent, a security with a β of 1.5 will be expected to earn an excess return of 15 per cent.

The CAPM thus indicates that the expected return on any particular capital asset consists of two components: (1) the return on a riskless security and (2) a premium for the non-diversifiable risk of the particular asset. Under CAPM, each security has an expected return which is related to its risk. This risk is measured by the security's systematic movements with the overall market and it cannot be eliminated by portfolio diversification.

As a measure of security risk, β is potentially of great importance to investors, the more so if β's are stable through time, since then, expectations of future returns may be formulated. Considerable research has been done into β stability and, on the whole, has concluded that portfolio β's are relatively stable, while β's of individual securities are considerably less stable.

Such results mean that it is important to attempt to explain the values of β for individual securities, and hence predict them. Of particular importance have been the numerous studies which have sought to explain β's in terms of accounting data. Ball and Brown (1968) found that there was an association between β and the covariability of the profits of individual companies with an aggregate level of corporate profits. Beaver, Kettler and Scholes (1970) investigated the relationship between β and various accounting variables (dividend pay-out ratio, growth in total assets, financial gearing, the current ratio and the standard deviation of earnings yield, amongst others) and found that accounting measures of risk were good predictors of β. Other studies reached similar conclusions, if with differing degrees of explanatory power (Gonedes, 1973; Breen and Lerner, 1973).

Efficient Markets Research

Whilst CAPM is concerned with the expected returns to securities, efficient markets research relates to descriptions of how capital markets operate and how their performance might be assessed. The most widespread description of the operation of capital markets is the efficient markets hypothesis (EMH). An efficient capital market is taken to be one where security prices fully reflect available information (Fama, 1970). Efficiency, generally speaking, is a desirable economic attribute. In a capital market it implies optimal asset prices and hence optimal resource allocation. An efficient capital market is characterised by dynamic equilibrium. New information which appears is assumed to be evaluated and incorporated into security prices almost immediately by numerous skilled and know-ledgeable investors. Such markets are assumed to be highly competitive with relevant economic information available to all.

In defining an efficient market, we referred to such markets as reflecting 'available information'. Now the boundary around 'available information' may be cast more or less widely. Consequently, three versions of the EMH have emerged, namely:

(a) The **strong form**: security prices reflect all information.
(b) The **semi-strong form**: the capital market responds accurately and instantaneously to reflect all publicly available new information on the security.
(c) The **weak form**: security prices reflect past series of share prices.

The EMH has important implications for accounting. The value of new pieces of accounting information may be determined through their effects on security prices: if there is a significant effect, the information has value. By extension, if there are alternative ways of recording or disclosing accounting information, the method with the largest impact on share prices is the most valuable. Further, if new information causes fluctuations around the long term equilibrium of the efficient market, the accounting alternatives which minimise those fluctuations are most valuable.

Financial reports seek to communicate the results of a series of economic events. Thus, the information contained in financial reports may be obtained from other sources, and thus may already be impounded in security prices by the time financial reports are published. Thus, any value which financial reports have will be in the new information which they may contain. Consequently, the semi-strong form of the EMH is most appropriate for assessing the effects of accounting information. The semi-strong form of the EMH implies that abnormal returns cannot be earned by investors, i.e. it is impossible for an investor to earn a portfolio return (based on the publicly available information) in excess of the return commensurate with the portfolio's risk.

In testing the EMH, researchers derive β's and risk-free asset returns from historical relationships, and market returns from actual data. The expected return to a security is compared with its actual returns to determine the security price response to new information specific to a company but not the market as a whole. In an efficient market, only new information can explain a difference in security price.

Research findings support the EMH to the extent that one leading finance academic in this field in the US has stated the following:

> I believe there is no other proposition in economics which has more solid empirical evidence supporting it than the EMH. That hypothesis has been tested and, with very few exceptions found consistent with the data in a wide variety of markets. (Jensen, 1978)

Although most of the research in this area has been conducted in the US, there is a growing body of research in the UK which shows the applicability of the model to UK stock markets (Henfrey *et al.*, 1977).

We consider the findings of efficient market research under two headings

(*i*)   The information content of accounting numbers, and
(*ii*) The impact of accounting alternatives.

The Information Content of Accounting Numbers

Many studies have been undertaken which investigate this topic. One of the earliest was carried out by Ball and Brown (1968) who tested the sensitivity of share prices to reported company profits. Using the data for 261 companies for the period 1946 to 1966, they concluded that profit was regarded as a significant source of information by investors, but that most of the information contained in published annual reports had been predicted and incorporated in share prices before the formal announcement of company results. Ball and Brown's study indicates that there is a correlation between earnings numbers and security returns, but that this earnings information is quickly impounded in security prices.

The Ball and Brown approach has been evaluated in numerous contexts with similar results. Kaplan (1978) summarises the findings as follows:

> These studies should put to rest the idea that accounting earnings are irrelevant. They have information content in that prior knowledge should enable an investor to earn superior returns, and they are timely since significant price and volume reactions do occur at the time they are released.

The Impact of Accounting Alternatives

If an association exists between security prices and accounting profit, the question arises as to whether the market reacts to changes in accounting profit due to economic events or to changes in accounting methods. Does the stock market react naively to changes in reported accounting profits (as if changes were always real) or does it distinguish between real and cosmetic changes due to accounting policy changes? There is evidence that company management has taken the view of a naive response. For example, there is evidence that many companies in the US have been reluctant to adopt LIFO stock valuation because of fear of an adverse effect on share prices which might result from a fall in reported profits.

Numerous studies have been undertaken in the US of stock market reactions to changes in accounting policy. Archibald (1972) examined the effects of changes in depreciation policy. Kaplan and Roll (1972) examined the influence of investment tax credit and depreciation policies. Sunder (1973) investigated the effects of different stock valuation methods. Dukes (1975) and Vigeland (1981) investigated the impact of accounting for research and development. Dukes (1978) and Shank, Dillard and Murdoch (1980) examined the effects of methods of foreign currency translation, and Abdel-Khalik (1981) the effects of accounting for leases. Gheyera and Boatsman (1980) and Beaver, Christie and Griffin (1980) considered market reactions to methods of inflation accounting. The balance of the evidence suggests that investors are able to separate cosmetic accounting changes from substantial economic events and purely accounting changes elicit little or no stock market reaction. Some studies have offered evidence of a counter view, as in Collins and Dent (1979) on oil and gas accounting and Noreen and Sepe (1981).

There is not a comparable volume of research work available for the UK, but such findings as there are tend to support those of US researchers. For example, it does appear that there has been no major readjustment of share prices in the UK since companies began to publish inflation-adjusted accounts in varying forms several years ago (Morris, 1975). These findings are consistent with the view that the market made its own assessment of the effects of inflation on company profits, and had already made the necessary adjustments for these effects.

Implications for Accounting Policy Makers

The impact of market research on accounting policy makers in the US may be seen in the difference between the objectives specified in the Trueblood Report and those of the later FASB conceptual framework. An objective of the Trueblood Report was that financial statements should 'serve primarily those users who have limited authority, ability or resources to obtain information and who rely on financial statements as their principal source of information about an enterprise's economic activities'. In contrast, the FASB's conceptual framework is geared towards the needs of the relatively sophisticated investor.

The extent to which policy makers should base their decisions on market research is controversial because the scope of the work is somewhat narrow. First, 'efficiency' in the context of efficient market theory simply means that the market impounds information quickly. It does not mean that the result of this process is a set of share prices which reflects the intrinsic worth of shares. The evidence says nothing of how the market ought to react to specific and different types of information and should not, therefore, be used by accounting policy makers for judging the desirability of accounting information. Secondly, policy makers have a broader mandate than that of providing information to investors. Other user groups such as employees, customers, government agencies and the general public may require financial information for their decisions. Thirdly, the EMH is concerned with informational efficiency rather than allocation efficiency, although, as noted above, the latter is implied by the former.

The contribution which tests of market efficiency have made in aiding standard setters is not clear (Beaver, 1973; Foster, 1980). EMH research has not provided a theory on which policy makers could rely to predict those circumstances or issues when a capital market reaction could be expected, or the extent of any anticipated reaction. *Ex-post* investigation of the stock market consequences following from a standard may produce results of value in revising a standard, but does not assist in initial policy deliberations. Further, the research has been confined to the identification of security price movements, without postulating or tracing wider economic effects in terms of income distribution or resource allocation. Movements in share prices constitutes only one possible source of economic consequences and accounting standards may affect the behaviour of other groups (Ketz and Wyatt, 1983). Some of these wider economic consequences are considered later in this chapter.

Increasing Disclosure

The above limitations of market research should be borne in mind when considering the case for increasing accounting disclosures. The arguments for this action have been made as follows (see Beaver, 1973; Henfrey, 1980).

1. Where there is a controversy over which of two alternative measurements should be reported to external users, and no additional costs are involved in reporting both measurements, the solution to the controversy lies in reporting both measurements. Use could be made of footnotes to the financial report. The market may be left to interpret the importance of such additional information.
2. Given the uncertainty attached to many accounting numbers, market research suggests the disclosure of probability ranges which communicate the uncertainty attached to future events (e.g. expected bad debts), would make financial statments more useful (Keane, 1980). Perhaps the main reason why this approach has not been used in the past is the thought that investors are incapable of handling this type of information.
3. Increased disclosure will benefit the naive investor. By improving the predictions which sophisticated investors are able to make, increased disclosure will reduce the speculative and destabilising influences which are associated with the uncertainties of stock market behaviour. In an efficient market, unsophisticated investors face a 'fair game' in which stocks are priced according to risk/return relationships. As long as these investors hold diversified portfolios,they can expect the same return for a given level of risk as more sophisticated investors.
4. The case for additional disclosure is strengthened by the recognition that failure to disclose may result in the existence of inside information which can lead to abnormal returns accruing to privileged individuals. Inside information is not reflected in security prices. Much information is circulating inside companies which could be disclosed to external users without incurring additional cost. There is a case for making this information public in order to prevent abnormal returns to privileged individuals who may secure such information.

Research on Other Economic Consequences

Although stock-market based research has dominated research into economic consequences, other issues have received attention.

Some research has been undertaken into how management decisions may be affected by the issuing of accounting standards. For example, Dukes, Dyckman and Elliot (1980) investigated the effects on the research and development decisions of companies following SFAS2 (FASB, 1974) and concluded that there was no evidence to support the assertion that the accounting standard had any effect on research and development expenditure. However, in the case of small, high-technology companies, Horowitz and Kolodny (1980 and 1981) claimed evidence of adverse effects on research and development.

In the case of accounting for leases, questionnaire evidence has been collected indicating that the requirement for lease capitalisation in SFAS13 (FASB, 1976) had an effect on managerial behaviour in the relative amounts of purchase and leasing in acquiring assets, the issuance of debt and equity finance, and the structuring of lease contracts (Abdel-Khalik, 1981).

Perhaps the accounting standard which has given rise to most investigation of managerial decision-making is SFAS8 (FASB, 1975) on the subject of foreign currency translation. These studies provide consistent evidence that SFAS8 had a significant impact on the foreign exchange management practices of companies (Evans, Folks and Jilling, 1978; Shank *et al*, 1980). Managerial decisions on investment policies, financing and hedging of foreign exchange risk were affected. Using a different methodology, Wilner (1982) obtained evidence supporting these conclusions.

Little work has been done on possible economic consequences following from the effects of accounting standards on other decision makers. Winn (in FASB, 1978) has postulated possible effects of historical cost versus current cost disclosures on certain government policies, while Abdel-Khalik (1981) has investigated the effects of lease capitalisation on bond prices and credit ratings.

Despite the fact that the scope of study of economic consequences has been broadened considerably, there remains the problem noted in Chapter 1 and repeated in the context of EMH research. Namely, what role evidence on economic consequences should play in accounting policy making (Taylor and Turley, 1982). Many writers accept the need for explicit considerations of economic effects in the deliberations of standard-setting bodies. This implies recognition that selection of accounting standards is a matter of social choice which gives rise to fundamental questions about the process of setting standards. It is not clear how economic consequences should be evaluated in the standard-setting process. Should the objective be to maximise or minimise economic impact? How much weight should be given to consideration of economic consequences and what is the balance between economic consequences and other criteria? What constitute acceptable or unacceptable economic consequences? How can a choice be made between conflicting sets of desirable and undesirable consequences? Does a private sector regulatory body possess the necessary authority to make such choices? (Zeff, 1978).

Predictive Properties of Accounting Numbers

The use of the predictive properties of accounting numbers as a criterion to guide the choice between accounting alternatives has received considerable support (Greenball, 1971; Carsberg, Hope and Scapens, 1974). Accounting numbers which are judged to be good predictors of the future and which thereby enable better decisions to be made are to be preferred to numbers which predict less well.

In this section we consider five topics to which a predictive ability approach has been taken:

1. The predictive value of past annual profits.
2. The predictive value of interim financial reports.
3. The prediction of credit worthiness.
4. The prediction of takeovers.
5. The prediction of corporate failure.

The Predictive Value of Past Annual Profits

Considerable academic research in recent years has been devoted to the question of whether or not there are patterns in the time series of annual earnings which may be used in making predictions about future earnings. The evidence indicates that past annual earnings are not usually repeated in the future, which leads one to suggest that extrapolating past trends is unlikely to be a fruitful exercise if one is aiming to forecast future profitability (Watts and Leftwich, 1977). With minor exceptions, the major conclusions of studies in this area have been that annual earnings appear to follow a random-walk, i.e. there is no empirical basis from which to predict future earnings growth from past growth. According to Foster (1978), 'it is difficult to find models that yield more efficient forecasts of the earnings of individual firms than does the random-walk model'.

The Predictive Value of Interim Financial Reports

Interim financial reports provide financial information for a period of less than one year. In the UK, listed companies have to deliver a six-monthly report of profitability and financial position to their shareholders. In the USA, the disclosure requirement is on a quarterly basis. Interim reports are not audited. One qualitative characteristic of the process of reporting to users discussed previously in this chapter is that of timeliness. The aim of interim reports is to provide users with more timely information about companies so as to alleviate the disadvantage of the significant time lag between annual reports.

The major conclusions of the research findings is that quarterly time-series models are able to predict annual earnings more accurately than are models based on past annual data (Brown and Rozeff, 1979; Lorek, 1979; Collins and Hopwood, 1980).

The Prediction of Credit Worthiness

Models have been developed for the explanation of risk premiums on fixed interest securities (Fisher, 1959) using, amongst other things, measures of accounting profit. Fisher's model, whilst not being strictly a predictive model, achieved quite a high explanatory power, indicating at least a potential for prediction. Others (Horrigan, 1966; Pinches and Mingo, 1969), constructed models to predict bond ratings and have achieved quite good results, particularly with variables measuring risk.

Predicting bank lending decisions has achieved less success. Deitrich and Kaplan (1982) have successfully modelled the risk classification process and Wojnilower (1962) found significant predictability in lending decisions. However, Orgler (1970) found virtually all financial reports to be statisticaly insignificant in explaining commercial loan credit scores.

The Prediction of Takeovers

Research has been undertaken to try to explain and predict takeovers using accounting variables (Singh, 1971; Stevens, 1973). These and similar studies have been able to associate taken-over companies and taking-over companies quite closely using accounting data, but formal prediction models have not emerged.

The Prediction of Corporate Failure

Empirical studies have been undertaken to determine the extent to which financial ratios may be used to predict business failure. The ability to predict company failure is particularly important from both the private investor's viewpoint and the social viewpoint, as it is an obvious indication of resource misallocation. An early warning signal of probable failure would enable both management and investors to take preventative measures.

In a study using more powerful statistical techniques than used by his predecessors, Beaver (1966) found that financial ratios proved to be useful in the prediction of failure in that such failure could be predicted at least five years before the event. He concluded that ratios could be used to distinguish correctly firms that would fail from those that would not, with much more success than would be possible by random prediction. One of his significant conclusions was that the most effective predictor of failure was the ratio of both short-term and long-term cash flow to total debt. The next best ratio was the ratio of net income to total assets. One of Beaver's most surprising findings was that the current ratio was among the worst predictors of failure. Turnover ratios were found to be at the bottom of the list of effective predictors. Generally, Beaver found that 'mixed ratios' which had income or cash flows compared to assets or liabilities, outperformed short-term solvency ratios which had been believed traditionally to be the best predictors of failure.

In a later study, Beaver (1968) suggested that business failure tends to be determined by permanent factors. He argued that if the basic financial position of a company was sound and profit prospects were good, it would recover from a temporary shortage of liquid assets, but that if the long-term prospects in these regards were not good, business failure could not be prevented by a good liquid position.

Altman (1968) extended Beaver's univeriate (single variable) analysis to allow for multiple predictors of business failure. He used a multiple discriminant analysis for the purpose of developing a linear function of a number of explanatory variables to predict failure. Altman used twenty-two financial ratios based on data obtained one year before failure, and selected five financial ratios for the purposes of establishing his final discriminant function. These five financial ratios were:

$X1$ = working capital/total assets, as an indicator of liquidity;
$X2$ = retained earnings/total assets, as an indicator of the age of the firm and its cumulative profitability;
$X3$ = earnings before interest and tax/total assets, as an indicator of profitability;
$X4$ = market value of the equity/book value of debt, as an indicator of financial structure;
$X5$ = sales/total assets, as an indicator of capital turnover.

The discriminant function chosen after numerous computer runs was

$$Z = .012X_1 + .014X_2 + .033X_3 + .006X_4 + .010X_5$$

The pass mark for Altman's Z score is 3.0. Companies scoring above that level should be safe, while companies scoring below 1.8 will be classified as potential failures. Altman's five-variable model correctly identified 95 per cent of the total sample of companies tested for failure. This percentage rate of success in predicting failure fell to 72 per cent when the data used was obtained two years prior to failure. As earlier data was used in testing the model, so its predictive ability became more unreliable.

A large number of Z-score equations now exist and although they all follow the concepts of the original one, they are all different (Altman *et al.*, 1977). Variations have been developed which use alternative statistical procedures (Ohlson, 1980). Taffler (1983) has applied multiple discriminant analysis to companies in the UK. Although his Z-score has not been published, the ratios and weightings given are as follows:

(*a*) Income before tax/current liabilities (53 per cent)
(*b*) Current assets/total liabilities (13 per cent)
(*c*) Current liabilities/total assets (16 per cent)
(*d*) Immediate assets (current liabilities/operating costs—depreciation) (16 per cent).

The major limitation of the research on corporate-distress prediction arises from the absence of a general theory of corporate failure with which to specify the variables to be included in the discriminant function. Furthermore, the research is of an *ex-post* nature. To demonstrate that the results have direct applicability for auditors and others, requires *ex-ante* predictions about the failure, and its timing, of firms currently non-failed. Another limitation of research based on discriminant analysis is that it does not show the cause of failure, but only the measurement of the failure of policies as they affect poor performance. Surprisingly, researchers have not been able to detect improvements if accounting alternatives are used in the equations. For example, Norton and Smith (1979) find little difference in price-level based predictions of failure versus predictions based on historical cost numbers.

Argenti (1983) studies non-financial signs of failure. He contends that most empirical studies have concentrated on the wrong things. Instead of watching for signs of financial deterioration, we should be looking for signs of managerial ineptitude. He considers six structural defects which lead to 'bad management'—one-man rule, non-participating board, unbalanced top team, lack of management depth, weak finance function and combined chairman-chief executive. He charts a process of failure which is followed by 'virtually all companies'.

Another 'theory' of bankruptcy is based on special stochastic models (e.g. the Markov process) as in Wilcox (1971) and (1973). More recent models have been offered by Santomero and Vinso (1979). According to Griffin (1982), 'the ability of such stochastic modelling approaches that attempt to integrate economic theory and statistical analysis is encouraging'.

Behavioural Research

This research uses field studies, interviews and questionnaires to seek explanations of how individuals use information and make decisions. In particular, studies have investigated the usefulness of financial statements data.

Surveys show that the sophisticated user tends to rely more heavily on the accounting data supplied to them in financial reports than the unsophisticated user. Backer (1970) found that the procedures used for forecasting profits employed by analysts closely parellel those used internally by companies. First, a projection of sales is required. Data about the general economy and industry in which a company operates are very useful for this purpose. Then, the analysis examines profit margins, and other significant ratios from the company published income statement. These are adjusted for changes in volume, price and cost and then applied to the sales forecast. Backer found that in this process 'historical accounting data plays a conspicuous role'. Since these procedures are used by analysts, it is not surprising that surveys of analysts' attitudes to financial reports find 'deficiences' in production cost data, economic industry developments and segmental reporting (Financial Analysts' Federation, 1977).

Surveys of shareholders find they have difficulty understanding financial statements. Lee and Tweedie (1976) based their research on 374 responses to a postal private survey and 320 interviews undertaken of private shareholders in a large public company. They found that annual reports appear to be used thoroughly by a minority of private shareholders and that their comprehension is not at a particularly high level. Research into the behaviour of sophisticated users of financial information have tended to investigate the decision model which they employ and the information which they use, rather than their degree of comprehension of information. Lee and Tweedie (1981) found that institutional investors perceived the annual profit and loss account, balance sheet and interim results to be the most influential information sources. However, the chairman's report, the source and application of funds statement and decisions involving personnel were also considered very important. Arnold and Moizer (1984) came to broadly the same conclusions on the information sources which were used and considered important by UK investment analysts appraising shares. One surprising finding was the popularity of historical cost balance sheet figures relative to current cost, realizable value and general price-level adjusted prices.

Hussey's (1979) study of the readability of financial statements by union officers and shop floor operatives reached similar conclusions. To overcome these problems, it has been suggested that accountants should employ more easily comprehensible measures such as cash flow statements. Other studies have identified the same behaviour by trades unionists and have reached much the same conclusions (Sherer *et al.*, 1981).

Apart from the biases which are an inevitable danger of surveys, the research suffers from severe problems. First, the surveys emphasise descriptive explanations of the world and as such are not particularly well suited to examining the desirability of alternative accounting standards (Gibbons and Brennan, 1982). Secondly, the fragmentary nature of these studies have lacked a theoretical underpinning. For example, there is no theory of attitudes to guide the studies. Thirdly, there has been no attempt to generalise from the studies: there has been no attempt to build up a theory of behaviour. Finally, a problem arises from the heterogeneous nature of decision makers. This implies that the usefulness of information depends on the particular decision taker (including his level of understanding and the other knowledge he has), the particular decision he has to take and the particular circumstances in which he has to take it (Macve, 1981). Even within a particular category of user there may be significant differences of usage of information. For example, investment analysts have been found to behave differently in share appraisals if they are portfolio managers rather than providers of share appraisals for others to use (Moizer and Arnold, 1984). Similarly differences have been found in investment analysts' behaviour between the UK and USA (Arnold, Moizer and Noreen, 1984). Therefore although potentially all information is useful for decisions, it is generally a subjective matter (i.e. peculiar to each individual) whether the value of a specific piece of information exceeds the cost of reporting it.

Despite the problems noted above, the results of behavioural research, particularly that applicable to investors, displays a marked consistency (Hines, 1982). All surveys conclude that investors use financial statements, and broadly the same patterns of use are noted. This is in marked contrast to EMH research, which may be interpreted to mean that financial reports are issued too late to be of use to investors. Hines suggests that this anomaly may be resolved if the possibility of abnormal returns provide the motivation for investors to use financial reports. Moreover, financial reports may provide inputs into long-term investment decisions rather than the short-term decisions of the EMH. As Hines concludes:

> short term market reaction is not an adequate indication of the usefulness of accounting information to investors.

QUESTIONS

1. What are the main components of the investor's normative decision model?
2. What kind of information is required to make the investor's normative decision model operational?
3. Define the phrase 'conceptual framework'.
4. Describe the five components of the FASB's approach to developing a conceptual framework.

5. What three objectives are included in the FASB's statement of Financial Accounting Concepts No. 1.
6. Examine the qualitative characteristics which are included in the FASB's statement of Financial Accounting Concepts No. 2. How do they differ from the qualitative characteristics of the conventional approach?
7. What particular problems do recognition and measurement concepts entail?
8. Consider the benefits claimed for a conceptual framework. What are its limitations?
9. The Corporate Report states that accounting information should be useful. Required:
   (a) Identify the characteristics of useful information and discuss each briefly.
   (b) Explain whether or not you consider that identification of desirable characteristics helps to improve financial reporting.
   (c) It has been suggested that corporate reports which possess these desirable characteristics sometimes recognise the economic substance of a transaction in preference to its legal form.
   Describe two examples of where this may occur.
                                 (Association of Certified Accountants)
10. The Corporate Report (ASC, 1975) recommended that firms produce employment reports.
   (a) Do you consider that employees need information in addition to that normally provided for shareholders? State your reasons.
   (b) Give five examples of information that might be usefully disclosed in an employment report. State how this information could be relevant to the decisions of employees.
                                 (Association of Certified Accountants)
11. What is 'Empirical Research'? How may it assist accounting policy makers?
12. What changes in behaviour give rise to economic consequences?
13. Explain the components of Capital Asset Pricing Model.
14. Differentiate between the:
   (a) strong
   (b) semi-strong
   (c) weak form of efficient market hypothesis (EMH).
15. What are the implications of capital market research for accounting policy makers?
16. Examine empirical research findings relating to the predictive value of:
   (a) past annual profits and,
   (b) interim financial reports.
17. To what extent do accounting ratios predict corporate failure?

18. Discuss the findings of behavioural research and their implications for accounting policy makers.

REFERENCES

Abdel-Khalik, A. R., *The Economic Effects on Leesees of FASB Statement No. 13, Accounting for Leases*, FASB, 1981.
Accounting Principles Board Statement No. 4, *Basic Concepts and Accounting, Principles Underlying Financial Statements of Business Enterprises*, AICPA, 1970.
Accounting Standards Committee, *The Corporate Report*, 1975.
Accounting Standards Committee, *Setting Accounting Standards*, 1978.
Altman, E., 'Financial Ratios, Discriminant Analysis and the Prediction of Corporate Bankruptcy', *Journal of Finance*, September, 1968.
Altman, E. I., *et al.*, 'ZETA Analysis: A New Model to Identify Bankruptcy Risk of Corporations', *Journal of Banking and Finance*, June 1977.
American Accounting Association, 'An Evaluation of External Reporting Practices—A Report of the 1966–1968 Committee on External Reporting', *Accounting Review*, Supplement to Vol. 44, 1969.
Archibald, T., 'Stock Market Reaction to the Depreciation Switch-Back', *The Accounting Review*, 1972.
Argenti, J., 'Predicting Corporate Failure', *Accountants' Digest No. 138*, ICAEW, 1983.
Arnold, J., and Moizer, P., 'A Survey of the Methods used by UK Investment Analysts to Appraise Investments in Ordinary Shares', *Accounting and Business Research*, Autumn, 1984.
Arnold, J. *et al.*, *Investment Appraisal Methods of Financial Analysts: A Comparative Survey of US and UK Practices*, Working Paper, Department of Accounting and Finance, University of Manchester, 1984.
Backer, M., *Financial Reporting for Security Investment and Credit Decisions*, NAA, 1970.
Ball, R. and Brown, P., 'An Evaluation of Accounting Income Numbers', *Journal of Accounting Research*, Autumn, 1968.
Beaver, W. H., 'Financial Ratios as Predictors of Failure', *Empirical Research in Accounting: Selected Studies 1966*. Supplement to *Journal of Accounting Research*.
Beaver, W. H., 'Alternative Accounting Measures as Predictors of Failure', *The Accounting Review*, January, 1968.
Beaver, W. H., 'What should be the FASB's Objectives?' *Journal of Accountancy*, August, 1973.
Beaver, W. H., *Financial Reporting—An Accounting Revolution*, Prentice Hall, 1981.
Beaver, W. H., *et al.*, 'The Information Content of SEC Accounting Series Release No. 190', *Journal of Accounting and Economics*, 1980.
Beaver, W., *et al.*, 'The Association Between Market Determined and Accounting Determined Risk Measures', *Accounting Review*, 1970.
Breen, W. J. and Lerner, E. M., 'Corporate Financial Strategies and Market Measures of Risk and Return', *Journal of Finance*, 1973.
Brown, L. D. and Rozeff, M. S., 'Univariate Time Series Models of Quarterly Accounting Earnings Per Share: A Proposed Model, *Journal of Accounting Research*, Spring 1979.

Carsberg, B. V., *et al.*, 'The Objectives of Published Accounting Reports', *Accounting and Business Research*, Summer, 1974.

Collins, W. A. and Hopwood, W. S., 'A Multivariate Analysis of Annual Earnings Forecasts Generated from Quarterly Forecasts of Financial Analysts and Univariate Time Series Models', *Journal of Accounting Research*, Autumn, 1980.

Collins, D. W. and Dent, W. T., 'The Proposed Elimination of Full Cost Accounting in the Extractive Petroleum Industry', *Journal of Accounting and Economics*, 1979.

Cooper, D. J. and Essex S., 'Accounting Information and Employee Decision Making', *Accounting, Organisations and Society*, 1977.

Dietrich, J. R. and Kaplan, R. S., 'Empirical Analysis of the Commercial Loan Classification Decision', *Accounting Review*, 1982.

Dukes, R. E., 'An Investigation of the Effects of Expensing Research and Development Costs on Security Prices' in M. Schiff and G. Sorter, *Proceedings of the Conference on Topical Research in Accounting*, Ross Institute of Accounting Research, New York, 1975.

Dukes, R. E., *An Empirical Investigation of the Effects of Statement of Financial Accounting Standard No. 8 on Security Return Behaviour*, FASB, 1978.

Evans, T. G. *et al.*, *The Impact of Statement of Financial Accounting Standards No. 8 on the Foreign Exchange Risk Management Practices of American Multinationals*, FASB, 1978.

Fama, E., 'Efficient Capital Markets: A Review of Theory and Empirical Work', *Journal of Finance*, 1970.

FASB, *Statement of Financial Accounting Standards No. 2, Accounting for Research and Development Costs*, 1974.

FASB, *Statement of Financial Accounting Standards No. 8, Accounting for the Translation of Foreign Currency Transactions and Foreign Currency Financial Statements*, October, 1975.

FASB, *Scope and Implications of the Conceptual Framework Project*, 1976a.

FASB, *Statement of Financial Accounting Standards No. 13, Accounting for Leases*, November, 1976b.

FASB, *Economic Consequences of Financial Accounting Standards—selected papers*, July 1978.

FASB, *Statement of Financial Accounting Concepts No. 2, Qualitative Characteristics of Accounting Information*, 1980.

FASB, *Reporting Income, Cash Flows, and Financial Position of Business Enterprises, Exposure Draft*, 1982.

FASB Status Report, *Status of Conceptual Framework Projects*, FASB, 1983.

Financial Analysis Federation, *Journal of Accountancy*, July, 1977.

Fisher, L., 'Determinants of Risk Premiums on Corporate Bonds', *Journal of Political Economy*, 1959.

Foster, G., *Financial Statement Analysis*, Prentice Hall, 1978.

Foster, G., 'Accounting Policy Decisions and Capital Market Research', *Journal of Accounting and Economics*, 1980.

Gheyara, K. and Boatsman, J., 'Market Reaction to the 1976 Replacement Cost Disclosures', *Journal of Accounting and Economics*, 1980.

Gibbons, M. and Brennan, P., 'Behavioural Research and Financial Accounting Standards', in P. A. Griffin, op. cit.

Gonedes, N., 'Evidence on the Information Content of Accounting Messages, Accounting Based and Market Based Estimates of Systematic Risk', *Journal of Financial and Quantitative Analysis*, 1973.

Greenball, M. N., 'The Predictive Ability Criterion: Its Relevance in Evaluating Accounting Data', *Abacus*, 1971.

Griffin, P. A., *Usefulness to Investors and Creditors of Information provided by Financial Reporting: A Review of Empirical Accounting Research*, FASB, 1982.

Hankhansson, N. H., 'Where we are in Accounting: a Review of Statement on Accounting Theory and Theory Acceptance', *The Accounting Review*, July 1978.

Henfrey, A. W., 'The Information Content of Accounting Disclosures—A US Perspective', *The Investment Analyst*, 1980.

Henfry, A. *et al.*, 'The UK Stockmarket and the Efficient Market Model: A Review', *The Investment Analyst*, September, 1977.

Hines, R. D., 'The Usefulness of Annual Reports: the Anomaly between the Efficient Markets Hypothesis and Shareholder Surveys', *Accounting and Business Research*, 1982.

Horngren, C. T., 'Uses and Limitations of a Conceptual Framework', *Journal of Accountancy*, April 1981.

Horowitz, B. N. and Kolodny, 'The Economic Effects of Involuntary Uniformity in the Financial Reporting of R and D Expenditures', *Journal of Accounting Research*, 1980.

Horowitz, B. and Kolodny, R., 'The Impact of Rule Making on R and D Investments of Small High Technology Firms', *Journal of Accounting, Auditing and Finance*, 1981.

Horrigan, J. O., 'The Determination of Long-Term Credit Standing with Financial Ratios', *Empirical Research in Accounting Selected Studies, Journal of Accounting Research*, 1966.

Hussey, R., *Who Reads Employee Reports?* Touche Ross, 1979.

Jensen, M. C., 'Some Anamolous Evidence Regarding Market Efficiency', *Journal of Financial Economics*, 1978.

Joyce, E. J. *et al.*, 'Using the FASB's Qualitative Characteristics in Accounting Policy Choices', *Journal of Accounting Research*, Autumn, 1982.

Kaplan, R., 'The Information Content of Financial Accounting Numbers: A Survey of Empirical Evidence' in *The Impact of Accounting Research on Practice and Disclosure*, A. R. Abdel-Kahlik and T. F. Keller (eds.), Duke University Press, 1978.

Kaplan, R. and Roll, R., 'Investor Evaluation of Accounting Information: Some Empirical Evidence', *Journal of Business*, 1972.

Keane, S. M., *The Efficient Market Hypothesis and the Implications for Financial Reporting*, Institute of Chartered Accountants of Scotland, Gee and Co., 1980.

Ketz, J. E. and Wyatt, A. R., 'The FASB in a World with Partially Efficient Markets', *Journal of Accounting, Auditing and Finance*, 1983.

Kirk, D. J., 'Concepts, Consensus, Compromise and Consequences: their Roles in Standard Setting', *Journal of Accountancy*, April 1981.

Lee, T. A. and Tweedie, D. P., *The Private Shareholder and the Corporate Report*, The Institute of Chartered Accountants in England and Wales, 1976.

Lee, T. A. and Tweedie, D. P., *Institutional Use and Understanding of Corporate Financial Information*, ICAEW, 1981.

Lintner, J., 'The Valuation of Risk Assets and the Selection of Risky Investments in Stock Portfolios and Capital Budgets', *Review of Economic Statistics*, February, 1965.

Lorek, K. S., 'Predicting Annual Net Earnings with Quarterly Earnings Time Series Models', *Journal of Accounting Research*, Spring, 1979.

Macve, R., *A Conceptual Framework for Financial Accounting and Reporting*, ICAEW, 1981.

Moizer, P. and Arnold, J., 'Share Appraisal by Investment Analysts—A Comparison of the Techniques used by Portfolio and Non-portfolio Managers', *Accounting and Business Research*, Summer, 1984.

Morris, R. G., 'Evidence of the Impact of Inflation on Share Prices', *Accounting and Business Research*, Spring, 1975.

Noreen, E. and Sepe, J., 'Market Reactions to Accounting Deliberations—the Inflation Accounting Case', *The Accounting Review*, 1981.

Norton, C. L. and Smith, R. E., 'A Comparison of General Price Level and Historical Cost Financial Statements in the Prediction of Bankruptcy', *The Accounting Review*, January, 1979.

Ohlson, J. A., 'Financial Ratios and the Probabilistic Prediction of Bankruptcy', *Journal of Accounting Research*, Spring, 1980.

Orgler, Y. E., 'A Credit Scoring Model for Commerical Loans', *Journal of Money, Credit and Banking*, 1970.

Pacter, P. A., 'The Conceptual Framework: Make no Mystique about it', *Journal of Accountancy*, July 1983.

Peasnell, K. V., 'The Function of a Conceptual Framework for Corporate Financial Reporting', *Accounting and Business Research*, Autumn, 1982.

Pinches, G. E., and Mingo, K. A., 'A Multivariate Analysis of Industrial Bond Ratings, *Journal of Financial and Quantative Analysis*, 1969.

Prakash, P. and Rappaport, A., 'Information Inductance and its Significance for Accounting', *Accounting, Organisations and Society*, 1977.

Revsine, L., *Replacement Cost Accounting*, Prentice Hall, 1973.

Ronen, J., 'A User Oriented Development of Accounting Information Requirements in Objectives of Financial Statements', AICPA, 1974.

Santomero, A. M. and Vinso, J. O., 'Estimating the Probability of Failure for Commercial Banks and Banking Systems', *Journal of Banking and Finance*, October, 1977.

Selto, F. H., 'Internal Adaptations to Effects of Changes in Financial Accounting Standards', *Accounting, Organisations and Society*, 1982.

Shank, J. K. *et al.*, 'FASB No. 8 and the Decision Makers', *Financial Executive*, 1980.

Sharpe, W. F., 'Capital Asset Prices: A Theory of Market Equilibrium under Conditions of Risk', *Journal of Finance*, September, 1964.

Sherer, M. *et al.*, 'An Empirical Investigation of Disclosure Usage and Usefulness of Corporate Accounting Information', *Managerial Finance*, 1981.

Singh, A., *Takeovers: Their Relevance to the Stock Market and the Theory of the Firm*, Cambridge University Press, 1971.

Solomons, D., 'The Political Implications of Accounting and Accounting Standard Setting', *Journal of Accounting and Business Research*, Spring, 1983.

Stevens, D. L., 'Financial Characteristics of Merged Firms: A Multivariate Analysis', *Journal of Financial and Quantitative Analysis*, 1973.

Sunder, S., 'Relationships between Accounting Changes and Stock Prices: Problems of Measurement and some Empirical Evidence', *Journal of Accounting Research*, 1973.

Taffler, R. J., 'The Assessment of Company Solvency and Performance using a Statistical Model', *Accounting and Business Research*, Autumn, 1983.

Taylor, P. J. and Turley, W. S., *Applying Economic Consequences Analysis in Accounting Standard Setting*, paper presented to the sixth Annual Congress of the European Accounting Association, Glasgow, 1982.

Vigeland, R. L., 'The Market Reaction to Statement of Financial Accounting Standards No. 2', *Accounting Review*, April 1981.

Vinso, J. D., A Determination of the Risk of Ruin, *Journal of Financial and Quantitative Analysis*, March, 1979.

Watts, R., and Leftwith, R., 'The Time Series of Annual Accounting Earnings', *Journal of Accounting Research*, Autumn, 1977.

Wilcox, J. W., 'A Simple Theory of Financial Ratios as Predictors of Failure', *Journal of Accounting Research*, Autumn, 1971.

Wilcox, J. W., 'A Prediction of Business Failure Using Accounting Data', *Journal of Accounting Research*, 1973.

Wilner, N. A., 'SFAS8 and Information Inductance—an Experiment', *Accounting, Organisations and Society*, 1982.

Winn, D. N., *The Potential Effect of Alternative Accounting Measures on Public Policy and Resource Allocation in FASB 1978*, op. cit.

Wojnilower, A. W., *The Quality of Bank Loans*, Occasional Paper, 82, NBER, 1952.

Zeff, S., 'The Rise of Economic Consequences', *Journal of Accountancy*, 1978.

CHAPTER 6

Income concepts

In this and the next two chapters we consider income as a basis for the provision of information to users of financial reports. Although our discussion in Chapter 5 showed that user needs were unlikely to be satisfied by income data alone, income numbers are used for many decisions and there is considerable evidence that many user groups (e.g. auditors, managers and shareholders), are income-orientated (Sprouse, 1978). A number of uses are cited for income data (Alexander, 1950):

1. The measurement of management performance.
2. The making of investment decisions.
3. The formulation of dividend policy.
4. The computation of tax liabilities.
5. The making of pricing and other management decisions.
6. The regulation of enterprises.

Moreover, the notion of income seems to have a marked psychological appeal and is strongly rooted in society (Bedford, 1971). Income is not directly observable and rules have to be devised for its measurement. Thus, approaches to income measurement are normative in character and arguments about income and its mesurement are conducted on a priori terms. Much of the debate on income has been directed towards the search for a single accounting measure of income which could correctly indentify the economic substance of business transactions. This 'true economic' approach was particularly characteristic of the early and mid-1960s. (AAA, 1977). However, as we shall see below, each of the major alternative income measures exhibits both advantages and inherent disadvantages and practical measurement problems. More significantly, the variety of objectives cited for income measurement imply that different income measures may be more appropriate for different purposes (Lee, 1974). Indeed, the reporting of several income measures based upon different models may be of greater usefulness to users than the traditional method of reporting one measure only, given the complexity of the economic environment.

Income, Capital and Wealth

Most writers on the subject relate the concepts of income, capital and wealth closely together. This is certainly true of economists who have contributed much to thought on income. For example, Adam Smith saw income as an increase in wealth. Later, Fisher (1919), an influential writer on the topic, reaffirmed this view and stated that the concepts of capital and income were related as follows:

> A stock of wealth existing at a given instant of time is called capital, a flow of benefit from wealth through a given period of time is called income.

In common with most other economists, Fisher was concerned with personal income and viewed 'the flow of benefit' as fundamentally a series of psychic experiences emanating from the consumption of goods and services, with income being a money measure of these consumption experiences. Capital, according to Fisher, could be valued as the present value of the flow of benefit, discounted at a personal discount rate.

The psychological basis of Fisher's income has lead it to be criticised as a basis for entity income (Taylor, 1975), although the relationship between income and capital is not questioned. More recently Hicks (1946) put forward a view of income which, whilst retaining the link with capital, is more applicable to the entity. Hicks defined the income of an individual as:

> the maximum value which he can consume during a week, and still expect to be as well-off at the end of the week as he was at the beginning.

Thus, Hicks' income can be expressed as:

$$Y^e t = C_t + (k_t - k_t - 1) \qquad \text{(Equation 1)}$$

Where $Y^e t$ is economic income, C_t consumption and k_t capital with t a time period. Similarly to Fisher, Hicks defined capital as the present value of prospective receipts. As we shall see below, Hicksian income represents interest on capital and is thus similar in character to that of Fisher, who viewed income as the fruit of the tree of capital. Hicks' model of personal income was adapted by Alexander (1950) (and subsequently revised by Solomons, 1962) to an equivalent concept of corporate income. Accordingly, Alexander defined corporate income as the maximum amount which a firm could distribute to its shareholders during a period and still remain as well off at the end of the period as at the begining, 'well-offness' being expressed in terms of residual equity and measured entirely as the present value of cash flows, discounted at a subjective rate of discount. Alexander argued that managers who sought to maximise shareholders 'well-offness' would use a discount rate at least equal to shareholders' marginal rate of time preference. Thus, in Equation 1, C_t would represent periodic net cash flow and k_t etc., the present value of future expected net cash flows suitably discounted.

Accounting income is also related to capital, but in somewhat different terms. Conventionally, an entity's assets less liabilities represents its accounting capital or residual equity (E). The change in residual equity over a period is conventionally viewed as accounting income $(Y^a t)$, thus:

$$Y^a_{t-1 \to t} = E_t - E_{t-1} \qquad \text{(Equation 2)}$$

Equation 2 applies where no dividends have been paid, no new capital subscribed, and no loans have been paid or received during a period. Such would reduce the closing value of net assets and must be added back to calculate accounting income, thus:

$$Y^a_{t-1 \to t} = D_t + (E_t - E_{t-1}) \qquad \text{(Equation 3)}$$

Periodic accounting income is therefore inseparable from asset and liability valuation.

Thus, we may identify two related approaches to income determination:

1. **Economic Income**. This approach bases income upon a comparison of present values of future benefits. For an entity these expected future benefits are the net cash flows and, when discounted, value the entity at a point in time in terms of a present value.
2. **Net Assets**. This approach is based upon the valuation of individual assets and liabilities and measures values in actual rather than the expected terms associated with economic income.

Economic Income

Hick's definition is generally accepted as the basis for economic income when adapted to the firm. Indeed, Hicksian income has gained wide acceptance as the best concept of income, economic or accounting. As Hansen (1962) has pointed out:

> Profit as capital interest . . . may be characterised as a theoretically complete concept, which is superior to other concepts of profit as a definition and as a guide point for an ideal practical procedure.

Several versions of economic income may be identified under different circumstances. These are considered below.

Ideal Economic Income

Under conditions of certainty ideal economic income may be calculated. Assume that a company is established at time $t=0$ with an investment of £7,855. For simplicity assume further that the company's operations generate net cash flows for three periods and at the end of the fourth, its net assets are disposed of. The cash flows arising in each period are as follows:

Period	£
$t0 \rightarrow 1$	1,000
$t1 \rightarrow 2$	2,000
$t2 \rightarrow 3$	2,500
$t3 \rightarrow 4$	5,000

An appropriate subjective discount rate for the company is assumed to be 10 per cent. Economic income for each period is shown in Table 6.1.

Economic income in column 5 is what may be distributed whilst keeping capital intact, and represents a 10 per cent return on the opening capital in each period. The differences between the cash flows of column 2 and economic income are what is retained in the company and, if reinvested,

Table 6.1.   Ideal economic income without interest income

Period	Cash flow	Capital value at the end of the period	Capital value at the opening of the period	Economic income
	$(C_{t-1 \rightarrow t})$	(K_t)	(K_{t-1})	$(Y^e_{t-1 \rightarrow t})$
(1)	(2) £	(3) £	(4) £	(5) £
$0 \rightarrow 1$	1,000 +	(7,641	− 7,855)	= 786
$1 \rightarrow 2$	2,000 +	(6,405	− 7,641)	= 764
$2 \rightarrow 3$	2,500 +	(4,545	− 6,404)	= 641
$3 \rightarrow 4$	5,000 +	(0	− 4,545)	= 455

Note: values are calculated as follows:

$$K_0 = \frac{£1,000}{1.1} + \frac{£2,000}{1.1^2} + \frac{£2,500}{1.1^3} + \frac{£5,000}{1.1^4} = £7,855$$

$$K_1 = \frac{£2,000}{1.1} + \frac{£2,500}{1.1^2} + \frac{£5,000}{1.1^3} = £7,641$$

$$K_2 = \frac{£2,500}{1.1} + \frac{£5,000}{1.1^2} = £6,405$$

$$K_3 = \frac{£5,000}{1.1} = £4,545$$

maintains capital and, assuming investment opportunities giving a 10 per cent return, gives additional income in subsequent periods.

The sum retained in one period maintains opening capital for that period and the cumulative effect is to maintain opening capital. Adding interest income to economic income gives a constant 10 per cent return on opening capital. Table 6.2 summarises these results.

The calculations underlying Tables 6.1 and 6.2 assume certainty, hence the resulting economic income is ideal since expectations about future cash flows are always realised. If uncertainty is introduced realism increases but so does the potential complexity of the computations. Expectations about future cash flows may alter and may not be realised. Thus, the point of time at which capital values are calculated may affect those values. Consequently, two versions of economic income are available to deal with uncertainty: *ex ante* and *ex post* income.

Ex Ante Economic Income

Dropping the assumption of certainty makes all variables expected. Thus, if we denote $\tilde{C}_{t-1\to t}$ as cash flow expected to be realised in period $t-1\to t$, $\tilde{k}_t$ the closing capital value expected at t, the economic income which is expected to be realised during a period is given by:

$$\tilde{Y}^e_{t-1\to t} = \tilde{C}_{t-1\to t} + (\tilde{k}_t - \tilde{k}_{t-1}) \qquad \text{(Equation 4)}$$

Both capital values are estimated at the beginning of the relevant period and the resulting economic income is *ex ante*. We shall assume that all the data used in the previous example apply. However, in addition we shall assume that at t=2 the estimate of the cash flow on disposal of the assets changes from £5,000 to £6,000 due to a change in expectations, and that in period $t_{3\to4}$ the actual cash flow realised on disposal is £7,000. Table 6.3 shows *ex ante* economic income.

The change to expectations and uncertainty do not change the mechanics of calculation of economic income. However, since expectations change at t=2 and are different from out-turn during $t_{3\to4}$, the *ex ante* calculations of economic income are affected. In $t_{2\to3}$, income is affected by the change in expected cash flow from £5,000 to £6,000 in t_{3-4}. The value of this change at t=2 (when valuation of capital for period $t_{2\to3}$ takes place) is £1,000÷1.12=£826. This represents a windfall gain for the period. Windfall gains or losses (the term was coined by Keynes), arise from changes in prior expectations, or from differences between expectations and outcomes. In the case just considered, the windfall gain of £826 is unrealised (unless capitalisation is considered as realisation, in the strict sense). Including the windfall gain in economic income gives a total for $t_{2\to3}$ of £1,549=£826+£723. Similarly, in period $t_{3\to4}$ a windfall gain of

Table 6.2.   Ideal economic income with interest income

Period (1)	Cash flow for the period (2) £	Economic income for the period (3) £	Cash retained to maintain capital		Interest income (6)	Total economic income (7)=(3)+(6) £
			For the period Cumu-lative (4) (5) £ £			
0→1	1,000	786	214	214	—	786
1→2	2,000	763	1,237	1,451	21	784
2→3	2,500	641	1,859	3,310	145	786
3→4	5,000	455	4,545	7,855	331	786

Table 6.3.   *Ex ante* economic income

Period (1)	Expected cash flow $(c_{t-1\to t})$ (2) £	Expected capital value at the end of the period (k_t) (3) £	Expected capital value at the opening of the period (k_{t-1}) (4) £	Economic income ex ante (5) £	Windfall gains (6)
0→1	1,000 +	(7,641	− 7,855) =	786	
1→2	2,000 +	(6,405	− 7,641) =	764	
2→3	2,500 +	(5,455	− 7,232) =	723	826
3→4	6,000 +	(0	− 5,455) =	545	1,000
			Total	2,818	+ 1,826=4,645

Note: Capital values are calculated as follows. The subscripts refer to the point of time to which capital is calculated; the superscripts refer to the point of time at which capital is calculated.

$$k_0^0 = \frac{£1,000}{1.1} + \frac{£2,000}{1.1^2} + \frac{£2,500}{1.1^3} + \frac{£5,000}{1.1^4} = £7,855$$

$$k_1^0 = \frac{£2,000}{1.1} + \frac{£2,500}{1.1^2} + \frac{£5,000}{1.1^3} = £7,641$$

$$k_2^1 = \frac{£2,500}{1.1} + \frac{£5,000}{1.1^2} = £7,232$$

$$k_3^2 = \frac{£6,000}{1.1} = £5,455$$

£1,000 is realised as the actual cash flow is £7,000 rather than the revised expectation of £6,000. This raises income to £1,545 in $t_{3\rightarrow4}$ and total economic income to £4,645.

Adding windfall gains, both realised and unrealised, to economic income implies that they may be distributed without adversely affecting the capital of the firm. Alternatively, if they are excluded from economic income and invested, the firm's capital expands. Thus, there is a choice between strict capital maintenance and expansion from the opening capital value in $t=0$.

Ex Post Economic Income

Ex post economic income is based upon realised cash flows and opening and closing capital values estimated at the end of the relevant period. Thus, whilst *ex ante* income is forward looking for all periods, *ex post* income is in part historical. *Ex post* income for the period $t-1\rightarrow t$ ($Y^e_{t-1\rightarrow t}$) is given by:

$$Y^e_{t-1\rightarrow t}=C_{t-1\rightarrow t}+(k'_t-k_t'-1) \qquad \text{(Equation 5)}$$

The primes on capital values denote that they are calculated at the end of the relevant period. With the data as in the previous example, *ex post* economic income is calculated in Table 6.4.

Again, windfall gains arise in two periods. The revision of expectations at $t=2$ affects income in the period $t_{1\rightarrow2}$ since capital values are established at $t=2$ based on the revised expectations. The revision changes capital valued at $t=1$ from £7,641 (valued from $t=1$) to £8,392 (valued from $t=2$), giving a gain of £751. The realisation of assets at $t=4$ generates a cash flow of £7,000 which can be incorporated into period $t_{3\rightarrow4}$ income (since income is measured from $t=4$), through the period cash flow and the change in capital value (£6,364−£5,455=£909).

Distributing economic income plus windfall gains maintains capital at the opening value $k^1_0=$ £7,855. Table 6.5 gives details.

As noted earlier, if windfall gains are excluded from income and retained, capital may be augmented rather than retained at its opening value. Re-investing all windfall gains gives a closing figure of capital of £(7,855+751+909)=£9,515.

The *ex post* economic incomes of Table 6.4 are calculated on a combination of expected and realised cash flows at the end of each period. An extension of this approach is to calculate ex post income from $t=4$ for each preceding period. Since all intervening cash flows are known with certainty, this represents ideal income. The difference from ideal income calculated earlier is that the former was based upon perfect foresight whilst the latter relies upon hindsight. Table 6.6 sets out ideal *ex post* income.

Table 6.4. Ex post economic income

Period	Realised cash flow ($c_{t-1 \to t}$)	Capital value at the end of the period (k_t^1)	Capital value at the opening of the period (k_{t-1}^1)	Economic income ex post	Windfall gains
(1)	(2) £	(3) £	(4) £	(5) £	(6) £
0→1	1,000 +	(7,641	− 7,855)	= 786	
1→2	2,000 +	(7,232	− 8,392)	= 840	751
2→3	2,500 +	(5,455	− 7,232)	= 725	
3→4	7,000 +	(0	− 6,364)	= 636	909
			Total	2,987	+ 1,660=4,647

Note: Capital values are calculated as follows. The subscripts refer to the point in time to which capital is calculated; the superscripts refer to the point in time at which capital is calculated, e.g. k_0^1 is capital at $t=0$ calculated from $t=1$.

$$k_0^4 = \frac{£1,000}{1.1} + \frac{£2,000}{1.1^2} + \frac{£2,500}{1.1^3} + \frac{£5,000}{1.1^4} = £7,855$$

$$k_1^1 = \frac{£2,000}{1.1} + \frac{£2,500}{1.1^2} + \frac{£5,000}{1.1^3} = £7,641$$

$$k_1^2 = \frac{£2,000}{1.1} + \frac{£2,500}{1.1^2} + \frac{£6,000}{1.1^3} = £8,392$$

$$k_2^2 = \frac{£2,500}{1.1} + \frac{£6,000}{1.1^2} = £7,232$$

$$k_2^3 = \frac{£6,000}{1.1} = £5,455$$

$$k_3^4 = \frac{£7,000}{1.1} = £6,364$$

Table 6.5. Capital maintenance under *ex post* economic income

Period	Cash flow realised	Economic income plus windfall gains	Cash retained to maintain capital — For the period	Cash retained to maintain capital — Cumulative	Capital maintenance required
(1)	(2) £	(3) £	(4) £	(5) £	(6)
0→1	1,000	786	214	214	= (7,641−7,855)
1→2	2,000	1,591	409	623	= (7,232−7,855)
2→3	2,500	723	1,777	2,400	= (5,455−7,855)
3→4	7,000	1,545	5,455	7,855	= (0 −7,855)

Table 6.6. Ideal *ex post* economic income

Period	Realised cash flow $C_{t-1\to t})$	Capital value at the end of the period k_t	Capital value at the opening of the period k_{t-1}	Ideal economic income ex post
	£	£	£	£
0→1	1,000	+ (9,143	− 9,221)	= 922
1→2	2,000	+ (8,058	− 9,143)	= 915
2→3	2,500	+ (6,364	− 8,058)	= 806
3→4	7,000	+ (0	− 6,364)	= 636

Note: Capital values are calculated as follows:– (The subscripts refer to the point in time to which capital is calculated; the superscripts refer to the point in time at which capital is calculated).

$$k_0^4 = \frac{£1,000}{1.1} + \frac{£2,000}{1.1^2} + \frac{£2,500}{1.1^3} + \frac{£7,000}{1.1^4} = £9,221$$

$$k_1^4 = \frac{£2,000}{1.1} + \frac{£2,500}{1.1^2} + \frac{£7,000}{1.1^3} = £9,143$$

$$k_2^4 = \frac{£2,500}{1.1} + \frac{£7,000}{1.1^2} = £8,058$$

$$k_3^4 = \frac{£7,000}{1.1} = £6,364$$

Table 6.7. Capital maintenance under ideal *ex post* economic income

Period	Cash flow realised	Economic income	Cash retained to maintain capital		Capital maintenance required
			For the period	Cumulative	
(1)	(2)	(3)	(4)	(5)	(6)
	£	£	£	£	
0→1	1,000	922	78	78	= (9,143−9,221)
1→2	2,000	915	1,085	1,163	= (8,058−9,221)
2→3	2,500	806	1,694	2,857	= (6,364−9,221)
3→4	7,000	636	6,364	9,221	= (0 −9,221)
	12,500	3,279			

The capital maintenance implied by the economic income figures of Table 6.6 is detailed in Table 6.7.

Adopting *ex post* certainty removes any need to revise expectations over time, and with it, the possibilities of windfall gains or losses due to such revisions. However, at t=0 the original investment was made at £7,855, which is £1,366 less than the present value of the returns to that investment. This difference does represent a windfall gain which increases economic income for t_{0-1} to £2,288, and total economic income to £4,645.

Evaluation of Economic Income

Periodic economic income figures on *ex ante*, *ex post* and ideal *ex post* bases are brought together in Table 6.8. Ideal economic income from Table 6.1 is omitted since the cash flows are not comparable. Total economic income (including windfall gains) under each of the bases is £4,645. This total is the same as conventional accounting income. With net assets maintained at their historical cost value of £7,855 in the first three periods, accounting income is equivalent to the net cash flows realised. In the final period, the realisation of net assets for £7,000 against their book value of £7,855 results in a loss of £855 giving total accounting income of:

Table 6.8.   Comparison of *ex ante* and *ex post* economic income

Period	Income ex ante		Income ex post		Ideal income ex post	
	Without windfalls	*With windfalls*	*Without windfalls*	*With windfalls*	*Without windfalls*	*With windfalls*
	£	£	£	£	£	£
0→1	786	786	786	786	922	2,288
1→2	764	764	840	1,591	915	915
2→3	723	1,549	725	725	806	806
3→4	545	1,545	636	1,545	636	636
	2,818	4,645	2,987	4,645	3,279	4,645

Period	Accounting Income £
0→1	1,000
1→2	2,000
2→3	2,500
3→4	(855)
	4,645

The three versions of economic income and accounting income appear equivalent due to the equality of the totals. However, this is illusory. The three versions of economic income give different patterns of periodic income from each other and from accounting income. Each of the four income bases reports the same real economic events differently, partly because they adopt different perspectives, but also because the versions of economic income rely to varying degrees upon expectations and therefore contain elements of subjectivity. Windfall gains and losses present difficulties of treatment as distributions or retentions for capital maintenance and expansion.

Ex ante and *ex post* economic income, being based upon expectations of future cash flows, appear to be relevant to economic decisions, and in a world of certainty expectations and estimates could be formed effortlessly. However, the need to predict under uncertainty reduces the benefits of the models as practical guides to action. This problem extends to the discount rate used in determining capital values and establishing the rate of corresponding uncertainties for re-investments. Indeed, the need to discount introduces significant additional subjectivity to the extent that there are differences in marginal rates of individual time preference.

Shwayder (1967) has questioned the theoretical soundness of economic income. He argues that in certain circumstances economic income allocates income to accounting periods in a manner which 'violates our intuitive notions concerning periodic income'. Economic income emphasises the timing and amount of cash flow and thus income does not reflect important economic events such as advantageous sales or purchases. Moreover, a firm's lifetime income may be allocated to periods when information is obtained about future operations; thus economic income may describe the timing of knowledge about economic events rather than the occurrence of the events themselves. This emphasis upon knowledge about timing leads to very liberal realisation criteria since capitalising future benefits implies realisation. Very distant benefits may thus be realised if expectations about those benefits are available. Indeed, if economic income is to be determined for firms in circumstances more realistic than those of the single venture of known finite life considered above, very distant, future benefits must be incorporated. At the limit, treating the firm as a going concern implies estimating cash flows to infinity, although distant cash flows may have an immaterial effect on present values once discounted. Of related concern are the complex problems involved in estimated future cash flows for complex entities with various operations.

Net Assets

As we noted earlier in the chapter, an alternative approach to valuation for income calculation is directed to the individual assets and liabilities of an enterprise. The valuation of individual assets and liabilities provides the basis for their aggregation in total net assets which are equivalent to residual equity, and whose change over time gives accounting income as in Equation 2 above. Several valuation bases are available:

1. Historical cost
2. Adjusted historical cost
3. Current replacement cost
4. Net realisable value
5. Present value
6. Value to the firm

Historical cost values assets and liabilities in accordance with the sacrifices incurred or benefits obtained at their date of acquisition. The longstanding and widespread acceptance of this basis of valuation can be attributed to its objectivity and its emphasis upon transactions. Acceptance of historical cost is based upon the view that accountants should measure and report only the external exchanges of an enterprise and not be concerned with events that do not involve transactions. Objectivity is assumed because cost data can be easily verified by reference to invoices and similar records.

Historical cost is part of the conventional approach to accounting. As well as the implicit assumption of price stability the historical cost approach to accounting consists of:

1. The definition of an accounting period.
2. The recognition of costs corresponding to that period.
3. The recognition of revenues of that period.
4. The matching of relevant costs to recognised revenues, carrying forward unallocated costs as assets for matching with revenues.

The assumption of price stability is unrealistic and raises doubts about the usefulness of historical cost information for decision making. Moreover, the recognition and realisation of items for valuation purposes and income measurement presents numerous conceptual and practical problems which are discussed more fully in Chapter 7. Aggregating the values of individual assets and liabilities, although similar in character, may produce meaningless totals if items were obtained at significantly different historical values.

Adjusted historical cost attempts to solve the problem of price instability by using a general price index to adjust values recorded at historical cost for changes in the general purchasing power of money. The basic rationale of these adjustments is to provide homogeneity to the measurement process so that all money equivalents are measured on the same scale. Furthermore, gains and losses resulting from holding monetary assets and liabilities during inflation my be identified. Monetary items are those assets and liabilities whose values are fixed by law or contract. Non-monetary items have values which may change with inflation. The historical cost values of non-monetary items such as fixed assets or stocks are adjusted to their current purchasing power equivalents by applying the ratio:

$$\frac{\text{index of general prices at the accounting date}}{\text{index of general prices at the transaction date}}$$

Such indexation aims to compensate for the effects of changes in the value of money on such items, as their prices change due to inflation. Holders of monetary items will experience changes in purchasing power as the result of inflation, since their own prices do not change. Holders of monetary assets, such as cash or debtors suffer a loss in purchasing power, whilst holders of monetary liabilities gain by settling their liabilities in currency of less purchasing power. The adjustment of accounting income for such gains or losses is consistent with the notion of accounting income as a change in net assets.

Example 6.1:

A company sold goods for £20,000 during the year 1.1.X0 to 31.12.X0. In the same period it purchased goods for £15,000, paid interest of £500, taxation of £2,000 and dividends of £1,000. Its opening cash balance was £1,500 and the closing balance £4,000. There were no debtors or creditors at the start of the period, but at the end they were £5,000 and £6,000 respectively. Over the period, the general index of prices moved regularly from 100 at the beginning to 112 at the end. The treatment of the monetary items was as follows:

Purchasing power gain or loss on monetary items
for the year 19X0

	Unadjusted data £	Conversion factor	Adjusted data £
Cash balance 1 January	1,500	112/100	1,680
Add sales	20,000	112/106	21,132
			22,812
Less purchases	15,000	112/106	15,849
			6,963

Purchasing power gain or loss on monetary items
for the year 19X0

Less other expenditure			
Interest	500		
Taxation	2,000		
Dividends	1,000		3,500
			3,463
Closing:			
Debtors	5,000		
Cash	4,000		
	9,000		
Less creditors	6,000		3,000
Loss on net monetary items			463

Income is reduced by the value of the loss on net monetary items. The above example does not include any loan finance. Had the company had a loan outstanding during the period of say, £5,000, the loss of purchasing power on this liability would have been $£5,000 \times \dfrac{(112-100)}{100} = £600$, equivalent to a gain to the company.

The treatment of such a gain is controversial. Adopting a proprietary view would identify a gain to shareholders due to the use of geared finance and would include this gain in income (Bourne, 1976). Alternatively, one might recognise the gain as accruing to the entity and, without any corresponding cash inflow, exclude the gain from income in order not to endanger the maintenance of capital (Gynther, 1966).

Current replacement cost values assets on the basis of the sacrifice which would be incurred today in replacing the asset or the service potential represented by the asset. This method of valuation divides income into:

1. Gains and losses from holding assets
2. Gains and losses from selling assets

The gains and losses from holding assets are equal to the increases or decreases in the replacement prices of the assets held and are reported in the periods the prices change. The gains and losses from selling assets equal the differences between the selling prices and the replacement prices of the assets at the time of sale, and are reported in the periods the assets are sold.

Example 6.2:

During the year ended 31 December 19X0, an asset was acquired at a cost of £40. By 31 December 19X0 its replacement cost had risen to £60. It was sold during the year ended 31 December 19XI for £100, and at the time of sale, its relacement cost was £65.

For the purpose of measuring historical cost accounting income, the income arising from the sale of the asset (assuming no depreciation) would accrue in the year ended 31 December 19XI and would be calculated as follows:

$$\text{HC income} = \text{Revenue—historical cost}$$
$$= £100 - £40$$
$$= £60$$

For the purpose of measuring replacement cost income three distinct gains are recognised which occur as follows:

(*i*)   A holding gain in the year ended 31 December 19X0 measured as the difference between the replacement cost at 31 December 19X0 and the acquisition cost during the year, that is £60—£40=£20.

(*ii*) A holding gain in the year ended 31 December 19X1 measured as the difference between the replacement cost at 31 December 19X0 and the replacement cost on the date of sale, that is, £65—£60=£5.

(*iii*) An operating gain resulting directly from the activity of selling measured as the difference between the realised sale price and the replacement cost at the date of sale, that is, £100—£65=£35.

These differing timings of income recognition may be compared as follows:

Year ended 31 December	*19X0* £	*19X1* £
Historical cost income	—	60
Replacement cost income		
Holding gains	20	5
Current operating gain	—	35

Holding gains on assets which have not been sold are termed 'unrealised', after sale they are said to be 'realised'.

It is clear from this example that the differences between historical and replacement cost relates to the timing of reported gains and losses since the total income over the two periods is £60 in each case. Furthermore, the replacement cost concept provides more detailed information than the historical cost accounting income for performance evaluation. Two arguments for the separation of income into holding and operating gains have been suggested (Drake and Dopuch, 1965). Firstly, the two income categories may be used to evaluate different aspects of management activity. Secondly, they permit better interperiod and interfirm comparisons.

One criticism of the current replacement cost concept is that the measurement process becomes more subjective. This applies particularly to depreciation, a problem we examine in Chapter 10. A related limitation is the difficulty of computing the replacement cost of assets. For many assets, especially physical plant, there may be no ready market in which to acquire replacement assets. In such cases specific price indices may be used, or management estimates. It follows that substantial technological change can make this concept difficult to apply.

Net realisable value of an asset may be defined as the estimated amount that would currently be received from the sale of the asset less the anticipated costs that would be incurred in its disposal. The valuations used by this method correspond to conditions of orderly, rather than forced, liquidation. This method abandons the realisation concept and gives rise to holding gains and losses different in character from those which emerge from the current replacement cost system. Operating gains are recognised as soon as production generates them, and subsequent price changes give rise to holding gains.

Example 6.3

The previous replacement cost example includes the following information. Selling price of the asset at 31 December 19X0 was £90. For the purpose of measuring realisable income, two distinct gains occur:

(*i*)   An operating gain which is recognised prior to realisation at 31 December 19X0, that is, £90–40=£50.
(*ii*) A holding gain in the year ended 31 December 19X1, that is £100–90=£10.

The different timings of income recognition may be compared as follows:

Year ended 31 December	19X0	19X1 £
Historical cost income	—	60
Replacement cost income		
Holding gains	20	5
Current operating gain	—	35
Realisable income		
Current operating gain	50	—
Holding gain	—	10

Once again, operating and holding gains total historical cost income. Because operating income is recognised prior to realisation, the timing at which operating income is recognised differs from that under the replacement cost system. However, both these systems contrast with the historical cost approach in that they provide a clear distinction between operating and holding activities.

The net realisable value approach possesses a number of advantages. It provides investors and creditors with some measure of the risks involved in investing in or lending to a company. Essentially this approach reflects the capacity of the enterprise to adapt to new alternatives, information which is not provided by other valuation systems. Another advantage of this approach is that the values represent the opportunity cost of using resources in the business, and this information is necessary for rational decisions as to whether the enterprise ought to retain individual assets for further use or dispose of them. Finally, this approach overcomes some of the criticisms of the conventional approach, concerning the problem of relating its concepts to the real world. It eliminates arbitrary cost allocations, a topic we discuss in Chapter 7.

The major disadvantage of using realisable values is that they imply a short-run approach to the analysis of business operations. All assets are valued at exit prices even though many assets are not held for resale. Although realisable values represent real world values based on market prices, they do not reflect the behaviour of enterprises. In reality, firms do not sell off their assets at frequent intervals: in practice they continue in the same line, or lines, of business for a considerable time. Another problem is that of determining selling prices for highly specific assets such as items of plant where there is no ready market. Scrap values may be the only alternative for valuing such assets.

Present value is defined as the sum of the future expected net cash flows associated with the use of an asset discounted to their present value. As such it is consistent with the concept of value contained in the economic theory of income. However, in this particular context this concept of value is used to value each asset individually rather than to value the firm as a whole. As we saw previously, the subjective nature of the computations based on this concept pose severe limitations for its practical application. Furthermore, it is only very rarely that cash flows can be identified with one individual asset. More commonly, cash flows are derived from a group of assets, with the result that wholly arbitrary allocations are necessary to assign them among individual assets. Because of these practical limitations, it is generally accepted that this approach is better applied to monetary resources and obligations whose cash flow timing and magnitude can be more readily estimated (APB 1971).

Value to the business is designed to indicate the value of an asset to an enterprise in the light of the economic context in which it is held. One method of computing this value is to measure the loss which would be suffered if the business was deprived of the asset. This reverses the opportunity cost concept and defines opportunity value as the least costly sacrifice avoided by owning the asset. It is based on the work of Bonbright (1937) who defined opportunity value in the following terms: 'The value of a property to its owner is identical in amount with the adverse value of the entire loss, direct and indirect, that the owner might expect to suffer if he were deprived of the property.'

In no sense may historical cost be measured as the value of an asset to the business because it is not related to the amount which would have to be paid for the asset, the amount that might be gained from disposing of it, or the amount to be gained by holding it. Deprival value is not based on a single type of value but on a combination of possible values which include the three bases of valuation already discussed:

(*a*) the current purchase price (replacement cost) of the asset (RC);
(*b*) the net realisable value of the asset (NRV);
(*c*) the present value of expected future earnings from the asset (PV).

It has been argued (Parker and Harcourt, 1969) that six hypothetical relationships exist between these three values:

	Correct valuation basis
(1) NRV>PV>RC	RC
(2) NRV>RC>PV	RC
(3) PV>RC>NRV	RC
(4) PV>NRV>RC	RC
(5) RC>PV>NRV	PV
(6) RC>NRV>PV	NRV

In (1) and (2) above, NRV is greater than PV. Hence, the firm would be better off selling rather than using the asset. The sale of the asset necessitates its replacement, if the NRV is to be restored. We may say, therefore, that the maximum loss which the firm would suffer by being deprived of the asset is RC.

In (3) and (4) above, PV is greater than NRV, so that the firm would be better off using the asset rather than selling it. The firm must replace the asset in order to maintain PV, so that the maximum loss which the firm would suffer by being deprived of the asset is again RC.

The general statement which may be made, therefore, in respect of the first four cases (1) to (4) is that, where either NRV or PV, or both, are higher than RC, RC is the appropriate value of the asset to the business. As regards a current asset, such as inventories, RC will be the current purchase price (entry value). In the case of a fixed asset, RC will be the written down current purchase price (replacement cost), since the value of such an asset will be the cost of replacing it in its existing condition, having regards to wear and tear.

As regards cases (5) and (6), RC does not represent the value of the asset to the business, for if the firm were to be deprived of the asset, the loss incurred would be less than RC. Case (5) is most likely to arise in industries where assets are highly specific, where NRV tends to zero and where RC is greater than PV, so that it would not be worth replacing the asset if it were destroyed, but it is worth using it rather than attempting to dispose of it.

Case (6) applies to assets held for resale, that is, where NRV must be greater than PV. If RC should prove to be greater than NRV, such assets would not be replaced. Hence, it implies that they should be valued at NRV or RC, whichever is the lower.

The Sandilands Report (1975) accepted the deprival value concept, but this action attracted criticism on two grounds. Firstly, the usefulness of aggregating a heterogeneous mixture of asset values was questioned. According to one writer, adding together RC, PV and NRV is 'logically and practically meaningless' (Chambers, 1976). In contrast, other writers argued that because these measures are subsets of a current value system based on the market opportunity costs of assets 'there is no inconsistency in adding them together in appropriate circumstances' (Barton, 1975). Secondly, a more important criticism is related to the practical implications of assessing PV which we have discussed above. This problem arises in Case (5) in the above table where RC>PV>NRV.

Gee and Peasnell (1976) argued that RC is likely to be the most satisfactory valuation basis for Case (5). They based their arguments on the view that valuation should be determined by the future role of the asset. This was the view adopted by the Australian Provisional Accounting Standard of 1978, which rejected the deprival value concept, which is the basis for Case (5), and recommended instead adoption of the 'recoverable amount' criterion. Accordingly, two questions should be asked about an asset:

1. Is the asset to continue in use? If yes—ask question 2. If no—value at net realisable value.
2. Can the current cost of the asset be expected to be recovered,

   (a) through charges against the revenues from the continued use of the asset, and/or
   (b) by its sale?

If yes—value at replacement cost. If no—value at the amount of replacement cost that can be recovered (the recoverable amount).

Similarly, SSAP16 abandoned the strict deprival value concept and prescribed a recoverable amount criterion where RC does not necessarily provide the value to the business. In SSAP16 the value to the business of an asset is defined as:

(*a*) RC or if a permanent diminution to below RC has been recognised,
(*b*) recoverable amount, which is the greater of NRV of an asset and, where applicable, the amount recoverable from its further use.

Capital Maintenance

The previous sections have shown how periodic income may be determined in different ways, but each method has resulted from a comparison of measures of capital at different points of time. Thus, capital measurement is central to income measurement and the idea of capital maintenance is fundamental to income. We have seen how different income figures may emerge if different approaches are taken to capital maintenance, especially with economic income. In this section we look at the issue of capital maintenance again, by bringing together a number of issues at raised different points in the chapter.

Although there is general agreement that income is a residue available for distribution once provision has been made for maintaining the value of capital intact difficulties begin to emerge when the discussion turns to the consideration of the meaning of 'capital maintenance'. Two measuring units may be used in an accounting system.

(*i*)   Money units of measurement are concerned with the number of £s received or expended in transactions. Money has a defect which makes its use as a measuring unit questionable: an increase in money value may not indicate an increase in general purchasing power.

(*ii*) General purchasing power (GPP) units are devised to adjust for changes in the general price level. This reflects the notion that money is not prized for its own sake but for the goods and services it may purchase. This is the measuring unit used in the adjusted historical cost approach to asset valuation discussed previously.

These two measuring units may be combined with the methods of valuing assets to give four concepts of capital maintenance.

Figure 6.1 illustrates that GPP and Current Value accounting are complementary rather than independent responses to changing prices (Rosenfield, 1972). The concepts of capital maintenance indicated in 6.1 figure are:

1. Money value
2. Purchasing power adjusted money value
3. Operating capability
4. Real value

Measuring unit	Asset valuation base	Historical cost	Current value
Money units		1	3
GPP units		2	4

Figure 6.1. Concepts of capital maintenance

1 Money Value

According to this concept, the measurement of periodic income should ensure that the monetary value of the shareholders' equity is maintained intact. In effect, the income of the period amounts to the increase in monetary terms in the shareholders' equity measured between the beginning and the end of the period. It is this amount which may be distributed as income to ensure that the money capital is maintained intact. The money capital maintenance concept is reflected in historical cost accounting.

During periods of inflation financial statements prepared under the historical cost concept lose their usefulness because:

(a) Not all balance sheets reveal the real value of all the assets and liabilities.
(b) Depreciation is inadequate to replace the fixed assets consumed during the year.
(c) The charge for the cost of stock consumed is inadequate to replace it because stock is charged at the cost of purchase and not at the cost of replacement.
(d) The effects of holding monetary assets or owing monetary liabilities are ignored.

As a result of these inadequacies:

(e) Growth is exaggerated because no allowance is made for the fall in the value of the money used to measure the results.
(f) Their uncritical use may lead to the situation where capital, although maintained in money terms, may not be maintained in real terms and may be distributed to shareholders, employees, customers or the

Inland Revenue to the detriment of the long-term viability of the business (Inflation Accounting Steering Group, 1976).

2 Purchasing-power-adjusted Money Value

The objective of this concept is to maintain the purchasing power of the shareholders' equity by constantly updating the historical cost of assets for changes in the value of money. The translation of historical asset cost is effected by a retail price index, and results in the representation of asset values in common units of purchasing power. This concept of capital maintenance purports to show to shareholders that their company kept pace with general inflationary pressures during the accounting period, by measuring income in such a way as to take into account changes in the price level. In effect, it intends to maintain the shareholders' capital in terms of monetary units of constant purchasing power. Therefore it reflects the proprietorship concept of the enterprise.

3 Operating Capability

According to this concept of capital maintenance capital is the operating capability provided by the resources (assets) of the entity. Income is considered to be the residue after provision has been made for maintaining the capability of the assets to continue operations at the same level which existed at the beginning of the period.

The operating capability concept implies that in times of rising prices increased funds will be required to maintain assets. These funds might not be available if income is determined without recognition of the rising costs of assets consumed in operations. For example, profit would not be earned on the sale for £1,000 of 100 units of inventory costing £800 if their replacement cost was £1,000. In this situation, an outlay of £1,000 would be required in order to maintain the operating capability of the business in terms of 100 units of inventory. In other words, the increase in the cost of the inventory necessitates the investment of additional funds in the business in order to maintain it as an operating unit.

The operating capability concept does not imply that the firm is committed to replacing assets with identical items. The entity, being dynamic, may extend, contract, or change its activities in which ever way desired. The concept simply means that the operating capability should be maintained at the same level at the end of a period as it was at the beginning.

In the previous section we saw how the purchasing power adjusted money value concept views the capital of the enterprise from the standpoint of the shareholders. By contrast, the operating capability concept views the problem of capital maintenance from the perspective of the enterprise itself. This notion underlies current cost accounting, but the method of its implementation is very controversial.

Real Value

This concept combines current replacement prices of assets with the general purchasing power property of the pound. Its objective is to preserve the purchasing power of shareholders' equity in real terms. During inflation holding gains may be divided into two components—fictitious and real. A fictitious gain is the amount required to maintain existing purchasing power. A real gain is the amount in excess of that necessary to preserve existing purchasing power. Therefore, during inflation a firm gains if it holds goods that increase in price faster than the general price level. But it loses if the goods it holds do not increase in price as fast as the general price level. Therefore, to measure real income we must take into account changes in the specific prices of goods and services and changes in the general purchasing power of the pound. This results in a form of accounting known as general price level-adjusted current cost accounting.

QUESTIONS

1. (a) Explain how far the measurement of income may be considered to be related to the measurement of capital.
   (b) What do you understand by the entity and proprietary concepts of capital, and what are their implications for capital maintenance?
   (Association of Certified Accountants)

2. Accounting income (Y_a) has been defined as:
   $$Y_a = D_t + (E_t - E_{t-1})$$
   Economic income (Y_e) has been defined as:
   $$Y_e = C_t + (K_t - K_{t-1})$$
   Apart from the fact that these two formulae employ different notation, they appear very similar!
   Explain the fundamental differences which lie behind these two income models.

3. On 1 January 19X1, Frank managed to buy a small established newsagent's shop in the face of keen competition. The assets, valued at replacement cost at 1 January, comprised:

	£
Premises	20,000
Stock	2,000
Debtors	800

Liabilities were settled by the previous owner, and the total purchase price of the business, including goodwill and £1,000 for legal costs, was £26,000 which Frank paid immediately. He estimated that he would be able to withdraw £5,000 from the business annually at the end of 19X1, 19X2 and 19X3. In addition, the business would probably be saleable at the end of 19X3 for £30,000. On 2 January 19X1 a disappointed rival offered Frank £27,000 in cash for the shop, but Frank refused to sell. At the end of 19X1, Frank's tangible assets and liabilities, valued at original cost, and before any drawings, were

	£
Premises	20,000
Stock	3,100
Debtors	1,040
Cash	8,000
Creditors	1,000

He estimated at that date that he could withdraw £7,000 immediately, and similar amounts at the end of 19X2 and 19X3, and then sell the business for £35,000. Alternatively, he believed that it would be possible for him to sell the premises immediately for £17,000 (net of any disposal costs), the stock for £4,000 and that debtors and creditors would be settled at face value. Frank's personal opportunity cost of capital is 20 per cent per annum.

Required:

(a) Making, but stating, any necessary assumptions, calculate for 19X1, the firm's—

    (i)   Accounting income
    (ii) Realisable income
    (iii) Economic income *ex ante*
    (iv) Economic income *ex post*, suitably analysed

(b) Evaluate the profit figures measured in (a) as indicators of Frank's performance and as guides to future conduct.

4. (a) In times of inflation, showing an asset at its current value will give a more meaningful picture of a business than will recording at historical cost.
'Current value' may be defined as replacement cost, net realisable value, economic value or deprival value. What arguments may be advanced for and against each definition?
(b) Compute the 'value to the business' in each of the following cases:

	Replacement Cost	Net Realisable	Economic Value
	£	£	£
(*i*)	1,000	600	500
(*ii*)	1,000	500	600
(*iii*)	600	500	1,000

5. Potts Ltd formed on 1 January 19X1. You are provided with the following basic information. Note that all transactions are on a cash basis.

(*a*) Issued share capital is 2,000 £1 ordinary shares.

(*b*) Fixtures and equipment were purchased on 2 January at a cost of £1,700. Depreciation is to be provided on a straight-line basis at the rate of 30 per cent per annum. The replacement cost of the fixtures on 30 June 19X1 is £1,900.

(*c*) During the year, sundry expenses (other than purchase of goods) amounted to £132.

(*d*) On the 3 January the company purchased 500 units at a cost of £2 per unit. These goods were sold on 18 February for proceeds of £3 per unit, and replaced by goods costing £2.15p per unit.

(*e*) The goods purchased on 18 February were then sold on 30 June 19X1 for proceeds of £3.10p per unit and immediately replaced by an equivalent quantity of goods costing £2.25p per unit.

You are required, in respect of the six months to 30 June 19X1 to:

(*i*) Prepare final accounts on a historical cost basis.

(*ii*) Prepare final accounts on a replacement (or current cost) basis.

(*iii*) Comment on the difference between the two profit figures.

REFERENCES

Accounting Principles Board Opinion 21, *Interest on Receivables and Payables*, 1971.

Alexander, S. S., 'Income Measurement in a Dynamic Economy. Five Monographs on Business Income', AICPA, 1950. Revised by D. Solomons in Baxter, W. T. and Davidson, S., (eds.), *Studies in Accounting Theory*, Sweet and Maxwell, 1962.

American Accounting Association, *Statement on Accounting Theory and Theory Acceptance*, 1977.

Barton, A. D., *An Analysis of Business Income Concepts*, International Centre for Research in Accounting, University of Lancaster, 1975.

Bedford, N. M., 'Income Concept Complex: Expansion or Decline', in Sterling, R. R., *Asset Valuation and Income Determination*, Scholars Book Co., 1971.

Bonbright, J. C., *The Valuation of Property*, McGraw-Hill, 1937.

Bourne, M., 'The "Gain" on Borrowing', *Journal of Business Finance and Accounting*, 1976.

Chambers, R. J., 'Accounting for Inflation—Part or Whole?' *Accountants Magazine*, March, 1976.

Drake, D. F. and Dopuch, N., 'On the Case for Dichotomizing Income', *Journal of Accounting Research*, Spring, 1965.

Fisher, I., *Elementary Principles of Economics*, New York, 1919.

Gee, K. P., and Peasnell, K. V., 'A Pragmatic Defence of Replacement Cost', *Accounting and Business Research*, Autumn, 1976.

Gynther, R. S., *Accounting for Price Level Changes: Theory and Procedures*, Pergaman, 1966.

Hansen, P., *Accounting Concepts of Profit: An Analysis and Evaluation in the Light of the Economic Theory of Income and Capital*, North-Holland Publishing Co., 1962.

Hicks, J. R., *Value and Capital*, second edition, Oxford University Press, 1946.

Lee, T. A., *Income and Value Measurement: Theory and Practice*, Nelson, 1985.

Inflation Accounting Steering Group, *Guidance Manual on CCA*, Tolley, 1976.

Parker, R. H. and Harcourt, G. C., *Readings in the Concept and Measurement of Income*, Cambridge University Press, 1969.

Rosenfield, P., 'The Confusion between General Price-level Restatement and Current Value Accounting, *Journal of Accountancy*, October, 1972.

Sandilands Report, *Report the Inflation Accounting Committee*, HMSO Cmnd Paper 6225, 1975.

Shwayder, K., 'A Critique of Economic Income as an Accounting Concept', *Abacus*, August, 1967.

Sprouse, R. T., 'The Importance of Earnings in the Conceptual Framework', *Journal of Accountancy*, January, 1978.

Taylor, P. J., 'The Nature and Determinants of Income: Some Further Comments', *Journal of Business Finance and Accounting*, Summer, 1975.

CHAPTER 7

Recognition, realisation and matching

The previous chapter considered income and related concepts. We noted the alternative approaches to income measurement and the various valuation bases which might be used to value assets and liabilities. In this chapter we consider two topics which were important elements in the discussion of Chapter 6, namely recognition and realisation, and their relationship to one of the most fundamental operating concepts of the conventional approach, matching.

Neither recognition nor realisation were defined in Chapter 6, but we shall interpret them as follows. Recognition is the process of formally recording or incorporating an item in the financial statements of an enterprise (FASB, 1985). This process allows the matching of revenues and expenses although the resulting profit may be termed unrealised if it does not satisfy the additional test of realisation. Realisation of profit means reporting profit in financial statements in a manner which indicates that uncertainty has been reduced to the point at which it could be regarded as available for distribution to investors, subject to constraints of a concept of capital maintenance and to the financing policy of the business (Weetman, 1980).

The conventional approach of Chapter 2 views recognition and realisation as occurring simultaneously. For example, SSAP2 states that 'revenue and profits are not anticipated, but are recognised by inclusion in the profit and loss account only when realised in the form either of cash or of other assets, the ultimate cash realisation of which can be assessed with reasonable certainty'. The 1981 Companies Act specifies that the profit and loss account must include only those profits which are realised at the balance sheet date. (The meaning of realisation is to be determined in accordance with accounting principles generally accepted at the time the accounts are prepared.)

The conventional approach breaks up the continuous stream of business activity into artificial segments known as accounting periods to which revenues and costs are allocated. Revenue is an inflow of cash or other assets, or a decrease in liabilities, resulting from the central operations of an enterprise. The most obvious example is sales of merchandise. Expenses are outflows of cash or other assets, or increase in liabilities, attributable to the process of generating revenue. Whereas the word 'cost' in accounting is used in the broadest sense to represent the amount given up to acquire goods and services, the word 'expense' refers to that portion of goods and services consumed in the process of earning revenue.

Accrual accounting requires that the effects of transactions and other financial events on the assets and liabilities of an enterprise should be recognised at the time they have their primary economic impact, not necessarily when cash is received or spent. The matching concept is an integral part of the accrual process and provides that, as far as it is practical, all costs should be associated with particular revenues and recorded in the same period in which the related revenues are given accounting recognition. Costs that are associated with future revenues should be maintained in asset accounts until the revenues are recognised when such costs can properly be charged as expenses.

The process of profit determination involves two basic steps:

(*i*) the identification of the revenues attributable to the period reported upon and,
(*ii*) the matching of the corresponding expenses with these revenues.

Thus, the matching concept links the recognition of revenues and costs and is a key element in the conventional approach to recognition and realisation. There has been an extensive and long-standing debate in accounting theory over the criteria adopted by the conventional approach to recognition, realisation and matching. There has been frequent criticism that the conventional approach places too much emphasis upon objectivity and conservatism at the expense of relevance to users of financial statements.

The Matching Concept

Many recent controversies in accounting have their origin in the allocation process which is guided by the matching concept. We have noted that the matching concept requires the allocation of costs and revenues together. Several criticisms can be levelled at allocation. Thomas (1974) has succinctly summarised these criticisms as follows:

> For each situation in which allocation is contemplated, there is a variety of possible allocation methods, each of which could be defended. The allocation

problem arises because there is no conclusive way to choose one method in preference to all others, except arbitrarily.

Thus, allocation may firstly be criticised as an arbitrary process. In Chapter 1, we saw that 'good theory' seeks to explain real-world occurrences. Allocations do refer to real-world events and objects in the life of an organisation. For example, depreciation is intended to reflect the decline in value of an asset through use. But there is an important difference between referring to real-world phonomena and measuring them directly. Allocations are measures of real world phonomena and they are arbitrary to some degree. This may not be judged a serious problem if an allocation method is supported by what is considered to be a satisfactory justification. However, a second criticism may be raised, and that is that accounting allocations are incorrigible and as such can neither be refuted nor verified (Thomas, 1974; 1982). Thus, no satisfactory justification is possible. Thomas' view is based upon a fundamental characteristic of production processes, namely the interaction of factor inputs. Because of managerial behaviour, total output from a process is likely to be different from the total of what each input would have yielded separately. For example, a machine operator and a machine interact with each other whenever the operator and the machine working together produce more than the total of what the operator could make with his bare hands and the machine could make untended. Therefore, whenever inputs interact there is no justifiable way of determining the contribution of any one service to the overall input. Thomas's conclusions are radical:

> Financial accounting has no defensible theory of allocation; the allocated magnitudes (such as depreciation), reported in financial statements are immediately arbitrary, and this problem is so severe that accountants should cease to allocate and instead should prepare reports that they can defend.

Even if this view were taken to be rejected and satisfactory justifications identified, a third criticism may be offered. The lack of definition of the allocation process allows a wide variety of allocation bases to exist. This provides management with an element of choice (with or without justification) and the ability and opportunity to manipulate accounting data. Efforts to narrow the range of alternatives have resulted in lengthy discussions about the relative merits of different methods of allocation. Much of this discussion has focused on a priori reasoning and little empirical evidence has been produced to support different viewpoints.

A fourth criticism is that the term 'matching' has a variety of meanings. The Accounting Principles Board's Statement No. 4 (1970), avoided using the term for this reason:

> The term matching is often used in the accounting literature to describe the entire process of income determination. The term is also often applied in

accounting, however, in a more limited sense to the process of expense recognition or in an even more limited sense to the recognition of expenses by associating costs with revenue on a cause and effect basis. Because of the variety of its meanings the term matching is not used in this statement.

Fifthly, the matching concept may be criticised on the grounds that it results in meaningless balance sheets which may be defined as 'what is left over after proper accounting has occurred'. Assets and liabilities are thereby regarded as residuals that must be carried forward to future periods. According to Sprouse (1971) the task of the analyst in evaluating financial position is bound to be complicated by the sheet of balance approach where the balance sheet serves as a dumping ground for balances that someone has decided should not be included in the income statement.

Is the Matching Concept Useful?

In the light of the above criticisms of the matching concept, should it be retained? If answered in the affirmative, are improvements possible at the operational level? These issues cannot be settled in abstract terms without reference to the needs of the users of financial statements. The matching concept need not be discarded merely because its application results in arbitrary allocations. If it can be shown that the resulting financial statements contain information content, and if this content is greater than can be included in allocation-free statements, allocations will remain an important part of financial reporting (Himmel, 1981).

The FASB has reaffirmed the importance of accrual accounting by asserting that it provides a better indicator of future long-run cash flows and dividend-paying ability than does cash flow accounting. Past cash flows, in isolation, may not be very good predictors. For example, large amounts spent on capital investment reduce past cash flows, but may have the effect of increasing future cash flows; also, a firm may sell its assets which increases current cash flow but reduces future cash generating ability. An objective of accrual accounting may be to 'lead' and 'lag' the movement of cash in either direction where necessary to help provide more meaningful information to the users of financial statements. As a consequence, the profit figure may give a better indication of the long-run cash-generating capacity of the firm and may give a better measure of management performance than net cash flows.

Allocations can be defended where they are verifiable by reference to markets, for example where the value of an asset entirely used up during a period is measured in replacement cost or net realisable value terms. But this is not a blanket approval for all current value methods. If the usage of a partly used asset is obtained by spreading a current value over useful life this is still an allocation procedure and open to the same criticisms as the allocation of historical costs.

The matching concept can be made more acceptable at the operating level if reliance is placed upon physical and causal relationships for guidance in associating costs with revenues. Physical relationships, such as arise when an identifiable economic event has incremental effects on revenues and costs, may allow a readily defensible allocation of costs and revenues. Similarly, causal relationships may provide a justifiable allocation. Causal relationships may be derived from quantitative correlation which is based upon statistical methods and qualitative causality which is deduced logically. One writer has suggested the following for choosing allocation bases:

1. If physical relationships are observable, use them as the allocation bases.
2. If causal relationships can be explicitly established via quantitative correlation analysis, use them as the allocation bases.
3. If causal relationships cannot be explicitly established as in 2, but can be implicitly established via qualitative causality, use them as the allocation bases.
4. If no discernible relationship can be established, do not allocate. If allocation is absolutely necessary, a uniform base must be used.

(Liao, 1979)

Liao argues that the use of physical or causal relationships would solve the identification problem which Thomas (1974) considered would lead to arbitrary allocations, by introducing the prospects of objective verification. A reliance upon physical or causal relationships would not preclude allocations on a time basis. Indeed, many costs, for example, costs of administration and costs of renting office space, are more closely related to time periods than to revenues realised and in such cases attempts to associate costs with revenues other than on a time basis may be contrary to economic reality.

Finally, the traditional view of the matching concept as matching cost to revenues may be replaced by one which seeks to match costs and revenues to time periods. The traditional view of matching implies the existence of the causal relationship which Liao explicitly advocates searching for. Unfortunately such a relationship may not exist, or be discernible. A more realistic definition of matching may be the relationship of the cost of assets used during a period with the value of revenues generated during the same period. In adopting this view, we are in reality allocating revenues and costs separately to the same time period (Skinner, 1979).

Implementing the Matching Concept

Having considered some of the issues associated with the matching concept we shall next investigate its implementation. On page 152 we identified two stages in profit determination: revenue recognition and the matching of expenses to revenues. Both of these we consider below.

Revenue Recognition

Because revenue may be described as being earned gradually and continuously, it may be recognised at a number of points during the production and sales cycle of a product. A common theme has been to associate the recognition of revenue with the occurrence of the 'critical event' (Myers, 1959). The literature provides guidelines as to when the critical event might occur as follows:

1. When the earning activities undertaken to create revenue have been substantiately completed.
2. When revenue is measurable.
3. When the costs incurred in the generation of revenue can be measured or estimated with reasonable accuracy.
4. When the eventual collection of cash can be reasonably assured.

The first and fourth guidelines refer to stages in the cycle of operations, but lack precision. The second and third guidelines are concerned with the ability to measure costs and revenues and are similarly vague. Thus, the 'critical event' may be interpreted in different ways, leading to a wide variety of bases for recognising revenue. However, the literature has tended to interpret the guidelines in five particular ways. These are considered below. The first four apply to companies generally and the fifth to oil and gas producers:

(*a*) at the time of sale,
(*b*) at the time of cash collection,
(*c*) during production,
(*d*) at the completion of production,
(*e*) when reserves are discovered.

At the Time of Sale

Time of sale is the most common point of revenue recognition for merchandise transactions or where services have been performed in service transactions. This delays recognition until most of the uncertainties about the earning process are removed. Generally, at the time of sale, all the five guidelines are satisfied, but where goods are sold on credit future costs of collection have to be estimated as well as allowances for defaulting debtors.

Delaying recognition of revenue until the time of sale does not always remove all important uncertainties inherent in accounting information. For example, a significant practical problem exists concerning collectibility if a right of return is present. In many industries, such as agricultural products, perishable foods, recording and publishing, products are commonly sold with a right of return. FASB No. 48 (1981) adopts the view that a 'sale' with right of return is not really a sale unless the following conditions are present:

(*a*) The selling price is substantially fixed.
(*b*) The buyer has paid the seller, or the buyer is obligated to pay the seller.
(*c*) The buyer's obligation would not be changed by theft or physical destruction or damage of the property.
(*d*) The buyer has economic substance apart from that provided by the seller.
(*e*) The seller does not have significant obligations for future performance which are necessary to bring about resale by the buyer.
(*f*) The amount of future returns can be reasonably estimated.

Of these conditions, probably the most troublesome is the last one. The ability to make a reasonable estimate of the amount of future returns depends on many factors that will vary from one case to the next. Factors such as the susceptibility of the product to technological obsolescence or changes in demand are important.

At the Time of Cash Collection

Some small firms use cash-based accounting with revenues and expenses being recorded at the time of cash collection and payment. This form of accounting is acceptable primarily in service enterprises which do not have a substantial volume of credit transactions or inventories. It is also used where sales are made on instalment or hire purchase terms. In these cases: 'revenue should be recognised at the date of sale. . . . If collection is not reasonably assured, revenue should be recognised by the instalment method as cash instalments are received' (IAS 18, 1983). Because this method delays the recognition of revenue beyond the time of sale it is generally accepted for accounting purposes only where extreme doubt exists as to the collectibility of the instalments due. Many writers reject the cash base as applied to the instalment method. It can be argued that if there is sufficient uncertainty regarding collectibility of a debt to justify delaying recognition after the sale, there is also the same degree of uncertainty about estimates of cash to be collected—estimates that need to be made to apply the instalment method (Jaenicke, 1981). Other writers question the view that accrual accounting must be set aside because accountants are unable to estimate satisfactorily doubtful instalment debts. Accountants 'have proved themselves able to cope with too many extremely difficult estimation problems in the past to warrant such a conclusion. The instalment method of accounting is illogical, internally inconsistent and riddled with flaws' (Scott and Scott, 1979).

In some cases cash is paid before the delivery of goods or on the signing of an agreement. For example, a magazine subscription may entitle the signer to receive magazines over a two-year period. Application of the guidelines suggests that this should not be treated as revenue because only three of the four have been fulfilled. The earning process has not been substantially completed because the magazines have not been written and produced. Revenue should not be recognised until the magazines are delivered to the reader.

During Production

When production on a contract basis extends over several accounting periods revenue may be recognised for the part of the contract completed each period. This is known as the percentage-of-completion method of recognising revenue. Under this method, if a job is half complete at the end of an accounting period, half of the total contract price is recognised as revenue for the period. The expenses of bringing the job to that stage of completion are matched with those revenues to determine net profit for the period. The advantage of this method is that profit is recognised periodically rather than irregularly when the entire job is completed. It may thus provide a better measure of current economic activity than shown by the completed contract method. The percentage-of-completion method is widely accepted as a production basis of revenue and expense recognition that attempts to achieve the goal of accrual accounting—namely to report the effects of transactions and other events in the period in which they occur.

The problem with the percentage-of-completion method is that it is subject to the risk of error in estimating the percentage of contract performance completed and the future costs that need to be incurred to complete a contract. In the construction industry, unlike many other industries, it is often necessary to set prices during the bidding or negotiating stage, before product costs can be determined. IAS 11 (1979) states that:

'The percentage-of-completion method may be used only if the outcome of the contract can be reliably estimated. In the case of fixed price contracts, this degree of reliability would be provided only if all the following conditions are satisfied:

(*a*) Total contract revenues to be received can be reliably estimated.

(b) Both the costs to complete the contract and the stage of contract performance completed at the reporting date can be reliably estimated.
(c) The costs attributable to the contract can be clearly identified so that actual experience can be compared with prior estimates.

In the case of cost-plus contracts, this degree of reliability would be provided only if both the following conditions are satisfied:

(a) The costs attributable to the contract can be clearly identified, and
(b) Costs other than those that will be specifically reimbursable under the contract can be reliably estimated.

In the UK, SSAP 9, *Stocks and Work in Progress*, sets out the standard accounting practice applicable to cases such as those considered in this section, and is discussed in Chapter 10.

At the Completion of Production

Businesses dealing in commodities which have ready markets and assured sales prices recognise revenue at the time goods are produced because the final sale is a mere formality in the earning process. Certain precious metals and farm commodities have established markets and sell for guaranteed prices. In these cases, production is viewed as the critical event which determines revenue.

When Reserves are Discovered

Given the ready marketability of discovered oil and gas reserves, the application of the realisation concept to accounting for oil and gas has been questioned in recent years. Critics of traditional accounting practice argue that the discovery of reserves is the critical event for a meaningful reporting of the assets and profit of oil and gas producers. Under the historical cost concept the capitalised acquisition, exploration and development costs associated with reserves are reported in the balance sheet. But these costs have little meaning, because they do not reflect the value of reserves. Similarly, the profit and loss account is deficient, because it is the discovery of reserves that gives rise to revenues. Unless additional reserves are acquired, there is a steady depletion of the reserve base, which implies that traditional accounting methods do not represent profit, but merely a conversion of oil and gas reserves already owned into inventories, debtors and cash. Therefore, unless the reserve base is maintained production only leads to the diminution of the enterprise's cash-generating ability.

In 1978 the SEC called for the development of a new approach to oil and gas accounting called reserve recognition accounting (RRA). Under RRA, the present value of expected net revenue from proved oil and gas reserves is recognised as an asset and as revenue when the reserves are discovered.

Subsequent increases or decreases in those assets are recognised when they occur. All acquisition and development costs are recognised as expenses when they are incurred. Thus, an enterprise's net profit is based in part on the net change in proven reserves. In FASB No. 19 (1977), the Board rejected RRA on the grounds that it is too subjective to be used for accounting purposes. In criticising RRA the Board observed that:

> Measurements of discovery value require estimates of
> (*a*) the quantity of reserves,
> (*b*) the amount and timing of costs to develop the reserves,
> (*c*) the timing of production of the reserves,
> (*d*) the production costs and income taxes,
> (*e*) selling prices and,
> (*f*) (for some valuation methods), appropriate discount rates that reflect both an interest element and a risk factor.

In reply to this criticism of RRA, one may say that they are some of the same estimates the analyst uses to assess risk and credit worthiness when companies in the extractive industry are seeking capital funds. The estimation of such things is difficult for the outsider and only management are in a position to estimate values with any high degree of accuracy.

In order to restrict the many subjective judgements inherent in RRA the use of standard assumptions is generally favoured as providing a comparative measure of the worth of reserves. This is reflected in a US Exposure Draft (1982) which uses the title '*Standardized measure of discounted future net cash flows relating to proved oil and gas reserves*'.

Expense Recognition

Earlier we defined expenses as outflows of cash or other assets, or increases in liabilities. Assets are economic resources for which there is an expectation of future benefits. Expenses are economic resources whose expectation of future benefits have been exhausted. In expense recognition the fundamental problem is to segregate the stream of incurred costs between those which represent the exhaustion of future expected benefits and those which are carried forward as assets. Practical measurement difficulties and consistency of treatment over time are important factors in determining expense recognition.

Expense recognition may be governed by (APB Statement No. 4, 1970):

1. Associating causes and effect
2. Systematic and rational allocation
3. Immediate recognition

Associating Cause and Effect

The argument for using physical or causal relationships as allocation bases for overcoming the interaction problem has already been made. An example of a physical relationship involves the computation of variable product costs, which can be directly associated with the manufacture of specific products and are capitalised as assets and charged as expenses in the period in which the goods manufactured are sold. However, even for costs that can be matched against revenues because they result directly or jointly from the same transaction, there may be problems involving allocation. For example, inventory cost-flow assumptions involve allocation assumptions: both LIFO and FIFO are considered systematic and rational methods of allocating inventory costs over time.

Systematic and Rational Allocation

In the absence of a direct means of associating cause and effect, costs are associated with specific accounting periods as expenses on the basis of an attempt to allocate costs in a systematic and rational manner among the periods in which benefits are provided. A systematic and rational pattern of expense recognition always involves assumptions about the benefits that will be received as well as the costs associated with these benefits. The depreciation of fixed assets and the amortisation of intangible assets are examples which involve this method of expense recognition. In order to match fixed asset costs with revenue in each period, some accountants favour relating the annual depreciation charge in some systematic manner to the pattern of revenues. But for most firms many factors interact in generating output, it is not easy to isolate the revenue from one given asset. In these cases, expense and revenue should be regarded as being independent. Expenses should be related to causal factors where they can be identified so that the resulting computations are more in keeping with the economic reality which accounting is assumed to reflect. For example, the allocation of individual asset costs to time periods may not only reflect economic reality, but may also overcome the interaction problem. This does not of course, solve the arbitrary nature of the allocation process. As we saw earlier in this chapter, a measurement method is said to be arbitrary if it cannot be defended logically and conclusively against all alternative methods. By their very nature, allocations involve subjective judgements.

Immediate Recognition

Some costs are charged to expenses in the current accounting period because:

1. Costs incurred during the period provide no discernible future benefits.
2. Costs recorded as assets in prior periods no longer provide discernible benefits.

It will be appreciated that some benefit to the future can be inferred as likely to result from almost any kind of business expenditure, otherwise it would not be incurred. However, it is not always possible to identify the benefits resulting from the expenditure. Future benefits may be unquantifiable as to time duration, or amount, or both. For example, the existence of a long-range planning department will undoubtedly benefit an enterprise. But in the absence of a cause and effect relationship, or a basis for systematically allocating the costs of this department to further periods, the expense would be recognised during the current periods.

Evaluation of Recognition Criteria

The guidelines for recognising revenue and expenses are often criticised for emphasising objectivity and prudence rather than relevance to users. Ijiri (1980) considers the role of qualitative characteristics in revenue recognition for contractual commitments where a sufficient period of time elapses between the initiation of a contract and subsequent performance under the contract. As a general rule for revenue recognition, Ijiri believes that relevance, completeness and comparability are factors that support earlier recognition and that costliness, verifiability and consistency support later recognition.

As we saw at the beginning of this chapter, the conventional approach views recognition and realisation as occurring simultaneously. These concepts provide a means of analysing and reporting uncertainty. Weetman (1982) suggests that dual uncertainty levels could be introduced if the two concepts were separated. One could then recognise an external event in the accounts earlier than is presently done, when the uncertainty level is still relatively high. Realisation would be deferred, as at present, until a somewhat lower uncertainty level is achieved (AAA, 1974).

The guidelines provided for expense recognition give less guidance to the accountant than those provided for revenue recognition and, therefore, are less reliable. This position is summarised by Jaenicke (1981) as follows:

> Revenue recognition principles generally specify how much revenue should be recognised at the same time that they specify when revenue should be recognised, e.g., recognition on the instalment basis defines the amount of revenue recognition each period i.e., the amount of cash received. Such is not the case with expenses. Principles can specify that the service potential of an asset should be allocated over its future benefit. But unless those principles also provide a means for determining how the asset releases its service potential, they provide little practical guidance.

QUESTIONS

1. Differentiate between recognition and realisation.
2. Why has the matching concept attracted criticism? Should it be retained?
3. What guidelines have been provided for recognising revenue?
4. Why is time of sale the most common point for revenue recognition? Should a sale with right of return be treated as a sale in the accounts?
5. Is time of cash collection an acceptable point for recognising revenue?
6. Evaluate the percentage-of-completion method of recognising revenue.
7. Under what circumstances is it appropriate to recognise revenue at the point of production?
8. Evaluate reserve recognition accounting for oil and gas.
9. Differentiate between the following methods of recognising expenses:
   (*a*) Associating cause and effect
   (*b*) Systematic and rational allocation
   (*c*) Immediate recognition.

REFERENCES

Accounting Principles Board, *Statement of Accounting Principles, No. 4, 1970.*
Accounting Standards Committee, *Accounting for Research and Development*, December 1977.
Accounting Standards Committee, *Stocks and Work in Progress*, May 1975.
American Accounting Association, 'Report of the 1972/73 Committee on Concepts and Standards—External Reporting', *The Accounting Review*, Supplement to Vol. 49, 1974.
Financial Accounting Standards Board, Statement No. 19, *Financial Accounting and Reporting by Oil and Gas Producing Companies*, December, 1977.
Financial Accounting Board, Concepts Statement No. 3, *Elements of Financial Statements of Business Enterprises*, 1980.
Financial Accounting Standards Board, Statement No. 48, *Revenue Recognition when Right of Return Exists*, 1981.
Financial Accounting Standards Board, Statement of Financial Accounting Concepts 5, *Recognition and Measurement in Financial Statements of Business Enterprises*, Stamford, 1985.
Himmel, S., 'Financial Allocations Justified', *C.A. Magazine*, October, 1981.
Ijiri, Y., *Recognition of Contractual Rights and Obligations*, FASB, 1980.
International Accounting Standards Committee, Statement No. 11, *Accounting for Construction Contracts*, March, 1979.
International Accounting Standards Committee, Statement No. 18, *Revenue Recognition*, 1983.
Jaenicke, H. R., *Survey of Present Practices in Recognising Revenues, Expenses, Gains and Losses*, FASB, 1981.
Liao, S. S., 'The Matching Concept and Cost Allocation', *Accounting and Business Research*, Summer 1979.

Myers, J. H., 'The Critical Event and the Recognition of Net Profit', *The Accounting Review*, October 1959.

Scott, R. A. and Scott, R. K., 'Instalment Accounting: Is it Consistent?', *Journal of Accountancy*, November, 1979.

Shank, J. H., 'Income Determination under Uncertainty: An Application of Markov Chains', *The Accounting Review*, April, 1971.

Skinner, R., 'Accounting for a Simplified Firm—The Search for Common Ground' in Sterling R. R. and Thomas A. L., (eds.), *Accounting for a Simplified Firm Owning Depreciable Assets*, Scholars Book Company, 1979.

Sprouse, R. T., *Foundations of Accounting Theory*, University of Florida Press, 1971.

Thomas, A. L., 'The Allocation Problem: Part Two', *Studies in Accounting Research No. 9*, American Accounting Association, 1974.

Thomas, A. L., 'Why Financial Allocations Can't be Justified', *C.A. Magazine*, April 1982.

Weetman, P., 'Accounting for Value Companies—The Barrier of Realisation', *Accountant's Magazine*, October, 1980.

Weetman, P., 'The Realisation Concept: A Principle or an Excuse?' *The Accountant's Magazine*, April, 1982.

CHAPTER 8

Accounting for price level changes

Chapter 6 considered conceptual problems inherent in the income approach. We saw how different measures of income may be required for different purposes. We also noted how each of the various methods of measuring income resulted from comparisons of capital value at different times and from the application of different concepts of capital maintenance. The four concepts of capital maintenance may be divided into those which adopt a proprietary viewpoint (money value, purchasing power adjusted money value, and real value), and those adopting an entity viewpoint (operating capability). The objective that income should be measured whilst an entity maintains its operating capability has wide support, although different definitions of operating capability have been proposed (Tweedie, 1979).

In this chapter, we discuss the extant proposals by standard setting bodies in the UK, USA, Australia, and New Zealand for implementing the income concepts considered in Chapter 6 in respect of accounting for price level changes. These proposals remain tentative in nature. For example, SSAP16 on current cost accounting was introduced in the UK in 1980 with the intention of review after three years while SFAS33, issued in 1979, was regarded by the FASB as 'experimental'. Recent developments in the UK have thrown SSAP16 back into the melting pot.

The Development of Inflation Accounting in the UK

SSAP16 and with it the adoption of current cost accounting was the result of an extended debate on inflation accounting. Table 8.1 indentifies some of the main events in this debate.

Contemporary interest in accounting for inflation was stimulated by the

Table 8.1.   History of UK proposals on inflation accounting

1971	Publication of a discussion paper on Accounting for Inflation by the ASC
1973	Publication of ED8 *Accounting for Changes in the Purchasing Power of Money*
1973	UK Government establishes the Inflation Accounting Committee (Sandilands Committee)
1974	Publication of Provisional SSAP7 *Accounting for Changes in the Purchasing Power of Money*
1975	Publication of *Report of the Inflation Accounting Committee*
1976	Inflation Accounting Steering Group (IASG) established to prepare a draft accounting standard on CCA
1976	Publication of ED18
1977	Rejection of current cost accounting by the membership of the ICAEW
1977	Publication of *Inflation Accounting—Interim Recommendation* (Hyde Guidelines)
1979	Publication of ED24 *Current Cost Accounting*
1980	Publication of SSAP16 *Current Cost Accounting*
1981	Companies Act 1981 introduces modified historical cost and current cost as permissible valuation bases
1983	ASC begins review of SSAP16
1984	Publication of Statement of Intent on SSAP16
1984	Publication of ICAEW—sponsored research into CCA
1984	Publication of ED35, *Accounting for Changing Prices*
1984	Publication of SOI on ED35
1985	Withdrawal of ED35 and suspension of mandatory status of SSAP16

accelerating rates of inflation experienced in the late 1960s and early 1970s. Their resulting effects, emphasised by high interest rates and credit restrictions, were reduced company profitability and liquidity problems.

The ASC's early proposals contained in ED8 were for inflation accounts supplementary to historical-cost accounts based upon changes-in-purchasing-power (CPP) principles. A full standard did not emerge from this exposure draft. Instead a standard was issued, again based upon CPP, which, because of its uniquely provisional character, requested rather than required compliance by preparers. Events overtook the ASC in the form of the Sandilands Committee, set up to inquire into inflation accounting. The Committee's report rejected CPP in favour of current cost accounting (CCA) and the ASC, responding to the Sandilands proposals, set up the Inflation Accounting Steering Group (IASG). The IASG was charged with putting the Sandilands proposals into effect. The result was ED18 which recommended CCA as the main medium for published financial statements and would have required a full CCA system. ED18 was widely and vigorously criticised for the revolutionary changes which many practitioners saw it introducing and it was subsequently rejected. The rejection of ED18 left a void, the bridging of which was entrusted to the Hyde Guidelines (after the chairman of the committee which drafted them). The Guidelines required supplementary CCA information turning upon a profit and loss account containing adjustments for current cost depreciation and cost of sales (concepts introduced by Sandilands) and an adjustment reflecting company financial structure (the gearing adjustment discussed more fully below). ED24, followed by SSAP16, built upon the Guidelines by requiring CCA balance sheet information and adding an adjustment for monetary working capital to the profit and loss account. As is emphasised by the foregoing, the progress to SSAP16 was lengthy and controversial (Westwick, 1980). The enshrinement of alternative valuation bases to historical cost in company law and moderation in inflation rates have not terminated the debate as the review of SSAP16 shows. The publication during 1984 of ED35 with proposals for modifications to SSAP16 provoked generally adverse comment and this, in part, stimulated the ASC to issue a second SOI before ED35's exposure period was over in an attempt to allay criticism. In the event the general tone of comment on ED35 by the end of its exposure remained unfavourable. The ASC's difficulties in formulating a revised standard were compounded by two further problems. The professional accountancy bodies displayed divergent views on ED35 The Irish Institute recommended the withdrawl of SSAP16 and its replacement by a SORP, a move which recognised the lack of consensus. In addition, the Association of Certified Accountants and the ICMA called for greater flexibility on inflation accounting methods. In June 1985 ED35 was withdrawn and the mandatory status of SSAP16 was suspended.

The four countries cited at the beginning of this chapter have produced broad similarities in the proposals made for accounting for price level changes. For instance, proposals for the treatment of stocks, cost of sales, fixed assets and depreciation are similar, but the treatment of monetary items in the profit and loss account is different in each country.

The standard-setting bodies in the UK, Australia and New Zealand have introduced current cost accounting systems in which the capital to be maintained is regarded as the operating capability provided by enterprise assets. Therefore, periodic profit is considered to be the total gain arising in a period which could be distributed in full whilst maintaining the operating capability in existence at the beginning of the period. The US proposals, on the other hand, adopt a more permissive view regarding capital maintenance and, moreover, require the disclosure of information on both a current-cost and general-purchasing-power basis. In the next section the proposals for current cost accounting in the UK, Australia and New Zealand are examined while in the final section the US proposals are considered.

Current Cost Accounting

The proposals discussed in this section are contained in SSAP16 for the UK (ASC, 1980); a proposed statement of Accounting Standard on Current Cost Accounting for Australia (Australian Accounting Research Foundation, 1981); and ED25 in New Zealand (New Zealand Accounting Research and Standards Board, 1981). After pointing out the similarities between the proposals we shall concentrate on SSAP16 and refer to the other documents as appropriate.

The main similarities between the three sets of proposals are as follows:

1. Current cost information may be published in addition to historical cost and should comprise a balance sheet and profit and loss account together with explanatory notes. Companies may also comply with SSAP16 by providing current cost information as the main financial reports with historical cost as supplementary.
2. The capital to be maintained by CCA is determined by the operating capability of the business as reflected in its existing resources.
3. The current costs of assets are to be determined on the lower of net replacement cost or recoverable amount. SSAP16 explicitly states that amounts are to represent value to the business (equivalent to deprival value, or the loss in value if the business were deprived of the item). While the Australian proposals do not specifically mention this requirement, their practical implications are similar in respect to the results obtained by applying the UK concept.
4. The results of any one period are determined by matching the revenue of the period with the current cost of producing that revenue. Therefore, the approach does not depart from that discussed in Chapter 2.
5. In the balance sheet the resources of the entity are stated at their value to the business at the balance sheet date.

There are two areas where differences do occur between the three proposals. The first relates to the treatment of monetary assets and liabilities. These are items (like debtors and creditors), whose value is fixed by law or contract, as opposed to non-monetary items (like stock or fixed assets), whose value may change. The second concerns differences in the focus of CCA profit as between the entity and proprietary views considered in Chapter 6.

Current Cost Profit in SSAP16

Two concepts of current cost profit are used in SSAP16. One is operating profit and the other profit attributable to shareholders. Current cost operating profit is obtained from historical cost profit before interest by applying three current cost adjustments. Profit attributable to shareholders results from the deduction of the gearing adjustment net of interest, thus:

	£	£
Historical cost profit before interest		X
Current cost operating adjustments:		
Cost of sales	X	
Depreciation	X	
Monetary working capital	X	(X)
Current cost operating profit		X
Gearing adjustment	X	
Interest	(X)	X (X)
Current cost profit attributable to shareholders		X

Current Cost Balance Sheet

According to SSAP16 non-monetary items are to be included at their value to the business. Following the discussion in Chapter 6, value to the business is associated with deprival value and may be determined by the criteria we examined. SSAP16 introduces the notion of 'recoverable amount' to refer to value to the business. Monetary items are entered at their historical cost values. Included in shareholders funds are two types of reserves: retained current cost profits (which are distributable), and the current cost reserve (which is not distributable). The current cost reserve contains the cost of sales, monetary working capital and gearing adjustments, and revaluation surpluses on fixed assets and stock.

Cost of Sales Adjustment (COSA)

The COSA refers to the difference between the value to the business of stock consumed during the period and the cost of stock charged in computing historical cost profit. Assuming, as is likely, that replacement cost represents value to the business, it may be calculated by identifying and revaluing individual items, by using current standard costs (provided that they approximate to current replacement cost), or by the application of appropriate specific indices to stocks for the average holding period between the date of acquisition and the accounting date.

COSAs will generally be calculated most easily using the averaging method. Averaging seeks to isolate the price and volume components in the movement between opening and closing stock values. Consider the following:

Example 8.1:

A Limited had historical cost values for stock as follows:

	£000
Closing (31 December 01)	2,240
Opening (1 January 01)	1,792

Stock is purchased during the last three months of each year and the specific index for stock items stood as follows:

30.09.00	194
31.12.00	206
30.09.01	236
31.12.01	244

Current cost of sales is calculated by revaluing opening and closing stock to the average index for the year, taking as their base value the index at the mid-point in their respective stock cycle (mid-November in each case). Thus COSA is given by:

	Historical cost £000				Average current cost £000
Closing	2,240	×	$\dfrac{225}{\frac{1}{2}(244+236)}$	=	2,100
Opening	1,792	×	$\dfrac{225}{\frac{1}{2}(194+206)}$	=	2,016
Movement	448				84

Since the historical cost and current cost values of purchases are taken to be the same, they cancel out and the COSA is the difference between the historical cost and current cost movement on stock:

$$COSA = £(84,000 - 448,000) = £364,000$$

The current cost profit and loss account is debited with £364,000.

Depreciation Adjustment

Accepted accounting principles for depreciation apply equally in current cost accounting. In principle current cost depreciation aims to charge in each accounting period the proportion of the current value to the business of a fixed asset consumed in the period. Thus, the depreciation adjustment reflects the difference between depreciation calculated on a current value to the business basis and depreciation charged to the historical cost profit.

As with stock, value to the business is determined by reference to deprival value. If we assume that net replacement cost reflects value to the business, this is determined from gross replacement cost which in turn is given by either the actual costs of similar assets, professional valuation, or specific price indices. However calculated, replacement cost should represent the value of an asset which is the modern equivalent of that being valued. Moreover, in calculating current cost depreciation it is required that a realistic estimate of useful life be used.

Example 8.2:

A company purchased machinery for £100,000 on 1 January X0. The assets were realistically estimated to have a useful life of ten years at the outset. Depreciation is calculated on a straight-line basis. The following indices apply to the current replacement costs of the machinery:

1 January X0	200
31 December X0	240
31 December X1	300
Average for X1	280

The current cost accounting entries for plant for the year ended 31 December 19X1 are obtained as follows:

	Historical Cost	Depreciation *(£000s)*	Net
Opening (1 January X1)	100	(10)	90
Revaluation surplus	20	(2)	18
Current cost (1 January X1) $\frac{(240)}{(200)}$	120 $\frac{(240)}{(200)}$	12 $\frac{(240)}{(200)}$	108

Historical cost depreciation for the year is £10,000.
Current cost depreciation may be calculated in three ways:

(*i*)   On indexed closing gross replacement cost (GRC) as proposed by Sandilands. This is applicable in the first year of preparing current cost accounts.

(*ii*)   On average indexed GRC.

(*iii*)   On the average of opening and closing indexed GRC.

These methods would give depreciation adjustments thus:

(*i*)   On closing GRC

Opening GRC		*Ratio of indices*		*Closing GRC*
£120,000	×	$\frac{300}{240}$	=	£150,000

Depreciation at 10 per cent is £15,000
Depreciation adjustment is £(15,000−10,000)=£5,000

(*ii*) On average indexed GRC
This method takes into account the timing of price changes during the year and satisfies matching requirements more closely.

Opening GRC		*Ratio of indices*		*Average GRC*
£120,000	×	$\dfrac{280}{240}$	=	£140,000

Depreciation at 10 per cent is £14,000
Depreciation adjustment is £(14,000−10,000)=£4,000

(*iii*) On Average of Opening and Closing GRC
This approximates to method (*ii*) unless there have been irregular movements in prices during the year.
Average GRC is £(120,000+150,000)/2=£135,000
Depreciation at 10 per cent is £13,500
Depreciation adjustment is £(13,500−10,000)=£3,500

In case (*i*) the current cost depreciation charge reflects the replacement cost at the balance sheet date, but cases (*ii*) and (*iii*) do not. They fall behind by £1,000 and £1,500 respectively. This represents a backlog of underprovided depreciation arising because the most recent index is not used. In fact this problem of backlog depreciation arises in case (*i*) as depreciation provided in early years falls behind current requirements. If we assume that the index stands at 350 on 31 December X2, by then the position would be:

Year end	*GRC at year end*	*CC deprecia- tion for year*	*Accumulated CC deprecia- tion charged*	*Accumulated CC deprecia- tion at current cost*	*Backlog (5−4)*
31 December X0	120	12	12	12	—
31 December X1	150	15	27	30	3
31 December X2	175	17.5	44.5	52.5	8

This backlog builds up in each year. However, if accumulated depreciation is revalued to current cost in addition to the GRC, this backlog is made good. Both revalued depreciation and the revaluation surplus due to revaluing GRC are taken to the current cost reserve. Backlog depreciation represents the effect of changing prices on past capital consumption and does not reflect current consumption and, therefore, it is not appropriate to match it against current revenues to obtain profit. Although depreciation charges create funds which may be re-invested in replacement assets, depreciation is not a replacement fund and asset replacement and its financing remains a financial management decision.

For the balance sheet at 31 December X1, the following is computed:

	Cost	£000s Depreciation	Net
Opening (1 January X1)	120	12	108
Revaluation	30	$(3)^4$	27^5
	150^1	$(15)^2$	135^3
Charge to current cost profit and loss account		$(14)^6$	
		(29)	
Backlog depreciation for the year		$(1)^5$	
Closing (31 December X1)	150	30^7	120

NOTES
1. £120,000 × $\dfrac{(300)}{(240)}$
2. £12,000 × $\dfrac{(300)}{(240)}$
3. £108,000 × $\dfrac{(300)}{(240)}$
4. Backlog depreciation for the year
5. Transferred to current cost reserve
6. On average indexed cost
7. Required balance on accumulated depreciation

The Monetary Working Capital Adjustment (MWCA)

The Sandilands Committee restricted their current cost valuation adjustments to the non-monetary fixed assets and stock. Operating capability was therefore defined as 'the physical assets possessed by the company, so that profit would be the amount that could be distributed after making sufficient provision to replace the physical assets held by the company as they are consumed or wear out' (Sandilands, 1975). The Sandilands approach excludes all monetary assets and liabilities from the inflation accounting framework. The report argues that since such assets and liabilities are designated in fixed monetary units they are of necessity expressed in terms of their value to the business. Secondly, assets are shown in the balance sheet at their value to the business, which is wholly expressed in terms of replacement cost. Thirdly, operating income results from matching the proceeds of sale with the cost of replacing the goods sold at the date of sale. Similarly, depreciation charges are calculated to reflect the current cost of the assets consumed during the period. No adjustment is required for other expenses for the period because such costs are already expressed in terms of the current prices of the goods or services to which they relate. This approach was widely criticised. A broader view of operating capability requires adjustments to total capital funds which includes losses and gains on net monetary items. Gynther (1976) illustrates the rationale of such adjustments with the aid of the following diagram:

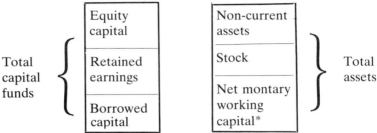

* Cash+Debtors−Creditors

This diagram shows adjustments are necessary to total assets if total capital funds are to be maintained. Working capital adjustments are just as necessary as those to cost of sales and depreciation. Holding monetary assets during a period of inflation will reduce cash available for distribution; holding monetary liabilities will increase this amount.

When prices are rising capital held in the form of cash is not maintained intact because it declines in terms of the assets (e.g. stock), which it could be used to purchase. This real loss should be reflected in the profit and loss account. Similarly, a real loss is made on debtors which, although appearing in the balance sheet in monetary terms, may be regarded as goods on loan to customers until paid for. Debtors and stock values increase in monetary terms during inflation and the increases must be financed, thereby draining the resources of the business. This will be reduced to the extent that trade creditors provide financing. Holding monetary liabilities such as trade credit will generate gains during inflation. Hence, the net financing needs associated with working capital appears to be a useful concept.

Where a business has net monetary assets, a current cost adjustment reflecting the capital maintenance needs for such items will represent a debit to profit and loss in addition to those for COSA and depreciation. Such a treatment of fixed assets, stock and net monetary assets would seem to be normal for a business. However, some businesses—for example, supermarkets—are likely to have a surplus of trade creditors over trade debtors since they will buy on credit and sell for cash. For such a business a MWCA may be treated as a credit to profit and loss. In effect, trade creditors finance stock and the MWCA serves to cancel the COSA. Alternatively a bank's operating capability will be dominated by monetary assets (advances, liquid assets and investments) and monetary liabilities (deposits). The arguments put forward above in favour of a MWCA apply strongly. However, banks have no stock in trade in the sense of a manufacturing company and a COSA will be absent. MWCA is likely to be a debit to profit and loss. Omission of a MWCA is likely to introduce biases into the treatment of different types of business in CCA.

Both the UK and New Zealand proposals on CCA specify the computation of a MWCA. They differ from the Australian proposals in this respect. However, the Australian approach does include an adjustment which produces a similar result. This is achieved in two steps:

1. by recognising the net gain (loss) on holding all monetary assets and liabilities and,
2. by transferring to a reserve that portion of this net gain (loss) which arises from holding loan capital.

We illustrate this adjustment later in this chapter.

First, we consider the UK adjustment for MWC which is paralled by the New Zealand proposals. SSAP16 defines MWC as the aggregate of—

(*a*) trade debtors,
(*b*) inventories not subject to a COSA less
(*c*) trade creditors,

insofar as they arise from the day-to-day operating activities of the business as distinct from transactions of a capital nature. Where the omission of cash floats and that part of bank balances or overdrafts arising from fluctuations in the volume of inventory, trade debtors and creditors can be shown to be misleading when calculating current cost profit, they may also be included.

As noted above, the MWCA supplements the COSA. The relationship between the MWCA made in respect of trade debtors and trade creditors and the COSA is as follows:

(*a*) when sales are made on credit the business has to finance the changes in its input prices until the sales result in a receipt of cash. The part of the MWCA related to trade debtors, in effect, extends the COSA to allow for this; and
(*b*) conversely, when materials and services are purchased from suppliers who offer trade credit, price changes are financed by the supplier during the credit period. To this extent extra funds do not have to be found by the business and this reduces the need for a COSA and in some cases for a MWCA on debtors. The part of the MWCA related to trade creditors reflects this reduction.

Owing to the close relationship between the two adjustments the method used to compute the MWCA should be compatible with that used to compute the COSA. For example, the sales of finished goods give rise to trade debtors. Thus, other things being equal, changes in the amount of finance required to support the increased level of trade debtors due to inflation will tend to be proportional to changes in the cost of goods finished. Consequently, the change in the index of finished goods prices may be used to calculate that part of MWC which relates to supporting trade debtors. Equally, since the purchase of raw materials by a manufacturing company gives rise to trade creditors, the change in the index of raw material prices is used to calculate that part of the monetary working capital which relates to trade creditors. In order to simplify the computations our example assumes that changes in the prices of sales and cost of sales are represented by the same index.

The MWCA is computed as follows:

Example 8.3:

	Opening £	Closing £
Debtors	0	5,000
Cash	1,500	4,000
	1,500	9,000
Creditors	0	4,000
Monetary working capital	1,500	5,000

Index numbers

Opening	100
Average	112
Closing	124

The increase in monetary working capital during the accounting period at average current cost is:

$$\left\{ £5{,}000 \times \frac{112}{124} \right\} \text{ less } \left\{ £1{,}500 \times \frac{112}{100} \right\} = £2{,}836$$

The MWCA is:

Increase at historical cost	£3,500
less	
Increase at average current cost	£2,836
MWCA	£664

Therefore, a charge of £664 is made. Of the increase of £3,500 at historical cost £664 was due to price increases and the remainder, £2,836 was due to an increase in volume.

Two problems which have created controversy in implementing the MWCA relate to the definition of MWC and the appropriate index to attach. The first problem is that of determining which monetary assets and liabilities are to be included in the adjustment. For example, how do we classify bank credit, such as overdraft, which is formally short-term but which is often hard-core (i.e., medium-term), borrowing? Management is required to answer such questions as 'what proportion of bank credit is short-term?' and to give unbiased answers. Some argue that identification can be achieved only by an arbitrary segregation of monetary assets and liabilities. The second problem is concerned with the choice between general or specific indices. According to one viewpoint the use of specific indices 'appears to imply that the firm is locked into a particular pattern of financing its purchase or sales whereas it is more likely that such decisions will depend, among other things on the value of money' (Wright and Papps, 1980). Many firms rearrange holdings of monetary items in the light of changing circumstances, a condition which suggests that a general index may be more appropriate. The accounting standards which have proposed a MWCA in the UK and New Zealand dismiss the 'general level of prices' approach as being inconsistent with the objective of maintaining the operating capability of the entity. According to the New Zealand Richardson Committee Report, 'the effects of inflation are specific in relation to monetary assets just as they are to non-monetary assets . . . we do not accept that because there has been a change in the general purchasing power of money this will necessarily lead to a similar change in the value to a particular enterprise of its monetary assets' (1976).

The Gearing Adjustment

The UK's SSAP16 and New Zealand proposals for a gearing adjustment mark a clear departure from the Australian system. The gearing adjustment seeks to recognise that, in a period of rising prices, the existence of borrowing provides a benefit to shareholders in that assets financed by borrowing do not need maintenance as the business has not used its own funds in obtaining these resources and, therefore, has nothing to maintain.

The purpose of the SSAP16 gearing adjustment is to allocate equitably the current cost adjustments in order that the full burden should not fall on ordinary shareholders where they themselves have not financed the entire assets in respect of which the adjustments are made. Therefore, a gearing adjustment is necessary where a proportion of the assets of the business is financed by borrowing. SSAP16 defines net borrowing 'as the amount by which liabilities (defined below [1]) exceed assets (defined below [2]):

1. the aggregate of all liabilities and provisions (including convertible debentures and deferred tax but excluding dividends) other than those included within monetary working capital,
2. the aggregate of all current assets other than those that are subject to a cost of sales adjustment and those that are included within monetary working capital' (ASC, 1980).

The gearing adjustment results from the application of the gearing proportion to the net adjustments made in converting the historical cost profit to current cost profit. The gearing proportion is the relationship between net borrowing (L) and the average ordinary shareholders' interest obtained from the opening and closing balance sheets (S), as follows:

Gearing proportion $\dfrac{L}{L+S}$

Three computations are involved in deriving the gearing adjustment:

(*i*)   computation of shareholders' interest and net borrowing
(*ii*) computation of the gearing proportion
(*iii*) application of the gearing proportion to the sum of the current cost operating adjustments.

These are considered in the following example.

Example 8.4:

Current Cost Balance Sheets

	19X0 £	19X1 £
Fixed Assets	215,548	241,341
Current Assets:		
Stock	44,366	57,000
Debtors	35,200	37,500
	79,566	94,500
Current liabilities		
Dividend (proposed)	4,800	6,250
Taxation	8,000	6,660

Creditors	22,000	27,083
Overdraft	20,000	16,660
	54,800	56,653

Net current assets	24,766	37,847
	240,314	279,188

Share captial	40,000	40,000
Current cost reserve	116,714	148,155
Retained profit	63,600	71,033
Loan stock	20,000	20,000
	240,314	279,188

Above are the current cost balance sheets for a company for the years ended 31 December X0 and X1. During the year to 31 December X1 the current cost operating adjustments were as follows:

	£
Depreciation	15,819
COSA	4,249
MWCA	1,116
Total	21,184

The company's overdraft has not met the criterion for inclusion in MWC. The gearing proportion to be applied to the total of operating adjustments is based upon the average of the opening and closing values of net borrowing and shareholders' interest. Net borrowing comprises the excess of all liabilities and provisions not included in MWC or shareholders' interest (loan stock, taxation and overdraft), over current assets not subject to COSA or included in MWC (in this example, none), thus:

	19X0 £		19X1 £
Loan stock	20,000		20,000
Taxation	8,000		6,660
Overdraft	20,000		16,660
	48,000		43,320
Average		£ 45,660	

Shareholders' interest, similarly averaged is:

	19X0 £	19X1 £
Share capital	40,000	40,000
Current cost reserve	116,714	148,155
Retained profit	63,600	71,033
	220,314	259,188

Average   £239,751

The gearing proportion for 19X1 is thus:

$$\frac{£45,660}{£(239,751+45,660)} = 0.160$$

and the gearing adjustment:

$$£21,184 \times 0.160 = £3,389$$

The gearing adjustment is credited to the current cost profit and loss account and debited to the current cost reserve. This latter requirement makes the foregoing example rather artificial since shareholders' interest includes the current cost reserve and cannot, therefore, be determined until the gearing adjustment is known. An alternative method which avoids this difficulty is to calculate the denominator of the gearing proportion by adding back to operating assets the equity and net borrowing items included in current liabilities (not included in MWC), thus:

	19X0 £	19X1 £
Net operating assets	240,314	279,188
Plus:		
Dividend	4,800	6,250
Taxation	8,000	6,660
Overdraft	20,000	16,660
	273,114	308,758

Average   £290,936

This gives a gearing proportion of:

$$\frac{£45,660}{£290,936} = 0.157$$

and a gearing adjustment as before.

The gearing adjustment is central to the dispute over whether an entity or proprietary view is appropriate for companies. As we have noted an entity view regards the company as an entity in itself and both shareholders and creditors are regarded as being outside the company. Both provide finance for the company and require to be compensated, but no distinction has to be made between their separate interests. On a proprietary view, the company belongs to the shareholders. Those who support the entity view argue that gains on borrowing should not be included in income because the gain is not represented by cash inflows. Therefore, distribution of the gain may impair the basic assets of the company. Some who support the proprietary view criticise SSAP16's gearing adjustment on the grounds that it does not reflect the full impact of inflation on monetary items. Instead, the benefits from net borrowings are associated with the other current cost adjustments and are not determined in their own right. According to this viewpoint, the COSA and depreciation adjustment arising in a particular period are unrelated to the benefit arising to shareholders from the existence of creditors.

The Australian proposals

We now consider how the Australian proposals have been designed to meet the controversial nature of the issues discussed in the previous paragraph. These proposals

(*i*)   reflect the full impact of inflation on monetary items,
(*ii*) distinguish clearly between entity and proprietary income.

The Australian proposals require the calculation of a loss or gain on all monetary items including loan capital, using a general price index.

Example 8.5:

The following current cost information applies to a company:

	£
Shareholders' interest at 1 January X1	10,000
Shareholders' interest 31 December X1	12,153
Average shareholders' interest for the period	11,077
Average net borrowing for year ended 31 December X1	5,000
Unrealised revaluation surpluses on fixed assets and investments	1,204
Operating adjustments for the period:	
Depreciation	100
COSA	207
MWCA	664

The following are extracts from the company's historical cost profit and loss account for the period:

	£
Profit before interest and tax	6,500
Depreciation	(2,000)
	4,500
Interest charges	(500)
	4,000
Taxation for the period	(2,000)
Profit after tax	2,000

A general price index stood as follows:

	£
1 January X1	100
31 December X1	124
Average for the period	112

According to the Australian proposals the net monetary items (average net borrowing for the year) would require an adjustment of:

$$£5,000 \times \frac{112}{100} = 5,600$$

	£
Less	5,000
Gain	600

The gain from holding net monetary liabilities may be offset against the loss on MWC of £664, giving a net loss of £64. The profit and loss account based upon the Australian proposals is given in Table 8.2 (page 184).

It will be noted that gains on loan capital are transferred out of the profit and loss account to a gain on loan capital reserve account. Therefore, these gains do not increase entity net profit, which is defined as 'the total gain, arising during a period, which can be distributed in full whilst still maintaining capital, in the sense of operating capability, at the level which existed at the beginning of the period.' The nature of the above profit and loss account enables a clear distinction to be made between gains to shareholders and gains to the firm.

The New Zealand Proposals

One criticism of SSAP16 involves the emphasis given to the prudence concept the gearing gain attributable to equity shareholders is limited to that proportion of the holding gains that have been charged as CCA adjustments to historical cost profits in the profit and loss account (i.e. the realised holding gains). Therefore, it is argued that the gearing ratio should be applied against the current cost reserve rather than the adjustments shown in the profit and loss account. This argument adopts the view that the increase in the current cost reserve attributable to the revaluation of assets represents real gains to the shareholders to the extent that such gains are financed by borrowed funds and should consequently be reflected in the profit attributable to shareholders. This view is adopted in the New Zealand proposals.

Using the same data as immediately above, the current cost reserve of the company would consist of:

	£	£
Unrealised revaluation surpluses on fixed assets and investments		1,204
Realised amounts equal to the cumulative total of the current cost adjustments:		
COSA	207	
Depreciation adjustment	100	
MWCA	664	971
		2,175

The gearing proportion is computed as that of SSAP16, thus:

$$\frac{£5,000}{£(11,077+5,000)} = 0.311$$

with a gearing adjustment of:

$$£2,175 \times 0.311 = £676$$

The gearing adjustment, according to SSAP16, would use the same gearing proportion, but would apply to the total of current cost operating adjustments thus:

	£
COSA	207
Depreciation adjustment	100
MWCA	664
	971

$$£971 \times 0.311 = £302$$

Comparison of profit and loss accounts

The current cost profit and loss accounts based upon the application of the proposals for the UK, Australia and New Zealand to the data of example 8.5 are shown in Table 8.2.

Table 8.2. Comparative profit and loss accounts

	UK		NZ	Australia		
	£		£			£
Historical cost profit before interest and tax	6,500		6,500	Historical cost profit before interest and tax		6,500
Less depreciation	(2,000)		(2,000)	*Less* depreciation		(2,000)
	4,500		4,500			4,500
				Less interest		(500)
						4,000
Less current cost adjustments:				*Less* current cost adjustments:		
COSA	207		207	COSA	207	
Depreciation	100		100	Depreciation	100	
MWCA	664	(971)	664	(971)	Loss of monetary items	64	(371)
Current cost operating profit		3,529		3,529	Entity profit before tax plus gain on loan capital		3,629
					Less transfer to gain on loan capital		
Gearing adjustment	302		676		reserve		(600)
Interest	(500)	(198)	(500)	176			
		3,331		3,705	Entity current cost profit before tax		3,029
Taxation		(2,000)		(2,000)	Taxation		(2,000)
Current cost profit attributable to shareholders		1,331		1,705	Entity current cost net profit		1,029

SSAP16 is similar to the Australian proposal in that the profit and loss accounts under both show a form of entity net profit and proprietorship net profit. However, the order in which they appear as between the body of the statement and the bottom line is reversed. Also, gearing gains under the Australian proposals are transferred from profit and loss to a reserve account. The UK gearing adjustment remains in the final net profit figure. A further difference applies to the treatment of interest. Under the Australian system interest is merely a deduction in arriving at the historical cost profit. The favoured presentation in the UK standard offsets interest against the gearing adjustment to show the net benefit arising to shareholders from borrowing, although an alternative presentation is available.

SSAP16 defines the resulting entity and proprietorship profit concepts as follows:

1. Current cost operating profit 'is the surplus arising from the ordinary activities of the business in the period after allowing for the impact of price changes on the funds needed to continue the existing business and maintain its operating capability, whether financed by share capital or borrowing. It is calculated before interest on net borrowing and taxation'.
2. Current cost profit attributable to shareholders 'is the surplus for the period after allowing for the impact of price changes on the funds needed to maintain their proportion of the operating capability'.

Both the UK and Australian proposals warn against the dangers of distributing gains from gearing as dividends. The Australian proposals state:

As gearing gains on loan capital do not increase entity net profit, distributions made to shareholders from the gearing gains reserve account constitute a reduction in the operating capability of the entity unless replaced by additional equity funds or loan capital.

SSAP16 says that

the current cost profit attributable to shareholders should not be assumed to measure the amount that can prudently be distributed. Although, the impact of price changes on the shareholders' interest in the net operating assets has been allowed for, other factors still need to be considered . . . such as capital expenditure plans, changes in the volume of working capital, the offset on funding requirements of changes in production methods and efficiency, liquidity and new financing arrangements.

Evaluation of SSAP16

A number of points of appraisal have emerged from our comparison of SSAP16 with the Australian and New Zealand proposals. In this section we consider some other questions which have been raised concerning the standard. SSAP16 is concerned to point out that other accounting standards, although specifically designed for historical cost accounts, apply to current cost accounts except, where a conflict exists between the two systems due to a conceptual difference. The implication is that SSAP16 represents a superior standard in such cases.

SSAP16 differs from other standards in that it is less permissive and more prescriptive on a number of points. For example, the guidance notes to the standard point out that in determining the GRC of an asset 'the objective is to make a realistic estimate of what it would now cost to acquire an asset which has the same service potential as that of the existing asset'. This refers to the concept of the modern equivalent asset for replacement purposes. Identification of such an asset may be problematical where technical progress takes place. The use of relative service potential may lead to counter-intuitive results in applying the standard as the following example shows.

Example 8.6:

A company operates an asset whose historical cost was £100,000. Its realistic useful life is four years and it is capable of producing 10,000 units of final product each year. The current version of the same asset costs £500,000 but produces 100,000 units each year. The depreciation adjustment is determined as follows. Historical cost depreciation, straight line, is £25,000 per annum. The GRC of the existing asset is derived from that of the new asset by reducing the latter's value in proportion to relative productive capacities, thus:

$$£500,000 \times \frac{10,000 \text{ units}}{100,000 \text{ units}} = £50,000$$

which gives a current cost depreciation charge of £12,500 with no change in useful life. The depreciation adjustment is £$(25,000-12,500)$=£12,500, which is credited to the profit and loss account to correct for the overprovision under historical cost. This treatment has been criticised on the grounds of imprudence and impracticality since the replacement output which is implied cannot be achieved.

Nobes and Cooke (1981) have pointed out that there are deficiencies in the guidance by SSAP16 on the revaluation of fixed assets and investments in subsidiaries and associated companies which, amongst other things, may allow scope for the manipulation of, and reduce the comparability of, financial statements. Further, they note the failure to deal with the problems posed by the inclusion in consolidated accounts of results which are not reported according to the requirements of SSAP16 (perhaps because the reporting companies are exempt from SSAP16, or as overseas subsidiaries, use the other methods).

As mentioned at the beginning of this chapter, SSAP16 was introduced with the prospect of a review after three years experience by users and preparers. The implementation of SSAP16 has been investigated on behalf of the ASC by the CCA Monitoring Working Party. In addition, an extensive programme of research has been undertaken into the usefulness of current cost accounting at the commission of the Research Board of the ICAEW.

The Monitoring Working Party recommended that SSAP16 be amended along the following lines:

1. The standard should require financial statements to show the effects of changing prices when they are material.
2. The standard should apply to all entities whose financial statements are intended to show a true and fair view.
3. The standard should permit different methods of calculating the effects of changing prices.
4. The standard should not require an adjusted balance sheet.
5. Where trend information is given the standard should require it to be adjusted by the Retail Price Index.
6. Information on the effects of changing prices should be incorporated in companies' main accounts.

Research into the usefulness of current cost information has concluded that certain types of information (e.g. current cost dividend cover) are used widely by certain users (sophisticated investors), and CCA is the main basis for performance evaluation for some entities (nationalised industries) (Carsberg and Page, 1984). Mixed evidence has been found about whether unexpected current cost information leads to changes in share prices, but CCA profit figures appear to be able to improve the explanation of share prices given by historical cost profits. Many preparers, it has been found, comply with SSAP16 from 'a sense of obligation', although preparation costs seem low. Although this research has been the subject of considerable controversy it has been interpreted in certain quarters as justification that CCA information should continue to be disclosed with limited exemptions where the concept of maintaining operating capability is not applicable.

At the end of its review process the ASC issued a Statement of Intent (SOI) on SSAP16 in March, 1984. The ASC concluded from evidence presented to it that information on the effects of changing prices is useful to users of financial statements and should be provided where

(*a*) the effects are material and,
(*b*) the usefulness of the information justifies its costs.

As an ultimate objective such information should be provided by all companies, irrespective of size or activity. The ASC acknowledge that this cannot be achieved in the short-term and propose that the basic methodology of SSAP16 apply to all publicly accountable companies regardless of size, except 'value-based companies' such as insurance companies and unit trusts. Such companies are already excluded from SSAP16.

Public accountability replaced size as the main criterion for the application of the standard and the ASC gave more main reasons for choosing the new criterion. First, the segregation of ownership and management in such companies. Secondly, a potential or actual capital market in their shares. Thirdly, the large number and range of users of accounts of other companies. Fourthly, the sophistication of many such users.

The SOI proposed the following:

1. Except where current cost accounts are adopted as the main accounts, the information should be given in notes in the accounts, not in separate accounts. This means that current cost information will form part of the company's statutory true and fair view, and compliance with the standard will be essential to a true and fair view.
2. The information to be required should include current cost adjustments for depreciation, cost of sales, MWC and gearing, the effect of these adjustments on the profit or loss for the year and the current cost of fixed assets.
3. Simplified methods for arriving at certain assets subject to valuation problems will be permitted.
4. Alternative methods are to be allowed for the calculation of the gearing adjustment (i) on the basis required by SSAP16 (ii) on a basis which would include unrealised holding gains (in addition to operating adjustments as in SSAP16), (iii) on a basis that reduces interest paid or received by an allowance for general inflation.

In July, 1984 and exposure draft, ED35 *Accounting for the Effects of Changing Prices*, was published and its proposals followed closely the intentions set out in the SOI referred to above. In doing so, the ASC maintained their position in the face of criticism that two of their proposals were inconsistent, namely, the inclusion of current cost information in 'true and fair view' disclosures and excluding certain categories of company from a requirement to disclose current cost information. The ASC took counsel's opinion, on this matter (further to that already taken on 'true and fair' more generally) and counsel reaffirmed their earlier opinion and emphasised the relevance of criteria of cost-effectiveness and expediency in the preparation of true and fair accounts, thereby supporting the exclusion of value-based companies from the requirement to disclose current cost information.

As noted above, the SOI which preceded ED35 proposed that simplified methods should be permitted to deal with practical valuation problems encountered under SSAP16. ED35 stated that these simplified methods would be dealt with in non-mandatory guidance notes accompanying the eventual standard, rather than in the standard itself. In an SOI issued in November 1984 the ASC set out some of the simplifications which it proposed to include in revised guidance notes to an inflation accounting standard. In issuing the SOI the ASC sought to stimulate (in their words) informed comment on the proposed standard. As noted above, this might be interpreted as an attempt to diffuse criticism of ED35. This view is strengthened by the observation in the SOI that the 'ASC recognises that there is widespread concern about the cost and complexity of current cost information and appreciates the importance of finding ways to make the information simple to produce'.

The main features of the proposed simplified approach were as follows:

(a) *Fixed assets and depreciation*: gross current cost and the associated depreciation adjustment may be calculated on the basis of the average age of principal categories of tangible fixed assets and by reference to suitable price indices for principal categories.

(b) *Stocks*: the current cost of stocks may be determined from the average age of all stocks and a single price index.

(c) *Working capital adjustment*: a working capital adjustment (combining the cost of sales and monetary working capital adjustments) may be determined by the averaging method and an appropriate price index (e.g. all-stocks index or general price index).

(d) *Gearing adjustment*: one of the three methods prescribed in ED35 should be used. Of these, the simplest will generally be the application of a general price index to net borrowings or net monetary assets (other than MWC).

(e) The methods described above are not intended to be prescriptive and companies may find it appropriate to adopt alternative simplifications appropriate to their circumstances. Companies should describe in the accounting policies note the approach they have adopted.

In June 1985 ED35 was withdrawn and the mandatory status of SSAP16 was suspended. The ASC announced that it intends to develop a new accounting standard on accounting for the effects of changing prices to replace SSAP16 '. . . in due course . . .'.

FASB Statement No. 33

In the background to the FASB's Exposure Draft its authors argued the case for the maintenance of the investor's purchasing power concept. FASB Statement No. 33, however, did not favour this concept as against that of maintaining operating capability. The statement considered that 'it should express no preference for either concept at this time and that enterprises should present information that would enable users to assess the amount of income under both concepts' in accordance with this the statement called for information which deals with both the effects of general inflation and changes in the price of certain specific types of assets. The statement argued that there are strong reasons to expect that both types of information will be useful and that further experimentation is required.

Specifically, major firms are required to report:

(*i*)   Income from continuing operations, adjusted for the effects of general inflation,

(*ii*)   the purchasing power gain or loss on net monetary items,

(*iii*)   income from continuing operations on a current cost basis,

(*iv*)   the current cost amounts of inventory and property, plant, and equipment at the end of the fiscal year,

(*v*)   increases or decreases in current cost amounts of inventory and property, plant and equipment, net of inflation.

Qualifying firms are also required to present a five-year summary of selected financial data, including information on income, sales and operating revenues, net assets, dividends per common share and market price per share. In the computation of net assets, only inventory and property, plant, and equipment need be adjusted for the effects of changing prices.

FASB Statement No. 33 calls for the disclosure of supplementary information on selected items rather than the publication of a complete income statement and balance sheet. This partial application of GPP accounting is intended to simplify the adjustment process by reporting only the items most frequently affected by inflation. The items disclosed should be measured in terms of the yearly average purchasing power using the *Consumer Price Index for Urban Consumers*. However, if a company chooses to disclose comprehensive GPP financial statements, rather than the minimum disclosures called for by FASB Statement No. 33, either yearly average or year-end purchasing power may be used. The use of the yearly average is a departure from the usual recommendations for implementing GPP accounting which suggest a year end index. This departure simplifies the computations of income from continuing operations in that revenue and expenses generally will reflect average purchasing power (except for cost of goods sold and depreciation), because revenues are usually earned and expenses usually incurred fairly evenly throughout the year.

The following is the format suggested by FASB Statement No. 33 for disclosure. Although the format uses both general and specific price information, it falls short of a general price-level adjusted CCA comprehensive approach.

	As reported in the primary statements £	Adjusted for general inflation £	Adjusted for changes in specific prices £
Net Sales and Operating Revenues	20,000	20,000	20,000
Cost of goods sold	13,500	13,673	13,707
Depreciation	2,000	2,120	2,100
Interest expense	500	500	500
Provision for taxation	2,000	2,000	2,000
Income from continuing operations	2,000	1,707	1,693
Gain on decline in purchasing power of net amounts owed		251	251
Increase in specific prices of stocks and fixed assets			1,204
Effect of increase in general price level			705
Excess of increase in specific prices over increase in the general price level			499

No supporting data or assumptions are provided for the above and it serves only to illustrate the form and content of FASB Statement No. 33. The concepts involved in each of the entries and the mechanics of calculation are contained in this chapter and in Chapter 6.

QUESTIONS

1. 'The Standard does not deal with the maintenance of financial capital in general purchasing power terms' (Statement of Standard Accounting Practice No. 16).

Required:

(a) What is the underlying concept of capital in SSAP16 *Current Cost Accounting*? Define any terms you use in your explanation.

(b) What voluntary disclosure does SSAP16 *Current Cost Accounting* suggest for reporting the impact of changes in general purchasing power on shareholders' equity interest? Explain whether you consider this to be necessary.

(Association of Certified Accountants)

2. SSAP16 *Current Cost Accounting* requires plant and machinery to be included in the Balance Sheet at its value to the business.

Required:

(a) Provide a definition of value to the business.

(b) An extract from the plant register of Tresilian Engineering is produced below:

Date of purchase	1 January 19X0
Description	Compressor
Cost	£10,000
Depreciation	25 per cent per annum straight line
Location	Workshop B
Supplier	Compress Limited

What additional information would you require about this asset before determining the amount to be included in a Current Cost Balance Sheet?

(c) What difficulties may arise as the result of rapid technological change when valuing plant and machinery under this valuation concept?

(Association of Certified Accountants)

3. (a) What is a holding gain? Explain the appropriate accounting treatment for such a gain.

(b) How does backlog depreciation arise?

(c) Provision for depreciation of fixed assets having a finite useful life should be made by allocating the cost (or revalued amount) less estimated residual values of the assets as fairly as possible to the periods expected to benefit from their use.

(Statement of Standard Accounting Practice No. 12)

To what extent do you consider that the replacement cost treatment of depreciation conforms to this intention?

(d) The following extract is taken from the historical cost balance sheet of Simpson Enterprises Limited.

	31 December 19X1 £000	31 December 19X2 £000
Plant and machinery at cost	200	300
Less aggregate depreciation	40	100
Net book value	160	200

The following facts are relevant:

(*i*)   Plant costing £200,000 was acquired on 1 January 19X1. The additional items were acquired on 1 January 19X2.

(*ii*)   No plant or machinery was sold or scrapped during 19X1 or 19X2.

(*iii*)   Of the year's depreciation written off in the 19X2 accounts, one-third is related to the items acquired on 1 January 19X2.

(*iv*)   Price index movements were as follows:

	General Price Index	Index of plant costs for the type of plant owned by Simpson
1 January 19X1	90	80
31 December 19X1	120	100
31 December 19X2	140	110

You are required to show the entries for plant and machinery in the final accounts of Simpson Enterprises Limited as at 31 December 19X1 and 19X2 on the assumption that the company used a system of replacement cost accounting making a charge for depreciation based on the relevant index at year end.

4. SSAP16 requires that three current cost adjustments should be made to the historical cost profit before interest and taxation, to arrive at a figure for current cost operating profit.

(*a*) Explain the reasons for the basic elements in the adjustments for:

(*i*)   cost of sales
(*ii*)   depreciation
(*iii*)   monetary working capital

(*b*) From the following data calculate the monetary working capital adjustment for Coe Limited:

	30 June 19X2 £	30 June 19X1 £
Per historical cost balance sheets		
Trade debtors	98,132	77,383
Trade creditors	77,072	66,313

Index numbers	*Finished goods*	*Raw materials*
At 30 June 19X1	134.6	136.1
Average for year ended 30 June 19X2	144.1	142.0
At 30 June 19X2	152.9	149.2

5. SSAP16 *Current Cost Accounting* states that 'where a proportion of the net operating assets is financed by net borrowing, a gearing adjustment is required in arriving at the current cost profit attributable to the shareholders.'

Required:

(*a*) Outline the reasons for the inclusion of a gearing adjustment in current cost accounts.

(*b*) The gearing adjustment described in SSAP16 has been criticised because:

(*i*)   it is based only on the current cost operating adjustments
(*ii*) it ignores negative net borrowings

Discuss each of these criticisms.

(Association of Certified Accountants)

6. It has been said that with the present success in controlling the rate of inflation the need for inflation-adjusted accounts has passed. After three years of operation of SSAP16 a review has recently been published by a working party under the Accounting Standards Committee. Among the main findings of the working party were that the public find two sets of figures, historical and current cost, confusing and that the requirement to produce current cost figures should be extended to cover all financial statements intended to give a true and fair view but subject to a 'cost benefit test'.

You are required to:

(*a*) comment, with reasons, on whether you agree with the remark that the need for inflation-adjusted accounts has passed, and

(*b*) consider the two main findings of the working party set out above and suggest how you would attempt to solve the problems involved.

(Institute of Chartered Accountants)

REFERENCES

Accounting Standards Committee, *Current Cost Accounting* (SSAP16), 1980.
Carsberg B. V. and Page M., *Current Cost Accounting: the Benefits and Costs* (four volumes), 1984, London, ICAEW and Prentice-Hall.
Cooke, T., and Nobes, C., 'Some Complexities in the Use of SSAP16', *Accountancy*, June and July, 1981.
Gynther, R. S., 'Some Problems Associated with the Implementation of Current Cost Accounting', *The Chartered Accountant in Australia*, July, 1976.
Richardson Report, 'Report of the Committee of Inquiry into Inflation' *Accounting*, New Zealand, 1976.
Sandilands Report, *Report of the Inflation Accounting Committee*, HMSO Cmmd paper 6225, 1975.
Tweedie, D., *Financial Reporting, Inflation and the Capital Maintenance Concept*, ICRA Occasional Paper No. 19, The University of Lancaster, 1979.
Westwick, C. A., 'The Lessons to be Learned from the Development of Inflation Accounting in the UK.', *Accounting and Business Research*, Autumn, 1980.
Wright, M., and Papps, I., 'The Use of a Monetary Working Capital Adjustment', *Accountancy*, July, 1980.

CHAPTER 9

Funds- and cash-flow statements

In previous chapters we examined financial reports from several perspectives. The view that user needs for decision making should be satisfied by financial reports has lead many authors to support funds-flow and cash-flow statements.

Funds-flow Statements

It is widely accepted that the balance sheet and profit and loss account do not provide ready or satisfactory answers to questions such as the following which users might pose. How much working capital has been generated by operations? Why does such a profitable company pay such relatively small dividends? How much reliance has been placed on external as opposed to internal funds for the finance of the business? How much was spent on new plant and equipment and how was it financed? (Mason, 1961). The funds statement is a medium for the provision of answers to such questions. The Corporate Report, discussed in Chapter 5, considered funds statements to be useful in assessing:

(a) corporate objectives;
(b) vulnerability of the entity;
(c) entity capacity to make future allocations of resources;
(d) future entity prospects;
(e) value of present or prospective interests in or claims on the entity.

A funds statement shows the sources from which funds have flowed into an entity and the uses to which such funds have been put. In the 1960s funds statements were increasingly included in the financial statements of North American corporations and have for a number of years been accepted as a basic element in financial reporting.

ED31 was published on the topic in the UK in 1974 and SSAP10 was issued in 1975. The aim of the standard was stated as being

> to establish the practice of providing source and application of funds statements as a part of audited accounts and lay down a minimum standard of disclosure in such statements.   (ASC, 1975)

There is no legal requirement for publication of a funds statement and evidence of company disclosure practices has shown a wide variety of practice despite SSAP10. One reason for this is a lack of precision in the definition of the term 'funds'.

Definitions of Funds

There are several definitions of funds. In this respect 'funds' are no different from many accounting concepts which although defined acceptably at a general level are subject to many practical interpretations. Here we consider three definitions: cash, working capital and all financial resources.

Cash Concept. Under the cash concept, funds represent changes in the entity's cash balance which occur over a period. The funds statement becomes, in effect, a statement of cash receipts and disbursements and the impact of those transactions on all other accounts. It does not group separately working capital items.

Table 9.1. Funds statement (cash concept)

	£000	£000
Opening cash balance		
Add Sources:		X
Profit before tax	X	
Adjustment for non-cash items		
Depreciation	X	X
	—	—
		X
Increase in creditors		X
		—
		X
Less Applications:		
Purchase of fixed assets	(X)	
Increase in stock	(X)	
Increase in debtors	(X)	
Taxation paid	(X)	
Dividends paid	(X)	(X)
		—
Closing cash balance		X(X)

A statement showing changes in cash funds could be prepared from the cash accounts of the business. Alternatively, the statement might be prepared (as in Table 9.1) from the company's published accounts and thus would provide an explanation of the change in the company's cash balance between opening and closing balance sheet positions. A serious limitation of the cash approach is that many important transactions of a non-cash variety which affect financial position are excluded from this statement.

Working Capital Concept. Statements based on the working capital definitions of funds report all transactions that result in a change in working capital (current assets minus current liabilities). Table 9.2 shows the components of such a statement.

Table 9.2. Working capital concept

	£000	£000
Working Capital from opening balance sheet		
Stocks	X	
Debtors	X	
Cash	X	
	X	
less creditors	(X)	X
Working Capital from closing balance sheet		
Stock	X	
Debtors	X	
Cash	X	
	X	
less creditors	(X)	X
Net increase (decrease) in working capital		X(X)
Other sources		
Profit before taxation	X	
Adjustment for non-cash items:		
Depreciation	X	X
		X
Other applications		
Purchase of fixed assets	(X)	
Taxation paid	(X)	
Dividends paid	(X)	(X)
Net source (application) of working capital		X(X)

All Financial Resources Concept. This concept expands the definition of funds to include all significant investment or financing transactions whether or not they directly or indirectly affect cash or working capital. For example, a company may acquire fixed assets by an issue of debentures or may exchange the form of a security for another. Under this concept, all such transactions should be shown.

Table 9.3. Statement of source and application of funds
Company without Subsidiaries Ltd.

	This Year			Last Year		
	£000	£000	£000	£000	£000	£000
Source of funds						
Profit before tax			1,430			440
Adjustments for items not involving the movement of funds:						
Depreciation			380			325
Total generated from operations			1,810			765
Funds from other sources						
Issue of shares for cash			100			80
Application of funds			1,910			845
Dividends paid		(400)			(400)	
Tax paid		(690)			(230)	
Purchase of fixed assets		(460)			(236)	
			(1,550)			(866)
			360			(21)
Increase/decrease in working capital						
Increase in stocks		80			114	
Increase in debtors		120			22	
(Increase) decrease in creditors —excluding taxation and proposed dividends		115			(107)	
Movement in net liquid funds: Increase (decrease) in:						
Cash balances	(5)			35		
Short-term investments	50			(85)		
		45			(50)	
			360			(21)

Note: The item 'total funds from operations' represents the increment in working capital from operations.
Source: ASC, 1975.

Accounting Policy Requirements

SSAP10 (ASC, 1975) does not specify directly a particular type of approach to be the basis of published funds statements. Indeed, it fails to discuss the relative merits of the three main concepts of funds statements or their implications for the disclosure of funds information.

However, SSAP10's approach may be inferred. The standard states:

> The figures from which the funds statement is constructed should generally be identifiable in the profit and loss account, balance sheet and related notes.

Since a statement of movements affecting working capital can be based on a rearrangement of information from the financial statements referred to above, this would appear to be the approach adopted implicitly by the Standard. Furthermore, the working capital concept is implied by all the illustrations cited by the Standard culminating in *Increase/decrease in working capital* as in Table 9.3 which is reproduced from the Appendix to SSAP10.

The Standard requires that the statement show:

1. Profit or loss adjusted for non-funds items.
2. Dividends paid.
3. Acquisitions or disposals of fixed and non-current assets.
4. Funds raised or expended by issuing or redeeming securities or loans.
5. Increase or decrease in working capital subdivided into its components, and movements in net liquid funds. The latter are defined as cash and cash equivalents (such as investments held as current assets) less bank overdrafts and other borrowings repayable within one year of the accounting date.

It is noteworthy that the above list excludes dividends proposed in favour of dividends paid. Also excluded are tax liabilities from the components of working capital. This suggests a cash concept of funds. Consequently SSAP10's approach appears to be based on a combination of the cash and working capital concepts.

SSAP10 requires public companies to include a funds statement, unless turnover is less than £25,000 a year. The standard permits considerable flexibility in practice, mainly because it allows alternative treatments of profit (before or after tax) and it does not define working capital (Knox, 1977). Consequently, the Institute's survey of published accounts reveals much diversity in the treatment of funds statements (ICAEW, 1982). Table 9.4 summarises the survey's findings on the form of published funds statements.

A limitation of SSAP10 originates from its implied emphasis on working capital. Because the statement is primarily a representation of net changes between two balance sheet dates, little or no new information is revealed.

Table 9.4. Formats used for funds statements, 1980–81

Forms of funds statement	% of survey
Current items	41
Working capital	21
Net borrowing	19
External financing	5
No focus: Sources=Applications	14

Note: The 'focus' refers to the method of arranging items so as to highlight or end with the movement of the particular items.
Source: ICAEW, 1982.

An analyst capable of interpreting such a statement would be capable of preparing it from other financial statements already at his disposal. Many writers suggest that the cash concept of funds provides more useful information than does the working capital approach. Unlike the cash view of funds, the working capital approach is consistent with the accruals concept. Revenue is a source of funds and cost of goods sold is a use of funds. Unfortunately, the accruals approach does not necessarily disclose the financial significance of the individual current assets and liabilities. For example, treating increases in investors and cash receipts as similar and decreases in prepayments and cash disbursements as similar may conceal short-term financial movements which are significant to the user. The working capital funds statement may reveal a favourable situation, and yet the enterprise may be unable to pay its bills. A statement of cash flows provides this additional information.

Reporting Cash Flows and their Components

The aim of this section is to consider the role of cash-flow reporting in providing inputs to the user's decision model. We examine the relationship of income and cash-flow accounting and conclude that they are complementary.

The Importance of Cash Flows

In Chapter 5 we noted how the normative investor's decision model is based on flows of cash from dividends. We considered how company financial statements could provide this information. Similarly, lenders and bankers are concerned with the cash receipt of interest and capital sums when due by the enterprise; creditors are mainly concerned with the enterprise's ability to meet its obligations in cash when due; employees within the enterprise consider their wage payments, future jobs and provision of benefits; and the government relies on the enterprise having sufficient cash to pay its taxation liability when due.

Cash has been called 'the key resource of most reporting enterprises' and 'the life blood of a business entity' (Lee, 1978). Although cash is essential to the existence of an enterprise, the importance of reporting cash-flow information has been virtually ignored by accounting policy makers. The Trueblood Report (AICPA, 1973) and FASB Concepts No. 1 (1979) state that an objective of accounting is to provide information useful to investors and creditors for predicting, comparing and evaluating potential cash flows in terms of amount, timing and related uncertainty. But both documents translate this objective into terms of reporting income which they state is 'the primary focus of financial reporting'. Two limitations of adopting an income basis for financial reporting are:

(*i*) Income is a mental construct and, therefore, is not represented by something which exists in the real world.
(*ii*) Income reporting conceals the timing of cash movements.

The first limitation is a result of the traditional accounting model based on matching. As we saw in Chapter 7, it is argued that the arbitrary nature of accounting allocations leads to false descriptions of reality (Thomas, 1974). The practice of depending on subjective judgements for allocation purposes introduces flexibility into the financial reporting process. There is no single income figure for a reporting entity for a defined period. Instead, there are many possible income measures, each dependent on the particular rules and judgements applied by the reporting accountant. It has been argued that the disclosure of the accounting methods adopted for income determination alleviate the users' problem. But some analysts point out the importance of disclosing the financial effects of alternative accounting policies on income. For example:

> The exact influence of LIFO stock valuation on financial ratios can be discovered only if one has information regarding the differences between the stock valuation under LIFO and what it would have been under some other method.
> (Holdren, 1964).

The second limitation of adopting an income basis for financial reporting originates from the differences between revenue recognition and cash receipts, and between cash payments and expense recognition. The amount of cash generated by a company during a short period of time, such as a year, will equal its reported profit for that period only by chance. The income statment is based on the accruals and matching concepts. Revenues are reported in the period they are earned; costs are charged to expenses in the same period that recognition is given to the revenues with which they are associated. As a consequence, the profit and loss account is deficient in that it fails to present a factual history of a firm's cash transactions. Furthermore, a profit and loss account provides an incomplete record of transactions involving cash. Several types of important financial events, such as the payment and repayment of debt, the issue of shares and the purchase of fixed assets are not revealed on this statement. These deficiencies conceal the timing of cash movements and have important implications for the users of financial statements. As we suggested in Chapter 5, investors and creditors need to evaluate the solvency as well as the profitability of companies in which they have an interest. Even if there is no imminent threat of insolvency, shortage of cash may force a company to forego profitable investment opportunities, thereby affecting long-run profitability.

The importance of cash-flow information in practice is illustrated by evidence on the behaviour of financial analysts. During the last twenty-five years the emphasis in solvency analysis by sophisticated users of financial information has shifted away from static analysis of working capital position to dynamic analysis of cash receipts and payments (Bradish, 1965). Also, empirical research findings into the predictive ability of accounting information support the importance of cash-flow information to the user. In Chapter 5 we saw their findings reveal the current ratio amongst the worst predictors of business failure. Of more significance for providing an early warning signal is information concerning the ability of the enterprise to generate cash from operations. For example, a study of the collapse in 1975 of the largest retailer in the U.S. found that 'whereas traditional ratio analysis of Grant's financial statements would not have revealed the existence of many of the company's problems until 1970 or 1971, careful analysis of the company's cash flows would have revealed impending doom as much as a decade before the collapse' (Largay and Stickney, 1980).

These findings question the usefulness of funds statements based on a profit-oriented, accrual-accounting system. According to one authority 'the working capital concept is an example of an accounting convention that has lingered in practice and in literature long after it has become obsolete for meaningful presentation of financial data' (Arthur Andersen, 1972). The emphasis on the working capital concept of funds statements, which emerged from our discussion earlier in this chapter may, therefore, be misplaced.

The Complementarity of Income and Cash Flow Reporting

Adoption of the user needs approach to financial reporting suggests that profit information supplemented by information about past cash flows will allow a more complete assessment of the current performance and future prospects of an enterprise to be made. This applies particularly to short-term assessments where the evaluation of solvency, that is, the ability of a company to pay its debts when due, may be more important than the evaluation of profitability. In the long-run, solvency and income are directly related: long-run solvency depends on profitability because cash can only be raised by profitable companies. In the short-run, as we discussed above, solvency and income do not necessarily coincide. The relationship between cash-flow and income reporting is summarised by Heath (1978) as follows:

> Income statements report the effects of a company's operations on its long-run cash generation; the question when cash has been or will be received or paid is ignored, except as it affects amounts at which receivables and payables are recorded. On the other hand, statements of cash receipts and payments report the effects of operations on cash movements during the year; whether these movements have affected or will affect income is ignored. Thus income statements and statements of cash receipts and payments are complementary, not competing, forms of disclosure.

In Chapter 5 we presented a format (Figure 5.1) for the disclosure of cash-flow information. It distinguished regular and irregular cash flows and allowed the comparison of forecast figures with actual on the assumption that past regular cash flows provide a satisfactory starting point for predicting future cash flows.

Generally, the greater the ability of an enterprise to generate regular net cash inflows from operations, the greater the ability of the enterprise to withstand adverse changes in operating conditions. Moreover, the reporting of forecast and actual cash flows allows users to evaluate the past forecasting ability of management, and with a profit and loss account available, the user is able to compare cash-flow data with profit data. Some suggestions for cash-flow statements include formats which reconcile net profit with closing cash balance (Page and Hooper, 1979).

A limitation of cash-flow statements is that they share with profit and loss accounts the potential for manipulation by management. For example, accelerating the collection of debts, delaying the payment of creditors and reducing inventory levels can increase cash from operations. Therefore, it is necessary for the user to examine changes in debtors, creditors and inventory levels in conjunction with cash-flow statements. The presentation of financial statements for several previous years should assist the user in his evaluation of the current year's results. Another limitation of cash-flow statements is that many important transactions of a non-cash variety, which have significant bearing on cash flows in the future, are omitted. Additional statements are required to provide details of these transactions. Heath (1978) suggests two such statements—Statement of Financing Activities and Statement of Investing Activities. Further alternatives are considered in the next part of the chapter.

Cash Flows and Financial Flexibility

An important consideration that affects the users' evaluation of future enterprise cash flows is the ability of the enterprise to adjust cash receipts and payments to survive a period of financial adversity, a concept called 'financial flexibility'. According to Heath (1978) a financially flexible company may be defined as

> One that can take corrective action that will eliminate any excess of required cash payments over expected cash receipts quickly and without major adverse effect on present or future earnings or on the market value of its stock.

Heath suggests that the ability of an enterprise to borrow money, liquidate assets, reduce costs, reduce dividends and issue capital stock determine its financial flexibility. An FASB discussion memorandum (FASB, 1980) discusses the types of information that would be helpful in assessing financial flexibility. For example, information about the amount of unused lines of credit may assist the user to evaluate an enterprise's ability to borrow money.

Lee (1981) has put forward the case for an integrated approach to reporting cash flows and net realisable values which emphasises the importance of accessibility to cash. As Lee points out:

1. Cash flow accounting details cash movements from various sources whilst net realisable values identify the current cash equivalent of assets.
2. Cash flows and net realisable values are free of allocations.
3. Both emphasise enterprise survival.
4. Both concentrate upon reporting the performance of the entity and its management without recourse to assumptions about continuity.

Lee has proposed three financial statements which make up such an integrated system. They comprise:

(a) **A statement of realised cash flows** for the year ended 31.12.19X4:

	£
Cash receipts from customers	X
less cash payments for materials, wages, overheads	(X)
Cash operating margin	X
less loan interest paid	(X)
Pre-tax cash flow	X
less tax paid	(X)
Distributable cash flow	X

less dividends paid	(X)
Operating cash flow after distribution	X
add long term loans received	X
Total cash flow available for investment	X
less cash payments for new assets	(X)
Total increase in cash resources	X

All items in the above represent actual realised cash flows. The potential for realisation of cash is detailed in the following statement of resources representing cash or its equivalent.

(b) Statement of Net Cash and Cash Equivalent Resources

	19X3		*19X4*	
Realised Cash Resources				
Bank, cash deposits		X		X
Readily realisable non-cash resources				
Debtors	X		X	
Stock of finished goods	X		X	
Vehicles	X		X	
Investments	X		X	
Land and buildings	X	X	X	X
Non-readily realisable non-cash resources				
Work in progress	X		X	
Non-specialist plant and machinery	X	X	X	
Non realisable non-cash resources				
Specialist plant and machinery		X		X
		X		X
Obligations				
Short-term obligations				
Creditors	X		X	
Taxation due	X		X	
Dividends	X	X	X	X
Long-term obligations				
Borrowings		X		X
Indefinite obligations				
Shareholders' funds		X		X
		X		X

Statement (b) may be interpreted as a rearrangement of balance sheet items (all expressed in net realisable values) under headings reflecting their nearness or otherwise to cash of both resources and obligations. This is the important difference between it and a balance sheet. The relationship between resources and obligations indicates financial flexibility (or vulnerability) at the accounting dates. The improvement or deterioration in flexibility or vulnerability may be determined from statement (c) below.

(c) Statement of total cash flow movements for year ended 31.12.19X4

		£
Realised cash flows		X
Readily realisable cash flows		
Potential cash flows represented by increase		
(decrease) in net realisable values of:		
Debtors	X	
Stocks of finished goods	X	
Vehicles	X	
Investments	X	X
Land and buildings	X	
Non-readily realisable cash flows		
Potential cash flows represented by increase		
(decrease) in net realisable values of:		
Work-in-progress	X	
Plant and machinery	X	X
Total potential increase in cash resources		X
Changes in short-term obligations		
Increases in:		
Creditors	X	
Taxation	X	
Dividends	X	X
Changes in long-term obligations		
Increase in:		
Borrowings		X
Change in indefinite obligations		
Indeterminate future cash outflows:		
		X
Total potential increase in obligations		X

The first entry in statement (c) 'Realised cash flows' corresponds in value to the final entry in statement (a) 'Total increase in cash resources'. The other entries in (c) are derived from the movements in the entries in statement (b). For example, the item 'debtors' under 'Readily realisable cash flows' represents the movement in the net realisable values of debtors from the position at 31.12.19X3 to that at 31.12.19X4 shown in (b). Since the cash flow potential of assets and liabilities derives from their net realisable values, such movements are the equivalent of cash flows and positive movements indicate an increase in financial flexibility.

QUESTIONS

1. Distinguish between (*a*) cash, (*b*) working capital and (*c*) all financial resources concepts of funds.

2. (*a*) What do you consider to be the functions of source and application of funds statements in financial reporting?

   (*b*) Explain briefly how you would account for the following five transactions in a statement of source and application of funds prepared in accordance with SSAP10 *Statements of Source and Application of Funds*:

      (*i*)   Corporation tax provided for the current accounting period and corporation tax paid for the previous period.

      (*ii*) The final dividend proposed for the current accounting period and last year's final dividend paid during the current period.

      (*iii*) The profit on the disposal of a fixed asset.

      (*iv*) The share of profits in an associated company.

      (*v*)   The acquisition of a subsidiary paid for partly by an issue of shares and partly by a payment of cash.

   (*c*) How generally might alternative definitions of funds influence the preparation of source and application of funds statements?

   (Association of Certified Accountants)

3. Evaluate the proposal that conventional financial statements should be replaced by reporting cash flows.

4.   *LINDOP LIMITED*

Summarised Balance Sheets	31 December 19X2 (£000)	31 December 19X1 (£000)
Fixed assets	1,400	960
Accumulated depreciation	(240)	(180)
Stock	880	720
Debtors	240	320

LINDOP LIMITED

Summarised Balance Sheets	31 December 19X2 (£000)	31 December 19X1 (£000)
Provisions for Doubtful Debts	(12)	(6)
Cash	120	102
	2,388	1,916
Ordinary share capital	1,800	1,200
Undistributed profits	308	236
Taxation	100	120
Trade Creditors	180	360
	2,388	1,916

*Summarised Income Statement for the year ended
31 December 19X2*

	(£000)	(£000)
Sales	1,600	
Investment income	20	
Profit on sale of machine (a)	4	1,624
Operating expenses and taxes (b)		(912)
Net profit for year		712
Undistributed profits brought forward		236
		948
Dividends	240	
Bonus issue of shares, one for every 3 held	400	640
Undistributed profits carried forward		308

(a) The machine which was sold for cash had cost £10,000 and its net book value at the time of sale was £4,000.
(b) Includes depreciation, £66,000; write-off of obsolete stocks, £8,000; and taxation £100,000.

You are required to:

Prepare a schedule of changes in working capital and statement of Source and Application of Funds for the year ended 31 December 19X2.

REFERENCES

Accounting Standards Committee, *Statements of Source and Application of Funds* (SSAP10), 1975.

American Institute of Certified Public Accountants, *Report of the Study Group on the Objectives of Financial Statements*, (Trueblood Report), New York, 1973.

Arthur Andersen, *Objectives of Financial Statements*, Arthur Andersen and Co., 1972.

Bradish, R. D., 'Corporate Reporting and the Financial Analyst', *The Accounting Review*, October, 1965.

Financial Accounting Standards Board, *Reporting Earnings, Discussion Memorandum*, 1979.

Financial Accounting Standards Board, *Reporting Funds Flows, Liquidity and Financial Flexibility, Discussion Memorandum*, 1980.

Heath, L. C., *Financial Reporting and the Evaluation of Solvency*, Accounting Research Monograph No. 3, AICPA, 1978.

Holdren, G. C., 'LIFO and Ratio Analysis', *The Accounting Review*, January, 1964.

Institute of Chartered Accountants in England and Wales, *Survey of Published Accounts, 1981–82*, London 1982.

Knox, R. W., *Statements of Source and Application of Funds—A Practical Guide to SSAP10*, ICAEW, 1977.

Largay, J. A. and Stickney, C. P., 'Cash Flows, Ratio Analysis and the W. T. Grant Company Bankruptcy', *Financial Analysts Journal*, July–August, 1980.

Lee, T. A., 'The Cash Flow Accounting Alternative for Corporate Financial Reporting' in C. van Dam (ed.) *Trends in Managerial and Financial Accounting*, Martinus Nijhoff, 1978.

Lee, T. A., 'Reporting Cash Flows and Net Realisable Values', *Accounting and Business Research*, 1981.

Mason, P., *Cash Flow Analysis and Funds Statements*, Accounting Research Study No. 2, American Institute of Certified Public Accountants, New York, 1961.

Page, J. R. and Hooper, P., 'Financial Statements for Security Analysts', *Financial Analysts' Journal*, September–October, 1979.

Thomas, A. R., *The Allocation Problem: Part 2, Studies in Accounting Research No. 9*, American Accounting Association, 1974.

CHAPTER 10

Specific issues in
financial reporting

Extraordinary items and prior-period adjustments—earnings per share
—deferred taxation—contingencies—post balance sheet events—stocks
and work-in-progress—depreciation—intangible assets—leases—pensions
—foreign currency translation—value added statements.

Extraordinary Items and Prior-period Adjustments

The treatment of extraordinary items has generated much controversy for
many years. This has been partly directed at the failure of companies to
disclose how material abnormal items are treated, thereby affecting the
comparability of financial statements. It also reflects a significant preoc-
cupation with a priori reasoning about how the net income figure should be
derived. The treatment of extraordinary items is considered important
because of its direct impact on the earnings per share figure. As we discuss
in the following section, SSAP3 chooses the figure of income after tax and
before extraordinary items for its definition of 'earnings'. Concern that
companies may be manipulating their earnings-per-share figure through
the use of extraordinary items has prompted recent scrutiny of policy
requirements in this area.

Two schools of thought—current operating and all-inclusive—have
debated the problem concerning which items should be included in the
profit and loss account and which should be relegated to reserves. The
proponents of the current operating approach would include only those
transactions in the profit and loss account which result from the ordinary,
normal operations of the entity during the current period. Other
transactions, those of an unusual, extraordinary nature should be
segregated from the ordinary transactions and relegated to reserves.

Current operating advocates maintain that investors are better served by information that is comparable from year to year. The proponents of the all-inclusive approach maintain the profit and loss account should provide a record of all such transactions. Its advocates believe that over the life of an entity the aggregate of net incomes should provide a complete history of the earnings of the enterprise. They maintain it is misleading to exclude extraordinary transactions from periodic profit and loss accounts. Furthermore, they argue that the all-inclusive concept avoids the necessity of making highly subjective judgements. These may lead to differences in the treatment of questionable items and create the danger of income manipulation. For example, losses may be relegated to reserves and gains to income.

Accounting Policy Requirements

SSAP6 adopts the all-inclusive concept of income for the following reasons:

(a) Inclusion and disclosure of extraordinary and prior-year items will enable the profit and loss account for the year to give a better view of a company's profitability and progress;

(b) Exclusion, being a matter of subjective judgement, could lead to variations and to a loss of comparability between the reported results of companies; and

(c) Exclusion could result in extraordinary and prior year items being overlooked in any consideration of results over a series of years.

The all-inclusive concept of income has been incorporated in legal requirements. As the appendix to Chapter 4 showed, the required formats for presentation of the profit and loss account under the Companies Act 1981 provide headings for *extraordinary income*, *extraordinary charges* and *tax on extraordinary profit or loss*. The Act does not define extraordinary items. These may be interpreted in the light of SSAP6 as 'those items which derive from events or transactions outside the ordinary activities of the business and which are both material and expected not to recur frequently or regularly. They do not include items which, though exceptional on account of size and incidence, derive from the ordinary activities of the business' (ASC, 1974). The classification of extraordinary items will depend on the particular circumstances of the business. SSAP6 gives the following examples of how extraordinary items may arise:

(a) The discontinuance of a significant part of a business.

(b) The sale of an investment not acquired with the intention of resale.

(c) Writing off intangibles, including goodwill, because of unusual events or developments during the period.

(d) The appropriation of assets.

Exceptional items are defined by SSAP6 as those which whilst deriving from the ordinary activities of the business should be disclosed separately because of their size and incidence. They would include:

(a) Abnormal charges for bad debts and write offs of stocks and work in progress and research and development expenditure.
(b) Abnormal provisions for losses on long-term contracts.
(c) Most adjustments of prior year taxation provisions.

Prior-year adjustments are defined as those material adjustments applicable to prior years arising from changes in accounting policies and from the correction of fundamental errors. They do not include the normal recurring corrections and adjustments of accounting estimates made in prior years. They should be accounted for by restating prior year profits resulting in the opening balance of retained profits being adjusted accordingly. The effect of the change should be disclosed where practicable by showing separately, in the restatement of the previous year, the amount involved.

In summary, all profits and losses, with the exception of prior-year adjustments (which are effected through adjustments to reserves) are required to go through the profit and loss account and exceptional and extraordinary items should be separated. This principle is enshrined in US practice and is consistent with IAS8.

Example 10.1:

The following information has been extracted from the records of Company Z for the year ended 31 December 19X1 with a view to inclusion in the financial statements for the period:

(i) Z has charged approximately £40,000 per year for bad debts for some time. This figure was increased to £150,000 for the past year due to a customer going into liquidation.
(ii) The auditors of Z have discovered that a senior employee has embezzled £250,000 during 19X1 and has left the country.
(iii) A court case for breach of contract by Z has been settled with Z having to meet a damages settlement of £80,000 to a former employee.
(iv) Stock worth £2.5m has been omitted from the value of closing stock for the year ended 31 December 19X0.
(v) Z's directors have decided to charge depreciation on the company's buildings after the issue of SSAP12 in the year to 31 December 19X1.
(vi) Z has agreed to pay £3m to the landlord of a leasehold property to cover repairs and renovations necessary at the end of a 10 year lease. The lease has been renewed for a further 15 years at a market rent.

In accordance with SSAP6 the suggested accounting treatments are as follows:

(*i*)   This item is likely to be viewed as exceptional since it arises out of Z's normal business. Whether it is disclosed separately as an exceptional item or included in operating profit depends on whether it is material or not.

(*ii*) This item is extraordinary being out of the normal business of Z and will be disclosed separately if considered material.

(*iii*) This item could be considered either exceptional or extraordinary. The contract derives from Z's ordinary business, but breaching contracts is not normal business activity. The latter is probably a more persuasive argument.

(*iv*) This omission, if material, will be considered a fundamental error and since it applies to the year ended 31 December 19X0, necessitates a prior-year adjustment. Thus Z's reserves will be adjusted by the addition of the value of omitted stock, and the profit for the year ended 31 December 19X1 computed as if the error had not been made.

(*v*)   According to SSAP12 (see the section on depreciation in this chapter), depreciation should be charged on freehold buildings and the directors' decision to do so represents a change of accounting policy (the second reason for a prior-year adjustment). Thus, Z's reserves should be adjusted accordingly.

(*vi*) Although only one payment is involved, the sum applies to the entire lease period which has expired. Thus, repairs and renovations (a normal part of a tenant's responsibilities in such cases as this), have not been carried out in previous years. However, this is neither a change of accounting policy nor a fundamental error and is thus not a prior-year adjustment. Since it derives from a normal aspect of business activity it is not extraordinary. Thus, if material, it is perhaps an exceptional item; if not, it should not be separately disclosed.

Evaluation of the Requirements

The publication of SSAP6 has encouraged companies to disclose more information about unusual items in the profit and loss account. However, *Surveys of Published Accounts* reveal considerable inconsistency between the treatment of apparently similar items in the financial statements of different companies. In 1983 the Society of Investment Analysts examined six breweries and looked at their treatment of property and related gains under SSAP6. Three breweries disclosed this item as extraordinary and three as not extraordinary. The two auditing firms concerned showed a similar inconsistency. Both firms appended a true and fair audit report to financial statements which treated property and related gains as both extraordinary and ordinary items.

An ASC working party concluded that the present broad definitions do not give adequate guidance. It stated that consistency of treatment should be the main objective of an accounting standard on this subject particularly in view of the standard formats for the profit and loss account introduced by the 1981 Companies Act which, additionally, specifically requires identification of exceptional and extraordinary items. The working party recommended that the definitions adopted by SSAP6 be supplemented by a list defining by nature whether items are normally to be treated as an undisclosed credit or charge, an exceptional item, an extraordinary item, or a reserve movement. The working party identified the items which should not normally be treated as extraordinary, although they may be exceptional where they are material:

(*a*) Redundancy costs relating to continuing business;
(*b*) Reorganisation costs unrelated to the discontinuance of a significant part of a business;
(*c*) Previously capitalised research and development expenditure written off;
(*d*) Profits appropriated to employee share schemes;
(*e*) Profit or loss on the disposal of depreciated fixed assets or intangible ones, unless they arise on the termination of activities;
(*f*) Abnormal charges for bad debts and write-offs of stock and work in progress, and
(*g*) Abnormal provisions for losses on long-term contracts.

The working party questioned the SSAP6 definition of extraordinary items that such items are 'expected not to recur frequently or regularly'. Experience has shown that, especially in the recent recession, categories of extraordinary items have recurred. The working party suggested that the restriction with regard to the frequency of occurrence should be deleted from the definition of extraordinary items or the standard should emphasise that it is the event or transaction leading to the extraordinary item which should not recur, rather than the category of extraordinary item. The working party identified the following items as being among those which they would expect to be treated as extraordinary:

(*a*) Redundancy costs relating to discontinued business;
(*b*) Terminal profits and losses;
(*c*) Profit or loss on the sale of investments where the purchase or sale of investments is not part of the normal trading activities;
(*d*) Provisions made for the permanent diminution in value of investments;

(*e*) Profit or loss arising on the sale of investments in subsidiary and associated companies, and

(*f*) Profit or loss arising on the expropriation or nationalisation of assets.

The working party suggested that a problem of classification of cost as extraordinary or exceptional relates to the treatment of costs arising from reorganisations and terminated activities. Reorganisations not involving the termination of a business will probably involve redundancies, etc. and should be shown as exceptional items. The decision to terminate will result in material costs and credits which do not relate to the continuing business and should be classified as extraordinary items.

In January 1985 the ASC issued ED36, *Extraordinary Items and Prior Year Adjustments*, based on the working party's review of SSAP6. The proposals contained in ED36 do not differ substantially from the principles set out in SSAP6. The changes which are proposed relate chiefly to matters of definition and disclosure, especially in regard to the effect of the issue of SSAPs 20 and 22 on foreign currency translation and goodwill respectively. A noteworthy modification is clarification of the phrase 'ordinary activities of the business' which is central to the definition of extraordinary items.

Empirical Research Findings

Some research findings have indicated manipulation by management of reported income figures through the classification of these items. Barnea *et al.* (1976) found that their results are consistent with the hypothesis that managements behaved as if they classified extraordinary items so as to smooth ordinary income over time (i.e. that used to compute earnings per share). Efficient market research findings, discussed in Chapter 5, lead us to the conclusion that, in addition to achieving greater consistency in the classification of items as either extraordinary or exceptional, there should be adequate disclosure of the nature and amount of the items in question. Then the analyst can adjust the data to suit his own preferences, if he feels the classification is inappropriate.

Earnings Per Share (EPS)

Earnings per share (EPS) is frequently cited as a financial accounting ratio which is widely used in shareholder investment decisions. EPS may be generally defined as the ratio:

$$\frac{\text{Profits attributable to shareholders}}{\text{Number of ordinary shares in issue and ranking for dividend}}$$

It may be used in conjunction with the price earnings ratio (PER) to estimate share price. Price earnings ratio is defined as:

$$\frac{\text{Current market price per share}}{\text{EPS}}$$

Thus, estimated share price is given as: PER×EPS

The circularity of calculation is removed from the above if it is recalled that the investment analyst will estimate an appropriate value for PER rather than use the current market estimate. This approach to share valuation may be considered less rigorous than the dividend model which is frequently used in cost of capital calculations. Arranging the well-known cost of equity formula in terms of share price we obtain:

$$P = \frac{D}{Ke-g}$$

Where P is share price, D is expected dividends per share, Ke the required yield on this equity share, and g the growth rate of dividends. If we define the proportion of EPS paid out in dividends as a, then we may re-write the foregoing as:

$$P = \frac{a\,\text{EPS}}{Ke-g}$$

Thus, with the introduction of dividend policy, EPS becomes important in the dividend model approach to share valuation.

However used, EPS will imply inter-company comparisons. Consequently, it is important that EPS figures be reliable and comparable. Difficulties may arise with the computation of the components of profits, the corporation tax system, or the number of shares in issue. The ASC issued SSAP3 on EPS in February 1972 and the standard was devoted to the latter two of the three areas of difficulty referred to, since other accounting standards are concerned with particular profit components.

Corporation Tax and EPS

The imputation system of corporation tax introduced in the UK in 1973 requires a company to make a payment of advance corporation tax (ACT) on distributions of dividends equal to a specified fraction of the amount distributed. The fraction has varied with the basic rate of income tax and we shall assume it to be three-sevenths. Amounts paid in ACT are available for offset against a company's basic corporation tax liability in computing mainstream liability. The amount which may be offset is restricted to the lower of:

(*a*) the ACT paid in an accounting period

(b) 30 per cent of UK income liable to corporation tax. For example, consider the following data:

	£000
Accounting profit	250
Excess capital allowances over depreciation	(90)
Taxable profit	160
Dividends paid	140

If we assume a corporation tax rate of 50 per cent the company's basic tax liability is 50 per cent of £160,000, namely £80,000. The company will be liable for ACT of three-sevenths of £140,000, namely £60,000. Now, since 30 per cent of the taxable profit of £160,000 is £48,000, the company may only claim the lower figure of £48,000 as relief against the basic liability of £80,000. Thus:

	£000		£000
ACT paid	60	Basic corporation tax liability	80
Offset against corporation tax	48	ACT offset	48
Unrelieved ACT	12	Mainstream corporation tax	32

Unrelieved ACT may be related back in time and (subject to the restrictions already noted), relieved against basic corporation tax on profits in the six preceding periods. Any ACT still unrelieved may be carried forward with no restriction to be relieved in future years. Alternatively, unrelieved ACT may be offset against the balance on deferred tax account.

However, if a company has had similar profits and distribution policies in earlier years and expects similar patterns to continue, unrelieved ACT may build up without any prospect of relief. In this case the application of the fundamental accounting principle of prudence might dictate that the unrelieved ACT be deemed irrecoverable. This raises the problem of how such ACT should be written off. The choice of accounting treatment may depend upon what the source of the unrelieved ACT is thought to be. Two views may be taken.

1. **Unrelieved ACT as an appropriation.** This view sees the unrelieved ACT as arising from a company's dividend policy, and acceptance of it implies that the ACT in question be treated as an appropriation. Thus, using the data given above, we have:

		£000
Profit before tax		250
Corporation tax on profit		
for the year		80
Profit after tax		170
Dividend paid	140	
Irrecoverable ACT	12	152
Retained profit		18

Given the definition of EPS above, if we assume that the company has four million ordinary shares in issue and ranking for dividend, EPS equals:

$$\frac{£170,000}{4,000,000} = 4.25p \text{ per share}$$

Treating unrelieved ACT as an appropriation means that EPS will always be 4.25p for all dividend distribution policies. Indeed, had the company paid no dividends EPS would have been calculated as:

	£000	
Profit before tax	250	
Corporation tax for year	80	(160,000×50 per cent)
Retained earnings	170	

In this case there is no ACT relieved or otherwise and

$$\text{EPS} = \frac{£170,000}{4,000,000} = 4.25p \text{ per share}$$

Since treating unrelieved ACT as an appropriation gives the same EPS as would arise if distributions were nil, this treatment is known as the nil basis method of computing EPS. The advantage of the nil basis is that it produces a figure for EPS which is not dependent upon a company's dividend policy and is, it is argued, more comparable between companies.

2. **Unrelieved ACT as part of the tax charge**. A contrary view is to treat unrelieved ACT as part of the tax charge on a company's profits, and not as an appropriation, arising as it does from the operation of the corporate tax system. Treating it thus would produce the following results for the data used above:

		£000
Profit before tax		250
Corporation tax for the year	80	
Unrelieved ACT	12	92
Profit after tax		158
Dividend paid		140
Retained profit		18

$$\text{EPS} = \frac{\pounds 158,000}{4,000,000} = 3.95\text{p}$$

Under this treatment, the company's dividend policy will influence EPS. For example, if the company distributed £120,000 in dividends, it would pay three-sevenths, if the company distributed £120,000 in dividends, it would pay three-sevenths or £51,429 of ACT and receive only £48,000 of relief leaving £3,429 unrelieved. This would give an EPS as follows:

		£000
Profit before tax		250.0
Corporation tax for the year	80.0	
Unrelieved ACT	3.4	83.4
		166.6
Dividend paid		120.0
Retained profit		46.6

$$\text{EPS} = \frac{\pounds 166,600}{4,000,000} = 4.17\text{p per share}$$

The reliance of EPS upon dividend policy is inevitable using this method since EPS is based upon earnings after tax. An argument in favour of this method of calculating EPS (known as the net basis) is that users of accounts wish to consider all relevant information in appraising company performance, and any extra tax liabilities arising from a company's dividend policy are relevant information. This would appear consistent with the acknowledged use of EPS in investment analysis. The ASC, despite justifying the issuing of a standard on EPS with reference to 'the increasing use of the price-earnings ratio as a standard stock market ratio', expressed favour for the net basis on grounds of improved accountability:

the net basis takes account of all relevant facts including the additional tax liabilities inherent in the dividend policy pursued by the company, for which the directors should be no less accountable to shareholders.

(ASC, SSAP3)

The foregoing is concerned with the implications of the corporate tax system for the numerator of the EPS formula. The denominator of that formula depends upon the number of shares in issue and ranking for dividend. The value of the denominator may change during an accounting period for several reasons. There may be:

(a) An issue of new equity at the full market price.
(b) A rights issue at less than full market price.
(c) A capitalisation issue.
(d) A share exchange.

Since EPS will be calculated from the earnings of an entire accounting period the calculation must be adjusted for such changes. Moreover, if the resulting EPS is to be used by analysts to make share investment decisions its predictive character is being stressed. Thus, if any factors exist which may make EPS unrepresentative of future trends they should be incorporated into the calculation. Amongst these factors are:

(a) Classes of shares not presently ranking for dividend but which will do so in the future.
(b) Convertible loan stock.
(c) Options or warrants to subscribe to equity.

If these factors increase the value of the denominator in EPS they will dilute the value of EPS. Hence, EPS may be calculated on the existing denominator (basic EPS) and the likely future denominator (full diluted EPS). We shall demonstrate the principles which may be applied in calculating EPS after considering the requirements of SSAP3.

Accounting Policy Requirements

SSAP3 applies to listed companies and requires that they disclose the following:

(a) Basic EPS calculated on the net basis for current and preceding accounting periods and disclosed on the face of the profit and loss account. If calculations on the nil basis are materially different it is desirable that this also be disclosed.
(b) Fully diluted EPS (where appropriate) and the difference between it and basic EPS if more than 5 per cent of basic EPS. The corresponding amount should be shown for the previous year if the assumptions made then no longer apply.

(c) Equal prominence should be given to both basic and fully diluted EPS.
(d) The basis of calculation for EPS, together with the amount of earnings and number of shares in issue and ranking for dividend.

An appendix to the standard sets out guidelines for the calculation of EPS and although these guidelines are not part of the standard, they will be used below to demonstrate certain of the relevant computations. In the appendix it is recommended that where losses are incurred EPS should be calculated in the normal way and loss per share should be reported.

Calculation of EPS

In the computations that follow, we shall use the data below which shows the consolidated profit and loss account for company A for the year ended 31 December 19X3.

	£000	£000
Net profit before tax		742.4
Less Corporation tax on the profits for the year	386.0	
Irrecoverable ACT	15.0	401.0
		341.4
Less Extraordinary item		104.4
		237.0
Less Dividends		
Preference paid	84.0	
Ordinary: interim paid	120.0	
Ordinary: final proposed	30.0	234.0
Retained profits for the year		3.0
Retained profits brought forward		100.0
Retained profits carried forward		103.0

The number of ordinary shares in issue and ranking for dividend at 1 January 19X3 was 5 million at £1 and there were 1.2 million £1 preference shares returning 7 per cent interest.

EPS on the Net Basis

As previously noted, the net basis involves treating irrecoverable ACT as part of the company's tax charge, so the profit and loss account above is arranged appropriately. The relevant earnings figure according to SSAP3 is earnings after tax and preference dividends (and if the company is a group, after minority interests) but before extraordinary items. According to SSAP6, extraordinary items are those which derive from events or transactions outside the normal activities of the business and are material and not expected to recur frequently or regularly. Thus, the argument runs, their inclusion in EPS would weaken it as an indicator of trends in company earnings.

Thus, basic EPS of the net basis is given as:

	£000
Net profit after tax	341.4
Less Preference dividends	84.0
	257.4

$$\frac{£257,400}{5,000,000} = 5.2\text{p per share}$$

EPS on the Nil Basis

Calculation on the nil basis requires that irrecoverable ACT be treated as an appropriation, not a tax charge, thus the relevant earnings are:

	£000
Net profit after tax	341.4
Add: Irrecoverable ACT	15.0
	356.4
Less: Preference dividends	84.0
	272.4

$$\frac{£272,400}{5,000,000} = 5.5\text{p per share}$$

EPS and Changes in Share Capital

New issue of shares at full market price

Let us assume that the company issued a further 300,000 £1 ordinary shares on 1 July 19X3 and that these shares carried an immediate right to receive a dividend. The new shares were issued at the full market price of £1.40 per share. With this additional data we shall compute EPS on both net and nil bases. On each basis it is necessary to combine existing and new shares. This is done by weighting the shares on the basis of the proportions of the year in which they have been in issue and ranking for dividend. Thus, to the 5 million shares in issue for the entire year we add the additional 300,000 weighted by six-twelfths for the proportion of the year they were in issue, giving 5,150,000 in total. EPS is:

Net basis	*Nil basis*
$\dfrac{£257,400}{5,150,000} = 5.0\text{p per share}$	$\dfrac{£272,400}{5,150,000} = 5.3\text{p per share}$

Capitalisation Issue

Let us assume that a capitalisation issue took place on 1 September 19X3 at the rate of one new share for each five held. Since the issue represents the capitalisation of reserves already held (and employed by the company), time weighting would not be appropriate and the shares are treated as being in issue for the entire year, thus EPS is:

Net basis
$$\frac{£257,400}{5,000,000+1,000,000)} = 4.3\text{p per share}$$

Nil basis
$$\frac{£272,400}{(5,000,000+1,000,000)} = 4.5\text{p per share}$$

Rights Issue

Let us assume that a rights issue of one share for each five shares held was made on 1 May 19X3 at a price of £1 per share. The market price (cum rights) immediately prior to the rights issue was £1.30. The rights issue alters the capital of the company in both volume and value terms and earnings could be apportioned to capital before and after the rights issue. Alternatively, the number of shares in issue could be weighted with respect to the relative capital values of shares in issue before and after the rights. This may be done by calculating a theoretical price per share after the rights issue to compare with the price immediately before the rights. This may be done as follows:

		£
Shares in issue pre-rights:	5 million at £1.30	6,500,000
Issue:	1 million at £1.00	1,000,000
	6 million	7,500,000

Theoretical price per share after the rights issue:

$$\frac{£7,500,000}{6 \text{ million}} = £1.25$$

The original 5 million shares were in issue for the months from January to the end of April. Their price before the rights issue was £1.30 which made them equivalent to more than 5 million shares at £1.25. From the 1 May there were 6 million shares at £1.25. Thus, the total number of time weighted and value weighted shares is:

					£
$\frac{4}{12}$	$\times$	5m	$\times \dfrac{£1.30}{£1.25}$	$=$	1,733,333
$\frac{8}{12}$	$\times$	6m		$=$	4,000,000
					5,733,333

Net basis	Nil basis
$\dfrac{£257,400}{5,733,333} = 4.5\text{p per share}$	$\dfrac{£272,400}{5,733,333} = 4.8\text{p per share}$

In circumstances such as this, the standard recommends that past earnings per share be adjusted to comparable values by the application of the reciprocal of the above ratio of share values. Thus:

$$\frac{\text{theoretical ex-rights price}}{\text{actual cum rights price on the last day of quotation cum rights}}$$

is the adjustment factor. If EPS, net and nil respectively, for the preceding year was 6.5p and 7.2p per share then their adjusted values are:

Net basis	Nil basis
$\dfrac{6.5\text{p} \times £1.25}{£1.30} = 6.3\text{p per share}$	$\dfrac{7.2\text{p} \times £1.25}{£1.30} = 6.9\text{p per share}$

This adjustment allows the EPS figures to be compared over the two years.

Share Exchange

Let us assume that a company A takes over another company, B, and uses as the consideration for the entire share capital of B, one million of its own £1 ordinary shares which are credited as fully paid. The exchange took place on 1 October 19X3 and the earnings of B have already been consolidated into A's profit and loss account from that date for the year ended 31 December 19X3. This is equivalent to a new issue of shares and EPS is calculated on a time weighted basis, thus:

Net basis

$$\frac{£257,400}{5,000,000+(3/12\times1,000,000)} = 4.9\text{p per share}$$

Nil basis

$$\frac{£272,400}{5,000,000+(3/12\times1,000,000)} = 5.2\text{ per share}$$

Fully diluted EPS (FDEPS)
As noted above, the shares in issue may change in the future as a result of a company's obligations. SSAP3 identifies three circumstances where such obligations might dilute EPS.

1. Shares ranking for dividend in the future. Let us assume that the 300,000 £1 ordinary shares issued at full market price on 1 July 19X3 did not rank for dividend until the accounting period beginning on 1 January 19X4. The basic EPS on net and nil bases are 5.2p and 5.5p as calculated above. Their fully diluted values are calculated as if the shares ranked for dividend for six-twelfths of the year giving EPS at 5.0p and 5.3p.

2. Convertible loan stock. Let us assume that the company has issued £1 million of 8 per cent convertible loan stock. These can be converted into equity between 1988 and 1993 at the option of the holder at the rate of £1.50 of loan stock for each £1 ordinary share. The standard requires that FDEPS be calculated on the basis of the maximum number of ordinary shares which might be created on conversion. Since only one rate of conversion is quoted, this must be used and gives:

$$\frac{£1,000,000}{£1.50} = 666,667\text{ ordinary shares}$$

Earnings must be adjusted to their post-conversion level by adding back loan interest saved less corporation tax, thus:

Net basis:

		£000
Net profit after tax and preference dividends		257.4
Add: Interest saved £1,000,000×8 per cent	80.0	
Less: Corporation tax at 52 per cent	41.6	38.4
		295.8

$$\text{FDEPS} = \frac{£295,800}{5,000,000+666,667} = 5.2\text{p per share}$$

Nil basis:

Net profit after tax (excluding irrecoverable ACT) and preference dividends		272.4
Add: Interest saved £1,000,000×8 per cent	80.0	
Less: Corporation tax at 52 per cent	41.6	38.4
		310.8

$$\text{FDEPS} = \frac{£310,800}{5,000,000+666,667} = 5.5\text{p per share}$$

3. Options to subscribe to equity. Let us assume that the company has issued options to its executives to subscribe £500,000 £1 ordinary shares at £1 per share. Now, should the options be exercised not only will the number of shares in issue increase, but company earnings should increase as the proceeds of the subscription are invested and generate returns. The standard requires that earnings be adjusted on the assumption that the proceeds of subscription had been invested in $2\frac{1}{2}$ per cent Consolidated Stock on the first day of the period at the closing price of the previous day. If that price were £25 per Consol, yield would be:

$$\frac{£2.5}{£25} = 0.10$$

This would give earnings and EPS as follows:

Net basis:

		£000
Earnings after tax and preference dividends		257.4
Add: potential earnings of 10 per cent on £500,000	50	
Less: corporation tax at 52 per cent	26	24.0
		281.4

$$\text{FDEPS} = \frac{£281,400}{5,000,000+500,000} = 5.1\text{p per share}$$

Nil basis:

Net profit after tax (excluding irrecoverable ACT) and preference dividends		272.4
Add: potential earnings of 10 per cent on £500,000	50	
Less: corporation tax at 52 per cent	26	24.0
		296.4

$$\text{FDEPS} = \frac{\pounds296,400}{5,000,000+500,000} = 5.4 \text{ per share}$$

Evaluation of the Requirements

The terms of the conversation or option, coupled with the assumption contained in the standard that conversion or option rights be exercised at the beginning of the period, may result in FDEPS being greater than basic EPS. In such cases, according to the standard it is likely that conversion or option rights would not be exercised. Consequently, SSAP3 recommends that FDEPS should not be shown if in excess of basic EPS. Skerrat and Peasnell (1975) have criticised both the realism of the foregoing assumption and the standard's assertion about likely investor behaviour. Decisions on the exercise of conversion or option rights are likely to involve the evaluation of a number of variables, whose inter-relationships will be difficult to assess without a formal decision model. Thus, it is difficult to accept the validity of SSAP3's recommendation on the non-disclosure of FDEPs in certain circumstances.

There has been considerable controversy over the most appropriate basis for calculating EPS. The Society of Investment Analysts has argued in favour of the nil basis on the grounds that:

1. Comparisons based upon net EPS could be difficult to draw if the same level of pre-tax profits led to different values for EPS.
2. In take-overs EPS on the net basis may understate earnings if otherwise irrecoverable ACT could be absorbed after takeover.

Ashton (1975) has argued that the net basis is more appropriate for comparisons if investors require cash flow forecasts (as most normative investor models presume), since irrecoverable ACT reduces company cash flows. Further, the sophisticated investors and analysts who are likely to be engaged in take-over decisions are unlikely to underestimate EPS prescribed on a net basis.

Accounting Practice

The 1982 *Survey of Published Accounts* found that of the 300 surveyed companies, 292 disclosed EPS information, although 2 companies did not disclose this information on the face of the profit and loss account as required. Of the 35 companies which made losses, 33 reported figures of loss per share as recommended by the standard and 2 reported EPS to be zero. 249 companies disclosed both earnings and the number of equity shares used in calculating EPS as required. 4 companies based EPS on earnings after extraordinary items and so did not comply with SSAP3.

The survey found that companies continue to disclose earnings after tax as charged in the profit and loss account. This use of actual tax charged may lead to volatility in EPS since actual tax charged may be volatile. A rise in pre-tax profits could be accompanied by a fall in EPS if tax charge rose sharply. Consequently, many investors and analysts have tended to calculate EPS after deducting a notional 52 per cent tax rate to smooth the trend of EPS and to facilitate comparisons between companies when, following the publication of SSAP15, not many companies made full provision for deferred tax. More recently, attention is switching to EPS after actual tax, as analysts note a stabilising of actual tax charges. In addition, use of actual tax reflects companies' tax management policies. However, the use of earnings after actual tax requires accurate estimation of the levels of tax changes in the future.

Some companies in the survey included EPS calculated on bases other than after tax charged in the profit and loss account. The policies adopted by companies making these voluntary disclosures were:

Basis of determining earnings	*Number of companies*
Before tax	7
With notional 52 per cent tax rate	7
With full potential deferred tax	12
Before release of deferred tax provisions relating to stock appreciation relief	11
Before release of deferred tax provisions relating to stock appreciation relief with a notional 52 per cent tax rate	1

35 companies in the survey reported FDEPS whilst 39 others made no disclosure since the potential dilution was stated not to be material. 7 companies made no disclosure of a material dilution.

The standard suggests that where material differences between EPS on net and nil bases exist, the latter should also be disclosed. 24 companies disclosed nil based EPS additionally. The standard gives no guidance on what may be considered to be a material difference, but if a 10 per cent difference is taken as the guideline, 74 companies did not disclose nil based EPS where such a difference existed.

In September 1983 the ASC set up a working party to consider whether SSAP3 required revision. The working party concluded that no revision was necessary for three reasons. First, many of the practical problems which might give cause for revision arise from issues related to SSAPs 6 and 15, both of which were being reviewed by the ASC. Second, following the changes introduced to corporation tax in the Budget of March 1984, much of the demand for the presentation of fully-taxed EPS has disappeared. Third, such changes as were envisaged by the working party were considered to be too minor to warrant a revised standard. The ASC accepted the working party's conclusion and have decided not to revise the standard.

Deferred Taxation

The attempts by the ASC to promulgate a standard for deferred taxation illustrate the political problems of accounting regulation which we discussed in Chapter 1. In 1976, difficulties arose when influential industrial opinion was at variance with the proposed accounting treatment for deferred taxation, which was based upon the framework provided by SSAP2. The ASC's proposal was withdrawn and replaced by a standard more acceptable to financial report preparers. This episode reveals the effect of power on the policy setting process, i.e., that companies and their representative bodies have power to overturn policy statements with which they disagree (Hope and Briggs, 1982).

Permanent and Timing Differences

A company's taxable income is often very different from the income reported in the financial statements. This difference arises from 'permanent' and 'timing' differences. Permanent differences arise because some items of revenue and expenditure which appear in the computation of accounting income are permanently omitted from taxable income. For example, items such as the entertaining expenses of home country customers, certain types of donations and subscriptions and franked investment income which appear in the profit and loss account are not included in taxable income. Another group of adjustments cause only a temporary difference between accounting and taxable income. These timing differences arise when an item is includable or deductible in taxable income in one period but in accounting income in another. These differences are said to originate in one period and reverse in one or more subsequent periods, for example where the government allows companies to accelerate items of income and expenditure (depreciation of plant) and transfer others (interest payments and receipts) to different periods.

SSAP15 identifies five categories of timing differences:

(*a*) Short-term timing differences from the use of the receipts and payments basis for taxation purposes and the accruals basis in financial statements: these differences normally reverse in the next accounting period.

(*b*) Availability of capital allowances in taxation computations which are in excess of the related depreciation charges in financial statements. As we note later, the system of capital allowances has been recently altered with implications for deferred taxation.

(c) Availability of stock appreciation relief in taxation computations for which there is no equivalent charge in financial statements. (As we note later, stock relief is no longer a timing difference for deferred taxation purposes.)

(d) Revaluation surpluses on fixed assets for which a taxation charge does not arise until the gain is realised on disposal.

(e) Surpluses on disposals of fixed assets which are subject to rollover relief.

Desirability of Providing for Deferred Taxation

The accounting procedure of allocating tax has developed to account for and explain differences between accounting and taxable income. Accounting policy makers have sought to bring a greater degree of uniformity to the accounting treatment of taxation where there are differences of timing between accounting and taxation recognition of revenue or expenditure. The effect of timing differences 'would be of little significance if taxation was not regarded as relevant to the performance of the business for the period, and the only accepted indication was the income before taxation. The view is widely held, however, that the income after taxation is an important indication of performance being the fund of earnings which supports (or perhaps does not support) the distribution of income by way of dividend' (SSAP15).

The fundamental principle underlying tax allocation is that the tax shown in the accounts is based on the accounting profit for the period.

Example 10.2:

A firm purchases a computer for £20,000 which is depreciated over four years, with no scrap value. For tax purposes a 100 per cent first-year allowance was claimed in year 1. Income before depreciation for the four years life of the computer is £10,000 per annum. Corporation tax rate is 50 per cent.

The computations below compare the resulting income with and without allocation. A timing difference originated in year 1 when £10,000 of the capital allowance claimed was utilised. The difference between the benefit in capital allowances received in year 1 and depreciation (£10,000 minus £5,000) represents £2,500 after taxation and appears as deferred taxation. Therefore, deferred taxation arises when the benefit received from capital allowances exceeds depreciation. In year 2 the computations are similar to year 1. In years 3 and 4 the tax benefits reverse because depreciation exceeded capital allowances. In these years, the difference between depreciation and capital allowances (£5,000 minus 0) at the current tax rate gave a deferred taxation charge of £2,500.

Profit and loss account without tax allocation

	1 £	2 £	3 £	4 £
Income before depreciation	10,000	10,000	10,000	10,000
Depreciation	5,000	5,000	5,000	5,000
Income before taxation	5,000	5,000	5,000	5,000
Tax payable[1]	—	—	5,000	5,000
Income after taxation	5,000	5,000	—	—
Income before depreciation	10,000	10,000	10,000	10,000
Capital allowances	(20,000)	(10,000)	—	—
Tax loss c/f	(10,000)	—	—	—
Taxable income	—	—	10,000	10,000
Tax payable			5,000	5,000

Profit and loss account with allocation

	1 £	2 £	3 £	4 £
Income after depreciation	5,000	5,000	5,000	5,000
Deferred taxation	2,500	2,500	2,500	2,500
Income after taxation	2,500	2,500	2,500	2,500

The computations above show that failure to allocate taxation can have a material impact on reported earnings. The objective of tax allocation is to reduce fluctuations in reported net income. This ensures equity between the shareholders of the same company in different periods of time, by ensuring that income is not inflated and dividends distributed in one year, while in subsequent years income is low and dividends have to be restricted.

Tax allocation has been developed to fit into the traditional financial accounting framework. In the United States *APB Opinion No. 11* (1967) provided the following rationale as theoretical justification for this practice:

(*a*) The operations of an entity subject to taxation are expected to continue on a going concern basis, in the absence of evidence to the contrary, and taxes are expected to continue to be assessed in the future.

(*b*) Taxes are an expense of business enterprises earning income subject to tax.

(*c*) Accounting for tax expense requires measurement and identification with the appropriate time period and therefore involves accrual, deferral and estimation concepts in the same manner as these concepts are applied in the measurement and time period identification of other expenses.

(*d*) Matching is one of the basic processes of income determination.

Objections to Providing for Deferred Taxation

Those who favour the tax payable method of accounting for corporate taxation criticise tax allocation on the following grounds.

1. It is taxable income which attracts taxation, not accounting income. This fact is supported by an enormous body of legislation which cannot be ignored. There is no legal reason, therefore, why taxation payable should bear any relationship to the amounts of income and expenditure appearing in the accounts (Chambers, 1968).

2. 'The primary complaint of those opposed to tax allocation is that the procedure attempts to normalize net income' (Keller, 1966). It is argued that attempts to allocate taxes between periods are conscious efforts to normalise income and should be avoided. Accordingly, it is bad accounting both in principle and practice to manipulate reporting with a view to equalising income as between periods when it is not in fact equal.

3. Taxation is not an expense to be deducted in arriving at a company's net earnings: it is more in the nature of a distribution of earnings. This objection is strongly refuted by many writers who argue that income tax possesses characteristics similar to other items which are treated as expense. Furthermore, distributions of earnings are under the control of the directors, whereas there is nothing voluntary about the payment of income taxes (Barton, 1970).

4. Deferred taxes fail to satisfy the traditional test necessary for their classification as liabilities. They are not a legal liability until they are accrued; they represent not what the firm is liable for, but what the firm expects to be liable for at some future date. This argument relies merely on legal concepts, whereas many writers draw attention to liabilities as economic phenomena (Rosenfield and Dent, 1983).

5. It is difficult to estimate the taxes ultimately payable with any degree of accuracy. Two unknowns which effect the computation are:

   (*a*) the tax rate schedules that will be effective in the periods of offset and,

   (*b*) the levels of earnings that the firm will experience in these future periods (Hill, 1957).

6. Taxes may be permanently deferred. There is no necessity to provide for an amount which will never become payable. To support this argument Davidson has posed two criteria which, in his opinion, must precede the assumptions of the proponents of tax allocation (Davidson, 1958). They are:

   (*i*)   are tax rules for depreciation methods expected to remain as generous as they are now? and

   (*ii*) will a policy of regular investment in assets subject to depreciation be maintained?

He proposed that if the answers are 'yes' there is no basis for the principle of allocation. It is the controversy arising from this objection to tax allocation which has given birth to two conflicting concepts which are considered in the following section.

Concepts of Providing for Deferred Taxation

Although there is wide agreement among accountants that taxes might be allocated there is disagreement about the extent to which it should apply. Two concepts have received support: partial allocation and comprehensive allocation.

Partial allocation. According to proponents of this viewpoint only non-recurring differences between tax payable and the financial accounting tax charge should be allocated between periods. When recurring differences between tax payable and accounting income lead, or are likely to lead, to the indefinite postponement of tax payable, then tax allocation should not be required. The most commonly cited example of a recurring difference which, it is argued, does not require tax allocation under the partial allocation concept is that arising from a stable or growing investment in fixed assets. We may illustrate the tax effects which arise from this kind of situation by considering the position of the firm discussed previously. However, rather than having just one £20,000 asset, assume the firm buys a new £20,000 asset each year until year 4 and in year 5 buys a new £20,000 asset to replace the retired one. The computations appear as follows:

Year	1	2	3	4	5
	£	£	£	£	£
Tax depreciation	20,000	20,000	20,000	20,000	20,000
Accounting depreciation	5,000	10,000	15,000	20,000	20,000
Difference	15,000	10,000	5,000	0	0
Deferred taxation (50 per cent)	7,500	5,000	2,500	0	0

This illustration shows how originating differences in years 1, 2 and 3 are not reversed. Over these years deferred taxation of £15,000 accumulates. Those who support the partial allocation concept argue that these taxes are unlikely ever to be paid and, therefore, should not be included in the financial statements. To do so involves overstating liabilities and correspondingly understating net earnings.

The proponents of partial allocation would allocate corporate tax to future periods only in those instances when non-recurring differences occur. In these cases it is expected that the tax will be paid in a reasonably short period of time.

Comprehensive allocation. Comprehensive allocation requires tax allocation for all timing differences, not just those of a non-recurring nature. Therefore, the current accounting period should be charged with all corporate taxes arising from the current accounting income, regardless of when the taxes are paid. Comprehensive tax allocation is consistent with accrual accounting. In contrast, partial tax allocation emphasises cash outlays.

The proponents of full deferral identify each source of timing differences separately. They trace the tax effects of each timing difference from its originating period through to its ultimate reversal. They do not find it relevant that similar transactions may currently be producing further originating differences which are larger than the reversals of previous timing differences. Each timing difference has its own distinct duration and the charge to income should reflect tax on each separate maturing and originating difference.

Those supporting comprehensive allocation state that the makeup of the balances of certain deferred tax amounts 'revolve' as the related differences reverse and are replaced by similar differences. These initial differences do reverse, and the tax effects thereof can be identified as readily as can those of other timing differences. While new differences may have an offsetting effect, this does not alter the fact of reversal; without reversal there would be different tax consequences. Accounting principles cannot be predicated on reliance that offsets will continue.

(APB Opinion No. 11).

Some critics of current accounting practice have argued that the only tenable basis for deferred tax accounting in relation to long-term assets is to discount the future liability. Accordingly, the tax benefit received on an asset would reverse over its life but the present value of that reversal is certainly not equal to its face value. This viewpoint was supported in the US by a research study, which recommended that deferred tax should be discounted wherever the time span is lengthy: 'to do otherwise grossly overstates liabilities and may significantly misstate periodic net income' (Black, 1966). Official pronouncements have not supported this recommendation.

Methods of Providing for Deferred Taxation

The foregoing discussion has assumed that the tax rate of 50 per cent did not change, but remains in effect over the period of time when originating and reversing differences take place. In these circumstances the balance on the deferred taxation account represents, at any point in time, 50 per cent of the difference between accounting income and the taxable income over the period of the timing differences. However, tax rates do change. This creates the problem: should the tax rate in effect when the timing difference originates be used to measure the tax effect, or should the tax rates expected to be in effect when timing differences reverse be used to measure the tax effect? Both alternatives have their devotees. The first alternative, called the deferral method has been adopted in the US, the second, the liability method, in Australia.

To illustrate these methods we employ the following data:

Year	1	2	3	Total
	£	£	£	£
Income before taxation	10,000	10,000	10,000	30,000
Taxable income	5,000	12,000	13,000	30,000
Tax rate	50%	40%	40%	

Deferral method. Since the tax rate is not adjusted to reflect subsequent changes which may occur, reversals take place at the same original rate. The accounting treatment may be explained with the use of journal entries.

Year	1	2	3	Total
	£	£	£	£
Tax charge	5,000	3,800	3,700	12,500
Deferred taxation	2,500	1,000	1,500	0
Tax payable	2,500	4,800	5,200	12,500

In year 1 a £5,000 originating difference is translated at the existing tax rate of 50 per cent into deferred taxation of £2,500. This difference reverses in years 2 and 3 by £2,000 and £3,000 respectively (i.e. two-fifths and three-fifths). Therefore, deferred taxation is allocated to years 2 and 3 on the basis of two-fifths (£1,000) and two-fifths (£1,500) respectively.

The tax effects of reducing taxes currently payable are not treated as liabilities, but as deferred credits. The deferral method is essentially income oriented.

Liability method. In contrast to the deferral method the liability method is a balance sheet approach to the problem of timing differences since these differences are considered to give rise to future liabilities. The taxes on the components of pre-tax income may be computed at different rates, depending upon the period in which the components were, or are expected to be, included in taxable income. For example, if it is expected that the tax rate will change in the next year, the current component of tax expense will be computed at the current rate, and the deferred components at the rates expected to prevail when reversals take place.

Using the above data, the computations are as follows:

Year	1	2	3	Total
	£	£	£	£
Tax charge	4,500	4,000	4,000	12,500
Deferred taxation	2,000	800	1,200	0
Tax payable	2,500	4,800	5,200	12,500

In year 1 the tax charge is computed as £2,500 tax payable (50 per cent of £5,000) plus £2,000 deferred taxation (40 per cent of £5,000). In years 2 and 3 reversals are computed at the current tax rate of 40 per cent (Year 2, 40 per cent of £2,000 equals £800; year 3, 40 per cent of £3,000 equals £1,200).

Net-of-tax Method. A third method of allocating taxation between periods is the net-of-tax method which is related to the deferral and liability methods. According to this method the tax effects (determined by either the deferral or liability methods) of timing differences are recognised in the valuation of individual assets and liabilities and the related revenues and expenses. Depreciation is held to reduce the value of an asset both because of a decline in economic usefulness and because of a loss of a portion of future tax deductibility. Therefore, financial statements should include, in addition to an amount for accounting depreciation, an amount equal to the tax effect of the excess of tax depreciation over book depreciation. To illustrate, assume the differences of the firm discussed, under the heading of 'Liability method' above were due to depreciation on a £15,000 asset. Accounting depreciation on a straight-line basis over the three years life is

£5,000 per year. Under the net-of-tax method the asset would be valued in the Year 1 balance sheet (assuming the liability procedure is used):

	£	£
Asset		15,000
Less accumulated depreciation	5,000	
Tax effects	2,000	
		7,000
Net asset		£8,000

Accounting Policy Requirements

Attempts to promulgate a standard for deferred taxation in the UK have been highly controversial. In the 1970s, the ASC produced two exposure drafts and two standards each of which advocated a different treatment. These differed from previous recommendations. The documents were:

1. Recommendation N27 (1968) advocated comprehensive allocation based on the liability method.

2. ED11 (1973) recommended comprehensive taxation, using the deferral method. No justification was given for choosing the deferral method, although APB Opinion No. 11 (1967) and the Accountants' International Study Group in 1971 had recommended this method as the most appropriate. ED11 followed the general framework established by SSAP2. Many comments on ED11 criticised the choice of the deferral method when most firms were using the liability method.

3. SSAP11 (1975) insisted on comprehensive tax allocations, but allowed companies the freedom to choose either the liability method or the deferral method to account for material timing differences. However, the granting in 1972 of 100 per cent First Year Allowances on qualifying capital and Stock Appreciation Relief in 1974 for increases both in value and volume of inventories produced large disparities between actual tax rates and the nominal tax rate. The outcome was a massive increase in the deferred tax balances in company balance sheets. By 1976 these balances were in some instances growing to be as large as the total of shareholders' funds. Many large firms united in a campaign to cancel the SSAP. They argued that the standard created unrealistically low earnings and balance sheet liabilities which may never become payable. Also, they feared the then Labour Government might use the large deferred tax balances as a pretext for a gradual nationalisation of UK industry.

4. ED19 (1977) reversed the requirements of SSAP11 and allowed for partial provision of deferred tax using the liability method. It stated that 'deferred taxation should be accounted for, on the liability method, in respect of the tax reduction arising from all originating timing differences of material amount, other than tax reduction which can be demonstrated with reasonable probability to continue for the foreseeable future'. Although industry was in broad agreement with ED19 many accounting firms criticised the provisions on the grounds that they lacked any conceptual basis, and introduced a higher level of subjectivity into the computations. Some firms believed the ED conflicted with the basic objective of the ASC, that of creating uniformity in accounting. ED19 was translated into SSAP15.

5. *SSAP15 (1978)* stated that deferred taxation should be accounted for on all short-term timing differences, except where the tax effects can be demonstrated with reasonable probability to continue in the future. Criteria which must be satisfied for directors to assume that timing differences will continue are:

(*i*)   The company is a going concern.
(*ii*) The directors are able to foresee a reasonable evidence that timing differences will not reverse for some considerable period (at least three years) ahead.
(*iii*) There is no indication that after this period the situation is likely to change so as to crystallise the liabilities.

Unlike ED19, SSAP15 did not provide guidance on whether the liability or deferred methods should be used. A technical release published by the ASC simultaneously with SSAP15 proposed that the liability method should be used to compute the deferred tax provision, although, for some companies, the deferral method may be equally or more convenient.

Disclosure in the profit and loss account was to be shown separately as a component of the total tax charge for the year. Also, there was to be an indication of the extent to which the taxation charge for the year had been reduced by timing differences. In the balance sheet, taxation balances was to be shown separately, and were not to be shown as part of shareholders' funds. A note were to indicate the nature and amount of the major elements of which the deferred tax balance was composed and a description of the method of calculation adopted.

Evaluation of the Requirements

1. The deferred taxation controversy illustrates the failure to develop agreed objectives for accounting: different groups who were affected by the standard setting process adopted different viewpoints as to the

objectives of accounting. Perhaps a user oriented approach as recommended by the Corporate Report provides a more realistic conceptual framework than SSAP2.

2. Investment analysts claim that the information provided by SSAP15 is of no use to them in analysing results because they may be heavily influenced by a reduced tax charge brought about by the purchase of more than usual amounts of plant (Gibbs, 1981). A small sample of companies over a five-year period showed that the percentage rate of tax charges in their accounts ranged from 5 to 52 per cent (Carty, 1983). According to Gibbs, financial analysts re-calculate reported profits using a 52 per cent standard tax rate charge.

The Recommendations of ED33

The ASC introduced further recommendations to accounting for deferred tax in ED33. ED33, whilst expressing general satisfactions with the existing accounting standard:

1. Incorporated certain comments which had been made in the light of experience in applying SSAP15.
2. Incorporated certain changes in rules for disclosure included in the Companies Act 1981.
3. Updated the standard for changes in the status of stock appreciation relief following the Finance Act 1981.

Moreover, the exposure draft altered the emphasis underlying the decision to provide for deferred tax. SSAP15 emphasised '. . . do provide unless . . .' whilst ED33 states:

> . . . provide to the extent that it is probable that a liability will crystallise and do not provide to the extent that a liability will not crystallise.

ED33 clarifies and specifies more closely the assumptions and evidence needed for decisions concerning provisions for deferred tax.

The ASC concluded that the 1984 budget provisions required no fundamental change to ED33. These provisions included the abolition of capital allowances over four years and the gradual reduction of corporation tax to 35 per cent. Where the impact of the deferred taxation account is significant, the adjustment should be treated as an extraordinary item.

A revised version of SSAP 15, based largely on the recommendations of ED33 and the SOI which followed it, was issued in March 1985. The main differences from the original version of SSAP15 are:

(*a*) Partial provision must be used as the basis for deferred tax computations.

(*b*) The deferral method is abandoned in favour of the liability method on the grounds that the former is more consistent with partial provision. This is in line with an IASC decision to withdraw the option to use the deferral method in IAS10.

(*c*) The guidance on provision for deferred tax is: provide to the extent that it is probable that an asset or liability will crystallise and do not provide to the extent to which it is probable that an asset or liability will not crystallise.

Contingencies

Sometimes companies may not wish to disclose information about contingencies because it would prejudice their position. To overcome this problem the 1948 Companies Act introduced a requirement that 'contingent liabilities are required to be disclosed with particulars of their general nature, together where practicable, with an estimate of the amount involved if material'. In 1980 the ASC issued SSAP18 which defined a contingency as a condition which exists at the balance sheet date where the outcome will be confirmed only by the occurrence or non-occurrence of one or more uncertain future events. It is not intended that uncertainties connected with accounting estimates fall within the scope of this standard (e.g. the lives of fixed assets, the amount of bad debts, the net realisable value of inventories, the expected outcome of longer-term contracts or the valuation of properties or foreign currency balances). Contingencies to which the standard refers are the existence of unresolved legal cases or insurance claims at the balance sheet date, for example.

The treatment of a contingency existing at balance sheet date is determined by its expected outcome:

1. Some contingent losses should be accrued in the financial statements although there are no particular disclosure requirements relating to them. This applies if,

   (*a*) the amounts are material and,
   (*b*) it is probable that a future event will confirm a loss and,
   (*c*) the amount of the loss can be estimated with reasonable certainty.

2. Some contingent losses should not be accrued but they necessitate disclosure. This applies to any material contingent loss that is not *probable* enough to be accrued, unless the possibility is remote. Disclosure requirements comprise the nature of the contingency, the uncertainties expected to affect the outcome and a prudent estimate of the potential financial effect (or a statement that it is impracticable to make such a statement).

The standard follows conventional principles in concluding that contingent gains should not be accrued. A material contingent gain should be disclosed in financial statements only if it is probable that the gain will be realised.

Post Balance Sheet Events

One may tend to assume that if the balance sheet date is 31 December, financial statements are prepared to show the results up to that date and events thereafter can be ignored. If financial statements were based on this assumption they may be misleading to users. Disclosure is required of other material events which provide evidence of conditions not existing at the balance sheet date. A post balance sheet event is defined for this purpose by SSAP17 (1983) as 'an event which occurs between the balance sheet date and the date on which the financial statements are approved by the directors'. The 1981 Companies Act recognised the importance of these items by requiring their disclosure in the directors' report. SSAP17 identifies two classes of post balance sheet event—adjusting and non-adjusting events.

Adjusting Events

These events provide more information relating to conditions existing at the balance sheet date and necessitate changes in the amounts reported in financial statements. This category could include, for example, a valuation of property which showed permanent diminution in value, a debtor who became insolvent, new information regarding rates of taxation or the discovery of frauds and error which show that the financial statements were incorrect. In all these cases the information relates to a time at or before the balance sheet date, although it does not become available until afterwards.

Non-adjusting Events

These events arise after the balance sheet date and concern characteristics which did not exist at that time. Consequently, they do not result in changes in amounts in financial statements, but they may be of such materiality that their disclosure is required by way of notes to ensure that financial statements are not misleading. This requirement necessitates the disclosure of 'window dressing' practices—entering into transactions at the end of the year which are primarily designed to improve the appearance of the balance sheet and which are reversed early in the following year. The standard does not require that such transactions should be eliminated from the financial statements but that their nature and effect should be disclosed.

Examples could include mergers and acquisitions, reconstructions, issues of shares and debentures, purchases and sales of fixed assets and investments, closing a significant part of trading activity or changes in foreign exchange rates. In such cases the nature of the event should be disclosed together with an estimate of the financial effect, or a statement that it is not practicable to make such an estimate.

Stocks and Work-in-progress

Surveys in the United States, Canada and the United Kingdom have shown that stocks generally constitute, after fixed assets, the largest balance sheet item in the financial reports of manufacturing firms. Furthermore, since the ratio of stocks to pre-tax income is generally high (about 2.5 to 1), relatively small changes in stock valuation can have a disproportionate effect on reported income.

Accounting Policy Requirements

As the preamble to SSAP9 points out, no area of accounting has produced wider differences than the valuation of stocks and work-in-progress. SSAP9 had two objectives:

(*i*)   To narrow the areas of differences and variations.
(*ii*) To ensure adequate disclosure in financial statements.

SSAP9 states that stocks and work-in-progress include goods for resale, consumable stores, raw materials, products partly completed and finished goods. The standard requires that stocks and work-in-progress, other than long-term contract work in progress, should be valued at the lower of cost or net realisable value. Cost is defined as the cost of purchase plus costs of conversion incurred in bringing the product or service to its present location and condition. The cost of conversion includes direct expenditure, production overheads and other relevant attributable overheads. Production overheads should be based on the normal level of activity. All overhead expenditure which relates to production should be included in stock, even though some of this may accrue on a time basis. All abnormal conversion costs such as exceptional spoilage and idle capacity, which are avoidable under normal operating conditions, should be excluded. Because the costs of general management are not directly related to current production, they are therefore excluded from costs of conversion.

In selecting the methods for ascertaining costs management must ensure they provide the fairest practical approximation to 'actual cost'. Methods such as LIFO and base stock are usually inappropriate for this purpose. In contrast, IAS2 states that LIFO or base stock methods may be used providing that there is disclosure of the difference between the amount at which stocks are stated in the balance sheet, and either the lower of the amount arrived at on an average cost or FIFO basis and net realisable value, or the lower of current cost and net realisable value. Furthermore, the Companies Act 1981, permits the use of LIFO and requires that the method chosen (FIFO, LIFO, weighted average or any other similar method) must be one which appears to the directors to be appropriate in the circumstances of the company.

Net realisable value (NRV) is defined as the actual or estimated selling price (net of trade but before settlement discounts), less—

(*a*) all further costs of completion and,
(*b*) all costs to be incurred in marketing, selling and distribution.

The comparison of cost and NRV needs to be made in respect of each item of stock separately. Where this is impracticable, groups or categories of stock items which are similar will need to be taken together.

Example 10.3:

Company Y processes and sells a single product. Raw material was purchased at a regular rate of 500 tons at the beginning of each week during 19X0. At the beginning of January the price was £50 per ton, which was increased to £75 per ton on 1 July, and thereafter remained constant until the end of the year. The transport costs to the factory were £10 per ton.

Variable processing costs were £30 per ton. The normal level of activity was 500 tons per week and annual fixed production costs were £260,000.

One ton of raw material is processed into one ton of finished product and sold at £130 per ton. Delivery costs to customers were £10 per ton and fixed selling expenses for the year were £20,000.

At 31 December, closing stocks of raw material and finished product were 3,000 tons and 1,000 tons respectively.

One might calculate the value of stock as follows:

(*a*) the value of stock at 31 December on a basis acceptable under SSAP9 and,
(*b*) the value of raw materials stock on a LIFO basis.

(*a*) Using a FIFO basis stock would be calculated as follows:

		Per Ton £	Stock Value £000
(*i*)	Raw material		
	Purchase price	75	
	Carriage	10	
	Value of 3,000 tons	85	255

		Per Ton £	Stock Value £000
(*ii*)	Finished goods		
	Raw material	85	
	Variable cost	30	
	Fixed production cost	10	
		125	
(*iii*)	Net realisable value		
	Selling price	130	
	Less delivery	10	
		120	
	Value of 1,000 tons	120	120
			375

Note that in accordance with SSAP9 stock is valued at the lower of cost or net realisable value.

(*b*) The value of raw material stock on a LIFO basis is calculated as follows:

	£
At 30 June (1,500 tons at £50 per ton)	75,000
At 31 December (1,500 tons at 75 per ton)	112,500
Add carriage (3,000 tons at £10 per ton)	30,000
	£217,500

The valuation of long-term contracts creates a conflict between two of the fundamental concepts discussed in Chapter 3: prudence and accruals. Prudence dictates that profit should not be taken until realised, which means at the satisfactory completion of the contract. Conversely, for a company which regularly undertakes long-term contracts, for example, in the construction industry, the accruals concept dictates that some profit be taken on contracts in progress, otherwise profit or loss would reflect the timing of completion of contracts rather than efforts expended. As we saw in Chapter 7, two alternative accounting methods have been proposed to deal with long-term contracts:

(*i*) Completed contract method, reflecting prudence by taking profit only on completion of a contract,

(*ii*) Percentage of completion basis, reflecting accruals by taking profit during the course of a contract.

SSAP9 requires that long-term contract profit be valued by:

(*i*)   the completed contract basis if the outcome of the contract cannot be foreseen with reasonable certainty; or by

(*ii*) the percentage of completion basis if the outcome of the contract can be foreseen with reasonable certainty.

The standard further requires that as soon as estimates of total contract costs exceed those of total contract revenues a loss be recognised.

The estimation of a contract's outcome depends upon a satisfactory ability to determine contract revenues and to define and estimate contract costs.

Example 10.4:

Company X is engaged in long-term construction contracts. At 30 June 19X1 it had three contracts in progress for which data was as follows:

Contract	1	2	3
	£000	*£000*	*£000*
Contract price	1,200	1,440	3,600
Costs to 30 June 19X0	432	132	—
Costs incurred during current year	372	392	120
Estimated costs to complete the contract	132	992	3,320
Work certified to 30 June 19X0	280	158	—
Work certified during current year	616	232	132
Profit taken on contract to 30 June 19X1	79	—	—

Each contract allows for X to receive progress payments from its clients equal to the value of work certified. All payments are prompt. The contracts may be accounted for as follows. Firstly, the contract profit or loss should be estimated. If a loss is foreseen this should be recognised in the profit and loss account immediately; if a profit is estimated, a judgement must be made on the attribution of profit. If profit is to be taken, several attribution bases are available. Two of the most widely used are based upon the value of work certified as a proportion of contract price (sales basis) and the value of cost as a proportion of total estimated contract costs (cost basis). The accounting treatments are as follows:

Contracts		1		2		3
		£000		*£000*		*£000*
Contract price		1,200		1,440		3,600
Costs: to 30 June 19X0	432		132		—	
for current year	372		392		120	

Contracts		1		2		3
		£000		£000		£000
to complete	132	936	992	1,516	3,320	3,440
Estimated profit (loss)		264		(76)		160

Since Contract 1 is substantially complete (around 75 per cent of the contract price is represented by total work certified), the sales basis seems appropriate. Thus, profit attributable thus far is:

$$\frac{£(280,000+£616,000)}{£1,200,000} \times £264,000 = £197,120$$

less profit taken to date of £79,000, giving profit attributable for the year of £118,120.

Since a loss is estimated on Contract 2, this should be recognised immediately in the profit and loss account.

With regard to Contract 3, although a profit is estimated, only a relatively small proportion has been satisfactorily completed (£132,000 of work certified out of a contract price of £3,600,000). Prudence would seem to prevail and prevent any recognition of profit so early.

The total profit recognised in the profit and loss account of X for the year ending 30 June 19X1 is:

	£
Contract 1	118,120
Contract 2	(76,000)
Contract 3	—
	42,120

Disclosure

The policies adopted in calculating cost, net realisable value, attributable profit and foreseeable losses (as appropriate) should be stated. Stocks and work-in-progress should be subclassified in the balance sheet or in the notes to the financial statements. This breakdown is also required under the 1981 Companies Act. This Act requires that where the balance sheet value of stocks differs materially from their replacement cost at the balance sheet date, the amount of the difference must be disclosed in a note to the accounts.

In relation to the amount at which long-term contracts are shown in the balance sheet there should be stated:

(a) the cost of work in progress plus attributable profit, less foreseeable losses,

(b) progress payments received and receivable at the accounting date.

Therefore, returning to the above example, Company X would show the value of long-term contract work in progress in the balance sheet as follows:

	Contract 1 £	Contract 2 £	Contract 3 £	Total £
Costs to date	804,000	524,000	120,000	1,448,000
Plus profit to date (less loss recognised)	197,120	(76,000)	—	121,120
	1,001,120 +	448,000 +	120,000 =	1,569,120

Progress payments

received and receivable	896,000 +	390,000 +	132,000 =	1,418,000

The balance sheet would record under 'current assets':

	£
Work-in-progress on long-term contracts at cost plus attributable profit less losses	1,569,120
Less: progress payments received and receivable	(1,418,000)
	155,120

Accounting Practice

The 1976 introduction of an accounting standard on stocks and work-in-progress has had considerable impact on the level of disclosure in financial reports. However, the degree of disclosure is usually limited to the minimum required by law and SSAP9; it is often obscure, and sometimes non-existent. Some companies have maintained bases of valuing stock which do not follow the rules set out in SSAP9. For example, the British Sugar Corporation values stock at selling price while Tate and Lyle values raw sugar on a base stock method. Both companies receive the blessing of the auditors but clearly this is an instance where the objective of narrowing the divergencies in practice so as to improve comparability between similar enterprises is not being achieved.

The 1982 *Survey of Published Accounts* showed that of the 297 companies carrying stocks and work in progress in all except 5 cases, the basis used was the lower of cost and net realisable value. The methods used were mentioned in 93 cases. Of these 40 used FIFO, 20 average cost, 18 retail price less a sales margin, 6 base stock, 5 standard cost and 4 LIFO. 220 companies disclosed which overhead costs were included in inventory. Of these, 5 companies specifically excluded some or all overheads.

72 companies were involved in long-term contracts. 68 of these included profit on uncompleted contracts. 3 companies did not mention this item and the one which specifically excluded profit on uncompleted contracts stated that the effect on profits and net assets would not be material. 68 companies mentioned provisions for losses and contingencies and indicated that these covered all losses to completion.

Evaluation of the Requirements

1. If the prime objective of financial reporting is to provide information which is useful for decision making, a strong case can be made for valuing stock at variable cost, thereby excluding fixed production overheads. Because SSAP9 requires the inclusion of these overheads in stock it adopts a full costing approach. The arguments in favour of providing variable costing information for assisting decision making by external users are very strong. Variable costing emphasises the behaviour of fixed and variable costs. This assists the prediction of future income in relation to volume changes.

In Chapter 7 we considered the importance of the critical event on income recognition. Management should not receive credit for increasing the net worth of the owners before the critical event has occurred. In most cases, sale is the critical event. Profits should vary with managerial achievement—which means occurrence of the critical event—and it is logical that where profits are limited by sales there should be a direct relationship between the two. With variable costing, profit can change only if revenue or cost incurrences vary from period to period. In contrast, the profit concept underlying full costing is obscure; profit is a function not only of revenue and cost incurrence, but of production.

Variable costing reduces some of the distortions which may occur where fixed costs are assigned to departments and products which bear only an arbitrary association.

2. SSAP9 requires stock to be valued at the lower of cost of NRV. However, where production is the 'critical event' it may be argued that valuation at NRV is more appropriate. Precious metals and agricultural commodities may have ready markets and assured sales prices.

3. There is a good case for producing supplementary balance sheets based on realisable values (Lyne, 1981). This would provide relevant information to the investors for assessing the risks associated with an investment.

4. SSAP9 adopts an historical cost approach to stock valuation. Many of the cost flow problems (FIFO *v.* LIFO) which have plagued accounting theorists for many years and created great variety in published financial statements, disappear under a CCA system.

Empirical Research Findings

SSAP9 provides a very broad framework for the valuation of stocks and work-in-progress. Companies are left very much to themselves when it comes to detailed practice. Considerable discretion is allowed, especially with regard to the valuation of long-term contracts. Full disclosure of accounting policies and their financial effects is necessary for users to get a full picture of corporate performance. That the market is able to assimulate such details is illustrated by Sunder's (1975) research which showed that the capital market may be able to assimilate changes in accounting alternatives. He investigated share price reactions to switches in the basis of inventory valuation from FIFO to LIFO and LIFO to FIFO. Firms switching from FIFO to LIFO will report lower earnings while at the same time lowering the tax bill. Sunder's research indicates that firms which made this switch experienced an average increase in the price of shares of 5 per cent more than would have been expected taking account of market movements during the year when the change in accounting policy occurred. This is in line with the implications of the efficient market model since it reflects the real economic impact of the change on the firm.

Depreciation

Depreciation is merely part of the larger subject of income measurement and asset valuation discussed in Chapter 6. Differences in views on depreciation reflects differences on these wider issues. For example, if assets are valued on a present value basis depreciation is regarded as the periodic reduction in the value of the assets estimated by discounting their future net services to their present value. If, on the other hand, accounting income is abandoned in favour of cash-flow accounting, or a net realisable asset base, the need to define depreciation disappears.

In an accrual based accounting system the estimates in computing depreciation are very subjective. The large amount of judgement involved (e.g. in estimating useful life) and the considerable variety of practices explain the importance of depreciation. Because of the significance of depreciation on the financial statements, it is essential that users understand the effects of alternatives on the statements so they may compare the statements of companies using different accounting policies. Efficient market research findings emphasise the importance of adequate disclosure.

Accrual accounting necessitates facing the problem of how one matches the benefits from depreciation. In this respect the role of revenue in computing depreciation has been a cause of much controversy. Some distinguished writers have explained an asset's depreciation in terms of net revenue, not merely in terms of age and costs. As Baxter (1981) points out, this treatment of depreciation cost is inconsistent with the accounting treatment of other costs. Depreciation cost ceases to be a matter of how much input is consumed and becomes instead a matter of how much revenue is earned. Another difficulty with the revenue approach is that usually a combination of assets is involved in making a product and one cannot sensibly isolate the revenue from any one given asset (Thomas, 1974).

Accounting Policy Requirements

According to the 1981 Companies Act,

1. Fixed assets having a limited useful life must be reduced by provisions for depreciation calculated to write off that amount systematically over the period of the asset's useful economic life.
2. If the diminution in value of a fixed asset is expected to be permanent, provision must be made in the accounts and disclosed in the profit and loss account or in a note to the accounts.
3. Where a provision no longer applies, it must be written back to the extent that it is no longer necessary.
4. The accounting policies adopted by the company in determining depreciation and diminution in the value of assets must be disclosed.

SSAP12 defines depreciation as the measure of the wearing out, consumption or other loss of value of a fixed asset whether arising from use, effluxion of time or obsolescence through technology and market changes. It requires that provision be made for depreciation of fixed assets having a finite useful life by allocating the cost (or revalued amount) of the fixed assets less residual values to the periods expected to benefit from their use.

The standard explains that depreciation is not related to market value and that the need for depreciation does not disappear merely because the market value of the asset at any particular time during its life is higher than the net book amount.

Where there is a revision of the estimated useful life of an asset, the unamortised cost should be charged over the revised remaining useful life. If any part of the unamortised cost becomes irrecoverable, it should be written off immediately and the recoverable amount charged over the remaining useful life. Where fixed assets are revalued in the financial accounts the depreciation provision must be based on the new valuation and on the revised estimate of the remaining useful life.

SSAP12 states that freehold land will not normally require a provision for depreciation, unless subject to depletion or loss of value for other reasons. Buildings have a limited life and should be depreciated using the same criteria applied to other fixed assets. There has been considerable resistance to this provision of SSAP12. In order to avoid making depreciation charges many companies argue that buildings are really an investment, not a depreciating asset. But where a company uses buildings for its own purposes the treatment proposed in SSAP12 should apply. Where properties are held as investments rather than used in the business SSAP19, *Accounting for Investment Properties*, requires that such assets should not be depreciated annually but should be revalued annually at open market value, the valuation being incorporated in the balance sheet. According to SSAP19, changes in value should be taken to an investment revaluation reserve, unless the balance on the reserve is insufficient to cover any deficit arising during the accounting period, in which case the excess amount of the deficit should be taken to the profit and loss account.

SSAP12 requires that the following be disclosed in the financial statements for each major class of depreciable asset:

(a) The depreciation methods used
(b) The useful lives or the depreciation rates used
(c) Total depreciation allocated for the period
(d) The gross amount of depreciable assets and the related accumulated depreciations.

Example 10.5:

The following data has been extracted from the records of W Limited for the purpose of preparing financial statements for the year ended 31 December 19X4:

	Purchase Date	Cost	Accumulated Depreciation at 31.12.X3	Net Book Value at 31.12.X3
		£	£	£
Machine A	1.1.X0	75,000	22,500	52,500
Machine B	1.1.X0	49,000	14,700	34,300

The useful life for each machine was estimated at 10 years at the time of purchase. The company uses straight line depreciation. At 1 January 19X4 the remaining useful life of machine A has been revised to 5 years (machine B's useful life is unchanged), and machine B has been revalued to £42,000.

Depreciation for the year ended 31 December 19X4 is calculated as follows:

Machine A The unamortised amount should be spread over the machine's remaining useful life, thus:

£52,500÷5 years=£10,500 charged to profit and loss account

Machine B The revalued amount should be spread over the remaining useful life, thus:

£42,000÷(10−3) years=£6,000 charged to profit and loss account

Accounting Practice

The 1982 *Survey of Published Accounts* found that the straight line method is used for all or most assets by 252 of the 300 companies. 18 other companies give no clear statement of the methods adopted. The remaining 30 use the reducing balance or a combination of methods.

Evaluation of the Requirements

1. The standard does not consider

(*a*) which method of depreciation should be used
(*b*) how asset lives should be computed.

It merely states that depreciation should be allocated 'as fairly as possible'. No criteria are provided by which individual companies can test the application of judgement in particular circumstances.

2. The standard does not consider the fact that traditional methods reduce the usefulness of income statement data for comparative purposes because they understate the costs of employing long-term assets compared with the costs of other items such as materials and labour. The cash payments associated with the latter are close in time to their associated expenses. The annuity method of assessing depreciation removes this difficulty by substituting a series of straight line charges in the form of an annuity which at an interest rate equal to the cost of capital for the enterprise, has a present value equal to the initial installed cost of the asset.

3. The 1982 *Survey of Published Accounts* found that out of 265 companies disclosing where CCA statements are produced, 51 adopted different asset lives for historical cost accounts (HCA) and CCA. This practice results from the failure of HCA to take into account price level changes. Because charges for HC depreciation do not reflect price changes there has been a tendency to underestimate the lives of assets in order to obtain a higher

depreciation charge. One researcher estimated that over 30 per cent of fixed assets held by companies are fully written off but still in use (Ross, 1980).

A Discussion Paper (ASC, 1983) stated that there is no logical justification for the same assets to have different lives in the CCA and HC statements. It argued that there should be a reassessment of asset lives (where they have been fully depreciated) and that if failure to charge depreciation on these assets would result in a material distortion of the results, a prior-year adjustment following the fundamental error provisions of SSAP6 should be made. The working party proposed that SSAP12 should be revised to make it clear that to charge supplementary depreciation without incorporating a revaluation of the asset(s) concerned contravenes the standard.

The conclusions of the 1982 working party on this and other matters were taken into account by the ASC in preparing an ED on revisions to SSAP12. Thus ED37 was published in March, 1985 and contained the following major points to be dealt with in a revised standard:

(*a*) The standard should continue to allow and encourage the inclusion of fixed assets at revalued amounts in accounts.

(*b*) Useful economic life for depreciation purposes should be that to the present owner, not the assets total useful economic life.

(*c*) The accounting treatment of fixed assets and depreciation in balance sheet and profit and loss account should be consistent. Thus, depreciation should be based on the assets value in the balance sheet.

(*d*) Identical asset lives should be used for historical cost and current cost depreciation.

(*e*) Differences in net book amount and revalued amount should be transferred to a revaluation reserve.

(*f*) The chosen depreciation method should most fairly reflect the allocation of cost of the asset to accounting periods based on type of asset and nature of its use.

4. The 1982 *Survey of Published Accounts* found that the usefulness and adequacy of the rates and lives shown is frequently questionable. For example, many companies give wide ranges of figures for each class of equipment. Where full information in respect of sub-classes of equipment is given, it is not always possible to ascertain the significance of these sub-classes from the fixed assets schedule.

5. As we saw in Chapter 7, many writers have questioned the feasibility of regarding depreciation as a process of allocation, not of valuation. This process results in entirely arbitrary measurements. Therefore, it is argued that accountants should avoid arbitrary allocations and that depreciation

should be related to measurable, market determinable, allocation-free parameters. The valuation of assets at second-hand replacement cost may provide more useful measurements.

Empirical Research Findings

Beaver and Dukes (1973) compared the price earnings ratios of firms that use accelerated methods of depreciation for both tax and reporting purposes with the price earnings ratios of firms that use accelerated methods for tax purposes but straight line for reporting purposes. They found that when the firms were placed on a uniform accounting method the price earnings differences disappeared. Thus, if the market is given appropriate information, it is able to adjust for differences in depreciation methods among firms.

Intangible Assets

The Companies Acts require that assets classified as intangible are shown separately in the balance sheet in order to inform users of the kinds of resources in which management has invested funds. In keeping with tangible assets, intangible assets represent rights to future benefits. The main characteristic of an intangible asset is the high degree of uncertainty concerning future benefits which result from its employment. As a consequence intangible assets are the subject of controversy.

A distinguishing feature of intangible assets is that they do not have physical substance. However, they are not unique in this respect: bank deposits, debtors and long-term investments lack physical substance, but are classified as tangible assets. The major problem in accounting for intangible assets is to decide whether they have future benefits and should be capitalised and amortised over a period of time, or whether they have no future benefits and thus are expenses of the period.

Accounting for intangible assets has conformed to the same accounting principles and procedures as for tangible assets. Therefore, in accordance with conventional principles:

(i) They should be recorded at cost. Cost includes all costs of acquisition and expenditures necessary to make the intangible asset ready for intended use.

(ii) The cost of intangible assets should be amortised to expense over the estimated periods of useful life just as the cost of tangible assets having a limited period of usefulness are depreciated. Depending on the type of intangible asset, its useful life may be limited by such factors as legal, contractual or regulatory provisions, demand and competition; life expectancies of employees; and economic factors.

APB Opinion No. 14 (1968) requires that intangibles be amortised over a period not exceeding forty years. Also, it states that 'the straight line method of amortisation—equal amounts—should be applied unless a company demonstrates that another systematic method is more appropriate'. These arbitrary guidelines were designed to introduce a measure of uniformity into practice.

Another principle which has governed the treatment of intangible assets is conservatism. This explains why the 'immediate recognition' method of recognising expenses discussed in Chapter 7 applies to much of the expenditure on intangible items, irrespective of any future benefits which may result. For example, a company may spend £1 million on advertising and training programmes which are beneficial to the company's future operations and yet not capitalise these costs. On the other hand, £1 million spent on an investment programme in tangible assets which is expected to produce less benefits would be capitalised.

In this chapter we limit our discussion of intangible assets to two topics: goodwill and research and development costs. These topics have been the subject of much controversy, a product of the lack of agreement on accounting objectives. Without a clear definition and agreement on these objectives, accounting problems will continue to be developed on a pragmatic basis.

Goodwill

Goodwill has been the subject of controversy for many years. Both its nature and treatment in financial statements have been disputed vigorously from time to time. However, general agreement exists on a number of points.

First,

> goodwill may be defined as an excess of the value of a business as a whole over the fair value of its accountable net identifiable assets (including identifiable intangibles such as patents, licenses and trademarks). The value of the business may be established, inter alia, by an assessment of the present value of the expected future streams of distributable earnings, and consequently the expected return on an investment in the company could directly affect the value attributed to the goodwill of that company. (ASC, 1980)

Second, inherent goodwill is present in most businesses in that, as going concerns, they are worth more than their fair net asset value and that the amount of goodwill fluctuates constantly. There is no provision within the framework of conventional accounting principles for recording inherent goodwill in the accounts.

Third, purchased goodwill arises when one business acquires another as a going concern. Therefore, the value of purchased goodwill is acquired at a particular point in time by a definitive market transaction.

The creation of purchased goodwill illustrates the fact that the value of a business can only be determined subjectively because it depends on the acquiring management's expectation of future cash flows, the expected opportunity rates of return and utility functions. This value may bear little resemblance to the aggregate value of individual assets which may play only a minor role in the acquiring management's calculations. On numerous occasions the buyer of another enterprise has been heard to remark, 'We were not buying assets, we were buying earning power' (Skinner, 1979). Rather than being reflected in the value of its balance sheet assets, the cash-generating ability of an enterprise may lie largely in its brand name, as in the case of Coca Cola, or in its formula for operations, as in the case of McDonald's, or in its technology as in IBM, or in a multitude of other things.

Treatment of purchased goodwill

Given the nature of goodwill it is not surprising that there are divergent views on the subject and how it should be treated in the financial statements. Four clearly recognised treatments are possible:

1. Write off goodwill to reserves at the time of acquisition. Proponents of this treatment support it by reference to the objectives of financial statements and the nature of goodwill. We have adopted the view that all accounting problems must be resolved against a background of the objectives of financial statements. Therefore, the main objective of financial statements is to communicate information to the user in a way which will assist his decision making. It is not the function of financial statements to value a firm: on the contrary, it is for investors to establish the value of the firm as an investment and to bear the risks involved. The evaluation of future expectations by investors—which collectively is what goodwill is based on—has no place in the statement of financial position of the very business from which expectations originate. Other arguments which support this treatment of goodwill are related to its nature:

(*a*) Goodwill is not an asset because it attaches to the business as a whole and, therefore, lacks the characteristics of exchangeability which assets generally possess. Many intangible attributes contribute to goodwill but these cannot be measured or evaluated separately. If severability is included in the definition of assets then goodwill is not an asset.

(*b*) Goodwill appears to accrue directly to the owner of the business rather than to the business itself. 'The goodwill of a going concern runs to the constituents, not to the firm. It is they who put valuations on expected superior returns' (Chambers, 1966). To the purchaser, goodwill is not an income producing asset, but rather is an advance distribution of anticipated future earnings. Therefore, goodwill should reduce the value of shareholders' equity.

(c) Unlike an asset goodwill has no reliable relationship to costs incurred in its creation. Many favourable conditions may explain the creation of goodwill without expenditures or efforts by a company. Furthermore, the value of goodwill does not have the general stability possessed by other resources, but can fluctuate erratically.

(d) Purchased goodwill arises merely because one enterprise acquires another. It is created over a relatively long period as internally generated goodwill and it is only because someone has spent money, or other consideration, that attention is focused on it. Furthermore, this book-keeping entry which tells an historical tale, becomes increasingly irrelevant as the years go by.

2. Retain goodwill as an asset indefinitely unless its value is permanently impaired. According to this treatment goodwill is regarded as a valid capital asset of economic significance. It is a cost incurred at the time of business acquisitions and the cash expenditure for goodwill is just as real as the cash invested in tangible assets. Why should the buying company be allowed to charge off this intangible expenditure to reserves when it cannot charge off other assets acquired in the same transactions? The arguments for retaining goodwill as an asset indefinitely are given below.

(a) Goodwill has no limited term of existence and, therefore, no sound basis for amortisation exists. 'Amortisation can neither be reasonably related to the revenue of a period nor reasonably associated in some other manner with specific time periods' (Catlett and Olson, 1968).

(b) Goodwill is not consumed in the production of revenue. Because the traditional assumption that 'costs attach' does not apply to goodwill, the cost of buying another company's goodwill cannot be realistically associated with future revenue.

(c) Goodwill may be enhanced. It is constantly replenished by the normal operations of the business. Where goodwill is obviously increasing, any sort of arbitrary amortisation of purchased goodwill is meaningless.

(d) The arbitrary allocation of goodwill may lessen the reliability and usefulness of financial statements for those external users who are concerned with evaluating the profitability or peformance of the enterprise.

3. Show goodwill as a separately identifiable deduction from shareholders' funds. This has become known as the 'dangling debit' treatment. This treatment compares with No. 1 above in the belief that goodwill is not an asset. This method achieves two objectives: it shows net assets less goodwill which is consistent with the value which would be placed on them by investment analysts; also the resultant value of net assets will be comparable with businesses of similar size which have expanded internally.

4. Retain goodwill as an asset to be amortised on a regular basis. The arguments for carrying goodwill as a fixed asset were stated in treatment No. 2 and are applicable here. The main arguments for amortising goodwill are based on the premise that a primary function of accounting is to match costs and revenues. This treatment is thereby considered conceptually sound because it is in accordance with traditional theory:

(*a*) Because goodwill is no different from another asset with a finite, useful life, it should be capitalised and amortised through the income statement. This treatment is in accordance with the matching concept which views all purchases as being made for the purpose of securing future revenues. Income will be overstated unless these costs are written off.

(*b*) Systematic and rational allocations are based on estimates. In this respect the amortisation of goodwill is no different from other items which involve the matching of costs and revenues.

(*c*) An ever-increasing proportion of internally-generated goodwill is gradually replacing goodwill originally purchased. This gradual diminution of purchased goodwill should be reflected in some sort of regularised policy on write-offs.

Accounting Practice

The 1982 *Survey of Published Accounts* showed the 300 sample companies following policies as follows:

Deducted from or written off reserves	138
Deducted from shareholders' funds	4
Written-off as an extraordinary item in the year of acquisition	38
Amortised on a regular basis	17
Retained as an asset at cost	31

Recommendations and Policy Requirements

In 1974 a working party was set up to examine goodwill but failed to reach agreement. The challenge of the EEC's Fourth Directive necessitated the setting up of a new panel in 1978 to consider what recommendations should be made by the Department of Trade. The Fourth Directive requires goodwill to be written off over five years or less, or at the option of the member state, over useful economic life, if longer. The panel produced the discussion paper *Accounting for Goodwill* (ASC, 1980) which recommended as follows:

1. Goodwill should not be carried forward indefinitely as a permanent item; it has a finite useful economic life and should be amortised over this life. Any unamortised goodwill should be classified under fixed assets.
2. The amortisation period is tentatively suggested (for discussion) as two-and-a-half times the price/earnings ratio with an absolute maximum in all cases of forty years.
3. Negative goodwill should be amortised in line with 'positive' goodwill.

The 1981 Companies Act bars the 'dangling debit' treatment. It states that goodwill must be written off over a period which does not exceed its useful economic life. The period over which it is being written off and the reasons for choosing that period must be disclosed in a note. SSAP22 requires that goodwill be eliminated either by immediate write-off on acquisition against reserves or by amortisation through the profit and loss account over its useful economic life. No maximum period is prescribed.

Research and Development Costs

The ASC experienced similar difficulties in promulgating a standard for research and development (R and D) to those which affected policy making for deferred taxation. Both cases illustrate the effect of corporate power on the standard-setting process. The ASC, it has been suggested, followed a 'survival strategy' in changing the tenor of original pronouncements (Hope and Gray, 1982). In both cases, on the key issues of accounting treatment and disclosure, the views of industrial opinion have prevailed.

Categories of Costs

R and D costs include those direct and indirect costs related to the creation and development of new processes, techniques, applications and products with commercial possibilities. SSAP13 placed these expenditures into three broad categories:

Pure research, which is directed primarily towards the advancement of knowledge and not towards any specific practical aim or application;

Applied research, which is directed primarily towards exploiting pure research, other than work defined below as development expenditure; and

Development, which is work directed towards the introduction or improvement of specific products or processes.

Within the conventional accounting system there are three methods of accounting for R and D costs: capitalise all costs as assets when incurred; treat all costs as expenses when incurred; capitalise those costs which meet a specified criterion (or criteria); and expense those costs that do not meet the criterion (or criteria).

Arguments for Capitalising

1. According to conventional practice, where costs are incurred in one period to produce an expected benefit in a future period these are expenses of future periods and should be deferred and amortised over the future periods they are expected to benefit. The immediate expensing of R and D costs could produce a distorted view of periodic income.
2. Balance sheets will not reflect reality if all past R and D expenditures are expensed, because to represent their continuing benefits as zero will not be in accordance with the facts of the situation.
3. A code of accounting procedure which requires immediate expensing of R and D costs may inhibit companies from engaging in large R and D expenditure because of the adverse effect on income.

Arguments for Expensing

1. The uncertainty of future benefits necessitates the expensing of R and D costs. According to this viewpoint the matching concept cannot by usefully applied. The financial stability of companies may be at risk if no worthwhile returns are forthcoming from R and D costs which have been capitalised.
2. The attempt to match expenditure and benefits is an arbitrary process because there is generally no direct or even indirect basis for relating costs to revenues. Therefore, there is a problem of deciding the method of amortisation and the period of amortisation. R and D costs are intangible assets that do not always have a clearly determinable life. Anything other than the immediate expensing of these costs may lead to the manipulation of reported results.
3. Because the future economic benefits of R and D expenditure cannot be objectively measured, it does not meet the accounting concept of an asset.

Accounting Policy Requirements

In 1971 SSAP2 drew attention to the importance of developing a standard for R and D. Companies were employing a variety of methods of accounting for R and D and there was a lack of information about R and D costs in company annual reports. The situation existed against the background of growing awareness of the importance of expenditure on R and D, particularly in high technology industries, and increasing expenditure on R and D by UK companies.

In 1975, ED14 was issued which followed the guidelines developed in SSAP2 that where the accruals concept is inconsistent with the prudence concept the latter prevails. Therefore, ED14 concluded that, on the grounds of prudence, uniformity and the avoidance of subjectivity, expenditure on R and D should be written off in the year in which it is incurred. No doubt another factor which influenced the ASC's decision was the criticism of accounting principles which allowed Rolls Royce in 1967 to change its accounting policy from expensing to capitalising R and D costs. At the time of the company's collapse, it was argued that this new policy had disguised the serious financial position of the company. The ASC was also influenced by considerations of international harmony (Watts, 1981): the US standard, FASB No. 2, which was issued in 1974 required R and D costs to be written off as incurred.

ED14 aroused bitter opposition from the electronics and aerospace industries who argued that the new policy, by reducing their profits, would limit their ability to attract new capital and thereby curtail their future growth and development. This pressure lead the ASC to withdraw ED14 and substitute ED17 which became SSAP13.

The new standard states that R and D costs in certain circumstances may be capitalised. At the beginning of this section we distinguished between pure research, applied research and development. SSAP13 regards expenditure falling within the first two categories as part of a continuing operation required to maintain a company's business and competitive position which should be written off against revenue in the year in which expenditure is incurred. The benefits from pure and applied research expenditures are usually uncertain: many costs are joint costs and a reasonable basis of allocation to specific products or processes cannot be developed. Therefore, on practical grounds it is expedient to recognise all costs of continuing research programmes as expenses at the time incurred. Recognising these costs immediately as expenses is an arbitrary allocation of costs, but so are all other treatments. Any other treatment would be more difficult to implement uniformily, leave greater scope for subjectivity and allow the possibility of very unconservative practices.

A different accounting treatment may be applied to expenditure on substantial development projects which have a definite purpose and separately indentifiable costs. Where projects are designed to develop products or processes which have already proved to be feasible, they involve a greater likelihood of success and the identification of future benefits is stronger than with pure and applied research. But many development projects are certain to produce benefits and have costs which are not separately identifiable. Therefore, it is necessary to develop criteria for establishing which costs shoud be deferred. SSAP13 recommended that a project should meet the following criteria if costs are to be deferred:

1. Clearly defined project
2. Separately identifiable expenditure
3. Technical feasibility
4. Commercial viability (in the light of competing products, public opinion, legislation, etc.)
5. Costs will be more than covered by expected revenues
6. Adequate resources exist to complete the project

Several additional criteria are considered in an American study (Gellein and Newman, 1973). These are:

1. The project should be of significant size
2. The Board of Directors should formally approve the project
3. The estimated amount and the probable timing of potential revenue should be reasonably established
4. Deferred costs should be limited to those that are reasonably allocatable to specific periods or future contracts.

According to this study 'a formal programme should be established to periodically evaluate the project to write off the costs that exceed expected revenue less completion and selling costs'. This finds support in SSAP13 which states 'At each accounting date the unamortised balance of development expenditure should be examined project by project to ensure that it still fulfills the criteria'.

With regard to disclosure, SSAP13 requires disclosure of—

1. Movements on deferred development expenditure, and the amount carried forward at the beginning and end of the period should be disclosed;
2. Deferred development expenditure should be separately disclosed and should not be included in current assets;
3. The accounting policy followed should be clearly explained.

The 1981 Companies Act requires that where development costs are included in a company's balance sheet there must be a note to the accounts which shows

1. the reasons for capitalising the expenditure and;
2. the period over which the costs are being written off.

SSAP13 does not require disclosure of the amounts expended on R and D. In contrast, SFAS does make the provision that 'disclosure shall be made in the financial statements of the total research and development costs charged to expense in each period for which an income statement is presented'. Similarly, IAS9 provides for this additional disclosure.

In the 1983 *Survey of Published Accounts*, of the 167 companies undertaking some R and D activity 33 did not give an accounting policy. The survey does reveal that the number of companies carrying forward development expenditure has declined over the last few years.

This episode highlights the problem of enforcing an accounting standard when influential parties are affected by that standard. It also illustrates a retreat from developing uniform standards which have a high degree of inflexibility. It is interesting to note that each document produced by the ASC was more flexible than its predecessor. For example, a comparison of ED17 with SSAP13 reveals that whereas the ED states that expenditure which satisfies the criteria *should* be carried forward the standard states that it *may* be.

Example 10.6:

Company T has a research and development programme which comprises two projects.

Project 1: To develop T's own version of a radio aerial to be incorporated into the glass of car rear windows. Several other versions of this product compete in a growing market.

Project 2: To develop a fuel cell relying on solar energy to power motor cars.

Both projects commenced on 1 January 19X1 and by 31 December 19X1 had incurred the following costs:

	Project 1 (£000)	Project 2 (£000)
Purchase of plant and machinery	150	40
Materials, salaries, overheads	102	28

The life of plant and machinery for each project is five years. The aerial developed by project 1 went into production on 1 October 19X1 and by 31 December 19X1, 10,000 units had been sold of an estimated 100,000 total sales over the product's life. The commercial prospects of project 1 were recognised at its inception.

The suggested accounting treatment is as follows:

Project 1: This seems to satisfy the criteria for a development project in the sense of SSAP13. Thus, costs associated with it may be capitalised. An appropriate basis for allocating costs to the year ended 31 December 19X1 may be sales. SSAP13 requires plant and machinery to be depreciated in accordance with SSAP12 irrespective of whether it is for research or development purposes. Thus, on a straight line basis, depreciation for project 1 is £150,000 divided by 5 years, or £30,000, making total costs of £132,000. Allocating on the basis of sales gives:

$$£132,000 \times \frac{10,000}{100,000} = £13,200 \text{ to be charged to profit and loss for 19X1}$$

The balance of £118,800 appears in the balance sheet as 'Intangible Asset: Development Expenditure', and is written off in subsequent years.

Project 2: This appears to be applied research and expenditure and it should be written off as incurred. Fixed assets will be depreciated.

Empirical Research Findings

Bierman and Dukes (1975) found a relationship between the amount of R and D expenditure incurred by a firm during a period and the security price of the firm. Although the firms they studied followed the policy of expensing R and D costs, the results were consistent with investors making capitalisation adjustments to R and D costs in estimating the future earnings potential of the firm.

Several studies have examined the behavioural effects of the US standard, FASB Statement No. 2, which was issued in 1974 and required R and D costs to be written off as incurred. No significant stock market reaction followed this standard (Vigeland, 1981). However, there is evidence to support the view that the standard caused a relative decline in the R and D outlays for small, high technology firms which had previously capitalised the expenditure (Horowitz and Kolodny, 1981).

Leases

The use of leasing by companies as a means of financing assets has increased rapidly in recent years (Bank of England, 1984). There are several reasons for this. The most important are the relatively low levels of profitability of UK industrial and commercial companies, and the substantial profits made by the major clearing banks. The former has meant that the purchase of assets has been made less attractive due to companies' inability to claim tax allowances because of insufficient taxable income. The latter has meant that the banks have had ample profits against which to set tax allowances on purchased assets. Consequently, the banks have set up leasing subsidiaries (lessors) which have leased assets to industry and commerce (lessees), with both groups sharing the tax benefits.

A lease is a contract between a lessor and a lessee for the hire of a specific asset. The lessor retains the ownership of the asset but conveys to the lessee the rights to use for an agreed period in return for the payment of specified rentals. There are two types of lease as follows:

Finance Lease

A finance lease is normally for the substantial part of the life of an asset. Thus, the lessee acquires the benefit, and risks of ownership of the asset, while the lessor seeks to make its entire profit from a particular asset, from one lease. Thus, a finance lease is a substitute for outright purchase of the asset.

Operating Lease

An operating lease is normally for a relatively short term, covering only part of the anticipated useful life of the asset. The lessor will arrange other leases for the asset at the expiry of the current one and aims to make a profit over the life of the asset. Thus the lessor retains the benefits and risks of ownership, and an operating lease is not a substitute for outright purchase.

Accounting for Leases

The conventional approach to accounting for leases has been to treat both types of lease as essentially the same, and to record the transactions in accordance with their legal form. Thus, a lessee would conventionally record its leases as follows:

Profit and loss account: rental expenses recorded as they fall due.
Balance sheet: no record of the leased asset as an asset and no corresponding liability associated with the lease.

A lessor on the other hand would conventionally record leases thus:

Profit and loss account: lease rental income recorded as it falls due, with depreciation charged on assets which are leased out.
Balance sheet: leased assets are recorded as fixed assets, at cost less accumulated depreciation.

The main disadvantage of this conventional approach is that, for finance leases, it does not reflect the substance of the transaction, nor the motivation of the parties involved. A lessee is acquiring the use of an asset without needing to buy it, and is thereby avoiding the need to raise finance for purchase. Had finance been raised, the liabilities incurred (perhaps through borrowing since this is the closest alternative to leasing), would have appeared on the balance sheet, as would the value of the asset acquired. Thus, leasing is frequently referred to as 'off-balance sheet financing', and empirical studies of the behaviour of lessees has found this to be a significant motivation for companies entering into leases (Fawthrop and Terry, 1975; Sykes, 1976).

The use of off-balance sheet finance may be seen as valuable if the management of lessee companies consider that there would be adverse effects following from an increase in gearing which might result from borrowing to buy rather than leasing.

The Companies Act 1981 requires the disclosure by lessees of the amount charged to revenue in respect of sums payable in respect of the hire of plant and machinery, and of particulars of financial commitments which have not been provided for and are relevant to assessing the company's state of affairs. Also it requires an analysis of creditor items falling due within and after one year, and those due after more than five years, with terms applicable and interest rates. Whilst this increases disclosure substantially over that required by the Companies Act 1967, it falls short of bringing leases on to balance sheets and may only partially mitigate problems of assessing company performance or risk from publishing accounting information.

Alternative Accounting Treatment

The alternative accounting treatment is based upon the notion of substance over form. It seeks to reflect the nature of the transaction by bringing finance leases on to balance sheets. Future commitments to finance leases are recorded as liabilities, balanced by the recording of assets subject to finance lease as fixed assets. Moreover, such assets are then depreciated as other fixed assets. The corresponding treatment in lessors accounts is no longer to treat assets subject to finance leases as fixed assets, but as debtors (corresponding to future lease rental income). This treatment was recommended by the ASC in ED29 and subsequently formed the basis of SSAP21, *Accounting for Leases and Hire Purchase Contracts*.

The Requirements of SSAP21

ED29 was published in November 1981 SSAP21 was issued in July 1984. The following are the main requirements of the accounting standard:

Lessees
1. Finance leases should be recorded in the balance sheet as an asset and an obligation to pay future rentals.
2. The initial value to be recorded as an asset and liability is either the fair value (i.e. purchase value), of the asset, or the present value of the minimum lease payments contained in the finance lease.
3. Assets subject to finance leases should be depreciated over the shorter of their useful life or the lease term.
4. Rentals for finance leases should be apportioned between a finance charge element and the amount which reduces the outstanding obligation for future amounts payable.
5. Assets subject to hire purchase agreements are to be treated like assets subject to their leasing counterparts.
6. Operating leases should be treated as an expense and not capitalised.

Lessors
1. Finance leases are to be recorded in the balance sheet as debtors at amounts equal to the value of the net investment in the leases.
2. Assets subject to operating leases are to be recorded as fixed assets and depreciated over their useful lives.

In putting these accounting policies into operation there are two fundamental problems. The first is distinguishing between finance and operating leases and the second is valuing leases to satisfy the disclosure requirements. ED29 defined finance and operating leases in terms generally accepted by leasing and finance specialists (Clark, 1978). A finance lease is defined as a lease which transfers substantially all the risks and rewards of ownership to the lessee. This may be presumed if the present value of the lease payments amounts to substantially all of the fair value of the asset. An operating lease is a lease other than a finance lease.

Lease valuation may be accomplished using several methods depending upon whether valuation is from the lessee's or lessor's point of view. For lessees three methods are identified by SSAP21:

1. Actuarial method.
2. Sum of years digits method.
3. Straight-line method.

The former is the favoured and more accurate method and the latter two are simpler alternatives. For lessors four valuation methods are:

1. Actuarial method before tax.
2. Sum of years' digits.
3. Actuarial method after tax.
4. Investment period method.

Example 10.7:

To illustrate some of these valuation methods we use the following. A finance lease commences on 1 January 19X4. Three annual rentals of £6,000 are payable in advance during the primary period. The secondary term is indefinite at a peppercorn rent. The purchase price of the asset is £16,500.

Lessee accounting
As we noted above, the nature of a finance lease is that it is a substitute for outright purchase. If the lease is considered as financing the purchase of the asset the annual lease rental of £6,000 is in part a charge for the provision of finance. The balance of the rental is equivalent to a capital repayment. The basis of lease capitalisation is the separation of these two elements of the rental. Since the purchase value of the asset is known, the total finance charge may be determined as:

	£
Minimum lease payment (3×£6,000)	18,000
Purchase price of asset	16,500
Total finance charge	£1,500

SSAP21 requires that the total finance charge to be allocated to accounting periods so as to maintain a constant periodic rate of return on the remaining balance of the lease liability. The acturial method referred to above achieves this by calculating the internal rate of return implicit in the lease thus:

$$£16,500 = £6,000 + £6,000 \, \overline{a2}|i$$

This expression sets the present value of the lease payments equal to the purchase price; paying the rentals in advance requires only the last two to be discounted at the internal rate of return $i\%$, $\overline{a2}|i$ being the two year annuity factor at this rate. Solving for $\overline{a2}|i$ gives:

$$£ \left\{ \frac{16,500 - 6,000}{6,000} \right\} = \overline{a2}|i = 1.75$$

The discount rate which gives a two-year annuity factor of 1.75 is 9.386 per cent. Now, having identified the finance charge we may set out the notional transactions implicit in the lease as follows:

Year	Capital sum at the start of year (1)	Rental (2)	Capital sum during the year (3)	Finance charge (4)	Capital sum at the end of the year (5)
One	16,500.00	6,000.00	10,500.00	985.53	11,485.53
Two	11,485.53	6,000.00	5,485.53	514.87	6,000.40
Three	6,000	6,000	—	—	—

The lessee is deemed to acquire capital of £16,500 with the lease of the asset. The first rental paid to the lessor reduces this to £10,500 on which a finance charge at 9.386 per cent is levied, raising the capital to the end-of-the-year figure. Repeating for the second and third years extinguishes the capital investment.

A simplified approach is to use the sum of the years' digits method thus:

Period	Number assigned to the period	Proportion of total finance charge	Finance charged per period
1	2	2/3	£1,000
2	1	1/3	£500
3	—	—	—
Total	3	Total	£1,500

These finance charges may be substituted for those in column (4) above with the other figures adjusted accordingly to give approximately the same result. The straight-line method simplifies the calculation for a small lease.

These calculations provide the basis for capitalisation. They may also be made for leases where the purchase price of the asset is not known. Without this price, an internal rate of return cannot be calculated. Instead, it is prescribed that lease capitalisation be based upon the present value of the minimum lease payments calculated using a commercial rate of interest. This is defined this as the rate which a lessee would be expected to pay on a loan over a similar period to finance the acquisition of the asset. If we assume that the appropriate commercial rate of interest is 15 per cent, the present value of the minimum lease payments is:

$$£6,000 + £6,000 \ ^{\overline{a}}\overline{2}|0.15 = £15,756$$

The transactions implicit in the lease now appear as:

Year	Capital sum at the start of the year	Rental	Capital sum during the year	Finance charge	Capital sum at the end of the year
One	15,756	6,000	9,756	1,463	11,219
Two	11,219	6,000	5,219	783	6,002
Three	6,002	6,000	—	—	—

The finance charge is now calculated at the commercial rate of interest of 15 per cent. The calculation may be repeated using the sum of years' digits.

Using the above calculations, the lease would appear in the lessee's accounts as follows (if we further assume that the leased asset is depreciated on a straight-line basis over the lease term):

	Balance sheet				Profit and loss account charges
Date	Asset		Obligation to pay future rentals		
		£		£	£
1.1.X4		15,756		15,756	
	Less depreciation	5,252	Interest	1,463	Interest 1,463
					Depreciation 5,252
			Less rental	6,000	
					6,715
31.12.X4		10,504		11,219	
	Less depreciation	5,252	Interest	783	Interest 783
					Depreciation 5,252
			Less rental	6,000	
					6,035
31.12.X5		5,252		6,002	
	Less depreciation	5,252	*Less* rental	6,000	Depreciation 5,252

Except at the beginning of the lease, asset and liability have different values. The treatment of leases according to SSAP21 is consistent with the 1981 Companies Act. The Act requires disclosure of accounting policy adopted and the commitments associated with the lease may be categorised as appropriate under creditors due within or after one year. The apportionments of lease rental are allocated to cost of sales and other operating expenses as appropriate.

Lessor Accounting
The substance of the leasing transaction from the lessor's viewpoint is that the asset has been acquired on behalf of the lessee in return for a contracted stream of rentals through time. Thus, the leased asset generates revenues for the lessor. Consequently, the accounting treatment recommended by SSAP21 is for the value of the lease to the lessor to be represented as a debtor rather than a fixed asset. This raises again the question of valuation. The question may be answered in much the same way as for lessees if we adopt the actuarial method before tax.

Actuarial Method Before Tax. Using the same data as Example 7 we would again calculate an internal (or actuarial) rate of return of 9.386 per cent implicit in the lease. This would give the same pattern of finance charges and capital repayments as above but in this case, column (5) showing 'capital sum at the end of the year' would represent the lessor's investment in the lease. Thus, the lease would appear in the lessor's balance sheet as:

Current Assets	19X4	19X5
	£	£
Net investment in finance leases	11,485	6,000

The sum of years' digits method would give (as we have noted) approximately the same result.

Both these approaches, though having the merit of simplicity, do suffer from the drawback that they ignore, amongst other things, taxation. Corporate taxation, as we have already noted has been an important influence upon leasing. The main financial benefit of leasing to the lessee is the ability to share in the tax allowances enjoyed by the lessor. There is evidence (Institute for Fiscal Studies, 1982) that the market has worked to provide lessees with significant shares in these tax benefits. Thus, it is necessary to reflect taxation in lease valuation in order to provide a comprehensive cash flow approach to leases from the lessor's viewpoint. This is achieved by using the actuarial method after tax and the investment period method to value leases. Each method involves significant cash flows in attempting to compute a constant periodic rate of return on net cash invested in a lease. We shall demonstrate by means of the investment period method, one which is widely used by lessors to evaluate leases.

Investment Period Method. We shall add to the earlier data by assuming that the lessor can claim 100 per cent first year capital allowances and pays corporation tax eighteen months after the balance sheet date. Thus, the net cash invested in the lease appears as follows:

Period to 31.12.X4	Expense or income £	Tax (relief) £	Outflow (inflow) £	Net Investment £
1.1.X4 Asset cost	16,500–			9,500
Less rental received	6,000			
Period to 31.12.X5				
1.1.X2 Rental received			(6,000)	3,500
Period to 31.12.X6				
1.1.X6 Rental received			(6,000)	
30.6.X6 Value of first year				
allowance		(8,250)		(7,750)
Tax on rental		3,000		

The total net cash invested in the lease is £(9,500+3,500)=£13,000 which gives rise to the total finance charge of £1,500. This may be allocated to the first two years when there is an investment in the lease (subsequently the lease contributes to lessor's funds):

$$\text{Year to 31.12.X4} \quad £ \left\{ \frac{9,500}{13,000} \times 1,500 \right\} = £1,096$$

$$\text{Year to 31.12.X5} \quad £ \left\{ \frac{3,500}{13,000} \times 1,500 \right\} = £404$$

Allocating the finance charges thus gives rates of return on net cash invested as:

$$\frac{£1,096}{£9,500} = 0.115 \text{ and } \frac{£404}{£3,500} = 0.115$$

Having identified the finance charges, the element of capital repayment is the balance of the rentals and the lessor's investment in the lease may be calculated as:

	19X4 £		19X5 £	19X6 £
Net investment at start of year	16,500		11,596	6,000
Less capital repayment (6,000–£1,096)	4,904	(£6,000–404)	5,596	6,000
Net investment at year end	11,596		6,000	

Economic Consequences

ED29 represented an important departure for the ASC in that it specified for the first time a concern with the economic consequences of an accounting standard. The exposure draft stated:

> While the ASC has no doubt that capitalisation of assets held under finance leases is the appropriate technical and practical solution to the accounting problem . . . there are some who argue that this solution . . . might have undesirable economic consequences

> (ASC, 1981, paragraphs 33 and 38)

The major adverse economic consequence specified was a reduction in investment and three possible sources were recognised by the ASC:

1. Capitalisation of a finance lease might cause companies to go to the limit of their legal borrowing powers.
2. Capitalisation might adversely affect the rate of return on capital employed and financial gearing.
3. The tax treatment of leased assets might be altered in response to lease capitalisation.

The Government pledged no change associated with the third cause at the time of issue of ED29. However, the law relating to capital allowances has subsequently been changed for other reasons. The second cause seems potentially most important and implies that various categories of decision maker may adjust their behaviour following lease capitalisation. Two broad categories of decision maker may be important here: the management of lessee companies and suppliers of finance, (including shareholders, bond holders and creditors). Table 10.1 sets out the main decisions and their possible consequences.

Investment may fall as a result of lease capitalisation if lessee management makes less use of leasing without replacing it with other sources of finance such as debt or equity, or if suppliers of finance (including lessors) restrict supplies or tighten terms.

We have noted that studies of lessee behaviour stress the importance of off-balance sheet financing as a benefit (Fawthrop and Terry 1975; Sykes 1976). This suggests the possibility of a retreat from leasing by some lessees. The willingness and ability to switch to non-leasing finance depends not only upon lessees but upon supplies of finance.

Lessors

Lessors would appear to be the suppliers of finance least likely to be 'fooled' by off-balance sheet financing and hence least likely to be influenced in their decisions by the introduction of lease capitalisation. However, there is little evidence available on how lessors appraise

Table 10.1. Leases: the main decisions and their possible consequences

	Management of the lessee	Suppliers of Finance	
		Lessors	*Others*
Decision areas	Leasing versus other sources of finance or no investment.	Terms on which lease granted.	Terms on which finance provided.
Consequences of lease capitalisation	Lease finance less attractive due to erosion of return on capital employed, or to changes in availability or terms of leases. Possible fall in investment. Increase in costs and prices. Fall in dividend payout, via profitability and increased retained earnings.	Market perception of additional risk may result in more onerous terms for lessee.	Possible perception of increased risk could lead to adjustment of risk premiums, demand for higher interest rates, restricted lines of credit, fall in share price, increase in required yield on equity.

potential lessees. Even the most recent and comprehensive analysis of lessors (see Flavell and Salkin, 1982) casts little light on this aspect of their activities. Flavell and Salkin do stress the importance of default risk to lessors but provide no information on how this is assessed in practice. Lessors have shown themselves to be responsive to the market and to changes in legislation by varying the terms of leases. This is borne out by Cranfield (1979) and Abdel-Khalik *et al.* (1981). This suggests that investment effects may be avoided by changes in the leasing product.

Other Long-Term Creditors

As with lessors, the likelihood of sophisticated financial institutions reassessing clients as a result of lease capitalisation seems, a priori, to be slight. However, as with lessors, little evidence is available on decision-making processes. As Dietrich and Kaplan (1982) have succinctly expressed it with regard to bank lending:

The risk classification of commerical bank loans is performed by loan officers, bank controllers, auditors and bank examiners. Despite the importance of this classification decision, little empirical research has been performed to explain this subjective evaluation process.

Such evidence as is available is mixed in its conclusions. Dietrich and Kaplan successfully modelled the risk classification process with variable measuring gearing, while Wojnilower (1962) found a significant degree of predictability in lending decisions, as did Wu (1969). However, Orgler (1970) found virtually all financial reports to be statistically insignificant in explaining commercial loan credit scores. (See Haslem and Longbrake, 1972, for criticism of Orgler). This evidence confuses rather than clarifies expectations of the likely effects of lease capitalisation on analysts' judgements. This view is confirmed by substantive research on SFAS13 in the USA. Abdel-Khalik, *et al.* (1981) found from responses to question-naires, that, on average, analysts would not downgrade the debt-paying ability of lessees following lease capitalisation. However, when asked to compare two companies equal in all other respects than the method of accounting for leases substantial percentages of the same analysts were found to assess the companies differently in terms of profitability and debt-paying ability. As Abdel-Khalik *et al.* put it:

> It is evident . . . that what responding users say they do and what they actually do may be substantially different
>
> (p. iv)

Some evidence is available from the USA on bond rating from which we may draw inferences about the effects of lease capitalisation on lending. Shakin argued that interest rates would increase and credit ratings decrease following SFAS13 (FASB, 1978). Abdel-Khalik *et al.* (1978), whilst examining off-balance sheet disclosure concluded that such disclosure did not appear to affect market assessment of lessees' default risk on bonds: in contrast they use observations of interest rate differentials in favour of companies using leasing rather than debt to argue that bringing leases on to balance sheets might raise interest rates. However, Abel-Khalik *et al.* (1981) discovered no adverse effects on market assessments of bond risks due to lease capitalisation.

Equity

The ability to use equity funds as an alternative to leases will be determined by a company's earnings, investment needs, dividend policy and market reactions to lease capitalisation. Management willingness to use equity finance may be limited in certain circumstances. Some of the survey evidence on lessee behaviour in the UK already cited indicated a preference for leasing over equity for some companies. The only area where evidence is available concerns stock market reactions to lease accounting policies. There is evidence of association between debt-based accounting measures of risk and stock market risk (see Beaver *et al.*, 1970; Ball, 1972; Gonedes, 1973; and Breen and Lerner, 1973), and Hamada (1972) found a relationship between gearing and beta.

Four studies have examined the association between methods of lease accounting and market assessments of risk. Ro (1978) investigated ASR No. 149 (see SEC, 1973) and found that reporting capitalised leases had a significant effect on distributions of securities returns, the more so as values of beta increased. Finnerty, *et al.* (1980) found no significant association between various accounting requirements for leases and market measures of risk. This conclusion was supported for SFAS13 by Abdel-Khalik *et al.* (1981). Interestingly, Cheung (1982) found that systematic risk decreased following disclosure of non-capitalised leases. One explanation of this result may be that the market had already impounded some lease data before disclosure (Bowman, 1980).

After a considerable delay the ASC issued SSAP 21. The main changes from the proposals contained in ED29 were as follows:

1. The allowance of a three-year transitional period during which lease capitalisation is not obligatory.
2. The method for capitalisation of leases should be the present value of the minimum lease payments unless fair value is a close approximation.
3. Finance leases are to be recorded in the balance sheets of lessors using the net cash investment method as the favoured method.

Pensions

Pension costs and liabilities have grown in recent years at a rapid rate and, today, pension costs form a significant proportion of a company's total employment costs. Despite this, UK companies typically provide little information about their pension arrangements in their financial statements. For example, the 1983 Survey of Published Accounts found that less than half the 300 companies surveyed disclosed one item of pension-related information. It is, therefore, difficult for the user to judge either the significance of pension costs in relation to a company's financial statements, or the extent of a company's potential future liabilities which, particularly in times of inflation, could be very substantial. The 1981 Companies Act introduced requirements for the disclosure of pension costs and pension commitments and, in 1983, the ASC issued ED32 which contained proposals for improving reporting in this area.

Nature of Pensions

A pension is deferred remuneration which accrues over the working life of the employee. Instead of making cash payments to the employee on an individual basis, the employer transfers funds to a pension scheme to be invested for the employee's ultimate benefit. A pension fund is a trust fund, administered by a trustee, such as an insurance company and is, therefore, separate and distinct from the employer. As Napier (1982) discusses, the funding process may be pictured as a bath, into which the contributions of employer and employee and the income from the fund's assets are fed and out of which the payments to beneficiaries flow. The objective of funding is seen in these terms as ensuring that the flows into the bath are sufficient both to meet the current outflows and to build up sufficient in the bath to meet future outflows if the inflows are stopped.

Pension schemes are of two types:

(i)   A *defined benefit* scheme is the most common. This specifies the amounts to be paid to retired employees, typically one-sixtieth of final salary for each year of service. The employee knows how this pension will be calculated but he does not know what his final salary will be. Under a defined benefit scheme the company bears the risks because, ultimately, it will carry the costs of the scheme in meeting defined benefits for the employees. Accounting for such schemes is difficult, because of the various uncertainties involved.

(ii) A *defined contribution* scheme is one where each year, in accordance with the pension contract, a predetermined amount is deposited in the pension fund e.g. 6 per cent of the individual's annual salary. Retirement benefits are then based upon the amounts accumulated in the pension fund at retirement age. The employee bears the risk of the scheme because he does not know what he will receive in pension payments; that depends on the success of the investment managers of the scheme. Accounting for defined contribution schemes is fairly simple because the annual cost is the contribution.

The attention of accountants has been directed towards defined benefit schemes because most of the problems which arise are associated with these and the majority of schemes are of this type.

Actuarial Cost Methods

Actuarial cost methods were developed primarily as funding techniques in that they provide the specific amounts for periodic funding payments. Since determination of the funding requirements explicitly requires estimation of the underlying pension costs, the actuarial cost methods are also useful in determining pension costs for accounting purposes. Although the various actuarial cost methods are alike in that they use present value concepts and rely on actuarial assumptions, they differ significantly in their approaches and can produce different results for the same situations.

There appears to be broad agreement that pension costs should be accounted for on an accrual basis (Archibald, 1980). Accordingly, accounting for pension schemes requires measurement of the cost and its identification with the appropriate time periods which involves application of the accrual, deferral and estimation concepts in the same manner that they are applied in the measurement and time period identification of other costs and expenses. Napier (1982) concluded that two actuarial funding methods are acceptable for allocating pension costs:

(*i*)   *Level contribution* methods are designed so that contributions over the working life of an employee remain constant, usually as a percentage of salary. The contributions are based on the ultimate projected salaries of employees.

(*ii*) *Accrued benefit* methods associate distinct units of projected retirement benefit with each year of service of an employee. The contribution required in any year is the actuarial present value (allowing for income earned on the contribution up to retirement and the possibility that the employee will leave the scheme before retirement of the unit of employee benefit associated with that year.

Simmonds (1983) uses the following example to illustrate these two methods of pension cost allocation:

Example 10.8:

Employee pension information

Name	Fred Bloggs
Age on joining company	25
Current age	30
Current salary	£10,000
Projected salary increases	5% per annum to retirement
Retirement age	65
Life expectancy	75

The Company is to credit Fred with his five years prior service to date, to give a total pensionable service period of forty years.

Contributions to the pension fund will be invested annually in arrears, and will earn 10 per cent per annum compound. Contributions will be charged to the profit and loss account.

At retirement, Fred will become entitled to a pension of one-half his final salary, payable annually in advance.

The fund will continue to attract investment income of 10 per cent per annum after retirement. No increase in pension benefits after retirement is envisaged.

The company require computations of:

(*a*) a lump sum to be paid into the fund at the end of the current year to cover the five years service credited to date, and

(*b*) the annual pension cost over the remaining period of employment. (For expediency, we will compare the cost in the sixth, tenth, twentieth, thirtieth and fortieth year of service).

From the data, the pension benefit and hence the required value of the pension fund at retirement is first computed.

Retirement salary $£10,000 \times (1.05)^{35}$	£55,160
Annual pension benefit $(\frac{1}{2} \times £55,160)$	£27,580
Value of pension fund at retirement age $\left(£27,580 \times (1 + \dfrac{1-(1.1)^{-9}}{0.1}) \right)$	£186,414

Level contribution method—level percentage of annual salary cost

The estimated pension benefit, based on projected final salary, is expressed as a constant percentage of annual salary costs. If salary costs increase by 5 per cent per annum, the pension cost will show a similar annual increase.

Suppose that the contribution in year one (of forty) was $£X$. Then the capitalised value of contributions at retirement age would be the following geometric progression:

$$£X (1.05)^0 (1.1)^{39} + £X (1.05)^1 (1.1)^{38} + \ldots + £X (1.05)^{39} (1.1)^0$$

The general formula for the sum of a geometric progression is:

$$\frac{a(1-r^n)}{1-r}$$

In this example:

a (the first term)	=	$£X (1.05)^0 (1.1)^{39}$
r (the constant multiplier)	=	$\dfrac{1.05}{1.1}$
n (the number of terms)	=	40

By inserting these values, and setting the whole sum equal to the value of the fund required at retirement age (£186,414), we find that $X=£244$.

In the fifth year, this would have increased to £296 $((£244 \times (1.05)^4)$ which represents 2.96 per cent of salary in that year.

The lump sum required at the end of the fifth year of service is a further geometric progression containing five terms. The first term is $£244 \times (1.1)^4$ and the constant multiplier is again $\dfrac{1.05}{1.1}$.

Lump sum	£1,631

$$\left(£244 \times (1.1) \times {}^{4}\left[\frac{1 - \dfrac{1.05}{1.1}^{5}}{1 - \dfrac{1.05}{1.1}} \right] \right)$$

The lump sum cost can be avoided by allocating the total cost over 36 periods, each of a higher amount. On this basis, the level percentage would be 3.71 per cent of annual salary costs.

Accrued benefits method
Simmonds defines the accrued benefit to the employee in any one period as the proportion of the estimated pension benefit, based on final projected salary, to which the employee has become entitled in that period. By discounting this proportion of the final benefit back to any one period, we find the pension cost for that period.

	£
Annual proportion of the final fund	4,660
(1/40×£186,414)	
Pension cost in year 6	182
($£4,550 \times (1.1)^{-34}$)	
Lump sum at end of year 5	829
($£4,660 \times .5 \times (1.1)^{-35}$)	

Again, this lump sum cost can be avoided by charging higher amounts over the 36 years remaining to retirement. These would be the present value of 1/36 of the total benefit.

On this basis, the cost in the sixth year of service would be £203.

Comparison of the two methods
Simonds makes a numerical comparison of the two methods, viz:

	Salary	Level Contribution		Accrued benefits	
	£	£	% of salary	£	% of salary
Lump sum payment in current year	10,000	1,631	—	829	—
Annual pension costs in selected years of service					
Year 6	10,500	311	2.96	182	1.73
Year 10	12,763	378	2.96	267	2.09
Year 20	20,789	615	2.96	693	3.33
Year 30	33,864	1,002	2.96	1,797	5.31
Year 40 (retirement)	55,160	1,633	2.96	4,660	8.45

Accounting policy requirements

The Companies Act 1981 requires the disclosure of wages and salaries paid to employees, social security costs and pension costs. Additionally, disclosure has to be made in notes to the accounts of any pension commitments for which no provision has been made in the accounts. In 1983, the ASC published ED32, *Disclosure of Pension Information in Company Accounts* which states:

Disclosure should be made in financial statements of sufficient information concerning pension arrangements to enable users of the statements to gain a broad understanding of the significance of pension costs in the accounting period and of actual and contingent liabilities and commitments at the balance sheet date. Towards this general objective, the disclosures should include at least the following, subject to any necessary modifications in the case of employees paid abroad and to summarising to a reasonable extent in the case of individual companies or groups with a number of different pension schemes:

(*a*) The nature of the pension schemes, (e.g. defined benefit or defined contribution), whether they are externally funded or internally financed and any legal obligations of the company (e.g. undertakings to meet the balance of cost);

(*b*) The accounting policy, and the funding policy if different from the accounting policy, indicating the basis used for allocating pension costs to accounting periods:

(*c*) Whether the pension costs and liabilities are assessed in accordance with the advice of a professionally qualified actuary and, if so, the date of the most recent actuarial valuation;

(*d*) The amount charged in the profit and loss account for pension costs, distinguishing between normal charges related to employees' pay and service in the accounting period and other charges and credits, (e.g. additional charges to cover the cost of post-retirement awards not covered by the normal charge, or reductions in the normal charge to take account of contribution holidays or a temporarily reduced contribution rate resulting from overfunding) with explanations of such charges or credits;

(*e*) Any commitments to change the rate of contributions or make special contributions;

(*f*) Any provision or prepayments in the balance sheet, resulting from a difference between the accounting policy and the funding policy;

(*g*) The amount of any deficiency on a discontinuance actuarial valuation or on the requirements of the Occupational Pensions Board, indicating the action, if any being taken to deal with it in future financial statements;

(*h*) The amount of any material self-investment;

(*i*) In the case of internally financed schemes, the amount of the provision at the balance sheet date and of any identifiable fund of assets representing the provision, and

(*j*) Expected significant effects on future financial statements of any changes which have occurred in the above, including the effects of any material improvements in benefits.

In a SOI issued in October 1984 the ASC stated that as ED32 was concerned primarily with disclosure, that exposure draft should not be converted into an accounting standard. Instead, the SOI sought to present the ASC's main conclusions on a broader range of issues than covered by ED32, although the majority of the disclosure recommendations of ED32 are included in the SOI. The main conclusions of the SOI are as follows:

(a) The accounting objective should be to charge the cost of pensions against profits on a systematic basis over the service lives of the employees concerned. Hence a periodic pension cost which is a substantially level percentage of the current and anticipated pensionable payroll, given current actuarial assumptions, should be produced.
(b) Any variations from regular costs should be prudently allocated over a period not exceeding employees remaining service lives.
(c) There should be no limit on actuarial methods or assumptions, so long as they are consistent with (a).
(d) The proposals would apply to all types of pension schemes.
(e) There should be no single, distinct method of accounting included in a standard.
(f) The emphasis in accounting for pension costs should be on the profit and loss account charge.
(g) The pension information disclosed should include substantially all that required by ED32.

Evaluation of Proposals

The ED32 proposals represent a first stage in the disclosure of pension information. They do not attempt to standardise the calculation of annual pension costs. Nor do they require detailed information to be made public such as they present value of pensions, discount rates and the market value of assets held in the pension scheme. In contrast, in the USA, APB Opinion No. 8 (1966) was issued to provide for a certain degree of uniformity in accounting for pensions and, particularly, to require that the accruals concept of accounting be applied to the area of pensions. SFAS No. 36 (1980) extended disclosure requirements and the following information now has to be shown in notes to the financial statements:

(a) The cost of pensions in each of the last three years.
(b) The estimated present value of providing pension benefits.
(c) The market value of assets held by the pension scheme to meet the promised benefits.
(d) The rate of interest used by the actuary in estimating the present value of the benefits.
(e) The date as of which the benefit information was determined.

Pension scheme accounts

The government has indicated that it intends to introduce legislation to regulate certain aspects of pension schemes, including the periodic provision of information to members, while leaving the content of the accounts to the accounting profession. However, as there is currently no statutory framework requiring the publication of pension scheme reports, or that they be distributed to members, the ASC considers it inappropriate to introduce an SSAP on the subject of annual accounts of pension schemes. Its preferred route is to put forward guidance on current best practice, in the form of a Statement of Recommended Practice, ED34 Pension Scheme accounts (ASC, 1984).

The principal features of the exposure draft are:

1. Pension scheme members are identified as the prime users of the scheme's annual report.
2. The annual report should inform members about the development of the scheme, fund value and performance, and the scheme's progress towards meeting its potential liabilities and obligations to members.
3. The annual report should comprise (a) a trustee's report, (b) accounts (c) an actuarial report and (d) an investment report.
4. Within the context of the full annual report the accounts should give a true and fair view of the transactions of the scheme for the period and of the disposition of its net assets at the accounting date.
5. The account should comprise (a) a revenue account (b) a net assets statement (c) a movement of funds statement and (d) such additional information, by way of a note, as is necessary to give a true and fair view.
6. Recommendations on the contents of each of the elements comprising the accounts noted in (5) above.

Foreign Currency Translation

The question of how transactions enumerated in foreign currencies should be dealt with in financial statements has generated a great deal of controversy. The problem of foreign currency translation only becomes important when exchange rates are floated and governments allow them to vary. Under the fixed exchange rates which generally prevailed under International Monetary Fund rules until the early 1970s, there was a very small range within which variation was possible and consequently limited difficulties for translation. However, with the floatation of exchange rates becoming common in the 1970s this relative stability evaporated.

There are many aspects to the problem of foreign currency translation, but two broad aspects may be identified:

1. The translation of transactions in which a company is directly involved. This may entail the export of goods and services, borrowing or lending, or foreign currency transactions. These transactions may broadly be described as direct.
2. The translation of the results of transactions undertaken by an overseas segment of the company. This broadly involves the problems of consolidating accounts which are expressed in foreign currencies. This has both profit and loss and balance sheet implications.

The majority of controversy and discussion has concerned the second of these aspects, and in particular the consolidation of balance sheet items (Nobes, 1980). There is a considerable degree of agreement on how direct transactions may be accounted for, thus:

1. They should be recorded in UK accounting records in sterling at the exchange rate applicable at the time of the transaction.
2. Under historical cost conventions, non-monetary items once converted into sterling will not require further restatement.
3. Monetary balances denominated in foreign currencies (e.g. debtors arising from export transactions) should be retranslated at year-end exchange rates in order to produce a current value statement.
4. Differences arising from variations in exchange rates between the date when transactions were first recorded in financial statements and when they were settled should be written off to profit and loss account since they arise from management decisions.
5. Where forward exchange rate transactions are entered into, the contracted exchange rate should be used for conversion and no translation difference arises.

The Consolidation of the Results of Overseas Segments

The foreign subsidiaries or associated companies, of, say, UK companies will generally maintain their accounting records in local currency. Indeed they may be required to do so by law. The need to consolidate accounts creates the need to translate foreign currencies into sterling. This presents two problems:

1. The choice of exchange rate for the valuation of individual balance sheet and profit and loss account items. When exchange rates vary valuation differences arise. This leads to the second problem.
2. How best to deal with exchange rate valuation differences.

A number of methods are available for dealing with these problems. Three exchange rates are used in these methods; they are:

(*a*) the historic rate (that ruling at the time a transaction occurred or when a revaluation took place);
(*b*) the closing rate (that ruling at the balance sheet date);
(*c*) the average rate (an average of exchange rates ruling during the accounting period).

Different methods are applied to balance sheets and profit and loss account.

Balance sheet. Four methods may be identified for consolidating balance sheet items:

1. *The temporal method*. According to this method the choice of exchange rates for valuation should be dictated by the valuation base adopted for the item to be translated. Thus if items are valued at historical cost, the historic rate is used; if valued at current cost, the closing rate; and if carried at valuation, the exchange rate ruling at the valuation date.

2. *The monetary—non-monetary method*. This method accords different treatments to monetary and non-monetary items. Monetary items are translated at closing rates and non-monetary items at historic rates. Where the historical cost convention applies as the valuation base (with no revaluation permitted) the temporal and the monetary—non-monetary methods generally coincide, since under historical cost fixed assets are valued at cost (historic rate), stock at the lower of cost (historic rate) or realisable value (closing rate), and monetary items at current value (closing rate).

3. *The Current—Non-Current Method*. This method distinguishes between current and non-current items and applies different treatments to each. Current assets and liabilities are translated at closing rates while non-current items are translated at relevant historic rates.

4. *The Closing Rate Method*. This method translates all balance sheet items at the closing rate. The four methods are summarised in Table 10.2.

Profit and Loss Account. Three methods may be used as follows:

1. *Historic rate method*. This applies the specific historic rate applying at the time of the transaction, e.g. for depreciation the rate applying when the fixed asset was acquired or revalued, and for items arising at particular times, whatever rate applied then.
2. *Average rate method*. An average rate for the accounting period is

Table 10.2. Translation methods for balance sheet items

Balance sheet item	Temporal	Monetary non-monetary	Current non-current	Closing rate
Fixed Assets	HR	HR	HR	CR
Stocks				
—at cost	HR	HR	CR	CR
—at market value	CR	HR	CR	CR
Debtors	CR	CR	CR	CR
Cash	CR	CR	CR	CR
Long-term liabilities	CR	CR	HR	CR
Current liabilities	CR	CR	CR	CR

Note: HR=historic rate; CR=closing rate.

applied to all items. This is a method often applied to recurring items as a practical simplification of the historic rate method.

3. *Closing rate method.* All items are translated at the closing rate.

Table 10.3 sets out the relationships between the various balance sheet and profit and loss account methods.

Table 10.3. The relationship between the various balance sheet and profit and loss account methods

	Balance sheet methods			
Profit and loss account methods	Temporal	Monetary— non-monetary	Current— non-current	Closing rate
Historic rate	√	√	√	
Average rate		√	√	
Closing rate				√

Note: √ denotes consistency.

Application of the methods

Before discussing accounting requirements and the relative merits of the various methods we shall examine the application of the methods. The following data will be used throughout:

Example 10.9:

Company X undertook the following transactions, all of which are enumerated in US dollars:

		$	$
30.6.X3	Issue of Share capital		3,000
	Issue of 10 per cent debentures		1,800
	Purchase of stock		600
	Purchase of fixed assets at a cost of:		3,600
31.12.X3	Sale of stock on credit for a total price of:		1,440
	This is to be paid in instalments as follows:		
	30.9.X4	840	
	31.12.X5	600	
31.12.X3	Wages paid		240
31.3.X4	Purchase of stock		900
30.6.X4	Payments of debenture interest		180

The following exchange rates apply:

	$ to £1
30.6.X3	1.50
30.9.X3	1.75
31.12.X3	2.00
31.3.X4	2.25
30.6.X4	2.50

It is assumed that exchange rates moved regularly during the year. Therefore the rate applying at 31.12.X3 is taken as average for the year.

The balance sheet and profit and loss account for company X in US dollars for the year to 30.6.X4 are given below:

Company X

Balance Sheet at 30.6.X4

Assets employed	$	$
Fixed assets: cost	3,600	
depreciation	(360)	3,240
Long-term advance		600
Current assets		
Stock	900	
Debtors	840	
	1,740	
less		
Current Liabilities		
Overdraft	(720)	1,020
		4,860

Profit and loss Account for year ended 30.6.X4

	$	$
Sales		1,440
Cost of Sales		(600)
Gross profit		840
Depreciation	360[1]	
Wages	240	
Interest	180	780
Net profit		60

Note:
1. Depreciation is calculated on the straight line basis on a life of 10 years.

Financed by
Capital
  Share capital 3,000
  Profit and Loss A/c 60
                          3,060

Long-term liability
  10% debentures 1,800
                          4,860

2. Overdraft is obtained as:

		$
Share issue		3,000
Debenture issue		1,800
		4,800
Purchase of plant		(3,600)
Purchases of stock	600	
	900	(1,500)
Wages		(240)
Interest		(180)
Excess of cash outflows over inflows		(720)

Temporal method. A combination of historic and average rates is used to translate the profit and loss account of X into sterling.

Profit and Loss Account for year ended 30.6.X4

		$	Rate of Exchange		£
Sales		1,440	£1: $2.00		720
Cost of sales		(600)	£1: $1.50		(400)
Gross profit		840			320
Depreciation	360		£1: $1.50	240	
Wages	240		£1: $2.00	120	
Interest	180	(780)	£1: $2.50	72	(432)
Net profit		60			(112)

Notes:
1. Sales occurred at 31.12.X3; translated ⁿᵗ the historic rate.
2. Stock was produced at 31.6.X3; translated at the historic rate.
3. Fixed assets were obtained at 31.6.X3, translated at the historic rate.
4. Since wages are paid regularly during the year the average rate is used.
5. Interest on debentures is paid at the year end; translated at the historic (=closing) rate.

The balance sheet of X is as follows:

Balance Sheet at 31.6.X4

	$		Rate of Exchange (£: $)	£	£	Note
Assets employed						
Fixed assets: Cost	3,600		1: 1.50	2,400		(1)
Depreciation	(360)	3,240	1: 1.50	(240)	2,160	(1)
Long term advance		600	1: 2.50		240	(2)
Current assets: Stock	900		1: 2.25		400	(3)
Debtors	840		1: 2.50		336	(2)
	1,740				3,136	

less current liabilities					
Overdraft	(720)	1,020	1: 2.50		(288)(2)
		4,860			2,848
Financed by:					
Capital					
Share capital		3,000	1: 1.50		2,000 (1)
Reserves:					
Profit and loss account		60			(112)
Differences on exchange					240
Long-term liability					
10% debentures		1,800	1: 2.50		720 (2)
		4,860			2,848

Notes:
1. Translated at the historic rate applicable at 31.6.X3.
2. Translated at the rate applicable at the balance sheet date.
3. Acquired at 31.3.X4; translated at the rate applicable then.
4. Translated at the closing rate.
5. Translated at the closing rate.
6. See profit and loss account.
7. Differences on exchange arises as follows:

	$ Value	Exchange variation between:		£ value of exchange difference
		Transaction (£: $)	Translation (£: $)	
Debenture	1,800	1: 1.50	1: 2.50	480
Long-term advance	600	1: 2.00	1: 2.50	(60)

Balance at bank/overdraft:

31.6.X3 to 31.12.X3

	$			
Share issue and debentures (+)	4,800			
Purchase of plant and stock (−)	4,200			
Balance at bank	600	1: 1.50	1: 2.00	(100)

31.12.X3 to 31.3.X4

Opening balance	600			
Wages paid (−)	240			
Balance at bank	360	1: 2.00	1: 2.25	(20)

31.12.X4 to 30.6.X4

Opening balance	360			
Purchase of stock (−)	900			
Overdraft	540	1: 2.25	1: 2.50	24

Debtor	840	1: 2.00	1: 2.50	(84)
Net gain (loss) on transaction				240

The exchange differences on debentures and overdraft are gains, while the differences on long term advance, cash balances and debtor are losses.

Since the temporal and monetary—non-monetary methods coincide under historical cost, the above represents both methods.

Current—Non-Current Method Since a profit and loss account translated at historical or average rates is consistent with the current—non-current method, the profit and loss account translated at the temporal method may be adopted. The net loss translated into sterling is £112. The balance sheet is given below:

Balance Sheet at 31.6.X4

	$		Rate of Exchange (£: $)	£	£
Assets employed:					
Fixed assets: Cost	3,600		1: 1.50	2,400	
Depreciation	(360)	3,240	1: 1.50	(240)	2,160
Long-term advance		600	1: 2.00		300
Current assets: Stock	900		1: 2.50	360	
Debtor	840		1: 2.50	336	
	1,740			696	
less Current liabilities					
Overdraft	(720)	1,020	1: 2.50	(288)	408
		4,860			2,868
Financed by:					
Capital					
Share capital		3,000	1: 1.50		2,000
Profit and loss account		60			(112)
Differences on exchange					(220)[1]
Long term liability					
10% debentures		1,800	1: 1.50		1,200
		4,860			2,868

Notes:
1. Differences on exchange arise as follows:

	$ Value	Exchange variation between		£ value of exchange difference
		Transaction £: $	Translation £: $	
Stock	900	1: 2.25	1: 2.50	(40)
Debtor	840			(84)[1]
Cash balance and overdraft				(96)[2]
Total loss on translation				(220)

1. As for temporal method.
2. As for temporal method.

Closing Rate Method. All items in the balance sheet and profit and loss accounts are translated at the closing rate. The balance sheet appears on page 292.

Profit for the year. Since all items are translated at the closing rate, profit for the year may be determined directly from its dollar value of $60 by translating at the closing rate of £1: $2.50 to give a sterling figure of £24.

The gain or loss on exchange variations may be found almost as directly. Because all items are translated at the same rate, the gain or loss for the period depends on the effect of exchange variation on the net investment in the overseas segment. The value of net assets at 30.6.X3 was (in dollar terms):

	$
Total assets	4,860
less profit for year	(60)
less debentures	(1,800)
Net assets	3,000

Now, translating opening net assets at opening and closing rates gives:

		£
Opening net assets at 30.6.X3	$3,000 at £1: $1.50 =	2,000
Opening net assets at 30.6.X4	$3,000 at £1: $2.50 =	1,200
Loss on exchange difference		800
less sterling profit for the year		(24)
Net exchange loss		776

The net exchange loss arises by translating opening and closing net investment in the overseas segments thus:

Opening net investment: $3,000 at £1: $1.50 =			2,000
Closing net investment: $3,060 at £1: $2.50 =			1,224
Net loss for the year			776

Balance Sheet at 30.6.X4

	$		Rate of Exchange (£: $)	£	£
Assets employed					
Fixed assets: Cost	3,600		1: 2.50	1,440	
Depreciation	(360)	3,240	1: 2.50	(144)	1,296
Long-term advance		600	1: 2.50		240
Current assets: Stock	900				
Debtors	840				
	1,740		1: 2.50	696	
Current liabilities					
Overdraft	(720)	1,020	1: 2.50	(288)	408
		4,860			1,944
Financed by					
Share capital	3,000				
Profit and loss account	60	3,060			1,224
Long-term liability					
10% debentures		1,800	1: 2.50		720
		4,860			1,944

Evaluation of the alternatives

Having demonstrated the application of the various methods we shall now consider their relative merits. For the purposes of this discussion, as for the computations, the temporal and monetary—non-monetary methods are equivalent, as they are under the historical cost convention.

The Temporal Method. The chief advantage claimed for the temporal method is that it preserves the underlying principles of valuation contained in financial statements (Lorensen, 1972; Flower, 1976). Thus, the method is in accordance with principles of historical cost, but would also give the same results as the closing rate method if CCA principles governed overseas segments' financial statements.

If the objective of consolidation of accounts is seen to be the presentation of the results of a group of companies as if the group were a single entity, then the accounting principles of the parent company ought to prevail, just as the currency of the parent company ought to be the unit of measurement. This leads to the idea that an overseas segment is merely an extension of the parent, and each transaction of the segment should have the same effect on the group as if undertaken by the parent. Thus, if an overseas segment buys an asset, the asset should be recorded at the historic rate since, had a parent company using historical cost principles bought the asset directly, it would be held at historic cost. Similarly, a parent company would hold debtors and creditors resulting from its own direct transactions at the closing rate (as we noted at the beginning of this section). Consequently, the temporal method is consistent with a view which sees the consolidation of accounts as a means of presenting the results of a unified entity. The temporal method meets the requirements of such an objective (FASB, 1975).

Several arguments may be levelled against the use of the temporal method. First, it may be argued that foreign segments are not organic extensions of the parent, but are entities in themselves and are subject to some independence of action and operate in their own environments (Patz, 1977). Thus, there may be no case for applying the accounting principles of the parent to its overseas segments. Second, the temporal method may be criticised as not reflecting economic reality. Assets were not purchased in the parent's currency; and perhaps could not have been bought at the historic costs indicated by the historic rate.

Current-Non Current Method. By using historic rates for non-current items no exchange gains or losses are reported since all such amounts are measured at historical cost. This is justified on the grounds that it is not appropriate to adjust for exchange rate variations on long term items since these may be reversed in the future. Also, by linking non-current assets and liabilities together there is an implied cancelling-out process. Current items, being transitory in nature, are translated at the closing rate, since their lifecycle may not encompass sufficient exchange rate reverses to cancel out gains and losses.

This method may be criticised on several grounds. First, it no longer reflects the economic reality of exchange rate behaviour. A cycle of exchange rate variations is more appropriate to fixed exchange rates than floating exchange rates. With the latter, movements tend to be in trends rather than cycles around a given (fixed) level, and the prospects of self-correcting gains and losses are more remote. Second, it is arguable that a more appropriate distinction is between monetary and non-monetary items. Current and non-current items are distinguished by classification and convention in the absence of more objective criteria.

Closing Rate Method. This method has been supported as being a more appropriate reflection of the nature of a parent company's interest in a foreign segment. According to this view the investment at risk in the foreign segment is represented by its net assets irrespective of the form in which those net assets are held. Thus, if exchange rates vary so does the amount of the investment and the closing rate indicates this by applying the closing rate to all assets and liabilities (Parkinson, 1972). Moreover, failure to use the single closing rate will disturb the relationship between various assets, liabilities and profit and loss items since every item is multiplied by the same translation factor. This adds the further advantages of simplicity and comparability. The latter is, of course, important to users. Finally, the method is sometimes supported as a means of overcoming disadvantages of historical cost accounts. However, it is perhaps better to make good the deficiencies of historical cost accounting directly, rather than by indirectly introducing elements of current value accounting through the closing rate method (Flower, 1976).

Critics of the closing rate method have argued that it may fail to preserve the accounting principles contained in the overseas segment's financial statements. For example, assets originally valued at historical cost no longer appear on that basis. Indeed, some writers have taken the view that the products of historical costs and closing rates are meaningless. More moderately, the closing rate method has been seen as a means to effect revaluations by exchange rates.

Accounting Policy Requirements

Statements on accounting policies by regulatory bodies in both the UK and USA have had a chequered history. The ASC has issued three exposure drafts and an accounting standard related to foreign currencies (ASC, 1975, 1977, 1980, 1983). ED16 considered foreign currency translation as an aspect of a broader problem of extraordinary items and prior-year adjustments, and took a permissive view in anticipation of the appearance of an exposure draft specifically devoted to the problem. ED21 was such a document, but recommended either the closing rate or temporal method. No standard resulted from ED21 and the considerable volume of comment on it, lead to the issue of ED27 in 1980. This exposure draft favoured the closing rate, net investment method and moved into line with the recommendations of the FASB's exposure draft issued in the wake of the withdrawal of FAS8. This common approach was more the fruit of co-ordination than coincidence. Indeed, a common approach to foreign currency translation based on the closing rate method was fostered by standard setters in the UK, USA and Canada in response to the problems posed for companies faced with conflicting policy requirements. Such problems arose for UK companies with US parents or listings on the New York Stock Exchange. SSAP20, published in April 1983, reflected this co-operation. Its main requirements are:

1. In individual financial statements (i.e., direct transactions) transactions are to be translated using the temporal method with exchange differences being taken to the profit and loss accounts.
2. In consolidated accounts a distinction is drawn between:
   (a) Overseas segments which are quasi-autonomous, which should use the closing rate method, with exchange differences being taken to reserve.
   (b) Overseas segments which are merely extensions overseas of the operations of the parent, which should use the temporal method with exchange differences being taken to profit and loss account.
3. Profit and loss items may be translated using either the closing rate or average rate of exchange.

The disclosure requirements of the standard are for:

1. The translation methods used;
2. The treatment given to exchange differences;
3. The net amount of exchange gains or losses, identifying separately amounts dealt with through reserves and through profit and loss account;
4. The net movement on reserves arising from exchange differences.

It is important to emphasise that the standard's requirements are dependent upon the circumstances of the overseas segment and in this respect meet the points raised on the temporal and closing rate methods concerning the nature of the relationship between parent and segment.

The FASB exposure draft (1981) issued to replace both its immediate predecessor and SFAS8 itself, stated of ED27 that the ASC 'has issued a proposed standard for foreign currency translation that is similar in all material respects to the standards set forth in this Statement'.

As the requirements set out above for SSAP20 are fundamentally those of ED27 the substance of the foregoing quotation is that a very close degree of harmonisation exists between UK and USA regulations. Since the IASC suspended work on an international standard until a joint UK–USA approach was agreed, the requirements of the international standard seem clear.

Economic Consequences and Currency Translation

Chapter 5 contained a brief review of some of the economic effects which researchers have found to follow from accounting regulations on foreign currency translation. Certain management decisions were found to change as a result of SFAS8. An alternative but related view of the relationships between translation methods and economic effects is that:

> much of the argument for and against particular methods, on both sides of the Atlantic, seems to be based on the acceptability of their effects on the consolidated historic cost profits of large companies under the exchange rate and inflation conditions that exist in that particular country at that particular time. (Nobes, 1980)

Thus, when exchange rates were fixed and strong in developed countries but weak in underdeveloped countries the closing rate method proved popular since it presented no problems for fixed exchange rates but provided a prudent solution for weak currencies. We have already noted the relevance of the monetary—non-monetary method in periods when exchange rates experience cyclical changes around a constant trend, but in the early 1970s when the US dollar was depreciating the method attracted criticism. By the mid 1970s many US corporations had adopted the temporal method and thus SFAS8's recommendation of this method accorded with common practice. However, as the US dollar depreciated against stronger currencies, translation losses arose and the temporal method began to lose its attractiveness.

The changes in popularity of different methods following from economic changes resulted in vigorous lobbying by interest groups for the adoption of accounting standards favourable to them. The selection of the closing rate method by standard setters in the UK, USA and Canada has introduced a degree of harmonisation which is somewhat strengthened by the growing use of CCA by companies. Whether this ends debate on foreign currency translation is doubtful.

Accounting Practice

The *Survey of Published Accounts* showed that a considerable majority of companies used the closing rate method. In 1980–1, 83 per cent of companies used this method, with only 4 per cent using historical rates. The policies of companies adopting these methods have remained roughly constant for several years. Much more variety is observed in the treatment of different types of exchange transactions and translation, and in the methods of disclosure of differences on exchange.

Value-Added Statements

Value added (VA) is the wealth created by an enterprise. It can be measured by finding the difference between the enterprise's turnover and the cost of bought-in goods and services used in the making of the goods and services sold. Depreciation, which is merely a proportion of the cost of fixed assets which have been acquired from outside suppliers, may also be deducted. VA can also be measured by adding the rewards to be distributed by the enterprise, i.e. wages, interest, dividends and taxes on profit. These two methods of measuring VA are incorporated in a VA statement which 'is the simplest and most immediate way of putting profit into proper perspective *vis-à-vis* the whole enterprise as a collective effort by capital, management and employees' (ASC, 1975).

Table 10.4. Statement of value added

		£ million
Turnover		100
Less: Bought in materials and services	55	
Depreciation	5	60
Value added		40
Applied as follows:		
To employees as pay, pension and welfare costs		30
To providers of capital:		
Interest on borrowing	2	
Dividends to shareholders	2	4
To pay government		4
Retained profits		2
		40

Table 10.4 illustrates how VA is a close relative of the profit and loss account. Indeed, it is a rearrangement of the figures included in the profit and loss account and the value of goods and services bought. But, whereas the profit and loss account shows the earnings that accrued to the shareholders, the VA statement represents the earnings of all groups which contributed to the company's performance. The VA statement represents a move in a new and different direction for financial accounting. Over the past decade accountants have given much attention to the question, 'How should we measure income?' The VA statement asks a different question: 'Whose income should we measure?' (Morley, 1978).

A Department of Trade consultative document *The Future of Company Reports* (1977), expressed the view that publication of such a statement should be incorporated in company law and that its presentation should be standardised. However, there are no statutory or Stock Exchange requirements relating to VA statements. Nor have exposure drafts been issued on the subject. Despite the absence of a formal reporting requirement one-third of the largest UK companies are publishing a VA statement.

Several advantages are claimed for the VA Statement. To date, these have been based essentially on a priori reasoning (Gray and Maunders, 1980; Morley, 1979):

1. Because the VA Statement reflects a broader view of the company's objectives and responsibilities it improves the attitudes of employees toward their employers.
2. It provides an alternative measure of performance and activity. The preparation of ratios for a VA Statement may be a useful means of interpreting that performance, e.g. comparison of value added per employee ratios across divisions of a company, or with competitors, may be employed.
3. It may be of assistance in the introduction of profit sharing or productivity schemes based on value added. A significant number of companies have, in recent years, introduced profit-sharing schemes based on productivity increases as measured by value added or related ratios.
4. It provides a good measure of the size and importance of a company and is superior to sales and capital in this respect. The sales figure may be inflated by large bought-in expenses which are passed straight on to customers. Capital employed may be a poor indicator of the number of workers employed in a company.
5. It reports a company's contribution to the national income and therefore, is of value to the macro economist.

The advantages which are sometimes claimed for VA Statements should not hide the fact that they are rearrangements of data available elsewhere in company reports. For example, although value added is not explicitly referred to in the Companies Act 1981, two of the alternative layouts for the profit and loss account would involve the disclosure of net turnover, raw materials and consumables and other external changes, thereby enabling a measure of value added to be derived for any company which adopted one of these alternatives.

Variety in Practice

There is at present no standard definition of value added, nor is there any universally accepted practice in its use in the reporting of business results. Consequently, as the 1983 *Survey of Published Accounts* shows there are different degrees of comprehensiveness and a wide variety of ways of incorporating VA information into company reports.

One problem is the existence of alternative ways of treating depreciation. This is normally shown as a disposal of value added, partly because of the view that depreciation is connected with asset replacement, and possibly also because the amount set aside is to some extent discretionary, dependent on manager assessment of asset lives. In Table 10.4 depreciation is treated as an external cost. This treatment ensures that a bought-in depreciable asset is treated in a manner similar to that of bought in materials (Morley, 1979). Furthermore, this treatment provides a better indicator of the wealth created by an enterprise. It is first necessary to maintain the capital of an enterprise before arriving at the amount of value added available for distribution. This argument necessitates the employment of some form of inflation accounting if added value is to be meaningful.

QUESTIONS

Extraordinary Items and Prior Period Adjustments

1. State the main objective of SSAP6.
2. Identify the main tests as to whether a particular item is an extraordinary item as a prior period adjustment.
3. Indicate the practical difficulties involved in applying the standard.
4. For a company which had a turnover of £100 million and pre-tax profit of £10 million classify the profits and losses listed below into the following categories:

(*a*) Extraordinary item
(*b*) Exceptional item
(*c*) Prior period adjustment
(*d*) Transferred directly to reserves

   (*i*) The taxation liability for prior years was agreed and showed that £10,000 had been under-provided.
   (*ii*) The directors have decided that the change in trading prospects evident during the year means that the goodwill shown at 30 June 19X1 at £200,000 has no value at 30 June 19X2.
   (*iii*) Research and development expenditure of £7 million incurred in the year, and written off due to the project being abandoned.
   (*iv*) Unrealised revaluation surplus of £10 million which arose on the revaluation of the company's buildings.
   (*v*) Provision for bad debts of £15 million on the collapse of the company's main customer.
   (*vi*) Loss of £1 million arising from the closure of the company's retailing activities.

(*vii*) Devaluation of land amounting to £4 million following the refusal of planning permission. The land had previously been revalued, and the surplus taken to a revaluation reserve.

(*viii*) Provision for loss of £5 million which is foreseeable on a civil engineering contract in the Middle East.

(*ix*) A balance brought forward in the balance sheet described as 'cash at bankers', of £3 million, which was in fact a bad debt.

(*x*) Uninsured losses which arose from damage caused by a freak tidal wave in the Thames, which was the result of a meteorite landing near Southend. The loss amounted to £6 million.

(*xi*) Exchange losses of £3 million. The company operates the temporal method of translating foreign subsidiary results.

Earnings Per Share

5. (*a*) State the main objective of SSAP3.
   (*b*) Define earnings per share.
   (*c*) Explain the difference between the *net* and *nil* bases of calculating earnings per share.

6. From the consolidated profit and loss account of Jameson Plc for the year ended 31 December 19X1:
   (*a*) Calculate and state the basic earnings per share for the year ending 31 December 19X1 using:
   (*i*) the *net* basis
   (*ii*) the *nil* basis
   (*b*) Calculate and state the fully diluted earnings per share on the *net* basis for the year ended 31 December 19X1.

	£	£
Net profit after all expenses including debenture interest		2,300,000
Less		
Corporation tax on profits for the year at 52%	1,100,000	
Irrecoverable ACT	100,000	1,200,000
		1,100,000
Less		
Extraordinary item after adjusting for Corporation Tax		80,000
		1,020,000
Less		
Dividends—Preference paid	120,000	

—Ordinary interim paid	200,000	
—Ordinary final, proposed	400,000	720,000
Retained profit for the year		300,000
Add		
Balance brought forward		150,000
Retained profits carried forward		£450,000

On 1 January 19X1 there were in issue 10 million £1 ordinary shares and 2 million 6 per cent £1 preference shares. In addition, the company had in issue £1,250,000 10 per cent convertible debentures carrying conversion rights into ordinary shares as follows:

Date	*Price per Share*
On 30 June 19X1	£1.10
On 30 June 19X2	£1.25
On 30 June 19X3	£1.75
On 30 June 19X4	£1.90

No debenture holders took up the option to convert on 30 June 19X1. No debenture or share issues took place during the year ending 31 December 19X1.

Deferred Taxation

7. Discuss the reasons for making full provision for deferred tax, and explain how this affects the profit and loss account and balance sheet.
8. Contrast this with the approach to deferred taxation under Statement of Standard Accounting Practice No. 15 revised, and identify the effects of the latter's adoption on company financial statements.
9. How did the recommendations of ED33 differ from the approach originally adopted by SSAP15?

Contingencies

10. According to SSAP18 *Accounting for Contingencies*:

   (a) What is a *contingency* in the context of the statement?
   (b) In what circumstances should contingent losses be accrued in financial statements?
   (c) How should contingent gains be dealt with in financial statements?

Post Balance Sheet Events

11. 'Financial statements should be prepared on the basis of conditions

existing at the balance sheet date'. (SSAP17 *Accounting for Post Balance Sheet Events*)

(*a*) Recognising the possibility of time lags in establishing what conditions actually exist at the balance sheet date, how does SSAP17 seek to ensure that financial accounts are prepared in accordance with this rule?

(*b*) How does SSAP17 seek to ensure that financial accounts prepared in accordance with this rule are not misleading?

Your answer should include THREE examples relating to (*a*) and a further THREE examples relating to (*b*).

(Association of Certified Accountants)

Stocks and Work-in-progress

12. Nite-nite Limited manufactures electric blankets. The thermostat of the 'super' model is less adjustable than that of the 'deluxe' version, but this is the only difference between them. The deluxe thermostat takes the same time to fit as the super version.

The unit costs of production are:

	Super £	*Deluxe* £
Raw materials	12	15
Direct labour	20	20

Normally 5,000 super blankets and 3,000 deluxe blankets are produced, but during August only 4,000 super blankets and 2,000 deluxe blankets were made.

Other costs incurred during August were:

	£
Factory overhead	24,000
Selling overhead	6,000
Administration overhead	8,000
Financial overhead	4,000

The selling prices of the blankets are £37 for the super and £45 for the deluxe.

The directors are unsure of how to value the stocks of blankets produced during August. Various suggestions have been put forward including

(*a*) valuation at selling price;

(*b*) divide the overheads equally between each unit giving valuations of £37.25 (super) and £40.25 (deluxe);

(*c*) divide overhead between units actually produced giving valuations of £39 (super) and £42 (deluxe);

(*d*) ignore overhead completely and value at prime cost.

You are required to comment on these suggestions in the light of SSAP9 and to compute valuations for the blankets in accordance with it.

13. Better Buildings Limited commenced business on the 1 June 19X1 as building contractors. The following details relate to the three uncompleted contracts in the company's books on 31 May 19X2:

Contract Name	Wallace	Fletcher	Arndale
Cost of work to 31 May 19X2, all certified (see note)	60,940	54,560	27,280
Value of work to 31 May 19X2 as certified by contractees' architects	77,000	44,000	28,600
Progress payments invoiced to 31 May 19X2	66,000	35,200	22,000
Progress payments received by 31 May 19X2	55,000	35,200	22,000
Estimate of:			
Final cost including future costs of rectification and guarantee work	66,000	77,000	132,000
Final contract price	83,600	61,600	176,000

Note:
The cost of work to 31 May 19X2 has been determined after crediting unused materials and the written down value of plant in use.
You are required:

(*a*) To prepare a statement for the board of directors showing your calculation for each contract of the valuation of work in progress at 31 May 19X2 and of the profit (loss) included therein.

(*b*) To show as an extract therefrom, the information which should appear in the balance sheet for work in progress.

The statement (*a*) should include any notes and recommendations that you consider necessary to assist the deliberations of the Board and should take into account the requirements of SSAP9.

Depreciation

14. (a) Why does an accountant provide for depreciation when he measures profit?
    (b) A company bought a moulding machine five years ago for £10,000. It is now fully written down, since straight line depreciation has been applied based on a five-year life.
    The company do not, however, intend to scrap the machine and propose to work on with it into the future.
    How would you account for this situation?
15. As the accountant of a small company you have had the following comments or suggestions from other staff regarding depreciation of fixed assets:
    (a) 'There is no point in depreciating the freehold buildings because the market value must be considerably in excess of cost.'
    (b) 'I estimate that the replacement cost of our machine shop equipment is a good 50 per cent more than we paid for it, so should we not increase the depreciation charge from 20 per cent to 30 per cent?'.
    (c) 'The trading prospects for the next year or two look good—I think we should change the depreciation method for machinery from 20 per cent straightline to 40 per cent reducing balance so as to get more written off whilst profits are high.'

Required:

Outline how you would respond to each of the above.
16. 'When a depreciating asset is first acquired, the accountant should try to forecast the net relevant cash-flow pattern.'

Required:

   (a) Explain what you understand by the 'net relevant cash-flow pattern'.
   (b) Explain why such a forecast may be necessary.

(Association of Certified Accountants)
17. Toumey Enterprises Plc owns three identical properties, North, and South and East. North is used as the head office of Toumey Enterprises Plc. South is let to, and is occupied by, a subsidiary. East is let to, and is occupied by, an associated company. A fourth property, West, is leased by Toumey Enterprises Plc and the unexpired term on the lease is fifteen years. West is let to, and is occupied by, a company outside the group.

Required

   (a) Which, if any, of these properties is likely to be an investment

property of Toumey Enterprises Plc and what additional information may be necessary for a final decision? State your reasons.
(*b*) Identify and justify the appropriate depreciation policy for each of
the properties.

(Association of Certified Accountants)

Goodwill

18. (*a*) How would you define goodwill?
   (*b*) Three accounting treatments of goodwill are:

   (*i*)   retain goodwill as an asset to be amortised over its estimated
          useful life;
   (*ii*) retain goodwill as an asset indefinitely;
   (*iii*) write off goodwill to reserves at the time of acquisition.

   Discuss briefly the principles underlying each of these three
   approaches.

(Association of Certified Accountants)

19. *Research and Development*
   (*a*) Discuss the criteria which SSAP13 *Accounting for Research and
        Development* states should be used when considering whether
        research and development expenditure should be written off in an
        accounting period or carried forward.
   (*b*) Discuss to what extent these criteria are consistent with fun-
        damental accounting concepts as defined in SSAP2 *Disclosure of
        Accounting Policies*.

(Association of Certified Accountants)

Leases

20. Define a finance lease and state the conditions under which it will be
   presumed that a lease is a finance lease.
21. From the lessee's point of view, contrast the difference between an
   operating lease and a finance lease.
22. Explain the arguments for and against the capitalisation of finance
   leases.
23. Show how the following transactions would appear in the published
   accounts of both Keepfit Limited and Blackstone Limited for the year
   ending 31 December 19X1:

   Keepfit Limited wishes to acquire the equipment for a small
   gymnasium and has decided to take up an agreement with Blackstone
   Limited whereby Blackstone Limited will lease the equipment on a

finance lease to Keepfit Limited for a period of eight years from 1 January 19X1. The equipment would cost £100,000 and, on the basis that it would have no value after eight years, it is to be depreciated at £12,500 per annum on a straight-line basis. The lease agreement specifies payments of £19,850 per annum to be paid annually in advance. The implicit rate of interest in the lease is 16 per cent per annum. Keepfit Limited has decided that the lease should be capitalised in its accounts. Both Keepfit Limited and Blackstone Limited have decided to allocate the interest element included in the rentals on a basis which takes into account the implicit rate of interest of 16 per cent per annum.

Pensions

24. Distinguish between a defined benefit and a defined contribution scheme.
25. 'Actuarial cost methods are basically funding and not cost allocation methods.' Discuss.
26. Evaluate the recommendations of ED32, *'Disclosure of Pension Information in Company Accounts'*

Foreign Currency Translation

27. What are the arguments for and against the use of the temporal and closing rate methods for the translation of foreign currency values?
28. X Plc operates in the UK. It has a wholly owned subsidiary, Y SA which is located in Switzerland. The following is Y's balance sheet at 31.12.X1:

		Swiss Francs
Share capital		200,000
Profit and loss account		100,000
		300,000
Loan		120,000
		420,000
Fixed assets		400,000
Depreciation		80,000
		320,000
Current assets	150,000	
Current liabilities	(50,000)	100,000
		420,000

Relevant exchange rates were:

	(£1:SF)
1.1.X1	3.38
Average for X1	3.33
31.12.X1	3.27

Depreciation is provided on a straight line basis at 20 per cent per annum. Y SA operates independently of X Plc.

Required:

Translate the items in the balance sheet of Y SA for inclusion in the accounts of X Plc on the closing rate method.

Value Added Statements

29. Do you consider the Value Added Statement to be a useful inclusion in a company's corporate report? Discuss your reasons.

(Association of Certified Accountants)

30. (*a*) Using the following summarised information prepare a value added statement:

	£000
Salaries and wages	400
Purchased materials used in production	600
Sales	1,480
Corporation tax on the profit for the year	120
Dividend proposed	48
Services purchased	120
Depreciation of fixed assets	80
Loan interest paid and payable	40

(*b*) There is an alternative view on the treatment of depreciation in Value Added Statements. What is this view and how would it affect the statement you have produced in answer to question (*a*)?

REFERENCES

APB Opinion No. 8, *Accounting for the Cost of Pension Plans*, American Institute of Certified Public Accountants, 1965.

APB Opinion No. 11, *Accounting for Income Taxes*, American Institute of Certified Public Accountants, 1967.

Accounting Standards Committee, *Earnings per share*, February 1972.

Accounting Standards Committee, *The Corporate Report*, 1975.

Accounting Standards Committee, ED21, *Accounting for foreign currency transactions*, September 1977.

Accounting Standards Committee, *Accounting for Goodwill: A Discussion Paper*, 1980(1).

Accounting Standards Committee, ED27, *Accounting for foreign currency translation*, October 1980(2).

Accounting Standards Committee, ED29, *Accounting for leases and hire purchase contracts*, October 1981.

Accounting Standards Committee, SSAP20, *Foreign Currency Translation*, 1983.

Abdel-Khalik *et al*, 'The Impact of Reporting Leases Off the Balance Sheet: Two Exploratory Studies', in *Economic Consequences of Financial Accounting Standards*, FASB, 1978 Stamford.

Abdel-Khalik *et al.*, *The Economic Effects on Lessees of FASB Statement No. 13, Accounting for Leases*, FASB, 1981.

Archibald, T. R., *Accounting for Pension Costs*, The Canadian Institute of Chartered Accountants, 1980.

Ashton, R. K., 'Earnings per share—net, nil or full', *Investment Analyst*, September 1975.

Ball, R. J., 'Changes in Accounting Techniques and Stock Prices', *Journal of Accounting Research: Empirical Research in Accounting, Selected Studies*, 1972.

Bank of England, *Equipment Leasing*, Quarterly Bulletin, 1984.

Barnea, A., *et al.*, 'Classificatory Smoothing of Income with Extraordinary Items', *The Accounting Review*, January 1976.

Barton, A. D., 'Company Income Tax and Interperiod Allocation', *Abacus*, September 1970

Baxter, W. T., *Depreciating Assets*, The Institute of Chartered Accountants of Scotland, Gee and Co., 1981.

Beaver, W. H., and Dukes, R. E., 'Tax Allocation and Definition—Depreciation Methods', *The Accounting Review*, July 1972.

Beaver, W. H., Ketter, T. P. and Scholes, M., 'The association between market determined and accounting determined risk measures, *The Accounting Review*, 1970.

Bierman, H. and Dukes, R. E., 'Accounting for Research and Development Costs', *Journal of Accountancy*, April 1975.

Black, H. A., *Interperiod Allocation of Corporate Income Taxes*, Accounting Research Study No. 9, AICPA, 1966.

Bowman, R., 'The debt-equivalence of leases: an empirical investigation', *The Accounting Review*, 1980.

Breen, W. J. and Lerner, E. M., 'Corporate Financial Strategies and Market Measures of Risk and Return', *Journal of Finance*, 1973.

Carty, J., 'Deferred Tax: ED33 is of Limited Value', *Certified Accountant*, July 1983.

Catlett, G. R. and Olson, N. O., *Accounting for Goodwill*, Accounting Research Study No. 10, AICPA 1968.

Chambers, R. J., *Accounting Evaluation and Economic Behaviour*, Prentice Hall, 1966.

Chambers, R. J., 'Tax Allocation and Financial Reporting', *Abacus*, December 1968.

Cheung, J. K., 'The Association Between Lease Disclosure and the Lessee's Systematic Risk', *Journal of Business Finance and Accounting* , 1982.

Clark, T., *Leasing*, McGraw Hill, 1978.

Cranfield School of Management, *Financial Leasing Report*, Bedford, 1979.

Davidson, S., 'Accelerated Depreciation and the Allocation of Income Taxes', *The Accounting Review*, January 1958.

Deitrich, J. R. and Kaplan, R. S., 'Empirical Analysis of the Commercial Loan Classification Decision', *The Accounting Review*, 1982.

Department of Trade, *The Future of Company Reports, A Consultative Document*, (HMSO Cmnd. 6888) 1977.

Fawthrop, R. A. and Terry, B., 'Debt management and the use of leasing finance in UK corporate financing strategies', *Journal of Business Finance and Accounting*, 1975

Financial Accounting Standards Board, FAS No. 8, *Accounting for the Translation of Foreign Currency Transactions and Foreign Currency Financial Statements*, 1975.

Financial Accounting Standards Board, *Economic Consequences of Financial Accounting Standards*, July 1978.

Finnerty, J. E., *et al.*, 'Lease Capitalisation and Systematic Risk', *The Accounting Review*, 1980.

Flavell, R. and Salkin, G. R., *A model of a lessor*, Omega, 1982.

Flower, J., *Accounting Treatment of Overseas Currencies*, ICAEW, 1976.

Gellein, O. S. and Newman, M. S., *Accounting for Research and Development Costs*, Accounting Research Study No. 14, AICPA, 1973.

Gibbs, M., 'Accounting Standards and Investment Analysis', in Leach, R. and Stamp, E. (eds.) *Setting Accounting Standards*, Woodhead Faulkner, 1981.

Gonedes, N., 'Evidence on the Information Content of Accounting Messages: Accounting Based or Market Based Estimates of Systematic Risks', *Journal of Financial and Quantitative Analysis*, 1973.

Gray, S. J. and Maunders, K. T., *Value Added Reporting: Uses and Measurement*, The Association of Certified Accountants, 1980.

Hamada, R. S., 'The Effect of the Firm's Capital Structure on the Systematic Risk of Common Stocks', *Journal of Finance*, 1972.

Haslem, J. A. and Longbrake, W. A., 'A Credit Scoring Model for Commercial Loans: A Comment', *Journal of Money, Credit and Banking*, 1972.

Hill, T. M., 'Some Arguments Against Interperiod Allocation of Income Taxes', *The Accounting Review*, July 1957.

Hope, T. and Briggs, J., 'Accounting Policy Making—Some Lessons from the Deferred Taxation Debate', *Accounting and Business Research*, Spring 1982.

Hope, T. and Gray R., 'Power and Policy Making: The Development of an R and D Standard', *Journal of Business Finance and Accounting*, Winter 1982.

Horowitz, B. and Kolodny, R., 'The FASB, the SEC and R and D', *Bell Journal of Economics*, Spring 1981.

Institute for Fiscal Studies, *Issues in Bank Taxation*, by J. S. S. Edwards and C. P. Mayer, 1982.

Keller, T. F., 'Interperiod Tax Allocation' in M. Backer (ed.), *Modern Accounting Theory*, Prentice Hall, 1966.

Lev, B., 'The Impact of Accounting Regulation on the Stock Market: The Case of Oil and Gas Companies', *The Accounting Review*, 1979.

Lorensen, L., in Accounting Research Study No. 12, *Reporting Foreign Operations of US Companies in US Dollars*, AICPA, 1972.

Lyne, S., 'Realisable Value—A Supplement to Current Cost Accounts', *Accountant's Magazine*, July 1981.

Morley, M. F., *The Value Added Statement—A Review of its Use in Corporate Reports*, Institute of Chartered Accountants of Scotland in Gee and Co., 1978.

Morley, M. F., 'The Value Added Statement in Britain', *The Accounting Review*, July 1979.

Napier, C. J., *Accounting for Pension Costs*, Accounting Standards Committee, 1982.

Nobes, C. W., 'A review of the translation debate', *Accounting and Business Research*, 1980.

Orgler, Y. E., 'A Credit Scoring Model for Commercial Loans', *Journal of Money Credit and Banking*, 1970.

Patz, D. H., 'The state of the art in translation theory', *Journal of Business Finance and Accounting*, 1977.

Parkinson, R. M., *Translation of Foreign Currencies*, Canadian Institute of Chartered Accountants, 1972.

Ro, B. T., 'The Disclosure of Capitalised Lease Information and Stock Prices', *Journal of Accounting Research*, 1978.

Rosenfield, P., and Dent, W. C., 'No More Deferred Taxes', *Journal of Accountancy*, February 1983.

Ross, D., 'CCA and the Asset Lives Bogey', *Accountancy*, September 1980.

Securities and Exchange Council, ASR No. 147, *Notice of Adoption of Amendments to Regulation S-X Requiring Improved Disclosure of Leases*, Chicago: Commerce Clearing House, 1973.

Simmonds, A., 'Pension Costs by Numbers', *Accountancy*, October 1983.

Skerrat, L. C. L. and Peasnell, K. V., 'Anti-dilution of earnings per share', *Accounting and Business Research*, 1975.

Skinner, R., 'Accounting for a Simplified Firm—The Search for Common Ground', in Sterling, R. R. and Thomas, A. L. (eds.) *Accounting for a Simplified Firm using Depreciable Assets*, Scholars Book Co., 1979.

Sunder, S., 'Accounting Changes in Inventory Valuation', *The Accounting Review*, April 1975.

Sykes, A., *The Lease-Buy Decision—A Survey of Current Practice in 202 Companies*, Management Survey Report No. 29, British Institute of Management, London, 1976.

Thomas, A. L., *The Allocation Problem, Studies in Accounting Research No. 9*, American Accounting Association, 1974.

Vigeland, R. L., 'The Market Reaction to Statement of Financial Accounting Standards No. 2', *The Accounting Review*, April, 1981.

Watts, T. R., 'Planning the Next Decade', in Leach and Stamp, op cit, 1981.

Wojnilower, A. W., *The Quality of Bank Loans*, Occasional Paper 82, National Bureau of Economic Research, 1962.

Wu, H. K., 'Bank examiners criticisms, bank loan defaults, and bank loan quality', *Journal of Finance*, 1969.

CHAPTER 11

Accounting for inter-company relationships

In previous chapters we have considered the problems of accounting theory and policy for the single entity. This emphasis has been largely implicit. In the present chapter we examine some of the issues raised by the need to account for inter-company relationships.

The method for accounting for a specific inter-company investment is determined by the nature of the particular investment. The most important factor which distinguishes different types of investment is the degree of control or influence which is exercised by one company over another. At one extreme a company may purchase shares in another in order to make profitable use of otherwise idle funds. At the other extreme a company may acquire all the share capital of another company and take control of its operations. In this chapter we examine three types of inter-company investments:

1. trade investments
2. associated companies
3. subsidiary companies

Trade Investments

An investment by one company in another may be held for short or long periods. If the former, it is in effect a current asset and if the latter a fixed asset. The conventional approach of Chapter 2 would value such assets at the lower of cost or net realisable value. In the case of a fixed asset investment this would be interpreted as reporting the asset at market value if this is judged to be permanently below cost. Dividends from trade investments are conventionally credited as income.

The Companies Act 1981 requires a trade investment to be classified as either a fixed or current asset as above (see the appendix to chapter 4). However, the Act requires additional disclosures of information if, at the end of an accounting period, a company holds in another either:

(*a*) more than 10 per cent of the nominal value of the allotted shares of any class of equity share capital, or

(*b*) more than 10 per cent of the nominal value of all allotted share capital, or

(*c*) share capital having a total book value exceeding 10 per cent of its own assets.

In such cases the disclosures required are the name of the investee company, its country of incorporation or registration, and a description and proportion of the nominal value of the allotted shares of each class held. The disclosure requirements refer to both preference and equity shares. Where the number of investee companies is large only those principally affecting the profit and assets of the investor company need be given. Further disclosures are required of companies holding more than 20 per cent of allotted share capital in other companies and those are considered below.

The methods described above are unsuitable for the presentation of information concerning large investments which give significant influence and control. In such cases treating the investments as trade investments give little indication of the profitability of the investment and of the way the profits of the investor company might be manipulated by changing the dividend policy of the investee company. For large investments law and accounting standards require that additional disclosures be made by investor companies so as to provide more information for users. This is considered in the next section.

Associated Companies

SSAP1, issued in January 1971 (ASC, 1971) and revised in 1982 defines an associated company as one

not being a subsidiary of the investing group or company in which:

(*a*) the interest of the investing group or company is effectively that of a partner in a joint venture or consortium and the investing group or company is in a position to exercise a significant influence over the company in which the investment is made; or

(*b*) the interest of the investing group or company is for the long term and is substantial and, having regard to the disposition of the other shareholdings, the investing group or company is in a position to exercise a significant influence over the company in which the investment is made.

(ASC, 1982)

The term 'significant influence' over a company basically involves participation in the financial and operating policies and decisions of that company (including dividend policy) but not necessarily control over those policies. Representation on the board of directors is an indicator of such participation but does not necessarily give conclusive evidence, nor is it the only method by which the investing company may participate in policy decisions.

Where the interest of the investing group or company is not in effect that of a partner in a joint venture or consortium but does amount to 20 per cent or more of the equity voting rights of a company, it should be presumed that the investor has the ability to exercise significant influence over that company unless it can clearly be demonstrated to the contrary.

The Companies Acts up to 1981 did not define associated companies nor prescribe any specific accounting treatment for them. The Companies Act 1981 did not use the term 'associated company' but instead introduced the term 'related company'. The definition of related company is very similar to that of associated company used in SSAP1 and in most circumstances will be the same. The term 'associated company' will be used hereafter.

An associated company is an intermediate stage between a trade investment and a subsidiary. The classification of an associated company involves a quantitative test. However, since a difference of kind as well as degree is identified an appropriate method of accounting for associated companies must be sought between those for trade investments and subsidiaries, as current or fixed assets in the case of the former, and consolidation in group accounts in the case of the latter. SSAP1 adopts the method known as equity accounting as the appropriate accounting treatment.

The Equity Method

The equity method is also known as one line consolidation because it involves the use in a modified form of the procedures adopted for subsidiary companies. Under the equity method the cost of the investment at its acquisition date is recorded by the investor as a debit on investment account. In each subsequent period the investment account is (*a*) increased for the investor's proportionate share in the reported profits of the investee, and (*b*) decreased by all dividends received from the investee. This treatment contrasts with that of the cost method under which dividends received from an investment are recorded as income, but the profits or losses of the investee company are not recorded in the investment account of the investor. We illustrate the application of the equity and cost methods in the following example.

Example 11.1:

Investor PLC has invested in 30 per cent of the shares of Investee Ltd at a cost of £10,000 on 1.1.19X1. The treatment of the investment under the two methods is as follows:

	Cost method	Equity method
1.1.19X1 Investor buys 30% of Investee's shares	Dr Investment in Associate £10,000	Dr Investment in Associate £10,000
	Cr Cash £10,000	Cr Cash £10,000
31.12.19X1 Investee Ltd reports profits of £1,500 for the year.	No entry	Dr Investment in Associate £450
		Cr Earnings of Associate £450
Investee pays dividends of £1,000	Dr Dividends Receivable £300	Dr Dividends Receivable £300
	Cr Dividend Income £300	Cr Investment in Associate £300

The above example illustrates how the initial investment in, and the subsequent profits and dividend distributions of the associate company are recorded. The carrying value of the investment under the equity method increases by the investor company's share of the net assets of the associate company.

The Accounting Requirements of SSAP1

The standard requires that the investing company's consolidated financial statements should record the relationships with associated companies on the equity method. In its own financial statements the investing company is recommended to use the cost method. In its consolidated profit and loss account the investing company should include the aggregate of its shares of the before-tax profits and losses of associated companies. This item should be shown separately and suitably described. The tax attributed to the share of associated company profits should be disclosed separately, and the investing group's share of extraordinary items should be included with the group's own extraordinary items. Also, the investing group's share of aggregate net profits less losses retained by associated companies should be shown separately. In the consolidated balance sheet of the investing group investments should be shown as the investing group's share of the net assets of associated companies.

Evaluation

Accounting for associated companies was considered important enough to be chosen as the subject of the first accounting standard issued in the UK. In the opinion of the first Chairman of the ASC the topic was chosen because of the circumstances existing when the concept of accounting standards was devised (Leach, 1981). At that time the wide variety in the bases on which profit forecasts and audited accounts were prepared tended to give rise to very different interpretations, especially where substantial equity interests in other companies amounting to less than a controlling interest were concerned.

The original standard was reviewed as part of the ASC's regular activities and ED25 (ASC, 1979) was issued during the review process. The exposure draft contained certain revisions which were subsequently incorporated into a revised accounting standard. ED25 and the revised standard were different from the original in the definition of an associated company and the specification of holdings to be aggregated in order to define an associated company. The equity method was proposed in the original standard and has been retained throughout.

The equity method presumes that the investor can exercise significant influence over the policies, both financial and operating, of the investee company. This includes dividend policy. The treatment recommended for profits and distributions of associated companies accords with the guidelines for revenue recognition discussed in Chapter 7. However, the resulting consolidated financial statements of the investing group do not necessarily provide useful information for the evaluation of the current financial position of the associated company nor for predicting the future earnings performance of the associate. Details of the components of costs and the composition of assets and liabilities which would serve such purposes are not disclosed by the equity method.

Subsidiary Companies

When a company goes beyond influencing the policies of another and acquires a controlling interest in it the investor company is usually referred to as the holding company and the investee company as the subsidiary. There is a legal requirement for the holding company to prepare group accounts, the term given to the financial statements of a group of companies. Consolidated accounts are one form of group accounts and they present the information contained in the separate financial statements of a holding company and its subsidiaries as if they were the financial statements of a single economic entity. Some aspects of the mechanics of preparing consolidated accounts are presented later in this chapter.

Legal Aspects

According to the 1948 Companies Act a company shall be deemed to be a subsidiary of another company if:

(*a*) that other company either:

(*i*)   is a member of it and controls the composition of the board of directors; or

(*ii*) holds more than half in nominal value of its equity share capital; or

(*b*) the first mentioned company is a subsidiary of any company which is that other's subsidiary.

To illustrate the circumstances of (*b*) consider the case where H owns 70 per cent of the equity share capital of S and S owns 60 per cent of the equity of SS. SS is a subsidiary of S and also of H. S must publish group accounts incorporating SS and H must publish group accounts incorporating all three.

Group accounts are not required under the 1948 Companies Act if:

(*a*) the company is itself the wholly owned subsidiary of another company; or

(*b*) the directors are of the opinion that:

(*i*)   it is impractical or of no real value because of the insignificant amounts involved,

(*ii*) undue expense would be involved,

(*iii*) it would be misleading or harmful to the business of the company or its subsidiaries,

(*iv*) the businesses are so different that they cannot reasonably be treated as a single undertaking.

Where group accounts are not produced on grounds (*b*) (*iii*) and (*iv*) above the approval of the Department of Trade is required.

If group accounts are not submitted the Companies Act 1967 requires that the following information be given:

(*a*) the reasons why such financial statements have not been provided,
(*b*) the aggregate profits or losses of subsidiaries which are attributable to the members of the holding company for the respective financial years of the subsidiaries ending with or during the holding company's financial year, and previous financial years of subsidiaries since they became subsidiaries.

The 1948 Act provides that the format of group financial statements shall be consolidated, comprising a consolidated balance sheet and consolidated profit and loss account unless the directors are of the opinion that the required information may be better or more clearly presented by another form of group financial statements such as:

(*a*) more than one set of consolidated financial statements,
(*b*) separate financial statements for each subsidiary and for the holding company,
(*c*) statements expanding the information about the subsidiaries in the holding company's own financial statements. Other forms of group financial statements must give the same or equivalent information as that required to be given by consolidated financial statements.

A holding company is not required to submit its own profit and loss account provided that a consolidated profit and loss account is produced and the amount of the consolidated profit or loss for the financial year dealt with in the holding company's financial statements is given. Virtually all large companies with subsidiaries present their results in this way.

Accounting Policy Requirements of SSAP14

In September 1978 the ASC issued SSAP14 entitled *Group Accounts*. The standard proposes that a holding company should usually prepare group accounts as a single set of consolidated accounts relating to the holding company and its subsidiaries at home and overseas. A subsidiary should be excluded from the consolidation if:

(*a*) its activities are so dissimilar from those of companies in the rest of the group that the needs of users would be better served if separate financial statements were to be provided for each of the subsidiary companies; or
(*b*) the holding company, despite holding more than half of the shares in the subsidiary does not own share capital carrying more than half of the votes, or has contractual or other restrictions placed upon its ability to appoint the majority of members of the board of directors; or
(*c*) the operations of the subsidiary are so severely restricted that the ability of the parent company to exercise control over it is significantly impaired; or

(*d*) control by the parent is indicated to be only temporary.

In case (*a*) group accounts should include separate financial statements for the subsidiary which is considered too dissimilar to consolidate. These should include a note showing the extent of the holding company's interest, particulars of any inter-company balances, particulars of the nature of any transactions between the subsidiary and the rest of the group, and a reconciliation with the amount included in the consolidated financial statements for the group's investment in the subsidiary which should be determined under the equity method.

In case (*b*) the subsidiary should be dealt with under the equity method in the consolidated financial statements if in all other aspects it satisfies the criteria for treatment as an associated company according to SSAP1. Alternatively, if the criteria are not met the investment in the subsidiary should be recorded as an investment at cost or valuation less any provision required.

In case (*c*) the subsidiary should be shown in the consolidated balance sheet of the group at the amount at which it would have been recorded under the equity method at the date at which the restrictions came into effect. Provision for any loss in value in the investment in the subsidiary should be made through the consolidated profit and loss account. The subsidiary's net assets, profit or loss for the period together with any amounts included in the consolidated profit and loss account in respect of dividends received and writing down of the investment should also be disclosed.

In case (*d*) a temporary investment in a subsidiary should be stated in the consolidated balance sheet as a current asset at the lower of cost and net realisable value.

Acquisition Versus Merger Accounting

There exist two methods of accounting for business combinations: the acquisition (or purchase) method and the merger (or pooling) method. These methods should not be viewed as alternatives. ED31 (ASC, 1982) proposed certain conditions which must be met for a business combination to be regarded as a merger and accounted for accordingly. Where these conditions are not met the combination must be recorded as an acquisition.

The Acquisition Method

The general characteristics of the acquisition method may be summarised as follows:

1. In the holding company's balance sheet shares purchased in a subsidiary

company are valued at cost, that is, the fair market value of the consideration given to acquire the shares. If the consideration is in the form of cash, the valuation process is relatively simple. Valuation is more difficult if the consideration involves an exchange of shares, i.e. where the holding company gives its own shares in exchange for those of the subsidiary. If the fair value of the consideration exceeds the par value of the shares issued a share premium account is required to be created.

2. The assets and liabilities of the subsidiary are required by SSAP14 to be revalued to their fair value at the date of acquisition.
3. The difference between the consideration given and the sum of the acquired company's net assets is treated as goodwill.
4. The pre-acquisition reserves of the acquired company are regarded as frozen and are therefore not available for distribution.
5. When a profit and loss account is prepared, the profit or loss of the acquiring company will include those of the acquired company only from the date of acquisition.

Example 11.2:

The following example illustrates acquisition accounting. Maxi Plc makes an offer for the shares of Mini Ltd as at 31 December 19X3. At that date the summarised balance sheets of the two companies were as follows:

	Maxi Plc *£000*	*Mini Ltd* *£000*
Net assets	600	300
Share capital (£1 shares)	400	200
Reserves (distributable)	200	100
	600	300

Maxi's offer comprises one of its own shares for every one share of Mini and the offer is accepted by the shareholders of Mini. Each Mini share is valued at £2 and the fair value of the net assets of Mini is £350,000.

Maxi would record the investment at a value of £400,000 (200,000 shares at £2 each) and the consolidated balance sheet of Maxi and Mini at 31 December 19X3 would appear as:

	£000
Net assets	950
Goodwill on consolidation	50
	1,000

Share capital (£1 shares)	600
Share premium account	200
Distributable reserves	200
	1,000

Several disadvantages have been claimed for the acquisition method (ASC, 1982):

(*i*) The pre-acquisition reserves of the acquired company are frozen and cannot be distributed even though the shareholders immediately before and after the acquisition are the same.

(*ii*) The method creates a share premium or similar account which is an unrealised reserve.

(*iii*) The method leads to the recognition of goodwill. As we noted in Chapter 10 goodwill creates a number of accounting problems. If it is capitalised it is required to be written off.

(*iv*) The requirement to revalue assets will increase the depreciation charges for acquired companies which use historical costs.

These objections are often voiced by management because of the depressive effects which they may have on net profit and EPS. But as we saw in Chapter 5, capital market research findings tend to conclude that the market can see beyond changes in accounting method to identify economic realities.

The Merger Method

The acquisition method does not appear to be suitable when companies of similar size combine by means of a share-for-share exchange, with neither of the combining companies being considered to have acquired the other or others. In such cases there is no purchase and no purchase price. Such combinations are best viewed as a merger or pooling of shareholders interests rather than as transactions involving the acquisition of assets. Merger accounting was originally developed to deal with such circumstances. Additionally with merger accounting the disadvantages of acquisition accounting do not arise.

Using the data from the previous example Maxi Plc would record the purchase of Mini's 200,000 £1 shares at £200,000 in its accounts and the consolidated balance sheet would appear thus:

	£000
Net assets	900
	900

Share capital	600
Distributable reserves	300
	900

Merger accounting results in distributable reserves of £300,000 compared with £200,000 under acquisition accounting. There is no share premium account, no goodwill on consolidation and no change in the value of net assets.

Requirements For Merger Accounting

In the UK merger accounting appeared to be prohibited by the provisions of the 1948 Companies Act which require that whenever shares are issued at a premium the excess above their nominal value should be credited to a share premium account. The case of Shearer versus Bercain Ltd (1980) confirmed the prohibition and lead to representations being made to the Department of Trade on the grounds that the Act inhibited mergers and frustrated intra-group reorganisation. The Companies Act 1981 introduced new requirements concerning goodwill, share premium and merger accounting. The provisions on merger accounting were set out in quite general terms on the understanding that other requirements, both legal and professional, would follow. A Statutory Instrument came into effect in November 1982 with other disclosure requirements and ED31 suggested additional disclosures. While the 1981 Companies Act specified circumstances in which merger accounting is permitted and where restrictions on the treatment of goodwill and pre-acquisition profits can be ignored, ED31 contained proposals which would establish more restrictive criteria. These were as follows:

(a) the business combination should result from an offer to all the holders of all equity shares and the holders of all voting shares which are not already held by the offerer; the offer should be approved by the holders of the voting shares of the company making the offer; and

(b) the offer should be accepted by the holders of at least 90 per cent of all equity shares and of the shares carrying at least 90 per cent of all votes of the offeree company; for this purpose any convertible stock is not to be regarded as equity except to the extent that it is converted into equity as a result of the business combination; and

(c) not less than 90 per cent of the fair value of the total consideration given for the equity share capital (including that given for the shares already held) should be in the form of equity capital; not less than 90 per cent of the fair value of the consideration given for voting non-equity share capital (including that given for shares already held) should be in the form of equity and/or voting non-equity share capital.

Where a business combination does not satisfy these criteria it should be treated as an acquisition. ED31 was more restrictive than the 1981 Act by specifying one transaction ('an offer' in (*a*) above) leading to the combination. The Act allows any number of transactions. Also, ED31 restricted the value of the consideration given in terms of equity alone (90 per cent) whilst the Act allows 90 per cent of any combination of equity and non-equity. ED31 required the approval of 90 per cent of equity and 90 per cent of voting shares but the Act makes no reference to voting shares.

Merger accounting is associated with two major problems. First, there is the difficulty of distinguishing a merger from an acquisition. ED31 (and the Companies Act 1981 to a lesser degree) distinguish on the basis of a series of quantitative tests. Second, critics of merger accounting argue that it may create artificial and instant profits. For example the profits of the combined businesses will include the results of all the merged companies for the complete accounting period irrespective of when in that period mergers took place.

The Accounting Requirements of ED31

ED31 contained the following recommendations for accounting requirements:

(*a*) Shares acquired by the holding company should be recorded in its accounts at the nominal value of the shares which are issued in exchange.

(*b*) Where there is some non-equity consideration, its fair value should be added to that of the nominal value of the shares issued to determine the carrying value to the holding company of the shares of the subsidiary.

(*c*) On consolidation the only difference to be dealt with will be between the amount at which the holding company carries the investment in the subsidiary (according to (*a*) and (*b*) above, the value of equity and non-equity considerations valued in nominal terms and at fair value respectively) and the nominal value of the shares acquired by the holding company. Any difference should be dealt with as follows:

   (*i*) if the carrying value of the investment is less than that of the shares transferred the difference should be treated as an undistributable reserve arising on consolidation; or

   (*ii*) if the carrying value of the investment is more than the value of the shares transferred the difference is to be viewed as the extent to which the reserves of the subsidiary have been capitalised as a result of the merger. The difference should be treated on consolidation as a reduction in reserves and should be applied first to undistributable reserves and then distributable reserves.

Subsequent to the issue of ED31, an SOI was published outlining the ASC's intentions for an accounting standard. However, when the standard itself, SSAP23 *Accounting for Acquisitions and Mergers* was issued, certain of its provisions differed from those of the SOI. In particular, whilst the SOI had proposed the substitution of an 80 per cent barrier for the equity consideration as the boundary between merger and acquisition accounting, the standard reverts to the criterion of ED31 namely a 90 per cent equity consideration. This revision to the proposals of ED31 was on the grounds that it would be unwise for the standard to conflict with the EEC's Seventh Directive which sets a limit of 10 per cent on the cash consideration, even though this Directive will not be implemented for several years. One important issue still unresolved in this context is that the Seventh Directive's provision refers to nominal value whilst the UK standard refers to fair value.

Consolidated Financial Statements

As we noted earlier, when a company acquires more than 50 per cent of the shares of another, consolidated financial statements are generally prepared. Such statements report the financial position and results of two or more companies as if they were a single economic entity. They are designed to give effect to the economic substance as opposed to the legal form of the corporate relationship. These statements are prepared from the point of view of the shareholder of the holding company who does not receive copies of the financial statements of the subsidiaries. Consolidated financial statements are prepared in addition to the financial statements of the member companies of a group which are prepared in whatever is the normal manner.

Consolidation requires the aggregation of all asset, liability, revenue and expense accounts of companies in the group to be consolidated. Any inter-company sales or loans are eliminated. The interest account of the holding company is also eliminated against the equity accounts of the subsidiaries. This procedure is accomplished by consolidating, adjusting and eliminating entries which are not recorded in the holding company or subsidiaries accounts but appear only in the consolidation worksheet. The following example shows some of the techniques and effects of consolidation. The example is in several stages and the consolidated worksheet referred to is on Table 11.1. The lower case letters at the margin in the example correspond with those by data in the worksheet.

Table 11.1. Example of a Consolidated Worksheet
Holding Company HC Plc and Subsidiary S Ltd Consolidated Worksheet for the year ended 31 December 19X3

	Holding Company	Subsidiary Company	Eliminations Dr	Eliminations Cr	Consolidation
	£	£	£	£	£
Sales	40,000	30,000	6,000(c)		64,000
Stock 31.12.X3	7,000	6,000	1,000(e)		12,000
	47,000	36,000			76,000
Stock 1.1.X3	6,000	5,000		6,000(e)	11,000
Purchases	6,000	12,000			12,000
Expenses	6,000	4,000			10,000
Amortisation of goodwill	–	–	1,000(b)		1,000
	18,000	21,000			34,000
Net profit	29,000	15,000			42,000
Minority shareholders' interest			3,000(a)		(3,000)
					39,000
Profit balance b/f 1.1.X3	85,000	60,000	60,000(a)	6,000	85,000
Profit balance c/f	114,000	75,000	71,000		124,000
Share capital	400,000	165,000	165,000(a)	6,000	400,000
Profit retained	114,000	75,000	71,000	48,000(a)	124,000
Minority shareholders' interest					48,000
Creditors	30,000	10,000	3,000(d)		37,000
Other liabilities	33,000	20,000			53,000
	577,000	270,000			662,000
Goodwill			20,000(a)	1,000(b)	19,000
Fixed assets	325,000	225,000		200,000(a)	550,000
Investment in subsidiary	200,000			1,000(e)	–
Stock	7,000	6,000		3,000(d)	12,000
Debtors	45,000	39,000			81,000
	577,000	270,000	259,000	259,000	662,000

Example 11.3:

(a) HC Plc paid £200,000 for 80 per cent of the shares of S Ltd which had a total book value of £225,000. The book value as evidenced by the balances in S's share account (£60,000), and retained profit account (£165,000) at 1.1.19X3 as shown in the consolidated worksheet above. Since the 80 per cent interest bought by H represents £180,000 of the book value the excess of cost over book value at the time of acquisition (£20,000) is the goodwill which has been bought by H. During 19X3 S had profits of £15,000. 20 per cent of these represent the minority shareholders. The elimination entries in the consolidated worksheet are as follows:

	£000	£000
Share capital S	165	
Profit balance brought forward	60	
Minority interest in profit	3	
Goodwill	20	
Investment in S		200
Minority interest		48

In consolidation only the equity of the holding company appears on the consolidated balance sheet. All the equity accounts of the subsidiaries—their share capital and retained profits on acquisition—must be eliminated. This elimination establishes the minority interest and eliminates the purchase price of the investment. In the consolidated profit and loss account the portion of subsidiary profit or loss that can be ascribed to the minority shareholders is deducted from the total consolidated profit or loss.

The figure for goodwill appears in respect of the group but not in respect of the minority interests. This is consistent with the usual accounting convention of recording intangible assets only when they are explicitly purchased. According to the entity concept of consolidation goodwill should be grossed up to the value of a 100 per cent acquisition and the difference added to the minority interest figure because the minority are entitled to a share of all assets. Three disadvantages of the entity concept of consolidation reduce its usefulness. First, having obtained 80 per cent of the shares in S the same proportionate price might not be applicable. Second, even if it had not been possible to compute a figure, no alteration would have occurred in the shareholders' funds section. Third, consolidated financial statements are prepared for the holding company's shareholders and therefore emphasise the perspective of the holding company. Minority shareholders do not receive any information of direct benefit from these statements. They must look to a particular company for the determination of the value of their equity, the likelihood of dividends and their prospects in the event of liquidation.

(b) Goodwill is amortised over twenty years and this is illustrated in the worksheet on Table 11.1.

The following inter-company transactions have occurred and require elimination entries:

(c) The holding company sold £6,000 of goods to the subsidiary company during 19X3. From the consolidation point of view these inter-company purchases and sales are internal to the group and should be eliminated.

(d) At the end of 19X3 S owes H £3,000 for purchases during the year. These transactions should be eliminated on consolidation.

(e) The closing stock of S contained stock purchased from H. S has recorded this stock at acquisition cost which includes £1,000 profit made by H. From a consolidation viewpoint this profit has not been realised and therefore must be eliminated from both the consolidated balance sheet and profit and loss accounts.

Evaluation

According to SSAP14:

> It is generally accepted that consolidated financial statements are usually the best means of achieving the objectives of group accounts which is to give a true and fair view of the profit and loss and of the state of affairs of the group.

However, there are several disadvantages which have been associated with consolidated financial statements. First, consolidating the results and position statements of several companies may serve to conceal the losses of some by the profits of others. Similarly the assets of certain companies may hide the liquidity problems of others. This is important since the assets of one company will not necessarily be used to settle the debts of others. Second, consolidating numbers which have been derived from different accounting policies may produce meaningless aggregates. Third, for groups which have significant degrees of diversification across industries or operations in different countries, consolidated financial statements may be of limited use in assessing current performance or future prospects. In recognition of these considerations accounting policy requirements necessitate the disclosure of information relating to different industry or geographic segments as supplements to consolidated financial statements. These requirements and the prospects and effects of extending them are discussed in the next chapter.

QUESTIONS

1. What is a trade investment? Describe the requirements of the Companies Act 1981 regarding their disclosure.
2. Define *associated company*.
3. What is meant by the term *equity method of accounting*. What are the advantages and disadvantages of preparing financial statements using this method?
4. Define a subsidiary company for the purpose of preparing group accounts under the Companies Acts. What do you consider to be the faults in this definition?
5. When does SSAP14 prescribe the preparation of consolidated accounts?
6. Distinguish between the acquisition and merger methods of accounting for business combinations. What advantages and disadvantages are claimed for each method?
7. Describe and evaluate the proposals for merger accounting contained in ED21.

REFERENCES

Accounting Standards Committee, *Accounting for the Results of Associated Companies*, SSAP1, 1971.

Accounting Standards Committee, *Group Accounts*, SSAP14, 1978.

Accounting Standards Committee, *Accounting for Associated Companies*, ED25, 1979.

Accounting Standards Committee, *Accounting for Associated Companies*, SSAP1 (revised), 1982.

Accounting Standards Committee, *Accounting for Acquisitions and Mergers*, ED31, 1982.

Leach, R., 'The Birth of British Accounting Standards', in R. Leach and E. Stamp (eds), *British Accounting Standards, The First Ten Years*, Woodhead-Faulkner, Cambridge, 1981.

CHAPTER 12

Increasing disclosure

In previous chapters we have reviewed many contributions to the development of accounting theory and policy making. Some trends are clearly discernible. We have seen how legislation has gradually increased the level of disclosure required from companies. The establishment of standard-setting bodies which regulate accounting practice has accelerated this process. The impetus for standard setting was in part the growing acceptance of the view that accounting data, particularly financial data, are important for economic decisions. The activities of the standard setters have further strengthened this view. The result of legislation and standard setting has been a trend towards financial reports which are user orientated rather than preparer orientated.

As is frequently the case, the stimulus for this change in financial reporting has come from changing economic and social conditions, or perceptions about them. For some, the justification for seeking improved disclosure is seen in a need to improve the traditional economic contribution which financial statements have been viewed as making, because 'lack of appropriate information promotes ignorance and uncertainty, causing both analyst and investors to make excessive allowances for errors in their forecast, thereby lessening the efficiency of the capital markets with consequently slower economic growth' (Belkaoui *et al.*, 1977).

Others have taken a broader perspective in distinguishing between the narrow traditional view of financial reporting which concerns itself with the provision of a minimal amount of strictly quantifiable data, and a wider doctrine of accountability to all groups identified as having a right to information about the activities of organisations:

We consider the responsibility to report publicly . . . is separate from and broader than the legal obligation to report and arises from the custodial role played in the community by economic entities. (ASC, 1975)

Although in this book we have concentrated upon the needs of investors, thereby reflecting the past and present emphasis of the literature, we have acknowledged the growing importance being given to non-investors who use financial statements. In the future, it seems inevitable that this emphasis will be increased.

The shift towards user needs has lead to an increased attention being placed upon the importance of financial data in predictive processes. As we noted in Chapter 5, the FASB, following the lead of the Trueblood Report, described the principle objective of financial reporting as providing information which would assist investors in predicting the amount, timing and uncertainty of future cash flows to the company. This aspect of disclosure is likely to be of increasing importance in the future. In Chapters 5 and 6 we considered the topic at a rather theoretical level, and in this chapter we consider some of the practical issues which are involved. In particular, we consider the case for increasing disclosure by reporting:

(*i*)   the components of income
(*ii*)   segmental information
(*iii*) interim information
(*iv*)   forecast information

Reporting Income Components

An FASB discussion memorandum, issued as part of the board's conceptual framework project stated that 'current earnings statements, invite an excessive emphasis on a single net earnings figure—the bottom line' (FASB, 1979). Disaggregation of income into relevant components is desirable for assessing company performance and for predicting future performance. Income statements may be disaggregated to disclose information about cost structures—

(*i*)   by behaviour and,
(*ii*)   by composition.

In Chapter 10 we argued the case for preparing income statements on a variable cost basis and saw how they may provide useful information to the user. A classification of costs by composition increases the amount of detail shown on the income statement. Variable costs could be detailed as raw materials, labour, manufacturing expenses, and selling. The disclosure of detailed cost breakdowns could improve the ability of the decision maker to assess the enterprise's past performance and future prospects. Backer

(1970), for example, found that the procedures used by analysts in estimating future prospects closely paralleled those used by management in the budgetary planning process where estimates of cost components is a necessary part of the process. A detailed study of the annual reports of 525 major American companies, from the point of view of the analyst, found they lacked detail in production costs and marketing information (Financial Analysts Federation, 1977).

The disclosure requirements of the Companies Act 1981 has moved UK practice some way towards improved reporting of income components by identifying certain cost components to be reported.

Reporting by Segments

A feature of business development that began in the 1960s has been the growth of diversified companies in which 'different segments of the operations are subject to significantly different rates of profitability, degrees of risk, and opportunity for growth'. (Accountants International Study Group, 1972). Adoption of the decision usefulness approach implies the disclosure of segmental information for diversified companies in order to provide the user with a better basis for the assessment of the enterprise's past performances and future prospects.

Support for segmental disclosure has come from groups of users of financial reports (Backer and McFarland, 1968) and aggregate market research studies (Kochanek, 1974; Barefield and Comiskey, 1975). This implies that segmental reporting brings improvements in capital market efficiency. Despite the existence of incentives for voluntary disclosure of segmental information (Ronen and Livnat, 1981), some companies may be rather hesitant to make disclosures. Several reasons are advanced for this (ICAEW, 1977). First, it is argued that investors participate in the company as a whole, not in particular segments. Secondly, additional disclosure may weaken the company's commercial position. Thirdly, the benefits which are likely to arise from producing such information are not likely to justify the expense. Fourthly, the wide variation amongst firms in the choice of segments, cost allocation and other accounting policies limits the usefulness of segmental information.

Segment Identification

The essential feature of diversified companies is that different segments of their operations may be subject to significantly different rates of profitability, degrees of risk and opportunities for growth. This description provides a definition of a diversified company and the conceptual basis for identifying segments for reporting purposes. Difficulties arise, however, in translating the concept into operational form. Several alternatives for identifying segments have received attention:

(*i*)   product line or industry
(*ii*) geographical area
(*iii*) internal structure of managerial control

Segmentation by product line or industrial categories is clearly preferred by most companies. One study found the majority of UK companies sampled made disclosures broadly in accordance with the Standard Industrial Classification (Emmanuel and Gray, 1977). However, this form of classification is very inflexible and may restrict management's ability to report information in the most useful manner. A geographical basis of segmentation may produce very relevant information for some companies especially where distinctions between domestic and foreign operations are important. Disclosing segments on a basis which conforms to the management control structure would in many cases be the most accurate and least costly alternative. There may be tenable managerial arguments for placing seemingly diverse activities under the control of one man (Emmanuel and Gray, 1978). Therefore, if internal reports are 'the best that management can produce to guide their own decisions, then there is an initial presumption that the same statements, or less detailed versions of them, are likely best to serve the investor in making his investment decisions' (Solomons, 1968). But where the organisational unit does not coincide with an industry or geographic area, disclosure by this means may not necessarily be regarded as consistent with the needs of external users.

Accounting Policy Requirements

In the UK the 1981 Companies Act now requires segmental information to be disclosed in the financial statements, where it is subject to audit, instead of in the directors' report in accordance with the 1948 Act. The Act states:

> If in the course of the financial year, the company has carried on business of two or more classes that, in the opinion of the directors, differ substantially from each other, there shall be stated in respect of each class (describing it):
>
> (*a*) the amount of the turnover attributable to that class, and
> (*b*) the amount of the profit or loss of the company before taxation which is in the opinion of the directors attributable to that class.

Additionally, the Act requires an analysis of turnover by geographical areas to be given where a company has supplied different markets.

The Act compares with previous legislation in the vagueness of its requirements. The amount of information provided is largely at the discretion of the directors, definitions of terms such as 'classes of business' and 'different markets' are not included. Also, the Act does not provide any guidance as to what are significantly different classes of business. There is no published proposal for a UK standard in this area, but IAS14 *Reporting Financial Information by Segment* (1981) proposes that listed companies should disclose certain financial information for each reported industry and geographical segment.

FASB Statement No. 14 (1976)

The US standard is a pioneering official attempt to provide a rigorous basis for the disclosure of segmental information. It calls for information to be presented on each of three topics:

(*i*)   the enterprise's operations in different industries;
(*ii*)   its foreign operations and export sales;
(*iii*) its major customers.

According to this Statement identifying the industrial segments of a firm requires that its products and services be grouped by industry. If export sales are significant in amount they should be reported in the aggregate and by appropriate geographical areas (such sales are considered significant if they amount to 10 per cent or more of the company's consolidated sales). Regarding major customers, if 10 per cent or more of the revenue of an enterprise is derived from sales to any single customer, that fact and the amount of revenue from each such customer must be reported.

The Statement supports our preceding discussion on the problem of segment identification. It states that no single system has developed for segmenting an enterprise that is by itself suitable for determining industry segments. Therefore, determination of an enterprise's industry segments must depend to a considerable extent on the judgement of management.

How finely should segments be drawn? The FASB requires an entity to present reports on each industry segment for which one or more of the following tests is satisfied during the accounting period:

(*a*) the segment's revenue is 10 per cent or more of the combined revenue of all segments of the entity;
(*b*) the absolute amount of the segment's operating profit or loss is 10 per cent or more of the greater, in absolute amount of:
  (*i*)   the combined operating profit of all industry segments of the entity that did not incur an operating loss, or
  (*ii*) the combined operating loss of all industry segments of the entity that did incur an operating loss,
(*c*) the segment's identifiable assets are 10 per cent or more of the combined identifiable assets of all industry segments.

In addition the total, revenue for all segments combined must be at least 75 per cent of the revenue of the company as a whole. If this test is not satisfied, management has not identified an adequate number of reportable segments and the delineation of additional segments is necessary.

Compared with the UK approach to segmental reporting the US requirements are highly prescriptive, but not without problems. They do not eliminate management discretion in the process of identifying segments and the significance criteria for determining when a segment should be disclosed are arbitrary.

Interim Reporting

In Chapter 5 we considered briefly the predictive ability of interim financial reports. We noted that a purpose of interim reports is to provide users with more timely information concerning companies in view of the time lag associated with annual reports. Evidence was quoted indicating that interim reports are useful for predictive purposes. However, on the question of how interim reports should be prepared, there are three viewpoints currently held. These are as follows (FASB, 1978):

1. The discrete approach which views each interim period as a basic accounting period.
2. The integral approach which views each interim period as an integral part of the annual period. This implies that results for the interim period are affected by judgements about results in the rest of the annual period.
3. The combination approach which adopts the view that certain items should be reported in accordance with the discrete approach and others according to the integral approach.

As Fried and Livnat (1981) point out the different views reflect differing views of the purpose of interim reports. Supporters of the discrete approach see the purpose of interim reports as satisfying users' interest in the actual realisations of the interim period itself for the purposes of monitoring performance. Interim reports have a limited function in aiding predictions according to this view and, like annual financial reports, are likely to be adapted by users to meet their own purposes. Application of the discrete approach would avoid allocations based on annual results which would have a smoothing effect on interim results. The integral approach, on the other hand, sees the objective of interim reports as the prediction of annual results, and thus interim reports ought to reflect estimates and judgements of annual operations.

APB Opinion 28 formally accepts the integral approach but its recommendations on the treatment of specific items implies a combination approach. Schiff (1978) in a survey of interim reporting in the USA concluded that the combination approach was generally adopted in practice. FASB (1978) has recommended that items be classified as follows:

1. costs which vary annually with revenues (e.g. advertising), and costs which are expected to be reversed in subsequent periods (e.g. material price variances), should be treated integrally,
2. costs which do not vary annually with revenue, or will not be reversed subsequently, should be treated discretely.

Such a classification aims to provide a clear reflection of the business's long-term performance by separating out permanent influences (1) from transitory influences (2).

Fried and Livnat (1981) evaluated the three approaches to interim reporting on the basis of their abilities to meet users needs for performance evaluation, the forecast of annual performance, and the forecast of future operations. This evaluation could serve as a test of the appropriateness of the FASB's choice of the combination approach as a mandated accounting policy. Fried and Livnat found the combination approach to rank poorly compared with the other approaches under individual objectives, but its performance increased greatly if items treated discretely and integrally were reported separately. More fundamentally, they found that the ranking of the three approaches depended largely upon the nature of the reporting environment, uncertainty, and correlations with periodic cash flows. This may be taken to imply that a uniform interim reporting policy should not be set, but rather that conditions prevailing in particular industries should be empirically determined before an accounting method is adopted.

Accounting Policy Requirements

In the UK there is no statutory requirement for the provision of interim reports unless it is necessary for a company to justify an interim dividend payment. However, the Stock Exchange Listing Agreement includes the requirement:

> To prepare a half-yearly or interim report which must be sent to the holders of securities or inserted as a paid advertisement in two leading daily newspapers not later than six months from the date of the notice convening the annual general meeting.

Although they are unaudited the Listing Agreement suggests that the accounting policies applied to them be consistent with those applied in final financial statements. The following is the minimum historical cost information to be supplied in interim reports: turnover, profit before tax and extraordinary items, taxation, minority interest, extraordinary items, profit attributable to shareholders, dividends paid and proposed, EPS and other information in the opinion of the directors necessary for a reasonable appreciation of results.

Comparative figures should also be provided. In addition some current cost information is now required: operating profit or loss, gearing adjustment, interest or income relating to net borrowing, taxation, current cost profit attributable to shareholders, current cost operating adjustments, and EPS.

In the USA disclosure requirements are on a quarterly basis. We have already referred to the FASB position on interim reports.

Evidence on Interim Reporting

The empirical evidence cited in Chapter 5 shows that interim reports possess important information content. Ball and Brown (1968), in their celebrated study conclude:

> Of all the information about an individual firm which becomes available during the year, one half or more is captured in that year's income number. Its content is therefore considerable. However, the annual income report does not rate highly as a timely medium since most of its content (about 85–90 per cent) is captured by more prompt media which perhaps include interim reports.

Subsequent findings of aggregate market research have shown that investors revise their expectations about annual profits throughout the year as they receive new information concerning the company. Research indicates that interim financial reports play an important feedback role in investment decisions by assisting the investor in judging the soundness and accuracy of earlier predictions.

These findings have been used to support the view that the frequency of interim reports should be increased in order to improve the quality of feedback information and the accuracy of predictions. The 1982 *Survey of UK Published Accounts* suggests that the timeliness of interim reports might be improved. The average interval between the publication date of interim reports and the date to which they referred for sample companies was 76 days, with the shortest interval 25 days and the longest 236 days.

Reporting Forecasts

Behavioural research findings reveal clearly opposing attitudes to published forecasts. Some studies indicate shareholder support (Epstein, 1975), but financial analysts view management forecasts with sceptism (Fuller and Metcalf, 1978). Corporate management oppose mandatory disclosure on the grounds of the potential danger of injuring the competitive advantage of companies and the doubtful reliability of forecast information. Aggregate user research studies have examined stock market reaction to management forecasts and have concluded that they possess information content (Penman, 1980). Numerous studies have investigated the accuracy of forecasts (Westwick, 1983). They conclude that forecast accuracy is generally unimpressive but that the level of accuracy varies from industry to industry depending on the stability of operating conditions (Abdel-Khalik and Thompson, 1977).

Usefulness of Forecasts

Some writers question the usefulness of forecasts on the grounds of their inaccuracy. However, the real question at issue is not whether, in an absolute sense, forecasts are sufficiently reliable, but whether the user of published financial reports finds them useful for decision-making purposes. Despite the difficulties of inaccuracy, management find them of value and one may assume that forecasts made within an enterprise will be more reliable than those attempted by naive investors. This assumption is supported by research findings which show that management forecasts are superior to those developed using the simple extrapolative models which we considered in Chapter 5 (Ruland, 1978). These findings suggest that management forecasts are useful information for the investing public.

Therefore, the publication of management forecasts, together with deviations from previously published forecasts, may provide information useful to a user for the purpose of assessing the enterprise's past performance and future prospects. This view received support from the UK Take-Over Panel which stated 'that the directors' opinions on the immediate future profitability of a company are the most important single element in the formation of the decision to invest or disinvest in that company' (Accountants International Study Group, 1974). Equity considerations provide further support for publishing forecasts. The tendency for companies to disclose expectations of earnings to individuals or groups of analysts without simultaneous release to shareholders may be prejudicial to shareholders' interests. In recent years support for such forecasts was provided by two officially sponsored study groups in the US and UK. The Trueblood Report stated that an 'objective of financial statements is to provide information useful for the predictive process. Financial forecasts should be provided when they will enhance the reliability of users' predictions' (AICPA, 1973). The Corporate Report suggested that company reports should include 'a statement of future prospects, showing likely future profit, employment and investment levels' (ASC, 1975).

The Importance of Assumptions

There is widespread agreement that disclosure of underlying assumptions is necessary to achieve meaningful forecast reporting. One survey of six hundred analysts found that 'when asked what items should be included in forecasts by management, the analysts overwhelmingly felt the assumptions underlying the forecasts were the most important consideration' (Fuller and Metcalf, 1978). Although the City Code argues that assumptions 'can be framed so as to be of maximum assistance to the reader' the limits of this assistance is unspecified. Corporate management is the only group that has complete access to all in-firm information. Only management knows all its goals and the plans to achieve them, for example, plans about adding to or dropping a product line, marketing effort, research and development and labour requirements. With published forecasts this internal information will be reflected in the financial results and may be revealed in the assumptions stated. As we discussed previously, the fear that forecast disclosures of micro assumptions may injure the competitive position of the firm has been cited on numerous occasions. How far this fear is justified depends on the amount of information contained in forecasts which may be useful to competitors. For example, if a firm were to reveal as part of a forecast report assumptions concerning proposed market strategies or new product developments, competitors could act on such knowledge and take steps to prevent the firm from achieving its objectives.

Accounting Policy

In the United Kingdom the 1981 Companies Act requires the Directors' Report to give an indication of likely future developments in the business. This does not necessitate a ratified profit forecast: a suitably formulated broad statement is sufficient. Forecasts must be published in a prospectus when a company is seeking listing on the London Stock Exchange. Although forecasts are considered desirable in a take-over they are not required. Auditing is compulsory for published profit forecasts found in prospectuses and take-over circulars. The principal requirements relating to profit forecasts in take-over bids was laid down in the City Code which first appeared in 1968. This requires disclosure of the assumptions upon which the forecast is based and for accountants to satisfy themselves that such assumptions are realistic.

In the United States, the SFAC No. 1 perspective is that accounting should provide information conducive to predictions but should not provide predictions *per se*. However, since 1978, the SEC has adopted a policy of encouraging companies to make voluntary disclosures of management projections in their filings with the SEC and elsewhere. The

Securities Act Release 5992 published in 1978 establishes guidelines to be followed in disclosing projections. At the same time, the SEC adopted a 'safeharbour' rule which offered legal protection to those who did prepare and disclose forecasts in good faith even if they were not subsequently achieved. In 1980 the SEC adopted a substantial expansion of the requirement for management's discussion and analysis which further emphasised the requirement for a discussion of future-oriented variables. The new requirement calls for a description of 'any known trends or uncertainties which had had, or which the registrant reasonably expects will have a materially favourable or unfavourable impact on net sales or revenues or income from continuing operations'.

Conclusion

According to one leading US observer the movement toward user-oriented disclosure is likely to continue and that, to a greater degree than in the past, accounting and reporting standards adopted in the future will be tested by the degree to which they assist users in the predictive process. 'We will see more disaggregation of historical information and more management explanation and interpretation of past data. Interpretation will inevitably be future-oriented; it will also, however, provide a better explanation of the past . . . ultimately since management has techniques for forecasting and estimating the future, it will be hard to deny them to investors, who will want to apply basically the same criteria to management as management applies to subordinates; namely, what did you think was going to happen and, if it didn't, why didn't it?' (Burton, 1980).

The trend towards user-orientated financial reports should not detract unduly from the importance of the actions of preparers on the disclosure process. Agency theory, by stressing the role of incentives for management to disclose or not disclose financial information to owners, has provided a framework for the analysis of financial reporting. Its recent popularity is likely to continue and the results of applications of agency theory are likely to play an increasing importance. As we saw in Chapter 10, difficulties arise in the formulation of acceptable accounting standards when business opinion is at variance with the proposed accounting treatment. Furthermore, requirements to increase disclosure are not always adhered to if those requirements are not enforced. Perk's (1983) survey showed that compliance with SSAPs overall was unsatisfactory. It seemed that companies tended to follow the parts of SSAPs that they liked but many sidestepped the parts they did not like.

This raises fundamental questions for standard setting. In the case of the UK, Watts (1981) has expressed it thus:

The touch-stone of accounting standards set in the private sector is the degree of compliance . . . At present the main sanction against enterprises which breach accounting standards is that they suffer a qualified audit report. This is in notable contrast to the United States . . . where the SEC will refuse the filing of Statements . . . with a qualified audit report. It is also in contrast with the position in Canada where the federal law requires compliance with accounting standards . . .

The need for a mechanism to ensure compliance, whether it be the direct rule of law, or the indirect influence of the audit report or the standard setting process itself, emphasises that a user orientation must be enforceable if it is to be applied in practice.

QUESTIONS

1. Should the ASC introduce comprehensive requirements for segmental disclosures along the lines of FASB Statement No. 14?
2. Evaluate the usefulness of interim reports and the different approaches to their preparation.
3. Should financial forecasts be provided to external users of financial statements?

REFERENCES

Abel-Khalik, A. R. and Thompson, R. B., 'Research on Earnings Forecasts: The State of the Art', *The Accounting Journal*, Winter, 1977/78.

American Institute of Certified Public Accountants, *Trueblood Report*, 1973.

American Institute of Certified Public Accountants, Accounting Principles Board, *Interim Financial Reporting*, Opinion No. 28, 1973.

Accountants International Study Group, *Reporting by Diversified Companies*, 1972.

Accountants International Study Group, *Published Profit Forecasts*, 1974.

Accounting Standards Committee, *The Corporate Report*, 1975.

Backer, M., 'Financial Reporting for Security Investment and Credit Decisions', *National Association of Accountants*, 1970, p. 18.

Backer, M., McFarland, W. B. 'External Reporting for Segments of a Business', *National Association of Accountants*, 1968, pp. 21–22.

Barefield, R. M. and Comiskey, E. E., 'Segmental Financial Disclosure by Diversified Firms and Security Prices: A Comment', *The Accounting Review*, October, 1975.

Belkaoui, A. *et al.*, 'Information Needs of Financial Analysts—An International Comparison', *International Journal of Accounting Education and Research*, Fall, 1977.

Burton, J. C., 'Financial Reporting in the 1980s', *Financial Analysts Journal*, 1980.

Emmanuel, C. R. and Gray, S. J., 'Segmental Disclosures and the Segment Identification Problem', *Accounting and Business Research*, Winter, 1977.

Emanuel, C. R. and Gray, S. J., 'Segmental Disclosures by Multibusiness

Multinational Companies: A proposal', *Accounting and Business Research*, Summer, 1978.

Epstein, M. J., 'Shareholders' view of Earnings Forecasts', *Management Planning*, November/December, 1975.

FASB, *Reporting Earnings*, Discussion Memorandum, 1979.

FASB, *Interim Financial Accounting and Reporting*, Discussion Memorandum, 1978.

Financial Analysts Federation, 'Areas of annual report deficiency identified in 525 companies' shareholders relations programmes in 1975–76', *Journal of Accountancy*, July, 1977.

Fried, D. and J. Livnat, 'Interim Statements: an analytical examination of alternative accounting techniques', *The Accounting Review*, 1981.

Fuller, R. J. and Metcalf, R. W., 'Management Disclosures: Analysts Prefer Facts to Management Predictions', *Financial Analysts Journal*, March/April, 1978.

Institute of Chartered Accountants in England and Wales: *Analysed Reporting*, 1977.

Kochanek, R. F., 'Segmental Financial Disclosure by Diversified Firms and Security Prices', *The Accounting Review*, April, 1974.

Penman, S. H., 'Empirical Investigation of the Voluntary Disclosure of Corporate Earnings Forecasts', *Journal of Accounting Research*, Spring, 1980.

Perks, B., 'The Implementation of SSAPs with particular reference to SSAP15', *Journal of the Association of University Teachers of Accounting*, 1983.

Ronen, J. and Livnat, J., 'Incentives for Segment Reporting', *Journal of Accounting Research*, 1981.

Ruland, W., 'The Accuracy of Forecasts by Management and by Financial Analysts', *The Accounting Review*, Apirl, 1978.

Schiff, M., *Accounting Reporting Problems—Interim Reporting*, Financial Executives Research Foundation, 1978.

Solomons, D., 'Accounting Problems and Some Proposed Solutions', in A. Rappaport, P. A. Firmin and S. A. Zeff (eds.), *Public Reporting by Conglomerates*, (Prentice-Hall, 1968).

Watts, T. R., 'Planning the next decade', in R. Leach and E. Stamp (eds.), *British Accounting Standards, The First 10 Years*, Woodhead-Faulkner, 1982.

Westwick, A., (ed), *Profit Forecasts, How they are Made, Reviewed and Used*, Gower, 1983.

INDEX

A priori research,
  decision usefulness, 91–104
  types, 4
Abdel-Khalik, R, 17, 109, 112, 274, 275, 276
Abdel-Khalik, R. and Thompson, R. B., 336
Accountants International Study Group, 330, 336
Accounting controversies, 5–6
Accounting policy making,
  agency theory, 15–16
  decision usefulness, 14–15
  efficient markets research, 110
  model of, 12–14
  political approach, 16
  prospects for future research, 19–20
  social welfare approach, 17
Accounting Principles Board, 12,
  Statement 4, 33, 99, 153, 160
  Opinions
    no. 8, 282
    no. 11, 232–3, 235, 238
    no. 14, 256
    no. 23, 141
    no. 28, 333
Accounting standards (see also
    Accounting Standards
    Committee and Statements of
    Standard Accounting Practice),
  case for, 39–40
  definition, 39

  emergence in the UK, 41–2
  relationship with company law, 67
  types of, 40–1
Accrual concept, 33
Advance Corporation Tax, 217–20
Accounting Standards Committee, 6,
  8, 12, 39, 41, 42, 47, 49, 167,
  178, 187, 188, 189, 197, 199,
  212, 220–21, 229, 238, 254, 256,
  260, 262, 273, 297, 329,
  aims, 42–3
  comparison with FASB, 52–3
  Discussion Paper, 51
  emergence of, 41–2
  evaluation of standard setting, 46–9
  Exposure draft, 44, 51
  reorganisation, 49
  standard setting process, 49–53
  Statement of Intent, 51
  Statement of Recommended
    Practice, 53, 283
  Statement of Standard Accounting
    Practice, 43–44
  work programme, 57–60
Accounting Standards Steering
    Committee (see Accounting
    Standards Committee)
Accounting theory
  conventional approach, 2–4, 24–38
  definition, 1
  purpose, 1
Acquisitions, 58

Agency theory, 15
Alexander, S. S., 125, 126
Altman, E., 115
Altman, E. *et al*, 115
American Accounting Association, 1,
    91, 92, 125, 162
American Institute of Certified Public
    Accountants, 12, 336
Archibald, T. R., 109, 278
Argenti, J., 116
Arnold, J. A., Moizer P. and Noreen,
    E., 118
Arnold, J. A. and Moizer, P., 117
Arthur Andersen, 203
Ashton, R. H., 34
Ashton, R. K., 228
Associated Companies,
    Companies Act 1981, 313
    equity method, 313–14
    evaluation of SSAP1, 315
    requirements of SSAP1, 314–15
    SSAP1 definition, 312–13
Auditing, 7, 12, 13, 27, 62, 69, 70, 337

Backer, M., 117, 329
Backer, M. and Gosman, M. L., 31
Backer, M. and McFarland, W. B., 330
Backlog depreciation, 172
Ball, R. J., 276
Ball, R. J. and Brown, P., 107, 108,
    335
Bank of England, 265
Barefield, R. M. and Comiskey, E. E.,
    330
Barnea, A., *et al.*, 216
Barton, A. D., 143, 233
Baxter, W., 40, 251
Beaver, W. H., 5, 17, 105, 110, 114,
    115
Beaver, W. H., Christie, A. A. and
    Griffin, P. A., 109
Beaver, W. H. and Dukes, R. E., 255
Beaver, W. H., Kettler, T.P. and
    Scholes, M., 107, 276
Bedford, N., 4, 5, 125
Belkaoui, A. *et al.*, 328
Benston, G., 9, 15, 25, 40
Bierman, H. and Drebin, A. R., 30
Bierman, H. and Dukes, R. E., 265
Black, H. A., 236
Bonbright, J. C., 142
Bourne, M., 138

Bowman, R., 276
Bradish, R. D., 203
Brault, R. and Houle, Y., 34
Breen, W. J. and Lerner, E. M., 107,
    276
Bromwich, M., 39
Brown, L. D. and Rozeff, M. S., 114
Business combinations:
    acquisition accounting, 318–20
    consolidated accounts, 323–6
    merger accounting, 320–1
    legal position, 321–2
    policy requirements, 322–3

Capital Asset Pricing Model, 105–7
Capital maintenance,
    concepts, 144
        operating capability, 146–7
        money value, 145–6
        purchasing power adjusted, 146
        real value, 147
    economic income, 131–4
Carty, J., 240
Carsberg, B. V., Hope, A., and
    Scapens, R. W., 113
Carsberg, B. V. and Page, M., 187
Cash flows,
    complementarity with income, 203–4
    financial flexibility, 205
    importance, 201–3
    integrated financial statements,
        205–8
    investors' needs, 92–4
    net realisable values, 205
Catlett, G. R. and Olsen, N. O., 258
Chambers, R. J., 4, 143, 233
Charities accounting, 59
Chau, T. T. M. C., 36
Cheung, J. K., 276
Chow, C., 15
City Code
    disclosure requirements, 88–9, 337
    effects on legislation, 28–9
    Listing Agreement, 85
Clark, T., 268
Cohen Committee, 27
Collins, D. W. and Dent, W. T., 109
Collins, D. W. and Hopwood, W. S.,
    114
Companies Acts,
    1844, 25
    1856, 25

1879, 27
1900, 26
1907, 26
1929, 26, 21
1948, 25, 61, 241, 316, 321, 331
1967, 26, 27, 61, 316
1980, 61, 62
  distributable profit, 62, 82–3
1981, 58, 61, 215, 240, 242, 247, 251,
    260, 263, 267, 271, 281, 298,
    312, 331, 337,
  accounting principles, 66–7
  balance sheet, 64
  changes arising from, 63–4
  Directors' Report, 65–6
  notes to the accounts, 64–5
  prescribed formats, 66, 73–81
  profit and loss account, 64
  realised profit, 151
  relationship with accounting
    standards, 67
  rules for publication of accounts,
    68–9
  true and fair view, 69–70
  valuation rules, 68
1985, 61, 70
Company law,
  changes in philosophy, 25–6
  Cohen Committee, 27
  growth of companies, effects, 26
  legislation lag, 27–8
  scandals, effects of, 26
Comparability, 98
Conceptual framework:
  ASC's approach, 60, 102–4
  FASB's approach, 93–102
    benefits, 101–2
    components, 94–5
    elements, 99–100
    presentation concepts, 100–1
    objectives, 96–7
    qualitative characteristics, 97–9
    recognition and measurement
      concepts, 100
Conservatism, 34
Consistency, 34
Consultative Committee of
    Accountancy Bodies, 42, 51, 52,
    53
Consolidated accounts, 323–6
Contingencies, 241–2
Council for the Securities Industry, 88

Conventional approach,
  assumptions, 30–5
    accruals, 33
    conservatism, 34
    consistency, 34
    cost, 32
    entity, 31
    full disclosure, 35
    going concern, 31
    materiality, 34–5
    money measurement, 31
    objectivity, 33–4
    periodicity, 32
    realisation, 33
  definition, 3
  stewardship, 35–6
  structure, 30
  true and fair view, 25
Cooper, D. J. and Essex, S. R., 10, 93
Corporate Report, 48, 102, 336
Cost concept, 32–3
Cranfield, 274
Cushing, B., 19
Cyert, R. M. and Ijiri, Y., 11

Davidson, S., 234
Decision usefulness, 90–124
  approach to policy making, 14
  behavioural research, 116–18
  conceptual framework, 93–104
  reporting cash flows, 92–4
  single investment model, 91–3
Deferred tax, 58,
  policy requirements, 238–41
  concepts of provision,
    comprehensive allocation, 235–6
    partial allocation, 234–5
  methods of provision,
    deferral method, 236–7
    liability method, 237
    net of tax method, 237–8
  objections to provision, 233–4
  permanent and timing differences,
    230–1
  reasons for provision, 231
Deitrich, J. R. and Kaplan, R., 114,
    274
Demski, J., 4, 19
Department of Trade, 51, 259, 297
Depreciation,
  accounting practice, 253
  backlog, 172

evaluation of requirements, 253–5
policy requirements, 251–3
Distributable profits,
  basic definition, 62
  insurance companies, 83
  investment companies, 83
  public companies, 82
  realised profits, 82
Dopuch, N. and Sunder, S., 16
Drake, D. F. and Dopuch, N., 139
Dukes, R. E., 109
Dukes, R. E., Dyckman, T. and
    Elliott, J. A., 111

Earnings per share,
  corporation tax, 217–20
  dividend policy, 220–1
  fully-diluted, 226, 229
  SSAP3, 221–30
Economic consequences,
  causes, 105
  definition, 17
  management decisions,
    foreign currency, 112
    leasing, 112
    research and development, 111–12
  role in policy making, 17, 112
  share prices, 108–10
Economic income,
  capital maintenance, 131–4
  evaluation, 134–5
  ex ante, 129–31
  ex post, 131–4
  windfall gains and losses, 129–31
  ideal, 128–9
Edey, H., 4, 40
Edwards, E. O. and Bell, P. W., 4
Edwards, J. R., 27, 28
E.E.C., 54, 63, 66, 259
  Directives, 61–2
Efficient Capital Markets Hypothesis,
  accounting numbers, 108–9
  alternative accounting policies, 109
  behavioural research, 118
  forms of efficiency, 107–8
  implications for policy makers, 110
  increasing disclosure, 111
Eggington, D. A., 62
Emmanuel, C. and Gray, S. J., 331
Empirical research,
  behavioural, 116–18
  capital market research, 105–7

types, 5
economic consequences, 105
efficient markets research, 107–11
predictive ability of accounting
    numbers, 113–16
Entity concept, 31
Epstein, M. J., 335
Evans, T. G., *et al.*, 112
Exposure drafts,
  no. 8, 166
  no. 11, 238
  no. 14, 262
  no. 16, 294
  no. 17, 262, 264
  no. 18, 166
  no. 19, 239
  no. 21, 294
  no. 24, 166, 167
  no. 25, 315
  no. 27, 294, 295
  no. 29, 267–276
  no. 30, 58
  no. 31, 58, 197, 318, 321, 322
  no. 32, 58, 277, 281
  no. 33, 240
  no. 34, 53, 59, 283
  no. 35, 166, 167, 188, 189
  no. 36, 58, 216
Extraordinary items, 211–16

Fair value, 59
Fama, E., 107
Fawthrop, R. and Terry, B., 266, 273
Financial Accounting Standards Board,
    5, 8, 17, 33, 41, 93, 100, 101,
    151, 154, 205, 293, 329, 333, 334
  Concepts Statement 1, 96, 202, 337
  Concepts Statement 2, 98
  Concepts Statement 3, 99
  Concepts Statement 4, 96
  Concepts Statement 5, 100, 151
  Statement no. 2, 112
  Statement no. 8, 294, 295
  Statement no. 13, 112, 275
  Statement no. 14, 332
  Statement no. 19, 160
  Statement no. 33,
  Statement no. 36,
  Statement no. 48, 157
Financial Analysts Federation, 330
Financial reporting:
  free-market approach, 9

influences on, 6–8
regulation of, 8–9
Finnerty, J. E., *et al.*, 276
Fisher, I., 126
Fisher, L., 114
Flavell, R. and Salkin, G. R., 274
Flint, D., 25, 35
Flower, J., 292, 294
Forecasts,
  assumptions, 337
  policy requirements, 337–8
  usefulness, 336
Foreign currency translation,
  accounting practice, 296
  accounting problem, 283–4
  balance sheet methods,
    closing rate, 285, 291–2
    current-non-current, 285, 290–1
    monetary-non-monetary, 285
    temporal, 285, 290–1
  economic consequences, 295–6
  evaluation of alternative methods,
    292–4
  policy requirements, 294–5
  profit and loss account methods,
    average rate, 285
    closing rate, 286
    historic rate, 285
  relationship between methods, 286
Foster, G., 113
Fried, D. and Livnat, J., 333, 334
Full disclosure, 35
Fuller, R. J. and Metcalf, R. W., 335,
  337
Funds flow statements,
  definition of funds,
    all financial resources, 199
    cash concept, 197–8
    working capital, 198
  uses, 196–7

Gearing adjustment,
  Australian proposal, 181–2
  New Zealand proposal, 182–3
  SSAP16, 177–81
Gellein, O. S. and Newman, M. S.,
  263
Gerborth, D. L., 16
Gheyera, K. and Boatsman, J., 109
Gibbons, M. and Brennan, P., 118
Gibbs, M., 240
Gilman, S., 30

Gjesdal, F., 36
Going concern concept, 31
Gonedes, N., 276
Goodwill, 58
  accounting practice, 259
  alternative accounting treatments
    amortise regularly, 259
    dangling debit, 258–9
    retain as asset indefinitely, 258
    write-off on acquisition, 257–8
  characteristics, 256–7
  policy requirements, 259–60
Grady, P., 30, 35, 47
Gray, S. J. and Coenenberg, A. G., 62
Gray, S. J. and Maunders, K. T., 297
Greenball, N., 113
Griffin, P. A., 104
Grinyer, J., 48
Gynther R. S., 138, 175

Hagerman, R. L. and Zmijewski, M.
  E., 17
Hakhansson, N. H., 90
Hamada, R. S., 276
Hansen, P., 127
Haslem, J. A. and Longbrake, W. A.,
  275
Heath, L. C., 204, 205
Henfrey, A., 111
Henfrey, A., *et al.*, 108
Hicks, J. R., 126
Hill, T. M., 234
Himmel, S., 154
Hines, R. D., 118
Holding gains, 138–40
  real and fictitious, 147
Holdren, G. C., 202
Hope, A. and Briggs, J., 230
Hope, A. and Gray, R., 17, 260
Horngren, C. T., 5, 6, 16, 101
Horowitz, B. and Kolodny, R., 112,
  265
Horrigan, J., 114
Hussey, R., 117
Hyde Guidelines, 166–7

Ijiri, Y., 4, 162
Ijiri, Y. and Jaedicke, R. K., 33
Impossibility Theorem, 19
Income,
  economic, 127–35
  limitations, 202–3

links with capital and wealth, 126–7
net assets approach, 127
   adjusted historical cost, 136–8
   current replacement cost, 138–40
   historical cost, 136
   net realisable value, 140–1
   present value, 141
   value to the business, 142–4
reporting components of, 329–30
uses of, 125
Inflation accounting,
Australian proposals, 181–2
comparison of approaches, 184–5
New Zealand proposals,
SSAP16, 168–81
UK requirements,
   history, 166
   ED35, 188–9
   review of SSAP16, 186–7
   Statement of Intent on SSAP16,
      187–8
US proposals, 189–91
Inflation Accounting Steering Group,
   146, 166
Institute for Fiscal Studies, 271
Institute of Chartered Accountants in
   England and Wales, 35, 42, 187,
   200, 330
Recommendations series, 29
Intangible assets,
characteristics, 255
conventional accounting practice,
   255–6
goodwill, 256–60
research and development, 260–5
Inter-company relationships,
associated companies, 312–13
subsidiary companies, 315–18
trade investments, 311–12
Interest, capitalisation of, 60
Interim reporting, 59:
alternative approaches, 333–4
evidence, 335
policy requirements, 334–5
International Accounting Standards,
IAS1, 55
IAS2, 55
IAS3, 55
IAS4, 55
IAS5, 55
IAS6, 55
IAS7, 55

IAS8, 55, 213
IAS9, 55, 263
IAS10, 55, 241
IAS11, 15, 55, 158–9
IAS12, 55
IAS13, 55
IAS14, 55, 332
IAS15, 55
IAS16, 55
IAS17, 55
IAS18, 55, 157
IAS19, 55
IAS20, 55
IAS21, 55
IAS22, 55
IAS23, 55
IAS24, 55
International Accounting Standards
   Committee, 53, 54, 295,
accounting standards, 55
   status in the UK, 53–4
objectives, 53, 54
Investments, accounting for, 60
Investment analysts, 117, 118

Jaenicke, H. R., 157, 162
Jensen, M., 108
Jensen, M. and Meckling, W. H., 15
Joyce, E. J., *et al.*, 102

Kaplan, R., 108
Kaplan, R. and Roll, R., 109
Keane, S., 111
Keller, T. F., 233
Ketz, J. E. and Wyatt, A. R., 110
Kirk, D. J., 101
Knox, R. W., 200
Kochanek, R. F., 330

Lafferty, M., 48
Largay, J. A., and Stickney, C. P., 203
Leach, R., 42, 44, 315
Leases,
alternative accounting treatment, 267
conventional accounting treatment,
   266–7
economic consequences, 273–6
finance lease, definition, 265–6
operating lease, definition, 266
policy requirements, 267–72
Lee, T. A., 31, 126, 202, 205
Lee, T. A., and Tweedie, D., 10, 117

Leftwich, R., 9
Liao, S. S., 155
Lindblom, C., 16
Lintner, J., 106
Littleton, A. C., 30
Lorek, K. S., 114
Lorensen L., 292
Lothian, N., 47
Lyne, S., 249

Macve, R., 52, 102, 118
Mason, P., 197
Matching concept,
  criticisms, 152–4
  implementation, 155–6
  usefulness, 154–5
Materiality, 34–5, 99
Mattesich, R., 4
Mautz, R. K. and May, W. G., 18
May, R. G. and Sundem, G., 12, 17,
  18
Mergers, 58
Moizer, P. and Arnold, J. A., 118
Monetary items, 137
Monetary working capital adjustment,
  173–7
Money measurement concept, 31–32
Moonitz, M., 4, 12, 47
Morley, M., 297, 299
Morris, R., 109
Muis, J., 17
Myers, J. H., 156

Napier, C. J., 277, 278
Net basis, earnings per share, 222–3
Neutrality, 99
Nil basis, earnings per share, 223
Nobes, C., 284, 296
Nobes, C. and Cooke, T., 186
Non-monetary items, 137
Noreen, E. and Sepe, J., 109
Norton, C. L. and Smith, R. E.,
  116

Objectives of accounting,
  advantages, 10
  approaches to formulation of, 11–12
  problems of formulation, 10
Objectivity, 33–4
Ohlson, J. A., 116
Operating gains, 138–40
Orgler, Y. E., 114, 275

Pacter, P. A., 101
Page, J. R. and Hooper, P., 204
Parker, R. H. and Harcourt, G. C.,
  142
Parkinson, R. M., 294
Paton, W. A., 30
Paton, W. A. and Littleton, A. C., 30
Pattillo, J. W., 35
Patz, D., 293
Peasnell, K., 12, 104
Penman, S. H., 336
Pensions,
  actuarial cost methods, 277–80
  characteristics, 276
  costs, 58
  evaluation of policy requirements,
    282
  pension scheme accounts, 59, 283
  policy requirements, 281–2
Periodicity concept, 32
Perks, R., 338
Pinches, G. E. and Mingo, K. A., 114
Post-balance sheet events,
  adjusting events, 242
  non-adjusting events, 242–3
Prakash, P. and Rappaport, A., 105
Predictive ability,
  decision usefulness, 98
  empirical tests
    corporate failure, 114–16
    credit worthiness, 114
    interim financial reports, 113–14
    past annual profits, 113
    prediction of takeovers, 114
Prior year adjustments, 211–16

Rappaport, A., 17
Realisation concept, 33
Recognition,
  criteria for expenses,
    cause and effect, 161
    immediate recognition, 161–2
    rational allocation, 161
  criteria for revenue,
    cash collection, 157–8
    completion of production, 159
    discovery of reserves, 159–60
    during production, 158–59
    sale, 156–7
  evaluation of criteria, 162
  FASB definition, 151
Regulation of financial reporting,

justification, 8–9
objectives, 10
Related party transactions, 59
Relevance, 99
Reliability, 99
Reporting economic reality, 14
Research and development,
  capitalisation, 261
  categories of cost, 260–1
  empirical research findings, 265
  expensing, 261
  policy requirements, 261–5
Research methods,
  a priori research, 4, 91–104
  empirical research, 5, 104–18
  purpose, 4
Reserve recognition accounting,
  159–60
Revsine, L., 91
Richardson Committee, 177
Ro, B. T., 276
Ronen, J. and Livnat, J., 330
Rose, H., 26
Rosenfield, P., 144
Rosenfield, P. and Dent, W. C., 233
Ruland, W., 336
Ryan, R. J., 3

Sanders, T. H., 30
Sandilands Committee, 32, 143, 166,
  167, 173,
  Corporate Report, 104
  operating capability, 173
  views on cost concept, 32–3
Santomero, A. M. and Vinso, V. O.,
  116
Schiff, M., 334
Scott, R. A. and Scott, R. K., 159
Securities and Exchange Commission,
  9, 41, 53, 159, 276, 337,
  reserve recognition accounting, 159
Segmental reporting, 59,
  FASB Statement no. 4, 332–3
  legal requirements, 331–2
  segment identification, 330–1
Selto, F. H., 105
Selto, F. H. and Newman, B. R., 17
Shank, J. K. *et al*, 109, 112
Shareholders, 117
Shearer *versus* Bercain, 321
Sharpe, W., 106
Sherer, M. *et al*, 117

Shwayder, K., 135
Simmonds, A., 278
Singh, A., 114
Skerrat, L. and Peasnell, K., 228
Skinner, R., 155, 257
Small businesses, 260
Solomons, D., 14, 52, 101, 126, 330
Sorter, G. H., 34
Sorter, G. H. and Gans, M. S., 10
Sprouse, R. T., 125, 154
Sprouse, R. T. and Moonitz, M., 4,
  12
Stamp, E., 10, 12, 48
Statement of Intent, 49
Statement of Recommended Practice,
  51, 53, 283,
  pension scheme accounts, 283
Statements of Standard Accounting
  Practice,
  no. 1, 44, 55, 312
  no. 2, 44, 46, 47, 55, 66, 67, 90, 151,
    230, 238, 261
    contents, 44–6
    realisation and recognition, 151
    relationship to other standards, 47
  no. 3, 44, 55, 211
    accounting practice, 228–30
    evaluation, 228
    requirements, 221–28
  no. 4, 44, 55
  no. 5, 44, 59
  no. 6, 44, 58, 67, 212–16, 254
    empirical research, 216
    evaluation, 214–15
    policy requirements, 212
    review, 215–16
  no. 7, 166
  no. 8, 44
  no. 9, 44, 47, 55, 67
    accounting practice, 248–9
    empirical research, 250, 255
    evaluation, 249–50
    policy requirements, 243–8
  no. 10, 44, 55, 60, 197, 200–1
  no. 11, 44, 48
  no. 12, 44, 59, 67, 214, 264
    accounting practice, 253
    evaluation, 253–5
    policy requirements, 251–3
  no. 13, 44, 55, 59, 67, 260, 262–3,
    264
    empirical research, 265

policy requirements, 262–5
no. 14, 44, 55, 317, 319, 326
no. 15, 44, 58, 239
  policy requirements, 239–41
no. 16, 44, 55, 67, 68, 86, 144, 165,
  166, 167, 168, 169, 175, 178,
  181, 182, 183, 184, 185, 191,
  212,
  backlog depreciation, 172
  balance sheet, 169
  cost of sales adjustment, 169–70
  current cost profit, 168–9
  depreciation adjustment, 170–3
  evaluation, 185–6
  gearing adjustment, 177–81
  monetary working capital adjust-
    ment, 173–7
no. 17, 44, 55, 67, 242–3
no. 18, 44, 55, 67, 241–2
no. 19, 44, 55, 252
no. 20, 44, 55, 216, 294–5
no. 21, 44, 55, 276
  economic consequences, 273–6
  requirements, 267–72
no. 22, 44, 58, 216, 260
no. 23, 44, 58, 323
Sterling, R., 3, 4, 34
Stevens, D. L., 114
Stewardship, 35–6
Stock Exchange,
  Listing Agreement, 28, 84–6, 334–5
  Unlisted Securities Market, 87
Stocks and work in progress, 248–9
  empirical research, 250
  evaluation, 249–50
  policy requirements, 243–8
Storey, R. K., 24, 33
Subsidiary companies,
  characteristics, 315–6
  legal aspects, 316–17
  SSAP14, 317
Sunder, S., 109, 250
Survey of Published Accounts, 228,
  248, 253, 254, 259, 263, 276,
  296, 298, 335
Survey research, 116–18
Sykes, A., 266, 273

Taffler, 116
Taffler, R. and Tisshaw, H., 31
Taylor, P. J., 126
Taylor, P. J. and Turley, W. S., 105,
  112
Terleckyj, N. E., 10
Theory, nature of, 2
Thomas, A. L., 152, 153, 202, 251
Tinker, A., 16
Trade investments,
  characteristics, 311–12
  Companies Act 1981, 312
Trades Unions, 117
True and fair view, 25,
  Companies Act 1981, 63, 69–70
Trueblood Report, 12, 53, 202, 329
Tweedie, D., 47, 165

Understandability, 98

Value-added statements:
  advantages, 297–8
  characteristics, 296–7
  practice, 298–9
  specimens, 298
Vigeland, R. L., 265

Watts, R., 8, 9
Watts, R. and Leftwich, R., 113
Watts, R. and Zimmerman, J. L., 8, 15
Watts, T. R., 49, 102, 262, 338
Weetman, P., 33, 48, 162
Westwick, C., 167, 336
Wilcox, J. W., 116
Williams, T. H. and Griffen, C. H., 4
Wilner, N. A., 112
Windfall gains and losses, 129–31
Winn, D. N., 112
Wojdak, J. F., 33
Wojnilower, A. W., 114, 275
Work in progress (see Stocks)
Wu, H. K., 275

Yamey, B., 29

Zeff, S., 17, 112